EARTHLY PARADISE

Colette

❦❦ An Autobiography

Drawn from her lifetime writings by ROBERT PHELPS
Translated by Herma Briffault, Derek Coltman,
and others
Farrar, Straus & Giroux   New York

EARTHLY PARADISE

❦ TRANSLATORS

The work of the various translators is identified in the text
as follows:

HB—*Herma Briffault*

DC—*Derek Coltman*

EMCC—*Enid McCleod*

HBk—*Helen Beauclerk*

UVT—*Una Vincenzo Troubridge*

AW—*Antonia White*

RS—*Roger Senhouse*

❧❧ Editor's Foreword

In her own lifetime, and especially outside of France, Colette was
best known as a novelist, as the creator of Gigi, Chéri, Claudine; and
as such, her place in twentieth-century fiction is very high, comparable among her countrymen only with that of Proust.

But over the same half century, she published a large body of
autobiographical prose—portraits, essays, memoirs, *chroniques;* and
now, hardly a decade after her death, it seems clear that it is this part
of her work, and the personality embodied there, which will fix her
final place in world literature.

For like Montaigne or Thoreau or Whitman, Colette appears
destined to become one of those writers whose literary achievement,
however extraordinary, is itself caught up in something ampler: a
personal myth, an emblematic image that merges the private life

and the public art into a greater whole which then comes to incarnate some perennial tendency, or tactic, in human experience.

This need be nothing so schematic as a philosophy. Indeed, it must involve the psyche and the senses as well as the mind, and use the total temperament rather than the mere intellect. Nor will the writer himself necessarily understand, or intend, this aspect of his work. It is we, his readers, who will discover his value. He will remain an instance of what Yeats meant when he said, "Man can embody truth, but he cannot know it."

Thus we see Montaigne as a man who forever asks himself, *"Que sçais-je? What can I know?"* He is our classic self-questioner. He doubts, therefore we can better perceive what a doubter is, see how he looks in action. Montaigne becomes more than a writer. He is a character in our human comedy.

In the same way, Colette forever exclaims *"Regarde! Look!"* If her autobiography, as assembled here, has any story, it is that of a born watcher. She did and said many things, but her deepest instinct, her readiest reflex, her surest hygiene, was to watch. (Advising a young writer, she once said, "Look for a long time at what pleases you, and longer still at what pains you . . .")

She has been called a pantheist—and pagan, sensuous, Dionysiac; and this is not untrue, but it is an oversimplification. Actually, her view of human life was austere, unsentimental, even harsh. She was not a wooly optimist, ever. She knew we are fallen creatures— "impure" was her word—for whom Freud's injunction to love and work is the only hope. She knew that, by our very nature, we must sooner or later lose the innocence we are born with, and that thereafter we can glimpse it only from afar, in children and in the prehuman kingdoms we call animal, vegetable, and mineral.

But she also knew—perhaps the word is "trusted"—that to be born sentient and watchful is a daily miracle: that the *paradis terrestre,* the earthly paradise around us, is as wondrous an index of heaven as any we shall ever know; and that to abide here, even as an exile, for seven or eight decades, is a blessing—because it is a chance to watch, to "look for a long time at what pleases you," and to find *"un mot meilleur, et meilleur que meilleur,* a better and better word," with which to secure it for others.

And when we, in turn, watch Colette watching, we realize that, along with love and work, this is the third great salvation, or form of prayer, which we have been given. For whenever someone is seriously watching, a form of his lost innocence is restored. It will not last, but during those minutes his self-consciousness is relieved. He is less corrupt. He forgets he is going to die. He is very close to that state of grace for which Colette reserved the word "pure."

Few of Colette's contemporaries were unmoved by her personality, and among others, Maurice Goudeket, her third husband, and Claude Chauvière, her onetime secretary and godchild, have left book-length portraits which impart some of the same cachet we get in her own writing. Of the shorter glimpses, one of the best, though less known, was published in the British weekly *Time and Tide* on August 14, 1954. It was written by Bertrand de Jouvenel, the elder son of Colette's second husband, and a distinguished political theorist in his own right. In a story called *The Watchman,* Colette has left a tender profile of his boyhood as her foster-son. This reciprocal remembrance seems to me the best possible introduction a volume of her autobiography could have:

"If you would know her, think of a garden in Brittany, by the sea. It is early morning and she has been awakened by the melancholy two-note whistling of those birds we call *courlis:* she has come down, carefully bypassing a small stack of sleeping cats, and the bulldog has followed her silently. She sits in delightful loneliness on the damp and salty grass and her hand enjoys the roughness of the herbs. The sound of the waves fills her mind, she looks now at them, now at the flowers, which are moving faintly upward as the weight of the dew dissolves.

"The Earthly Paradise is here: it is not lost for her; others merely fail to see it, indeed shut themselves out from it. From the still silent house, by and by will emerge a husband weighed down by the cares of state, a bookish foster-son, a friend obsessed by the recapture of a lost lover, another whose mind is on the obtaining of a given professional position. Either selfishly or unselfishly, their concern is with the world of men: to all of them, the newspapers, the mail are a life-line to what matters. Not to Colette. She is completely unconscious of political events, wholly devoid of any ambition. What matters to her is the rapidly changing color of the sky, the increasing roar of the incoming sea, the polish of a pebble which she has now picked up, and, venturing farther, the prompt dartings of a shrimp which feels that the tide will soon liberate it from its narrow pool. It is also the gait of her husband when he comes out: she will watch whether it is lightened by the enjoyment of the crisp air. I have seen her made happy because a new friend, as his bare feet experienced the cool firm sand, sprang up in a little dance of joy . . . And when her small daughter, long ago, suddenly stopped in her jumping, having become conscious of the perfume of the flowering *troènes,* Colette's hands went out in an instinctive hushing gesture: something important had happened, and she drank in this graceful picture of awareness . . ."

❦❦ Chronology

[Nothing seems less appropriate to a book of Colette's self-portraiture than footnotes, explication, apparatus of any kind. As Henry de Montherlant said in his *Notebooks*, "When you finish *Chéri*, you say 'That's it.' Just two syllables, and no praise could be greater; only you can't make Colette Studies with two syllables. Yet what glosses or commentaries does a Colette book need? A critic has nowhere to take hold, since there is nothing to explain, nothing even to criticize. He has only to admire."

Of course, one day we shall doubtless have a variorum *Chéri* and an annotated *Gigi*. Meantime, for present purposes, I have tried to let Colette speak as entirely as possible for herself, using an editorial parenthesis only when the circumstances of a particular text seemed to require it for understanding. Otherwise, as a general margin to her own story, I have assembled the following chronology, which includes the dates of her principal publications and milestones, as well as occasional glimpses of her over half a century by friends and associates.]

❦❦❦

1865 : Madame Sidonie Landoy Robineau-Duclos, a Paris-born, thirty-year-old widow, remarried. Her new husband was a handsome ex-captain of the select Zouave infantry, who had been born in Toulon, had been trained at Saint-Cyr, and had lost his left leg in Italy in 1859. His name was Jules-Joseph Colette, and with his wife, whom he called "Sido," he now settled at her manor farm in Saint-Sauveur-en-Puisaye, a county seat of some 1,700 inhabitants in Yonne, about a hundred miles from Paris. The house was full of cats, flowers, books, love, and children, for besides a son and daughter from her first marriage, Sido soon had a second son, and then another daughter, named after herself, Sidonie and Gabrielle.

January 28, 1873 : "In a room which no stove could ever sufficiently heat . . . laboriously, half-choked, but showing a determined will to live" (*Le Fanal bleu*), was born Sidonie-Gabrielle Colette—by her birthplace Burgundian, by her father *méridionale*, by her mother Parisian, and by her maternal grandfather, one sixteenth Negro.

1890 : The house in Saint-Sauveur was sold at public auction, and with her parents, Colette moved to the neighboring village of Châtillon-Coligny, where she lived with her elder half-brother Achille, now married and a country doctor. About this time, her father was in correspondence with the firm of Gauthier-Villars et Fils, the leading scientific publishers in Paris, and when young Gauthier-Villars came to call one day, he met seventeen-year-old Gabrielle and fell in love.

May 15, 1893 : Colette was married to Henri Gauthier-Villars and settled in Paris, on the Left Bank, at 28, rue Jacob. In his early thirties, with a genius for public relations, Henri had already established himself in the newspaper jungle of the Belle Époque— publishing caustic music criticism under his own name, and under the pen name of "Willy," masses of ghost-written semi-pulp reading matter of every kind. He and his young wife were soon being noticed in smart cafés and theater lobbies, and what must be the first appearance of Colette's name in the annals of French literature occurs in a November 1894 entry in the *Journal* of Jules Renard. At the opening night of Maeterlinck's translation of *'Tis Pity She's a Whore*, she was conspicuous for her laugh and "a braid of hair long enough to let the bucket down a well with."

March 1900 :   Publication of *Claudine à l'école,* which "Willy" had urged his wife to write some years before and which now, retouched by one or more of his ghosts, became a sudden best-seller. Three sequels followed, all published under Willy's name only, with himself shrewdly promoted as Claudine's creator, and his wife as the real-life model. Jean Cocteau, then in his teens, remembered them as celebrities artfully on view at the old Palais de Glace: "At one of the rink-side tables sat Willy, Colette and her bulldog: Willy, with his walrus mustache and goatee, his heavy eyelids and flowing tie, his wide-brimmed top hat and his bishop's hands clasped on the knob of his cane; and beside him Colette . . . a thin, thin Colette, a sort of miniature fox in cycling dress . . ." (*Portraits-souvenir*)

1904 :   *Dialogues de Bêtes,* four conversation pieces between Colette's bulldog and her Angora cat, were published under her own name or at least under a combination of her own surname and her husband's pen name: Colette Willy. (As her legal self, Gabrielle Gauthier-Villars, she would barely have been recognized even by her mother, who still called her "Minet-Chéri.") In 1905, with three additional dialogues, and an introduction by the poet Francis Jammes, the book was reprinted and enjoyed a *succès d'estime.* In September of that year, Captain Colette died in Châtillon-Coligny.

1906 :   After various amateur appearances, Colette made her professional debut as a mime dancer in a drama called *Le Désir, l'a-*

mour et la chimère. Having separated from "Willy," she received a divorce and went to live with a friend, the ex-Marquise de Belboeuf, daughter of the Duc de Morny, known intimately as "Missy." In his semi-documentary novel, *l'Exilé de Capri,* Roger Peyrefitte has described them both as members of the circle around the poetess Renée Vivien: "Colette wore bracelets engraved 'I belong to Missy,' in honor of the Marquise de Belboeuf, while the latter, dressed in a tuxedo, would reminisce, between two puffs on her cigar, about 'the great Morny, my father.' "

January 3, 1907 : *"Le Scandale du Moulin-Rouge"*—in a pantomime entitled *Rêve d'Egypte,* Colette appeared with the Marquise de Belboeuf (billed as Yssim). At the climax, there was a kiss which brought a clamor from the audience, and further performances were forbidden by the police. This same year saw the publication of *La Retraite sentimentale,* a novel with only "Colette Willy" on the title page, and a note to the reader declaring that "for reasons which have nothing to do with literature, I have ceased to collaborate with Willy . . ."

1908–11 : The Music Hall years—while miming in Paris and on tour, Colette continued to live with "Missy" and to write the books which brought her increasing recognition as not just a scandalous young lady but a distinguished prose stylist. *Les Vrilles de la vigne* (1908) was a collection of autobiographical essays and stories; *L'Ingénue libertine* (1909) a novel reforged from two earlier ones she had written under Willy's aegis; and *La Vagabonde* (1910) her first masterpiece and a candidate for the year's Prix Goncourt. About the same time, she began to write regularly for one of the leading Paris newspapers, *Le Matin,* though, since her name was thought too notorious for a family paper, she was required for a while to use still another pen name: Rosine. It was in connection with *Le Matin* that she met its handsome and ambitious young editor-in-chief Henri de Jouvenel, who was to become her second husband.

September 25, 1912 : Death of Sido at Châtillon-Coligny.

December 19, 1912 :   Married to Henri de Jouvenel.

July 3, 1913 :   Birth of a daughter, Colette de Jouvenel, called "Bel-Gazou." Publication of *L'Envers du Music-Hall,* stories of backstage life, and of *L'Entrave,* a sequel to *La Vagabonde.*

1914–18 :   In the first winter of the war, Henri de Jouvenel was stationed at Verdun, and Colette managed to get through the lines and join him for a number of weeks. The rest of the time she lived in Paris, writing theater criticism for one paper and a weekly "Journal de Colette" for another. "Bel-Gazou" remained for the most part at the Jouvenel estate near Brive, in Corrèze. In 1915 Colette was in Rome, where her husband had been sent on a diplomatic mission, and in 1916 she was there again, this time as scenarist for a film based on *La Vagabonde.* Her wartime publications included *La Paix chez les bêtes* (1916), a collection of animal sketches which Rilke called "a *delicious* book"; *Les Heures longues* (1917), reportage about the war; and *Dans la foule* (1918), prewar sketches of public events and faces "in the crowd."

1919 :   A play, *En Camarades,* in which Colette herself appeared; and a short novel, *Mitsou,* which made Proust weep, and whose final chapter, lost in the Métro, had to be rewritten while the presses waited.

1920 :   With the publication of *Chéri,* which appeared first as a serial in *Le Matin* and then in the late spring as a book, Colette took her place, at forty-seven, as one of the living masters of French prose. Later in the year, she gathered up enough short stories to make *La Chambre éclairée,* at the same time continuing to serve as dramatic critic and literary editor for *Le Matin.* In the latter capacity, she published some of the earliest stories of Georges Simenon: "One day I was told, 'Madame Colette would like to see you,' and there she was, marvelous to behold in her editorial chair, suddenly addressing me as *'Mon petit Sim'* . . . 'You know,' she said, 'I've read your last story, and I ought to have returned it weeks ago. It isn't right. It's almost right. It almost works. But not quite. You are too literary. You must not be literary. Suppress all the literature and it will work . . .' That was the most useful advice I've ever had in my life, and I owe a grateful candle to Colette for having given it to me." (*Portraits-souvenir*)

1921–4 : Dramatized with Leopold Marchand, *Chéri* reached the stage in December 1921, and in 1922 Colette collected a number of stories about her childhood in Saint-Sauveur into *La Maison de Claudine*. In 1923, *Le Blé en herbe,* her classic portrait of young love, was published, and again there was a scandal. The early chapters had appeared in *Le Matin,* but when it became clear that the teen-aged hero and heroine were, indeed, going to consummate their romance, there was a barrage of protest from readers, and serialization was stopped. Perhaps it was on this occasion that Henri de Jouvenel, Colette's editor-in-chief as well as her husband, wearily asked: "But is it impossible for you to write a book that isn't about love, adultery, semi-incestuous relations? Aren't there other things in life?" In any case, by December they had separated, and as of 1924, with a further collection of stories called *La Femme cachée,* Colette began to publish everything under her family name alone.

1925 : Divorced from Jouvenel, Colette toured in *Chéri,* playing Lea herself, and during the Easter holidays, in the South of France, she met Maurice Goudeket, the man who was finally to set her hectic life in order and to become her third husband and "best friend." *L'Enfant et les sortilèges,* the opera Ravel had made from a libretto written by Colette during the war, had its première in December.

1926 : Publication, in March, of *La Fin de Chéri.* About the same time, Colette gave an interview in which, once and for all, she established her claim to the Claudine books (showing manuscripts which had been saved by one of Willy's ghost writers) and publicly discarded some of the many disguises behind which she had lived and worked for so much of her life. Thus, in the new novel she had begun, *La Naissance du jour,* she was able to declare: "Both legally and familiarly, as well as in my books, I now have only one name, which is my own . . ." In 1926, she also made two important changes of residence. In what was then the relatively quiet fishing village of Saint-Tropez, in the South of France, she bought a house which she called "La Treille Muscate"; and in Paris she left her town house near the Bois de Boulogne and settled in a snug, tunnel-like apartment under the colonnades of the Palais-Royal.

1927–31 : Colette lectured widely—in North Africa, Hungary, Germany, and throughout France; translations of her work were appearing regularly in England, America, Italy, Germany; two whole books were devoted to her work and personality. With a company made up entirely of actors who were also writers, she played the lead in a stage adaptation of *La Vagabonde,* and in three vintage years published three of her best books: *La Naissance du jour* (1928), a lyric evocation of her Provençal house, with a token love story interwoven; *La Seconde* (1929), a more formal novel about a *ménage à trois;* and *Sido* (1930), a full-length portrait of her mother and father. As a Parisian personality, Colette was now chic and distinguished, rather than scandalous. Janet Flanner, one of her earliest and best translators into English, described her in 1929 as "a short, hearty-bodied woman with a crop of wood-colored hair, with long, gray luminous eyes and a deep alto voice . . . [who] still speaks French with a racy Burgundian accent." Julian Green's diary for May 1929 records a glimpse of her mellowness, as well as her tart unsentimentality: "Colette listened and joined in our laughter while she 'browsed' on apples. She too contributed to the store of anecdotes (about Victor Hugo) and spoke to us of his 'armchairs with secrets.' As he arrived, Cocteau showed us a sick bird which he had found in the Champs-Élysées. Colette took it, examined it, and went and wrung its neck in the garden." (*Personal Record*) And another young writer, Pierre Scize, has remembered that "if we said to her, 'Colette, I'm unhappy,' we would hear her voice of a grumbling laborer reply, 'Nobody asked you to be happy. Work. Do you hear me complaining?' "

1932 : Publication of *Ces Plaisirs . . .* (whose title was changed in 1942 to *Le Pur et l'impur*). In an interview, Colette said,

"It will be a very moral book. Unfortunately the publisher will write on the title page, 'A Novel.' But it will not be a real novel." A decade later, she called it the book which "will perhaps one day be recognized as my best . . ." Again, readers protested when it was serialized in a weekly magazine called *Gringoire,* and the text was cut off, as Colette indignantly pointed out, "in the middle of a sentence!" In June, backed by a list of stockholders which included the Princess de Polignac, the Pasha of Marrakesh, and the banker Daniel Dreyfus, Colette inaugurated a Salon de Beauté, with her own cosmetic products, and shops in Paris and Saint-Tropez. "The human face was always my great landscape," she wrote, and for the rest of the year she was nourished and refreshed, if also exhausted, by her schedule of lecture demonstrations. In November, *Prisons et paradis,* another collection of essays and texts written for limited editions was published.

1933 : *La Chatte,* Colette's first novel in four years, and one of her most original and best-selling. By this time, she had also begun to work in films, having collaborated, in 1931, on a second version of *La Vagabonde* (in which her bulldog played a role) and having written the French subtitles for *Maedchen in Uniform.* Now she wrote the dialogue for *Lac aux dames,* to be directed by Gide's protégé, Marc Allegret, and by the end of the summer she contracted to write a weekly column of dramatic criticism for *Le Journal,* a stint she continued for the next five seasons.

1934 : *Duo,* a novel, and further film work, including an original scenario, *Divine,* directed by Max Ophüls.

April 3, 1935 : Married to Maurice Goudeket.

June 1935 : To New York for two and a half days, on the maiden voyage of the *Normandie.* At a party given by her American publisher, she was introduced to novelist Glenway Wescott:

"I remember her strong hands—serious writing is a manual labor!—and her fine feet in sandals, perhaps larger than most, rather like the feet of Greek goddesses. I remember her slightly frizzly hair fetched forward almost to her eyebrows, because (as she has told her readers) she has a square boyish or mannish forehead. I remember her delicate nostrils and her painted thin lips . . . She gave it as her opinion that there was nothing at all surprising about skyscrapers; man having been all through the ages a mountain-climber, a tower-builder. I then expressed my pleasure in the little conversation I had had with Maurice Goudeket, her distinguished, interesting third husband. 'He is a very good friend,' she said, and she emphasized friend a little . . ." (Introduction to *Short Novels of Colette*)

October 5, 1935 : Death of Henri de Jouvenel.

1936 : Publication of *Mes Apprentissages*, Colette's memoirs of "Monsieur Willy" (who had died in 1931) and her beginnings as a writer. In his *Journal,* fastidious André Gide noted that he had read the book "with a very lively interest. There is more than talent here: there is a very particularly feminine genius and a great intelligence. What choice, what order, what happy proportions in so apparently unbridled a story! What perfect tact, what courteous discretion in matters of confidence (in the portraits of Polaire, of Jean Lorrain, and above all, of Willy, of "Monsieur Willy"); there is not a line which does not count, which is not written as though at random, as if in play, yet with such subtle, accomplished art. I myself encountered this world Colette describes, and I recognize here its artificiality, its pseudo-sophistication, its hideousness. Happily, an unconscious residue of Puritanism kept me on guard against it. For all her superiority, it does not seem to me that Colette quite escaped a little contamination . . ." (*Journal: 1889–1939*)

April 4, 1936 : Wearing sandals, with her toenails lacquered a brilliant red, Colette was received into the Académie Royale de Langue et de Littérature Françaises de Belgique, her chair being the one formerly held by the Comtesse de Noailles.

1937–9 : Years of continuing fame, fulfillment, hard work. *Life* magazine quoted her as claiming to write "as easily as frying an egg," but to Somerset Maugham, she was more truthful. "I think no one in France now writes more admirably than Colette," he declared in 1938, "and such is the ease of her expression that you cannot bring yourself to believe that she takes any trouble over it . . . I asked her. I was exceedingly surprised to hear that she wrote everything over and over again. She told me that she would often spend a whole morning working upon a single page . . ." (*The Summing Up*) *Bella-Vista* (1938) contained the first of a series of novellas in which Colette perfected a hybrid form of story—part memoir-narrative, part lyric essay, with the whole shot through with her own vulnerable watchfulness—which will certainly come to be her most influential contribution to the art of the novel. Four annual volumes called *La Jumelle noire* collected her astute but generous ("I am not a headsman!") theater criticism; and in 1939 there was a short sequel to *Duo,* called *Le Toutounier.* Meantime, after experimenting with rooms atop the Hotel Claridge overlooking the Champs-Élysées, Colette moved back to the Palais-Royal, to a large, sunny apartment directly over the one she had occupied formerly and where she was now to live for the remaining fifteen years of her life.

1939–45 : With the outbreak of World War II, Colette promptly returned from Dieppe, where she had spent the month of August, to Paris, and began making overseas broadcasts to America. It was on a dark cold day on the following December that the novelist Lise Deharme saw her walking along the Left Bank's rue de Bellechasse, "barefoot in her sandals, with a rose in her hand . . ." (*Les Années perdues*) In the spring, she bought a small house in Méré, a suburb of Paris, but she had barely moved in before the Germans entered the city in June. With Maurice Goudeket and Pauline (*La servante au grand coeur,* who had entered her service during World War I and who was to remain with her as long as she lived), she escaped by car to Curemonte, in Corrèze, where she lived for the summer with her daughter. But in September, in spite of the gasoline shortage, she managed to get back to the Palais-Royal

("I'm used to spending my wars in Paris!") and began writing a weekly chronicle of life under the Occupation. *Chambre d'hôtel,* consisting of two novellas, was published in November, and in 1941 she finished her last full-length novel, *Julie de Carneilhan,* whose heroine's initials reverse her own when she was Madame Colette de Jouvenel, and whose story is as close a reckoning with the elements of her second marriage as she ever allowed herself.

December 12, 1941 : Maurice Goudeket, as a Jew, was arrested by the Gestapo and interned until the following February at a camp in Compiègne.

1942–3 : Colette had already begun to suffer from arthritic pains, which had perhaps originated in a broken fibula bone in 1931 and which were eventually to leave her wholly bedridden. In the spring, she had an extensive series of X-ray treatments for sciatica, and during the summer, to relieve her anxiety over his possible re-arrest, Maurice Goudeket withdrew beyond the Occupation Zone and stayed with friends in Saint-Tropez, while Colette remained with Pauline in Paris. It was in these months, "while I trembled for what was dearest to me," that she wrote *Gigi,* which first appeared that autumn in a Free Zone weekly called *Présent.* The following year, 1943, she published *Le Képi,* another gathering of novellas and assorted works of nonfiction: *Flore et pomone,* about gardens and fruits; *De la Patte a l'aile,* about birds and animals; and *Nudité,* about human attitudes toward nakedness. In October came the death of Renée Hamon—a young writer and South Seas voyager whom Colette had nicknamed "The Little Pirate," who had come to be one of her most cherished friends and whose *Journal* has left us some of the most candid images of Colette yet published:

"Colette, I'm in love!"

"Ah! With whom?"

". . . With a woman."

"So? Is she nice?"

"Oh, she's a love. Beautiful to look at, intelligent, sweet-natured, and so prudent . . ."

"Now don't be carried away. Look out. You are a migratory bird. Don't be too quick to attach yourself."

"It's happened all the same. I'm going to live with her."

Colette looks at me, astonished.

"But that's very serious."

"Oh, yes. But I won't be seeing her all day."

"Very good. There is nothing like separation to preserve love . . ." (*Lettres au petit corsaire*)

1944–5 : After the liberation of Paris in August 1944, Colette published *Paris de ma fenêtre,* and by the following May, when the European war was over, she had become world-famous, not only as a novelist but as an emblem of everything that is most profoundly French. *Gigi* was published in book form and became a best-seller. Colette was elected to the powerful Académie Goncourt, and in an interview she said that her future projects included "flowers, strawberries, and living in a more tranquil universe." Her photographs, such as the one that appeared in *Life* that month, now showed her on her divan bed, with a fur rug drawn over her legs; her papers, pens, scissors, and glasses strewn on a small, bridgelike table drawn across her lap; with a bowl of flowers at hand, mounted butterflies on the bookshelves in front of her, and over her left shoulder the extension lamp with a shade made from a piece of her favorite blue writing paper, which she called her *fanal bleu,* or blue beacon light, and which, as Cocteau said, ghosts in the arcades of the Palais-Royal would always defer to, saying, "Let's disappear. Colette is working."

1946–54 : She had thought a volume of memoirs, called *L'Étoile vesper* and published on Bastille Day, 1946, would be her last book, but there were more to come. *Pour un herbier* in 1948, *Le Fanal bleu* in 1949, and beginning in December of that year, fifteen volumes of her *Oeuvres complètes.* *Chéri* was revived on stage; a number of her novels were made into films; there was even a film of her life, imaginatively using old photographs and newsreels, with scenes of herself and Maurice Goudeket and Pauline and Cocteau in her

room in the Palais-Royal. In 1950 there was another book of portraits and landscapes, *En Pays connu;* and there were visits—from
Julian Green:

Her great eyes are among the most beautiful woman's eyes I
know, as beautiful as those of an animal, brimming with soul and
sadness . . . There is a huge pile of letters on the long table beside
her bed, letters which she says will go unanswered. She takes one at
random and murmurs: "Who is this jackass who talks to me about
my 'long experience'?" . . . Then she tells me the story of two
swallows which she took to school as a little girl and which had to
be fed . . . "Worms?" I asked. "Worms!" she scoffed. "Heavens,
no, my son. Living flies! You don't know swallows. They have a
superb scornfulness, superb . . ." At this moment an elderly gentleman comes in who talks about pornographic books. He leaves and
Colette says to me: "How young you look! You're right. Old men
are ugly . . ." (*Journal: 1950–1954*)

—from Glenway Wescott:

"What is it, Pauline? Who is it, Pauline? But no, but no, not
that vase, not for roses. Oh, they're magnificent, aren't they? So long-
legged and in such quantity! Leave them here on my bed, for the
moment."

Though the furthest thing in the world from a young voice, it
had a sound of unabated femininity, and it could never have been
livelier at any age. It was slightly hoarse, but with the healthy
hoarseness of certain birds; nothing sore-throated about it.

"Who brought them, Pauline? What young man? The one of
the other day, the Swiss one? But, my poor dear Pauline, if he's gray-
haired, what makes you think he's young? If only you'd remember
names, so much simpler."

Thus she sputtered or, to be more exact, warbled, and I gathered that Pauline withdrew from the room in midsentence; the
hoarse and sweet phrases murmured to a close. . . .

I have never seen a woman of any age so impeccable and immaculate and (so to speak) gleaming . . . There was evidence of
pain in her face but not the least suggestion of illness. What came

uppermost in my mind at the sight of her was just rejoicing. Oh, oh, I said to myself, she is not going to die for a long while!

"Please sit on my bed," she said. "Yes, there at the foot, where I can look straight at you. Arthritic as I am, it wearies me—or perhaps I should say it bores me—to turn my head too often . . . Do you see? I have excellent feet . . . I have always worn sandals, indifferent to severe criticism, braving inclement weather; and now I have my reward for it . . ." (*Images of Truth*)

—and from her neighbor Jean Cocteau:

And I repeat, don't ever take Madame Colette to have been merely a nice little lady. Her velvet paws had real claws, which could leave scars. For the most part, these scars marked only those who had dared to attack people her heart respected. Friendship could make her ferocious. For instance, if an insult directed at me happened to come to her attention, she would recoil as though confronted with a bad smell. She would scowl, pucker her nostrils, pinch her lips, and there would be a lash of lightning in her beautiful eyes. She would murmur, "What a horror!," rolling the r's, and shaking her hair, she would excommunicate, with a thrust of her freckled hand, the newspaper article which had so gravely offended her soul. (*Colette*)

August 3, 1954 : At about 8:30 in the evening, Colette died in her bed, overlooking the summer gardens of the Palais-Royal. A final scandal remained: Cardinal Feltin, the Archbishop of Paris, refused her family's request for burial service at the Église Saint-Roche, and the English novelist Graham Greene admonished him in an open letter published on the front page of the weekly *Figaro Littéraire:* "To non-Catholics it could seem that the Church itself lacked charity . . . Of course, Catholics, upon reflection, can decide that the voice of an archbishop is not necessarily the voice of the Church . . ." After a state funeral in the Cour d'Honneur of the Palais-Royal, Colette was buried in the Père-Lachaise cemetery. In *La Douceur de vieillir,* the second volume of memoirs Maurice Goudeket has devoted to his wife, he graciously acknowledges the Church's attitude, but adds: "All the same, I should love to see a cross affixed on the tombstone of black- and rose-colored granite which I have erected to her . . . partly out of a certain taste for harmony, partly in regard for my own understanding of this glorious emblem, and partly, too, because I fear that a day will come when passers-by will no longer know whether it was the Church, or Colette herself, who refused to allow it there."

❦❦ Contents

Chronology   xi

Part One ❦ [1873-1893]
Childhood—Family—Early Signs

The Past (*Paysages et portraits*)   3

Sido

    Always up at dawn . . . (*Sido*)   5
    It was the reflected glow . . . (*Sido*)   6
    In her garden my mother . . . (*Sido*)   8
    "I could live in Paris . . ." (*Sido*)   10
    In those days there were bitter winters . . . (*Sido*)   15
    "There is about a very beautiful child . . ."
        (*La Naissance du jour*)   16

The time came . . . (*La Maison de Claudine*)   19
"Sir, you ask me . . ." (*La Naissance du jour*)   22

Sido and I

"You've thrown a chestnut hull . . ."
        (*Journal à rebours*)   24
"As sure as I'm here . . ." (*Sido*)   28
Mothers and children . . . (*En Pays connu*)   31
In the countryside where I was born . . .
        (*En Pays connu*)   36

The Captain

It seems strange to me now . . . (*Sido*)   40
When I was eight . . . (*La Maison de Claudine*)   45
My father, a born writer . . . (*Le Képi*)   48
He was a poet and a townsman . . . (*Sido*)   50
I never surprised them . . . (*Sido*)   54
He died in his seventy-fourth year . . .
        (*La Maison de Claudine*)   57
"I've just been sorting . . ." (*La Naissance du jour*)   59
I can still see . . . (*Sido*)   59

The Children

The house was large . . . (*La Maison de Claudine*)   61
"Savages . . ." (*Sido*)   66
My half-sister . . . (*Sido*)   72

The Footwarmer (*Journal à rebours*)   75

Part Two ❧ [1893-1910]
Marriage—Literary Apprenticeship—Masks

Wedding Day (*Noces, Oeuvres complètes, VII*)   81

Monsieur Willy

His constant cry . . . (*Mes Apprentissages*)   88
I have known people . . . (*Mes Apprentissages*)   91

A third floor . . . (*Mes Apprentissages*) 93
Judging from various . . . (*Mes Apprentissages*) 95
Is it hard to understand . . . (*Mes Apprentissages*) 96
The memories of my first . . . (*Mes Apprentissages*) 99
Winter months . . . (*Mes Apprentissages*) 106

Literary Apprenticeship: "Claudine"

At first . . . (*Mes Apprentissages*) 108
I have often thought . . . (*Mes Apprentissages*) 110
It must be acknowledged . . . (*Mes Apprentissages*) 112
What Polaire made . . . (*Mes Apprentissages*) 114
From the day . . . (*Mes Apprentissages*) 120
[Meantime] . . . (*Mes Apprentissages*) 122
At the faintest stir . . . (*Mes Apprentissages*) 123
Above the flat . . . (*Mes Apprentissages*) 127

Freedom

A fable: the tendrils of the vine
  (*Les Vrilles de la vigne*) 135

ALONE

During the loneliest years . . . (*Bella-Vista*) 137
Behold me then . . . (*La Vagabonde*) 138
Having rescued . . . (*Trois . . . six . . . neuf*) 141

The Sémiramis bar (*Paysages et portraits*) 144
Renée Vivien (*Le Pur et l'impur*) 150
Letter to Léon Hamel (*Lettres de la vagabonde*) 163
Night without sleep (*Les Vrilles de la vigne*) 164

Part Three ❧ [1910-1920]
Music Halls—Motherhood—World War I

Music Halls

Was I, in those days . . . (*Bella-Vista*) 171
Rehearsal (*Les Vrilles de la vigne*) 173
Provincial tour (*Belles saisons*) 176

Remarriage and Motherhood

Letter to Léon Hamel (*Lettres de la vagabonde*) 193

My mother was twice a widow . . . (*La Naissance du jour*) 195

The always unexpected blast of air . . . (*Trois . . . six . . . neuf*) 196

Letter to Christiane Mendelys (*Lettres de la vagabonde*) 198

I was forty . . . (*L'Étoile vesper*) 199

Bel-Gazou

At the sea (*Oeuvres complètes, III*) 206

The lighted room (*La Chambre éclairée*) 207

The hollow nut (*La Maison de Claudine*) 212

The sempstress (*La Maison de Claudine*) 214

The watchman (*La Maison de Claudine*) 217

World War I

Saint-Malo, August 1914 (*Les Heures longues*) 223

Paris: the wounded (*Les Heures longues*) 225

Verdun, December–January 1915 (*Les Heures longues*) 227

Venice, 1915 (*Les Heures longues*) 233

Rome, 1915 (*Les Heures longues*) 235

Middle Age: A New Year Reverie

(*Les Vrilles de la vigne*) 237

Part Four ❦ [1920-1939]
Work—Appetites—La Grande Colette

Lady of Letters

Origins of *Chéri* (*Oeuvres complètes, VI*) 245

The poetry I love (*Paysages et portraits*) 250

LESSONS IN WRITING

To Marguerite Moreno (*Lettres à Marguerite Moreno*) 253

From the preface to Renée Hamon's *Aux Îles de lumière*
    (*Lettres au petit corsaire*) 254
Fate has decreed . . . (*Le Fanal bleu*) 255

Making movies (*Paysages et portraits*) 255
On being elected to the Belgian Academy (*Belles
    saisons*) 258

The South of France
In love (*Lettres à Marguerite Moreno*) 259
"La treille muscate" (*Prisons et paradis*) 261
The door leading to the vines . . . (*La Naissance du
    jour*) 265

Gastronomy
Recriminations (*Prisons et paradis*) 270
Wines (*Prisons et paradis*) 274
Cheese (*Paysages et portraits*) 278
Truffles (*Prisons et paradis*) 281

Portraits and Tributes
Honoré de Balzac (*Belles saisons*) 283
Marcel Proust (*Belles saisons*) 285
Eleonora Duse (*Aventures quotidiennes*) 288
Sarah Bernhardt (*En Pays connu*) 290
Claude Debussy (*En Pays connu*) 291
Maurice Ravel (*Journal à rebours, En Pays connu*) 292
Jean Cocteau (*Le Fanal bleu*) 296
La Belle Otéro (*Mes Apprentissages*) 297

Human Nature

BEAUTY SALON
. . . The first time . . . (*En Pays connu*) 300
In all the time . . . (*Les Vrilles de la vigne*) 301

Nudity (*Belles saisons*) 303
Landru (1921) (*Prisons et paradis*) 307
Stavisky (1934) (*Paysages et portraits*) 311
Temptations (*En Pays connu*) 313
Desert flower (*Prisons et paradis*) 317
The bliss of confession (*Mes Apprentissages*) 320

Animal Nature
The heart of animals (*Journal à rebours*) 321
A lizard (*Prisons et paradis*) 328
Bitterness (*En Pays connu*) 332
Leopards (*Prisons et paradis*) 336
Snakes (*Prisons et paradis*) 338
Fame (*La Naissance du jour*) 340

The Palais-Royal (*En Pays connu*) 344

Part Five ❧ [1932]
The Pure and the Impure

Don Juan (*Le Pur et l'impur*) 351

La Chevalière (*Le Pur et l'impur*) 373

Amalia X. (*Le Pur et l'impur*) 386

Sodom (*Le Pur et l'impur*) 393

The Pure and the Impure (*Le Pur et l'impur*) 408

Part Six ❧ [1939-1954]
Another War—Old Age—The Blue Lantern

World War II
Letters to Renée Hamon (*Lettres au petit corsaire*) 425
"Colette speaking" (*Paysages et portraits*) 426

June 1940 (*L'Étoile vesper*) 429
Late June 1940 (*Journal à rebours*) 431
Letter to Renée Hamon (*Lettres au petit corsaire*) 435
Ruins (*Journal à rebours*) 435

The Occupation

PARIS FROM MY WINDOW: 1940–41
A pink roof, guttered tiles . . . (*Paris de ma fenêtre*) 442
Like flies after honey . . . (*Paris de ma fenêtre*) 446
Every morning . . . (*Paris de ma fenêtre*) 448
"I'd like to see you in my place!" (*Paris de ma fenêtre*) 452
A dry spring . . . (*Paris de ma fenêtre*) 455

Three letters (*Lettres à Marguerite Moreno, Lettres
au petit corsaire*) 457
Fifteen hundred days: liberation, August 1944
(*L'Étoile vesper*) 458

The Evening Star

"I'm going out" (*L'Étoile vesper*) 465

FLOWERS
They say now . . . (*Prisons et paradis*) 472
I used to love to visit the flower shows . . . (*Flore
et pomone*) 477
. . . If I had a garden. . . . (*Flore et pomone*) 480

Autumn (*Journal à rebours*) 483

Under the Blue Lantern

We should not be unreasonably perturbed . . . (*Le Fanal
bleu*) 493
My juniors in the prime of life . . . (*Le Fanal bleu*) 494
In anticipation of the time . . . (*Le Fanal bleu*) 495
Beyond the need to see . . . (*L'Étoile vesper*) 495

The only living animal left to me . . . (*Le Fanal bleu*) 498

I grow less and less afraid . . . (*Paysages et portraits*) 501

We have close friends . . . (*Belles saisons*) 501

It has taken me a great deal of time . . . (*L'Étoile vesper*) 502

EARTHLY PARADISE

Ma poésie est à ras de terre . . .

My poetry is earthbound . . .

PART **One** ❧❧ [1873-1893]

Childhood—Family—Early Signs

J'appartiens à un pays que j'ai quitté . . .

I belong to a land I have left . . .

❧❧ The Past

To call to mind everything a child's heart encompasses, to delight again in all it holds of goodness, decency, cunning, and suspicion— at the same time to describe the marvelous instinct that impels a child to suppress what should be hidden, the instinct that makes him keep a childlike aspect while, safe behind that façade of a frisky little body, formless features, tousled hair, he gravely looks out at the world, deliberating, judging, and suffering with proud reserve . . . This is what I must do if I am to write the story of a child-hood, of my childhood. I want to write it, but already, as I begin, I see failure ahead. For how modest, how easy it is to write a love story by comparison with the romance of growing from infancy to girl-hood, when the idea of love is overshadowed by other passions and does not seem the be-all and end-all of life, but merely an uncertain crowning achievement, as impressive as the hazardous and fragile capital of a pillar, a splendid but superfluous ornament . . .

Other passions? Yes, passions, since I can find no better word for the compelling, fierce, and secret rapport I had with the earth and everything that gushes from its breast, and for that jealous and anxious passion I had for solitude. O solitude of my young days! You were my refuge, my panacea, the citadel of my youthful pride. With what might and main did I cling to you, and how afraid I was, even then, of losing you! I trembled at the mere thought of the more ruthless and less rare ecstasy of love! At the thought of losing you I felt already demeaned. And yet . . . who can resist the pull of love? To become only a woman—how paltry. Yet I hastened eagerly toward that common goal.

Did I hesitate a minute, one solitary minute, standing there between your beloved specter, O solitude, and the menacing apparition of love? Perhaps. I don't know, it is still too close to me. An infallible memory guides my recollections only through the tangled garden of my infancy. I do not at all remember if, the first time I saw him, the man I loved was wearing a grayish coat to match the weather, and I have forgotten the words he spoke that day. But ask me to tell you the shape and tint of every separate leaf of those brown wallflowers that the frost and snow preserved every winter in the garden and which, seized with the cold on the white ground, looked like scalded salad greens . . . Ask me if the two-centuries-old wisteria flowered twice every year and if the perfume shed by the scrawny clusters of its second blooming seemed to be only a faint souvenir of the first blooming . . . I could tell you the names of my dead cats and dogs, and I could repeat for you the dirge, the moaning in a minor key of the two pine trees that lulled my sleep, and the youthful voice, sweetly shrill, of my mother calling my name in the garden. I could open for you the books over which was bent my forehead framed by long braids, and in a puff I could blow away, still damp, the petals of the pink peonies, the dark wrinkled faces of the pansies, the water-blue forget-me-nots which, innocent young pagan that I was, I pressed between the pages of a book. You

will hear the hooting of my shy owl, and you will feel the warmth of
the low wall, embroidered with snails, where I propped my elbow,
you will warm your arms, folded one upon the other, and . . .
Quick! Shut your hand, shut your hand quickly on the dry, hot,
tense little lizard. Oh-ho! You shuddered! So you were caught up in
my dream? Pray, give me, the better to delude you, give me some
soft pastel crayons, of colors as yet without names, give me sparkling
powders and a fairy brush, and . . . Well, no! For there are no
words, no crayons, no colors that could paint for you, above a mauve
slate roof adorned with russet mosses, the sky of my homeland, as it
beamed down upon my childhood!

HB

❧❧ Sido

Always up at dawn . . .

Always up at dawn and sometimes before day, my mother attached particular importance to the cardinal points of the compass,
as much for the good as for the harm they might bring. It is because
of her and my deep-rooted love for her that first thing every morning, and while I am still snug in bed, I always ask: "Where is the
wind coming from?" only to be told in reply: "It's a lovely day," or
"The Palais-Royal's full of sparrows," or "The weather's vile" or
"seasonable." So nowadays I have to rely on myself for the answer,
by watching which way a cloud is moving, listening for ocean rum-
blings in the chimney, and letting my skin enjoy the breath of the
West wind, a breath as moist and vital and laden with portents as
the twofold divergent snortings of some friendly monster. Or it may
be that I shrink into myself with hatred before that fine cold dry

enemy the East wind, and his cousin of the North. That was what my mother used to do, as she covered with paper cornets all the little plant creatures threatened by the russet moon. "It's going to freeze," she would say, "the cat's dancing."

Her hearing, which remained keen, kept her informed too, and she would intercept Aeolian warnings.

"Listen over Moûtiers!" she used to say, lifting her forefinger where she stood near the pump, between the hydrangeas and the group of rose bushes. That was her reception point for the information coming from the west over the lowest of the garden walls. "Do you hear? Take the garden chairs indoors, and your book and hat. It's raining over Moûtiers; in two or three minutes more it'll be raining here."

I strained my ears "over Moûtiers"; from the horizon came a steady sound of beads plopping into water and the flat smell of the rain-pitted pond as it sluiced up against its slimy green banks. And I would wait for a second or two, so that the gentle drops of a summer shower, falling on my cheeks and lips, might bear witness to the infallibility of her whom only one person in the world—my father —called "Sido."

EMCC

It was the reflected glow . . .

It was the reflected glow of your blazing line along the terrace, O geraniums, and yours, O foxgloves, springing up amid the coppice, that gave my childish cheeks their rosy warmth. For Sido loved red and pink in the garden, the burning shades of roses, lychnis, hydrangeas, and red-hot pokers. She even loved the winter cherry, although she declared that its pulpy pink flowers, veined with red, reminded her of the lights of a freshly killed calf. She made a reluctant pact with the East wind. "I know how to get on with him," she would say. But she remained suspicious and, out of all the cardinal and collateral points of the compass, it was on that icy treacherous point, with its murderous pranks, that she kept her eye. But she trusted him with lily-of-the-valley bulbs, some begonias, and mauve autumn crocuses, those dim lanterns of cold twilights.

Except for one mound with a clump of cherry laurels over-shadowed by a maidenhair tree—whose skate-shaped leaves I used to give to my school friends to press between the pages of their atlases—the whole warm garden basked in a yellow light that shimmered into red and violet; but whether this red and violet sprang then, and still spring, from feelings of happiness or from dazzled sight, I could not tell. Those were summers when the heat quivered up from the hot yellow gravel and pierced the plaited rushes of my wide-brimmed hats, summers almost without nights. For even then I so loved the dawn that my mother granted it to me as a reward. She used to agree to wake me at half past three and off I would go, an empty basket on each arm, toward the kitchen gardens that sheltered in the narrow bend of the river, in search of strawberries, black currants, and hairy gooseberries.

At half past three, everything slumbered still in a primal blue, blurred and dewy, and as I went down the sandy road the mist, grounded by its own weight, bathed first my legs, then my well-built little body, reaching at last to my mouth and ears, and finally to that most sensitive part of all, my nostrils. I went alone, for there were no dangers in that freethinking countryside. It was on that road and at that hour that I first became aware of my own self, experienced an inexpressible state of grace, and felt one with the first breath of air that stirred, the first bird, and the sun so newly born that it still looked not quite round.

"Beauty," my mother would call me, and "Jewel of pure gold"; then she would let me go, watching her creation—her masterpiece, as she said—grow smaller as I ran down the slope. I may have been pretty; my mother and the pictures of me at that period do not always agree. But what made me pretty at that moment was my youth and the dawn, my blue eyes deepened by the greenery all around me, my fair locks that would only be brushed smooth on my return, and my pride at being awake when other children were asleep.

I came back when the bell rang for the first Mass. But not before I had eaten my fill, not before I had described a great circle in the woods, like a dog out hunting on its own, and tasted the water of the two hidden springs which I worshipped. One of them bubbled out of the ground with a crystalline spurt and a sort of sob, and then carved its own sandy bed. But it was no sooner born than it lost confidence and plunged underground again. The other spring, almost invisible, brushed over the grass like a snake and spread itself out secretly in the middle of a meadow where the narcissus, flowering in a ring, alone bore witness to its presence. The first spring tasted of oak leaves, the second of iron and hyacinth stalks. The mere mention of them makes me hope that their savor may fill my mouth when my time comes, and that I may carry hence with me that imagined draught.

BMCC

In her garden my mother . . .

In her garden my mother had a habit of addressing to the four cardinal points not only direct remarks and replies that sounded, when heard from our sitting room, like brief inspired soliloquies, but the actual manifestations of her courtesy, which generally took the form of plants and flowers. But in addition to these points—to Cèbe and the rue des Vignes, to Mother Adolphe, and Maître de Fourolles—there was also a zone of collateral points, more distant and less defined, whose contact with us was by means of stifled sounds and signals. My childish pride and imagination saw our house as the central point of a mariner's chart of gardens, winds, and rays of light, no section of which lay quite beyond my mother's influence.

I could gain my liberty at any moment by means of an easy climb over a gate, a wall, or a little sloping roof, but as soon as I landed back on the gravel of our own garden, illusion and faith returned to me. For as soon as she had asked me: "Where have you come from?" and frowned the ritual frown, my mother would resume her placid, radiant garden face, so much more beautiful than her anxious indoor face. And merely because she held sway there and watched over it all, the walls grew higher, the enclosures which I had so easily traversed by jumping from wall to wall and branch to branch, became unknown lands, and I found myself once more among the familiar wonders.

"Is that you I hear, Cèbe?" my mother would call. "Have you seen my cat? "

She pushed back her wide-brimmed hat of burnt straw until it slid down her shoulders, held by a brown taffeta ribbon around her neck, and threw her head back to confront the sky with her fearless gray glance and her face the color of an autumn apple. Did her voice strike the bird on the weathercock, the hovering honey buzzard, the last leaf on the walnut tree or the dormer window which, at the first light, swallowed up the barn owls? Then—though it was certain to happen, the surprise was never failing—from a cloud on the left the voice of a prophet with a bad cold would let fall a "No, Madame Colê—ê—tte!" which seemed to be making its way with great difficulty through a curly beard and blankets of fog, and slithering over ponds vaporous with cold. Or perhaps: "Ye—es, Madame Colê—ê—tte!," the voice of a shrill angel would sing on the right, probably perched on the spindle-shaped cirrus cloud which was sailing along to meet the young moon. "She's he—e—ard you. She's go—oing through the li—i—lacs."

"Thank you!" called my mother at random. "If that's you, Cèbe, just give me back my stake and my planting-out line, will you! I need them to get my lettuces straight. But be careful. I'm close to the hydrangeas!" As if it were the offering of a dream, the prank of a witches' Sabbath, or an act of magical levitation, the stake, wound around with ten yards of small cord, sailed through the air and came to rest at my mother's feet.

On other occasions she would offer to lesser, invisible spirits a tribute of flowers. Faithful to her ritual, she threw back her head and scanned the sky: "Who wants some of my double red violets?" she cried.

"I do, Madame Colê—ê—tte!" answered the mysterious one to the East, in her plaintive, feminine voice.

"Here you are, then!" and the little bunch, tied together with a juicy jonquil leaf, flew through the air, to be gratefully received by the plaintive Orient. "How lovely they smell! To think I can't grow any as good!"

"Of course you can't," I would think, and felt inclined to add: "It's all a question of the air they breathe."

EMCC

"I could live in Paris . . ."

"I could live in Paris only if I had a beautiful garden," she would confess to me. "And even then! I can't imagine a Parisian garden where I could pick those big bearded oats I sew on a bit of cardboard for you because they make such sensitive barometers." I chide myself for having lost the very last of those rustic barometers made of oat grains whose two awns, as long as a shrimp's feelers, crucified on a card, would turn to the left or the right according to whether it was going to be fine or wet.

No one could equal Sido, either, at separating and counting the talc-like skins of onions. "One—two—three coats; three coats on the onions!" And letting her spectacles or her lorgnette fall on her lap, she would add pensively: "That means a hard winter. I must have the pump wrapped in straw. Besides, the tortoise has dug itself in already, and the squirrels round about Guillemette have stolen quantities of walnuts and cobnuts for their stores. Squirrels always know everything."

If the newspapers foretold a thaw, my mother would shrug her shoulders and laugh scornfully. "A thaw? Those Paris meteorologists can't teach me anything about that! Look at the cat's paws!" Feeling chilly, the cat had indeed folded her paws out of sight beneath her, and shut her eyes tight. "When there's only going to be a short spell of cold," went on Sido, "the cat rolls herself into a turban with her nose against the root of her tail. But when it's going to be really bitter, she tucks in the pads of her front paws and rolls them up like a muff."

All the year round she kept racks full of plants in pots standing on green-painted wooden steps. There were rare geraniums, dwarf rose bushes, spiraeas with misty white and pink plumes, a few "succulents," hairy and squat as crabs, and murderous cacti. Two warm walls formed an angle which kept the harsh winds from her trial ground, which consisted of some red earthenware bowls in which I could see nothing but loose, dormant earth.

"Don't touch!"

"But nothing's coming up!"

"And what do you know about it? Is it for you to decide? Read what's written on the labels stuck in the pots! These are seeds of blue lupin; that's a narcissus bulb from Holland; those are seeds of winter cherry; that's a cutting of hibiscus—no, of course it isn't a dead twig!—and those are some seeds of sweet peas whose flowers have ears like little hares. And that . . . and that . . ."

"Yes, and that?"

My mother pushed her hat back, nibbled the chain of her lorgnette, and put the problem frankly to me:

"I'm really very worried. I can't remember whether it was a family of crocus bulbs I planted there, or the chrysalis of an emperor moth."

"We've only got to scratch to find out."

A swift hand stopped mine. Why did no one ever model or paint or carve that hand of Sido's, tanned and wrinkled early by household tasks, gardening, cold water, and the sun, with its long, finely tapering fingers and its beautiful, convex, oval nails?

"Not on your life! If it's the chrysalis, it'll die as soon as the air touches it, and if it's the crocus, the light will shrivel its little white shoot and we'll have to begin all over again. Are you taking in what I say? You won't touch it?"

"No, Mother."

As she spoke, her face, alight with faith and an all-embracing curiosity, was hidden by another, older face, resigned and gentle. She knew that I should not be able to resist, any more than she could, the desire to know, and that like herself I should ferret in the earth of that flowerpot until it had given up its secret. I never thought of our resemblance, but she knew I was her own daughter and that, child though I was, I was already seeking for that sense of shock, the quickened heartbeat, and the sudden stoppage of the breath—symptoms of the private ecstasy of the treasure seeker. A treasure is not merely something hidden under the earth or the rocks or the sea. The vision of gold and gems is but a blurred mirage. To me the important thing is to lay bare and bring to light something that no human eye before mine has gazed upon.

She knew then that I was going to scratch on the sly in her trial ground until I came upon the upward-climbing claw of the cotyledon, the sturdy sprout urged out of its sheath by the spring. I thwarted the blind purpose of the bilious-looking, black-brown chrysalis, and hurled it from its temporary death into a final nothingness.

"You don't understand . . . you can't understand. You're nothing but a little eight-year-old murderess—or is it ten? You just can't understand something that wants to live." That was the only punishment I got for my misdeeds; but that was hard enough for me to bear.

Sido loathed flowers to be sacrificed. Although her one idea was to give, I have seen her refuse a request for flowers to adorn a hearse or a grave. She would harden her heart, frown, and answer "No" with a vindictive look.

"But it's for poor Monsieur Enfert, who died last night! Poor Madame Enfert's so pathetic, she says if she could see her husband depart covered with flowers, it would console her! And you've got such lovely moss roses, Madame Colette."

"My moss roses on a corpse! What an outrage!"

It was an involuntary cry, but even after she had pulled herself together she still said: "No. My roses have not been condemned to die at the same time as Monsieur Enfert."

But she gladly sacrificed a very beautiful flower to a very small child, a child not yet able to speak, like the little boy whom a neighbor to the east proudly brought into the garden one day, to show him off to her. My mother found fault with the infant's swaddling clothes, for being too tight, untied his three-piece bonnet and his unnecessary woolen shawl, and then gazed to her heart's content on his bronze ringlets, his cheeks, and the enormous, stern black eyes of a ten months' old baby boy, really so much more beautiful than any other boy of ten months! She gave him a *cuisse-de-nymphe-émue* rose, and he accepted it with delight, put it in his mouth, and sucked it; then he kneaded it with his powerful little hands and tore off the petals, as curved and carmine as his own lips.

"Stop it, you naughty boy!" cried his young mother.

But mine, with looks and words, applauded his massacre of the rose, and in my jealousy I said nothing.

She also regularly refused to lend double geraniums, pelargoniums, lobelias, dwarf rose bushes and spiraea for the wayside altars on Corpus Christi day, for although she was baptized and married in church, she always held aloof from Catholic trivialities and pageantries. But she gave me permission, when I was between eleven and twelve, to attend catechism classes and to join in the hymns at the evening service.

On the first of May, with my comrades of the catechism class, I laid lilac, camomile, and roses before the altar of the Virgin, and returned full of pride to show my "blessed posy." My mother laughed her irreverent laugh and, looking at my bunch of flowers, which was bringing the May bugs into the sitting room right under the lamp, she said: "Do you suppose it wasn't already blessed before?"

I do not know where she got her aloofness from any form of worship. I ought to have tried to find out. My biographers, who get little information from me, sometimes depict her as a simple farmer's wife and sometimes make her out to be a "whimsical bohemian." One of them, to my astonishment, goes so far as to accuse her of having written short literary works for young persons!

In reality, this Frenchwoman spent her childhood in the Yonne, her adolescence among painters, journalists, and musicians in Belgium, where her two elder brothers had settled, and then returned to the Yonne, where she married twice. But whence, or from whom, she got her sensitive understanding of country matters and her discriminating appreciation of the provinces, I am unable to say. I sing her praises as best I may, and celebrate the native lucidity which, in her, dimmed and often extinguished the lesser lights painfully lit through the contact of what she called "the common run of mankind."

I once saw her hang up a scarecrow in a cherry tree to frighten the blackbirds, because our kindly neighbor of the west, who always had a cold and was shaken with bouts of sneezing, never failed to disguise his cherry trees as old tramps and crown his currant bushes with battered opera hats. A few days later I found my mother beneath the tree, motionless with excitement, her head turned toward the heavens in which she would allow human religions no place.

"Sssh! Look!"

A blackbird, with a green and violet sheen on his dark plumage, was pecking at the cherries, drinking their juice and lacerating their rosy pulp.

"How beautiful he is!" whispered my mother. "Do you see how he uses his claw? And the movements of his head and that arrogance of his? See how he twists his beak to dig out the stone! And you notice that he only goes for the ripest ones."

"But, mother, the scarecrow!"

"Sssh! The scarecrow doesn't worry him!"

"But, mother, the cherries!"

My mother brought the glance of her rain-colored eyes back to earth: "The cherries? Yes, of course, the cherries."

In those eyes there flickered a sort of wild gaiety, a contempt for the whole world, a lighthearted disdain which cheerfully spurned me along with everything else. It was only momentary, and it was not the first time I had seen it. Now that I know her better, I can interpret those sudden gleams in her face. They were, I feel, kindled by an urge to escape from everyone and everything, to soar to some high place where only her own writ ran. If I am mistaken, leave me to my delusion.

But there, under the cherry tree, she returned to earth once more among us, weighed down with anxieties, and love, and a husband and children who clung to her. Faced with the common round of life, she became good and comforting and humble again.

"Yes, of course, the cherries . . . you must have cherries too."

The blackbird, gorged, had flown off, and the scarecrow waggled his empty opera hat in the breeze.

BMCC

In those days there were bitter winters . . .

In those days there were bitter winters and burning summers. Since then I have known summers which, when I close my eyes, are the color of ocher-yellow earth, cracking between stalks of corn; and beneath the giant umbels of wild parsnip, the blue or gray of the sea. But no summer, save those of my childhood, enshrines the memory of scarlet geraniums and the glowing spikes of foxgloves. No winter now is ever pure white beneath a sky charged with slate-colored clouds foretelling a storm of thicker snowflakes yet to come, and thereafter a thaw glittering with a thousand waterdrops and bright with spear-shaped buds. How that sky used to lower over the snow-laden roof of the haylofts, the weathercock, and the bare boughs of the walnut tree, making the she-cats flatten their ears! The quiet vertical fall of the snow became oblique and, as I wandered about the garden catching its flying flakes in my mouth, a faint booming as of a distant sea arose above my hooded head. Warned by her antennae, my mother would come out on the terrace, sample the weather, and call out to me:

"A gale from the west! Run and shut the skylights in the barn! And the door of the coachhouse! And the window of the back room!"

Eager cabin boy of the family vessel, I would rush off, my
sabots clattering, thrilled if, from the depths of that hissing turmoil
of white and blue-black, a flash of lightning and a brief mutter of
thunder, children of February and the West wind, together filled one
of the abysses of the sky. I would try then to shudder and believe
that the end of the world had come.

But when the din was at its height, there would be my mother,
peering through a big brass-rimmed magnifying glass, lost in wonder as she counted the branched crystals of a handful of snow she
had just snatched from the very jaws of the West wind as it flung
itself upon our garden.

EMCC

"There is about a very beautiful child . . ."

"There is about a very beautiful child something I can't define which makes me sad. How can I make myself clear? Your
little niece C. is at this moment ravishingly beautiful. Full-face
she's still nothing much, but when she turns her profile in a certain way and you see the proud outline of her pure little nose below her lovely lashes, I am seized with an admiration that somehow disturbs me. They say that great lovers feel like that before
the object of their passion. Can it be then that, in my way, I am
a great lover? That's a discovery that would much have astonished
my two husbands!"

So she was able, was she, to bend over a human flower with no
harm to herself, no harm save for that "sadness"; was sadness her
word for that melancholy ecstasy, that sense of exaltation which up-
lifts us when we see the waxen purity of faces dissolving into an
arabesque never resembling its original, never twice the same: the
dual fires of the eyes, the nostrils like twin calyxes, the little sea cave
of the mouth quivering as it waits for its prey? When she bent over
a glorious childish creature she would tremble and sigh, seized with
an anguish she could not explain, whose name is temptation. For it

would never have occurred to her that from a youthful face there
could emanate a perturbation, a mist like that which floats above
grapes in their vat, or that one could succumb to it. My first com-
munings with myself taught me the lesson, though I failed to observe it sometimes: "Never touch a butterfly's wing with your
finger."

"I certainly won't . . . or only just lightly . . . just at the
tawny-black place where you see that violet glow, that moon lick,
without being able to say exactly where it starts or where it dies
away."

"No, don't touch it. The whole thing will vanish if you merely
brush it."

"But only just lightly! Perhaps this will be the time when I
shall feel under this particular finger, my fourth, the most sensitive,
the cold blue flame and the way it vanishes into the skin of the
wing—the feathers of the wing—the dew of the wing . . ." A trace
of lifeless ash on the tip of my finger, the wing dishonored, the tiny
creature weakened.

There is no doubt that my mother, who only learned, as she
said, "by getting burnt," knew that one possesses through abstaining,
and only through abstaining. For a "great lover" of her sort—of our
sort—there is not much difference between the sin of abstention and
that of consummation. Serene and gay in presence of her husband,
she became disturbed, and distracted with an unexplained passion,
when she came in contact with someone who was passing through a
sublime experience. Confined to her village by her two successive
husbands and four children, she had the power of conjuring up
everywhere unexpected crises, burgeonings, metamorphoses, and
dramatic miracles, which she herself provoked and whose value she
savored to the full. She who nursed animals, cared for children, and
looked after plants was spared the discovery that some creatures
want to die, that certain children long to be defiled, that one of the
buds is determined to be forced open and then trampled underfoot.
Her form of inconstancy was to fly from the bee to the mouse, from
a newborn child to a tree, from a poor person to a poorer, from

laughter to torment! How pure are those who lavish themselves in this way! In her life there was never the memory of a dishonored wing, and if she trembled with longing in the presence of a closed calyx, a chrysalis still rolled in its vanished cocoon, at least she respectfully awaited the moment. How pure are those who have never forced anything open! To bring my mother close to me again I have to think back to those dramatic dreams she dreamed throughout the adolescence of her elder son, who was so beautiful and so seductive. At that time I was aware that she was wild, full of false gaiety, given to maledictions, ordinary, plain-looking, and on the alert. Oh, if only I could see her again thus diminished, her cheeks flushed red with jealousy and rage! If only I could see her thus, and could she but understand me well enough to recognize herself in what she would most strongly have reproved! If only I, grown wise in my turn, could show her how much her own image, though coarsened and impure, survives in me, her faithful servant, whose job is the menial tasks! She gave me life and the mission to pursue those things which she, a poet, seized and cast aside as one snatches a fragment of a floating melody drifting through space. What does the melody matter to one whose concern is the bow and the hand that holds the bow?

She pursued her innocent ends with increasing anxiety. She rose early, then earlier, then earlier still. She wanted to have the world to herself, deserted, in the form of a little enclosure with a trellis and a sloping roof. She wanted the jungle to be virgin but, even so, inhabited only by swallows, cats, and bees, and the huge spider balancing atop his wheel of lace silvered by the night. The neighbor's shutter, banging against the wall, spoiled her dream of being an unchallengeable explorer, a dream repeated every day at the hour when the cold dew seems to be falling, with little irregular plops, from the beaks of the blackbirds. She got up at six, then at five, and at the end of her life a little red lamp wakened her, in winter, long before the Angelus smote the black air. In those moments while it was still night my mother used to sing, falling silent as soon as anyone was able to hear. The lark also sings while it is

mounting toward the palest, least inhabited part of the sky. My
mother climbed too, mounting ceaselessly up the ladder of the
hours, trying to possess the beginning of the beginning. I know what
that particular intoxication is like. But what she sought was a red,
horizontal ray, and the pale sulphur that comes before the red ray;
she wanted the damp wing that the first bee stretches out like an
arm. The summer wind, which springs up at the approach of the
sun, gave her its first fruits in scents of acacia and woodsmoke; when
a horse pawed the ground and whinnied softly in the neighboring
stable, she was the first to hear it. On an autumn morning she was
the only one to see herself reflected in the first disk of ephemeral ice
in the well bucket, before her nail cracked it.

BMCC

The time came . . .

The time came when all her strength left her. She was amazed
beyond measure and would not believe it. Whenever I arrived from
Paris to see her, as soon as we were alone in the afternoon in her
little house, she had always some sin to confess to me. On one occasion she turned up the hem of her dress, rolled her stocking down
over her shin, and displayed a purple bruise, the skin nearly broken.

"Just look at that!"

"What on earth have you done to yourself this time, Mother?"

She opened wide eyes, full of innocence and embarrassment.

"You wouldn't believe it, but I fell downstairs!"

"How do you mean—'fell'?"

"Just what I said. I fell, for no reason. I was going downstairs
and I fell. I can't understand it."

"Were you going down too quickly?"

"Too quickly? What do you call too quickly? I was going down
quickly. Have I time to go downstairs majestically like the Sun
King? And if that were all . . . But look at this!"

On her pretty arm, still so young above the faded hand, was a
scald forming a large blister.

"Oh goodness! Whatever's that!"

"My footwarmer."

"The old copper footwarmer? The one that holds five quarts?"

"That's the one. Can I trust anything, when that footwarmer has known me for forty years? I can't imagine what possessed it, it was boiling fast, I went to take it off the fire, and crack, something gave in my wrist. I was lucky to get nothing worse than the blister. But what a thing to happen! After that I let the cupboard alone. . . ."

She broke off, blushing furiously.

"What cupboard?" I demanded severely.

My mother fenced, tossing her head as though I were trying to put her on a lead.

"Oh, nothing! No cupboard at all!"

"Mother! I shall get cross!"

"Since I've said, 'I let the cupboard alone,' can't you do the same for my sake? The cupboard hasn't moved from its place, has it? So, shut up about it!"

The cupboard was a massive object of old walnut, almost as broad as it was high, with no carving save the circular hole made by a Prussian bullet that had entered by the right-hand door and passed out through the back panel.

"Do you want it moved from the landing, Mother?"

An expression like that of a young she-cat, false and glittery, appeared on her wrinkled face.

"I? No, it seems to me all right there—let it stay where it is!"

All the same, my doctor brother and I agreed that we must be on the watch. He saw my mother every day, since she had followed him and lived in the same village, and he looked after her with a passionate devotion which he hid. She fought against all her ills with amazing elasticity, forgot them, baffled them, inflicted on them signal if temporary defeats, recovered, during entire days, her vanished strength; and the sound of her battles, whenever I spent a few days with her, could be heard all over the house till I was irresistibly reminded of a terrier tackling a rat.

At five o'clock in the morning I would be awakened by the clank of a full bucket being set down in the kitchen sink immediately opposite my room.

"What are you doing with that bucket, Mother? Couldn't you wait until Josephine arrives?"

And out I hurried. But the fire was already blazing, fed with dry wood. The milk was boiling on the blue-tiled charcoal stove. Nearby, a bar of chocolate was melting in a little water for my breakfast, and, seated squarely in her cane armchair, my mother was grinding the fragrant coffee which she roasted herself. The morning hours were always kind to her. She wore their rosy colors in her cheeks. Flushed with a brief return to health, she would gaze at the rising sun, while the church bell rang for early Mass, and rejoice at having tasted, while we still slept, so many forbidden fruits.

The forbidden fruits were the overheavy bucket drawn up from the well, the firewood split with a billhook on an oaken block, the spade, the mattock, and above all the double steps propped against the gable window of the woodhouse. There were the climbing vine whose shoots she trained up to the gable windows of the attic, the flowery spikes of the too-tall lilacs, the dizzy cat that had to be rescued from the ridge of the roof. All the accomplices of her old existence as a plump and sturdy little woman, all the minor rustic divinities who once obeyed her and made her so proud of doing without servants, now assumed the appearance and position of adversaries. But they reckoned without that love of combat which my mother was to keep till the end of her life. At seventy-one, dawn still found her undaunted, if not always undamaged. Burnt by the fire, cut with the pruning knife, soaked by melting snow or spilled water, she had always managed to enjoy her best moments of independence before the earliest risers had opened their shutters. She was able to tell us of the cats' awakening, of what was going on in the nests, of news gleaned, together with the morning's milk and the warm loaf, from the milkmaid and the baker's girl, the record in fact of the birth of a new day.

It was not until one morning when I found the kitchen un-warmed, and the blue enamel saucepan hanging on the wall, that I felt my mother's end to be near. Her illness knew many respites, during which the fire flared up again on the hearth, and the smell of fresh bread and melting chocolate stole under the door together with the cat's impatient paw. These respites were periods of unexpected alarms. My mother and the big walnut cupboard were discovered together in a heap at the foot of the stairs, she having determined to transport it in secret from the upper landing to the ground floor. Whereupon my elder brother insisted that my mother should keep still and that an old servant should sleep in the little house. But how could an old servant prevail against a vital energy so youthful and mischievous that it contrived to tempt and lead astray a body already half fettered by death? My brother, returning before sunrise from attending a distant patient, one day caught my mother red-handed in the most wanton of crimes. Dressed in her nightgown, but wearing heavy gardening sabots, her little gray septuagenarian's plait of hair turning up like a scorpion's tail on the nape of her neck, one foot firmly planted on the crosspiece of the beech trestle, her back bent in the attitude of the expert jobber, my mother, rejuvenated by an inde-scribable expression of guilty enjoyment, in defiance of all her prom-ises and of the freezing morning dew, was sawing logs in her own yard.

UVT/EMCC

"Sir, you ask me . . ."

"Sir,

"You ask me to come and spend a week with you, which means I would be near my daughter, whom I adore. You who live with her know how rarely I see her, how much her presence de-lights me, and I'm touched that you should ask me to come and see her. All the same I'm not going to accept your kind invitation, for the time being at any rate. The reason is that my pink cactus is probably going to flower. It's a very rare plant I've been given, and I'm told that in our climate it flowers only once every four years. Now, I am already a very old woman, and if I went away when my pink cactus is about to flower, I am certain I shouldn't see it flower again.

"So I beg you, sir, to accept my sincere thanks and my regrets, together with my kind regards."

This note, signed *"Sidonie Colette, née Landoy,"* was written by my mother to one of my husbands, the second. A year later she died, at the age of seventy-seven.

Whenever I feel myself inferior to everything about me, threatened by my own mediocrity, frightened by the discovery that a muscle is losing its strength, a desire its power, or a pain the keen edge of its bite, I can still hold up my head and say to myself: "I am the daughter of the woman who wrote that letter—that letter and so many more that I have kept. This one tells me in ten lines that at the age of seventy-six she was planning journeys and undertaking them, but that waiting for the possible bursting into bloom of a tropical flower held everything up and silenced even her heart, made for love. I am the daughter of a woman who, in a mean, close-fisted, confined little place, opened her village home to stray cats, tramps, and pregnant servant girls. I am the daughter of a woman who many a time, when she was in despair at not having enough money for others, ran through the wind-whipped snow to cry from door to door, at the houses of the rich, that a child had just been born in a poverty-stricken home to parents whose feeble, empty hands had no swaddling clothes for it. Let me not forget that I am the daughter of a woman who bent her head, trembling, between the blades of a cactus, her wrinkled face full of ecstasy over the promise of a flower, a woman who herself never ceased to flower, untiringly, during three quarters of a century."

BMCC

❧❧ Sido and I

"You've thrown a chestnut hull . . ."

"You've thrown a chestnut hull into the fireplace again, Minet-Chéri."

"No, Mamma."

"Oh yes, my child."

And Sido, my mother, picked out the offending object with the tongs and brandished it under my nose. ("Just why did you choose to inherit my nose, you little duffer?")

"My clean ashes! To soil my precious ashes of applewood, poplar, and elm! What about my washing? I've told you twenty times . . ."

It was not out of disrespect that I did not listen to what she said then, although it was an old story. A child's attention obeys the keenest of its five senses, and even at that early age mine was the sense of smell. Scarcely had my mother pronounced the word "washing" than I seemed to smell the sweetish odor of the ashes spread on the hempen cloth stretched over the big caldron in the washhouse. At regular intervals, the washerwoman poured a jug of boiling water on the layer of ashes, which filtered the lye into the mass of soiled linen . . . The darkened air, blue with vapor, rolled out in distinct clouds, veiling the great round stove and its pipe that pierced the ceiling. Enormous, armored in her big apron, the washerwoman floated from one side of the room to the other, in defiance of the laws of gravity, it would seem. A bundle of iris roots, bone-white, hung from a nail. The smooth and smoking lava of the layer of ashes retained a few small black cinders—raisins in the cake, truffles in the *foie gras*—and I burned my fingers as I plucked them out. "All you had to do was not touch them, *ma petite servante*," said the washerwoman. For the sweetest names a nurse, a domestic, or a mother can bestow upon a child they've known since it came into the world, is "my little helper."

"I've told you twenty times," Sido went on, "that the tannin in chestnut hulls makes a yellow stain. When will you learn the things a woman should know, if you don't learn them now?"

"When I'm married," I fatuously replied.

The effect of such a retort on my mother Sido went beyond what I expected. Snatching off her distance glasses, she seized her lorgnette, which had been mended with wire, leveled it on me as if to make sure that my reply had not cast an evil spell and already deposited me, aged only fifteen, in the arms of an abductor. Her brows drew together in a frown, deepening the vertical wrinkle, narrowing her eyes.

"How delightful!" she exclaimed. "You take after your father, who is also fond of joking!"

"Why, I wasn't joking, Mamma. I hope to marry. After all, you were married twice."

"Do as I say, not as I do," quoted Sido, sententiously.

"If Papa heard you . . ."

"I hear her," said a magnificent male voice from behind the wide-opened newspaper *Le Temps*.

"And he dares pretend he's hard of hearing!" murmured Sido indignantly.

She flushed, however. Although past fifty, she still had the pink cheeks of a young girl, and they reddened twenty times a day, whenever she battled her children or broke a blue cup or was caught in a loving attitude with my father.

Did I give her a great deal of trouble? Maybe yes, maybe no. She counted on me and took me seriously, so long as practical notions and housekeeping procedures were not concerned. I listened and retained all she taught me, and I have still forgotten none of it. But although I knew how to carve a raddish rose, and although no one could equal me when it came to turning a blade of grass into a flute or polishing up an old ten-centime piece until it gleamed like gold, or skimming—to my own benefit—the pink foam that rises on strawberries or currants simmering in the preserving kettle, on the other hand I burnt the butter, my sewing was worse than a soldier's, and in the midst of wiping the mirror over my fireplace I would stop to read, standing there with an open book on the mantelshelf.

"And if only my washing was concerned!" Sido went on. "But what about the ashes for the potatoes? You surely know they have to be impeccably clean . . ."

The ashes for the potatoes reposed in an urn, as if they were the ashes of a hero. By urn I mean a three-legged black cast-iron kettle, standing rather high on its outspread legs and provided with a convex lid with one sole flange. Seeing it at a distance in the gloom, one thought, "What is that strange animal?" In the ashes it contained, fine grayish-white and sifted ashes, we carefully buried a few big unpeeled potatoes, then planted the whole thing in the glowing coals, over which we heaped more ashes. Cooked without water or steam, the potatoes became marvelously "floury"; you needed only to add some fresh butter and a pinch of salt. Under their powdery skin I found both the main course and the dessert, for I also mixed in with their crumbly flesh some very sweet apple sauce. In the same way, we cooked those beetroots that go so well with lamb's lettuce in a salad . . .

"Since you can't wait for the time to come when you'll be leaving me," said Sido, "go out now to the fields and fetch me some lamb's lettuce. Take the knife with the blunt blade."

She did not have to repeat the command. On the instant, I was running down the street, Sido standing in the doorway and shouting her final urgent injunctions:

"Don't go by way of the Petit-Moulin fields, they're flooded! And don't go toward Thury—gypsy wagons are there! And see that you get back before dark! Mind you don't eat any spindle berries or sloes in the hedges! And don't put the salad with all its dirt in your pockets!"

Out of sight, I furiously shrugged and muttered to myself, "No, really, for goodness' sake!" What kind of opinion did parents have of their children, and would my mother—"Oh, for heaven's sake!" —would she ever realize that I was practically fifteen years old?

Beyond the reach of the maternal voice—a modulated soprano with a wide range but never harsh—I determinedly went toward Petit-Moulin and its flooded meadows. Five hundred steps farther on, I stuffed myself with the sloes and spindle berries in the hedges; the one almost tasteless, the other so acid it almost took off the roof of my mouth. And since I kept getting farther and farther away from the broken old basket I had set down, as I went from one bunch of field salad to another, I stuffed my harvest into my pockets . . .

Ritual gestures, in which calculated disobedience played no part. Ever since I could walk, the deserted countryside had constituted my unmapped domain. Who else could have known as I did when the juniper berry and the wild strawberry and the hazelnut were ripe? Who else kept secret as I did the preferred habitat of the May lily, the white narcissi, the squirrels? To each one his fief. Did I dispute with Sido the sovereignty of our household? The discovery of a fairy ring of mushrooms led me to look for another, and still another. I gathered a bouquet of mauve meadow saffron, those votive candles of the fields, along with some late-blooming scabious. The autumn twilight descended, with its thrilling odor of damp oak leaves underfoot and of the fertile swamp. It was the hour when Sido planted herself on the doorstep of our house to watch for my return. Would she see me appear at the bottom of the street or at the top? She turned her head from right to left, from left to right, like a mother bird sitting on the edge of its nest. This was the hour of her great torment. To wait for me, she threw around her shoulders and over her head whatever piece of clothing she had snatched up as she passed the coat hanger in the front hall. Thus I sometimes saw her with one of my father's overcoats or my little old hooded cape that was barely good enough for gardening, and sometimes even a blue apron knotted by its strings under her chin. She was Worry Incarnate, beneath these varying insignia . . . Other attributes—a pair of spectacles, two pairs of spectacles, a pair of spyglasses, a magnifying glass—proclaimed that she was also Discovery.

Sido's great word was "Look!" And it could signify "Look at the hairy caterpillar, it's like a little golden bear! Look at the first bean sprout that is raising up on its head a little hat of dried earth . . . Look at the wasp, see how it cuts with its scissors mandibles a bit of raw meat." At sunset she would say, "Look at that red sky, it forecasts a high wind and storm." What matters the high wind of tomorrow, provided we admire that fiery furnace today? Or it would be, "Look, be quick, the bud of the purple iris is opening! Be quick, or it will open before you can see it . . ."

However, the minute I turned the corner of the street, at the top or at the bottom, Sido disappeared indoors so as not to seem to have been waiting for me. For my part, I pretended not to know that she had followed at a distance my youthful figure adorned with long hair, recalling my little cat face with its wide forehead and pointed chin, thinking of my fifteen years and my confidence in the familiar countryside, where I had never experienced a nasty encounter . . . Under the pale green dome of the hanging lamp, her eyes scrutinized me, with a sharp, almost hard look, surveying me from head to foot, deciphering the reason for my scratched cheek, my muddy shoes, totting up the damages: "A trickle of blood on her cheek, a snag near one shoulder, the hem of her skirt ripped and wet, shoes and stockings soaked like sponges . . . That's all. That's all there is. Once more, that's all there is, thank God . . ."

HB

"As sure as I'm here . . ."

"As sure as I'm here," she used to tell me, "I've seen it snowing in the month of July."

"In the month of July!"

"Yes, on a day like this."

"Like this . . ."

I had a habit of repeating the ends of her sentences. My voice was already lower than hers, but I used to imitate her way of talking, and I still do.

"Yes, like this," said my mother, blowing away an airy wisp of silvery fluff, pulled from the coat of the Havanese bitch she was combing. The fluff, finer than spun glass, was caught gently up in a little stream of ascending air, rose to the ceiling, and was lost to view in the dazzle of light there.

"It was a lovely day," my mother went on, "lovely and warm. All of a sudden the wind changed, caught the tail end of a storm, and piled it all up, to the East of course. Next came a spatter of very cold, fine hail, and finally a heavy fall of big, thick snowflakes. Snow covered the roses and lay on the ripe cherries and the tomatoes. The red geraniums had had no time to cool down, and they melted the snow as fast as it covered them. All *his* tricks, of course," she concluded, with a jerk of her elbow and a defiant thrust of her chin, toward the lofty throne, the invisible Judgment Seat, of her enemy the East, whom I tried to see beyond the warm, white, tumbling clouds of a fine summer day.

"But I've seen something much stranger than that!" my mother went on.

"Stranger than that?"

Could it be that one day, on her way to Bel-Air or on the road to Thury, she had met the East in person? Perhaps a huge foot, blue with cold, and the frozen pool of an immense eyeball, had cleft the clouds so that she might describe them to me?

"I was expecting your brother Léo at the time, and one day I was out driving the mare, in the victoria."

"The same mare we have now?"

"Why of course the same mare. You're only ten. Do you suppose one changes a mare as one does a chemise? In those days our mare was a beautiful creature, a bit on the young side, and sometimes I let Antoine drive her. But I always went in the victoria to reassure her."

I remember wanting to ask: "To reassure whom?" but I refrained, so that I could go on believing in the possible ambiguity: after all, why should not my mother's presence have reassured the victoria?

"You see, when she heard my voice she felt quieter."

Of course she did, very quiet and all spick and span, in her blue upholstery between her two handsome carriage lamps with their brass crowns of cloverleaf pattern. The very image of a reassured victoria, couldn't be more so!

"My goodness, daughter, what a silly look you've got on your face at this moment! Are you listening to me?"

"Yes, Mother."

"Well, then, it was one of those terribly hot days, and we'd been for a long drive. I was enormous and I felt very heavy. We were on our way back at a walking pace, and I remember I'd been cutting flowering broom. We'd just drawn level with the cemetery —no, this isn't a ghost story—when a cloud, a real southern cloud, copper-colored with a little rim of quicksilver all around it, began to climb rapidly up the sky, gave a clap of thunder, and shot out water like a bucket with a hole in it. Down got Antoine and wanted to put up the hood to shelter me. But I said to him: 'No, the first thing is to hold the mare's head, because if it hails, she'll bolt while you're putting up the hood.' So he held the mare, who was dancing a bit where she stood, and I started talking to her just as if it had neither rained nor thundered, you know, just as if we were going out for a quiet drive in fine weather. Meanwhile an unbelievable downpour of water was falling on my wretched little sunshade. When the cloud had passed, I was left sitting in a hip bath, Antoine was wet through and the hood full of water, and what was more, quite warm water. And when Antoine went to empty the hood, what do you think we found in it? Frogs, tiny live frogs, at least thirty of them. They'd been carried through the air, owing to some freak of the southern atmosphere, by one of those hot whirlwinds or tornadoes whose corkscrew foot picks up a tuft of sand and seeds and insects and carries them a hundred leagues away. And that I've seen with my own eyes!"

She brandished the steel comb we used for unraveling the knots in the coats of the Havanese bitch and the angoras, not in the least astonished that meteorological marvels should have waited for her to pass that way, and treated her so familiarly.

You can easily understand how the South wind, conjured up by Sido, rose before my mind's eye, swirling on its corkscrew foot rooted in the Libyan Desert, and bedecked with seeds and sand and dead butterflies. It shook its shapeless, disheveled head and out fell water and the rain of frogs. I can see it still.

BMCC

Mothers and children . . .

Mothers and children; bitches and their puppies; female cats and their kittens, a dozen or so per head or, rather, per cat belly; the cow Violette, her calf that was taken away from her; swallows that lined their nest with chicken down laced together with some of my long hairs; the litter of mice, six tiny ones the size of wasps, all being suckled at once by their tiny mother . . . There were few male animals. Now and then there was an interminable tomcat, black as a wet eel, and a stray dog, a bloodhound offered us as a gift which we dared not refuse . . . But mothers and their offspring, in their turn fertile! There was never any lack of these during the first twenty years of my life. This was the natural order of things, as inevitable as the course of a river. Did I perhaps think less about my own mother than about all these mother creatures surrounding me? Perhaps. We never think about the presence of the air.

"Is your mommy coming to fetch you at four o'clock?" I asked my schoolmates.

"Yes, she's coming to fetch me."

But mine, my "mommy," did not come for me. She disliked the

sight of my school face, a bit dirty, and my hair and clothes steeped in the smell of other children . . . I believe she never came to fetch me. I always encountered her at the boundaries of her empire, standing on our doorstep, turned in the direction of the narrow street, the rue des Soeurs, when I was late. If I didn't dawdle on the way, if I didn't make a detour to accompany Camille Corneau or Jeanne David, then there was no vigil behind the wrought-iron grille—which bore the initials of my mother's first husband. She would not be out there watching for me, and I would go into the garden to look for her.

There I would find her bending over a plant, searching for the mole cricket that was decimating the lettuce, or crouching down to fumble among the dense foliage of the double violets—when and upon what marvels did I not see her bent over, absorbed? One day I surprised her kneeling beside the basket that had been arranged for the mother cat.

"Don't disturb her, she's having her babies. She's already had two, and the third is coming. Don't make a noise, she's in labor."

She did not add, "Now be off with you," but said, "Look!" And it wasn't her fault if I turned away.

I did not learn from her that between mothers and offspring there exists a strict and perfect love called sacred, which cannot be broken except at great cost and great scandal. On the contrary, with an imperious hand she waved away the fruits of these teachings that I had acquired at school or in my books.

"Mamma! The mother cat's daughter is fighting her! Oh! And she's really hitting her!"

"Well, the time for that has come. What can we do? It is written."

"Where, written?"

"Everywhere."

"That I will fight you?"

"No. I'd no longer be young enough. But . . . you will leave me."

"Why?"

"Because it is written, it's fate. Look, Louise Thomazeau has left her mother, to get married."

"Yes, I know. That's what makes Madame Thomazeau so sad, that's why she stays in bed."

Sido jumped as if stung, then turned her neat plump self toward me, grasping her shears and planter, her gray eyes flashing with sudden wrath.

"Madame Thomazeau is a harpy, a bad mother, an old horror, a dangerous fool, a fake, a criminal—and I'm not saying all I think! At a distance Madame Thomazeau is cleverly poisoning the life of her daughter and son-in-law, she's carrying out an abominable blackmail to get back her daughter! And you go into ecstasies over her grief!"

"Oh, I didn't go into ecstasies over . . ."

"And you think I ought to take some roses to Madame Thomazeau!"

"Why, I never said I wanted you to go taking . . ."

Her exasperation expired in a sigh, and what she then said changed everything.

"I know, I know, Minet-Chéri. But all the same, I will go. That Madame Thomazeau who is aging visibly, on purpose . . . Those windows kept shut in fine weather . . . That photograph of her daughter at her bedside, a wedding picture—every time she looks at it she casts an evil spell. Oh!"

With the flat of her hand she pushed my hair out of my eyes, exposing the wide forehead which I concealed and which she considered beautiful.

"Well, it's that woman," she continued, "who is teaching me everything a mother should take care *not* to do . . ."

It may seem strange that anyone with such a spontaneous and watchful maternal feeling as hers should abominate large families. Capable of coming to their assistance, she regarded them with a kind of consternation. According to her moral standards, which derived from no ethical system, an imposing series of offspring was a thing to be blamed.

"We're not made for bearing such broods," she said. "I always feel that the children in such large families are jerry-built."

"But, Mamma, there are four of us, that's a pretty big family." She blushed hotly.

"I beg your pardon! I've had two husbands. And so I've been the mother of two children twice. And you are all so different! What terrifies me is when the children in a family are all alike. Look at those pitiful little Pluvier children! Nine pairs of blue eyes, nine heads of curly fair hair, nine straight little noses, nine sets of teeth all alike, with the incisors far apart. Ugh!"

"But, Mamma, they are pretty children, aren't they?" She shook her head, her eyes again wrathful.

"Pretty? Oh yes, they're pretty. A nightmare of pretty children . . ."

But her greatest horror was the Sarcus family, its name and physical characteristics branding it as of Jewish or Gypsy origin. Twenty-two times had the enormous Sarcus mother discharged the fruit of her loins haphazardly, beside the washtub, in the plot of carrots, in front of the cold fireplace, as if absent-mindedly. Even so, she had lost some, but she consoled herself with the eighteen survivors, all of them skinny and swarthy, the very image of their father. My mother heard and relayed the Sarcus family news as if the subject were a ruinous hailstorm or an invasion. All the same, her exasperation was not unproductive but found expression in turning out the chests of drawers and delving into the depths of the huge cupboards, searching for and bringing to light the soft old blanket that would cover the eighteenth little Sarcus. Her good deeds and her pity were then accompanied by a string of muttered maledictions, all the more spellbinding since they concerned a certain "old billy goat of a tailor"—by which appelation I did not yet recognize Sarcus *père,* a little man but imperturbably prolific.

However, I could not help remarking from my very early years that Sido's kindness lavished upon the newborn, all and any newborn, and upon anxious mothers nearing their time, did not extend to the progenitor. She had a cutting way of puncturing the fatuity of young fathers who blissfully sat at the side of a weakened young mother in childbed. Moffino, our hunting dog, was roughly relieved of the benevolent guard he was keeping beside a basket full of puppies.

"But, Mamma, they're his children!" I sobbed.

On my mother's face sparkled that impenetrable and combative gaiety that so often disconcerted me.

"Exactly," she said.

"Oh, poor Moffino," I sniveled, "where can he go?"

"Wherever his role as father takes him," retorted my mother. "To the tavern. Or to play cards with Landre. Or to flirt with the washerwoman."

Her joking never condescended to our level. Too proud, and having confidence in her children, she let us run our chance of catching up with her, of recognizing a joke beneath an allusion or a play on words; in this way she sharpened our wits and made us a bit disdainful of outsiders and infatuated with a family argot, which did not concern language alone but shaped our feelings and sentiments.

"How ugly you are, child, when you cry. Come, Minet-Chéri, let me prettify you again."

She assigned the dog to a place in the background, where he lay down with a great rumble and thump that sounded like a bag of potatoes being emptied.

And I curled up at the feet of Sido, my head at her knees. The three-o'clock sunlight closed my eyelids and the to-and-fro movement of the comb made me drowsy. In the depths of a rattan armchair slept a pregnant cat; stretching out my hand, I felt her inhabited flanks, the round heads of the imprisoned litter, and its dolphin leaps beneath the flood. Blissful, the mongrel bitch suckled her mongrel pups, a mixture of pointer and griffon and heaven knows what. No half-grown males anywhere, no sign of a man. Mothers. Children still ignorant of their sex. The deep peace of a harem, under the nests of May and the wisteria shot with sunlight. I was no longer linked with the real world except by the purring of the cat, the clear ringing of a nearby anvil, and the hands of my mother at the back of my neck, deftly braiding my hair . . .

HB

In the countryside where I was born . . .

In the countryside where I was born, Christmas did not count for much when I was a child. The free-thinking citizens of my part of the country suppressed as much as possible a feast day nineteen centuries old and the festival of all children. My mother, my dearly beloved atheist Sido, did not attend the midnight Mass, where congregated, as they did on Sundays, all the exemplary families and a few of the gentry who came from their châteaux in closed carriages. She was afraid I might catch a cold in the church with its blasted belfry, its drafts, its cracked flagstones. Possibly, too, she was afraid I might be charmed and ensnared by the Catholic incense, the flowers, the spellbinding canticles, the sweet vertigo of the responses . . . She did not discuss all this with me, a ten-year-old child. I have told elsewhere how the old parish priest, while preferring her to his pious congregation, was still never able to overcome her resistance to religion. Between them there was no least casuistry, there was no question of anything but me, my religious instruction, the catechism, my first communion. And Sido, brows knitted, bit a fingernail.

It goes without saying that I allied myself ardently with Father Millot, who had baptized me, and that I wanted everything the Church offered: catechism, sung vespers, white dress and ruched cap. I wanted and had the Hail Marys in the month of May, the Month of Mary, when the days are so long that through the wide-open great portal of the church, facing the high altar, you saw the sun set beyond the tapers, while the odor of the sheep flocks climbing the hill toward the village mingled with the scent of camomille, the first lilies and the white roses surrounding the plaster Virgin . . . Who could have given to the parish that great big Virgin of bygone days, white, with a blue sash? The statue was discolored, but not with age;

the dampness of our poor church had told against her, and a retouching with paint—the black pupil of the eye which had been brightened by an inexpert hand—had deprived her of serenity.

It was during my first months of catechism, at the start of the October term, that I came in contact with the pupils of the free church school. Usually, we of the laity kept them at a distance, because childish opinions are fiercely and savagely held. But in the catechism lessons and in the divine services, we breathed an air of sweetness that was bound to captivate the miscreants ten years old and over. And what a delight it is to make friends with someone you have despised! That day when I felt my little girl's shoulder pressed by a similar shoulder, when a flaxen braid slid against one of my braids and hung over my open book, and an ink-stained finger with a black nail underscored the Latin text and I heard a voice murmur in my ear: "That's where we take up again with *O-ra pro no-bis*," I was subjugated.

Subjugated—but not in the least by piety. Rather, I was subjugated by the unknown, by the childish refrains that my school did not teach, by the "selected verses" that were more moving than ours and full of God, by the genuflections and glib prayers, the exchanges of medals and rosaries, and above all by the fascinating tales of the gifts the Christ Child left in one's shoes early on Christmas morning.

I remember the first time a little girl spoke to me about this and I remember my reply.

The little girl was one of those whose "dedication" to the Holy Virgin showed in her blue-and-white attire—blue dress, white pinafore, a blue cord tying her braid, a silver medal at her throat.

"What did the Christ Child put in your shoes this Christmas?" she asked.

"My shoes? You make me laugh!" I almost roared. "How many times must I tell you it's our parents who put gifts in our shoes and not the Christ Child? Anyway, Christmas doesn't count, the best day of all is New Year's Day."

Covering their mouths with their hands, the "nun's pets" ran away, with exclamations of horror.

"Oh! Did you hear? Oh, did you hear what she said!"

I can still hear their wooden shoes clattering in the distance, and their exclamations transformed into a chorus: "Ohdidjahear, didjahear whatshesaid!"

By December I had become less uncouth and was almost soulful. I reread the tales of Hans Christian Andersen, on account of the snow and Christmas. I asked my mother to tell me Christmas stories. Her penetrating gray eyes met mine, she felt my forehead and took my pulse, made me show my tongue and drink some sweetened hot wine, in my battered little silver cup.

In lower Burgundy, the goblet of mulled wine is a panacea. Even diluted with a few drops of water, it loosened my tongue as I sat by the fire of apple-wood logs. My wooden shoes, filled with hot cinders, were steaming as they slowly dried out, and I wriggled my toes in their woolen socks as I talked.

"Mamma, Gabrielle Vallée told me that last Christmas, in her wooden shoes . . . Mamma, Julotte des Gendrons, she told me that at Christmas she had seen a comet in the fireplace . . . And Fifine, but really, Mamma, this is true, cross my heart and hope to die if I'm telling a lie, Fifine saw something like a moon fall into her sabots, on Christmas morning, and a crown all of flowers, and next day . . ."

"Calm yourself, drink," said my mother.

She said "drink" as if she meant to say, "Get drunk and talk." She listened to me, unsmiling, and with the kind of consideration she often showed with children. Becoming confidential, the Treigny wine reddening my cheeks, I recounted and invented:

"Anyway, Father Millot did say that it's always on Christmas Eve that . . . And Mathilde's brother! Two years ago on Christmas Eve he went to look at his cows, and above the tool shed he saw in the sky a great big star that said to him . . ."

My beloved Sido laid her quick hand on my arm and peered at me so intently that I was struck dumb.

"You believe all that? Do you really believe all that, Minet-Chéri? If you do believe . . ."

I was abashed. A frost flower that I alone could see and could hear tinkling as it hung in the air, a frost flower that was called Christmas drifted away from me.

"But I'm not scolding you," said my mother. "You've done nothing bad. Give me that cup. It's empty."

Only a few days, a few nights afterward I was wakened before daylight by a presence rather than by a sound. Used to sleeping in a chilly room, I opened my eyes without moving and gently pulled the blanket up to my nose, taking care to keep the down quilt over my feet, which were set against the stoneware hot-water bottle. The winter dawn and my pink night light in the form of a crenelated tower divided my room into two parts, one cheerful, the other gloomy. Wearing her thick dressing gown of purple flannel lined with gray flannel, my mother was standing in front of the fireplace, looking toward my bed. Very softly she whispered, "Are you asleep?" and I almost replied, quite sincerely, "Yes, Mamma."

In one hand she was holding my sabots, which she now set down noiselessly in front of the empty fireplace, and on them she balanced a square parcel, then an oblong bag, decorating the ensemble with a bouquet of hellebore, the ones that blossom every winter under the snow in the gardens and are called Christmas roses. I thought then that she would go out, but instead she went to the window and absent-mindedly pulled aside the curtains.

Beneath her eyes, perhaps without seeing, she had the garden opposite, black under a thin and mottled layer of snow, the steep street, the house of Tatave the madman, the evergreen arborvitae of Mme Saint-Aubin, and the winter sky, which was slow in brightening. Perplexed, she bit a fingernail.

Suddenly she turned back, gliding quietly in her felt slippers toward the chimney piece, picked up the two parcels by their strings and thrust the hellebore between two buttonholes on her bosom. With her other hand she picked up my sabots by their straps, inclined her head for a moment in my direction, like a bird, and left.

On the morning of January 1, I found, beside the cup of thick and steaming hot breakfast chocolate, the two parcels, tied with golden thread, containing books and sweets. But never again in all my youth did I receive Christmas gifts, other than those Sido brought me that one night and took away, the entire incident bespeaking her scruples, the doubt and hesitation of her quick pure heart, the furtive homage that her love conceded to the excited mind of a ten-year-old little girl.

HB

🌿🌿 The Captain

It seems strange to me now . . .

It seems strange to me, now, that I knew him so little. My attention, my fervent admiration, were all for Sido and only fitfully strayed from her. It was just the same with my father. His eyes dwelt on Sido. On thinking it over, I believe that she did not know him well either. She was content with a few broad and clumsy truths: his love for her was boundless—it was in trying to enrich her that he lost her fortune—she loved him with an unwavering love, treating him lightly in everyday matters but respecting all his decisions.

All that was so glaringly obvious that it prevented us, except at moments, from perceiving his character as a man. When I was a child, what in fact did I know of him? That he was wonderfully skillful at building me "cockchafers' houses" with glazed windows and doors, and boats too. That he sang. That he handed out to us— and hid too—colored pencils, white paper, rosewood rulers, gold dust, and big, white sealing wafers which I ate by the fistful. That he swam with his one leg faster and better than his rivals with all four limbs.

But I knew also that, outwardly at least, he took little interest in his children. "Outwardly," I say. Since those days I have pondered much on the curious shyness of fathers in their relations with their children. Mine was never at ease with my mother's two eldest children by her first marriage—a girl with her head always full of romantic visions of heroes, so lost in legends that she was hardly present, and a boy who looked haughty but was secretly affectionate. He was naïve enough to believe that you can conquer a child with presents. He refused to recognize in his son—the "lazzarone," as my mother called him—his own carefree musical extravagances. I was the one he set most store by, and I was still quite small when he began to appeal to my critical sense. Later on, thank goodness, I proved less precocious, but I well remember how severe a judge I was at ten years old.

"Listen to this," my father would say, and I would listen, very sternly. Perhaps it would be a purple passage of oratorical prose, or an ode in flowing verse, with a great parade of rhythm and rhyme, resounding as a mountain storm.

"Well?" my father would ask. "I really believe that this time. . . . Go on, say!"

I would toss my head with its fair plaits, a forehead too high to look amiable, and a little marble of a chin, and let fall my censure: "Too many adjectives, as usual!"

At that my father exploded, thundering abuse on me: I was dust, vermin, a conceited louse. But the vermin, unperturbed, went on: "I told you the same thing last week, about the *Ode à Paul Bert.* Too many adjectives!"

No doubt he laughed at me behind my back, and I daresay he felt proud of me too. But at the moment we glared at each other as equals, already on a fraternal footing. There can be no doubt that it is his influence I am under when music or a display of dancing—not words, never words!—move me to tears. And it was he, longing to express himself, who inspired my first fumbling attempts to write, and earned for me that most biting, and assuredly most useful praise from my husband: "Can it be that I've married the last of the lyric poets?"

Nowadays I am wise enough, and proud enough too, to distinguish what in me is my father's lyricism, and what my mother's humor and spontaneity, all mingled and superimposed; and to rejoice in dichotomy in which there is nothing and no one to blush for on either side.

Yes, all we four children certainly made my father uncomfortable. How can it be otherwise in families where the father, though almost past the age for passion, remains in love with his mate? All his life long we had disturbed the tête-à-tête of which he had dreamed. Sometimes a pedagogic turn of mind can draw a father closer to his children. In the absence of affection, which is much rarer than is generally admitted, the vainglorious pleasure of teaching may bind a man to his sons. But Jules-Joseph Colette, though a cultivated man, made no parade of any learning. He had at first enjoyed shining for "Her," but as his love increased, he came to abandon even his desire to dazzle Sido.

I could go straight to the corner of our garden where the snowdrops bloomed. And I could paint from memory the climbing rose, and the trellis that supported it, as well as the hole in the wall and the worn flagstone. But I can only see my father's face vaguely and intermittently. He is clear enough sitting in the big, rep-covered armchair. The two oval mirrors of his open pince-nez gleam on his chest, and the red line of his peculiar lower lip, like a rolled rim, protrudes a little beneath the mustache which joins his beard. In that position he is fixed forever.

But elsewhere he is a wandering, floating figure, full of gaps, obscured by clouds and only visible in patches. I can always see his white hands, particularly since I've begun to hold my thumb bent out awkwardly, as he did, and found my hands crumpling and rolling and destroying paper with explosive rage, just as his hands used to. And talking of anger! But I won't enlarge on my own rages, which I inherit from him. One has only to go to Saint-Sauveur, and see the state to which my father reduced the marble chimney piece there, with two kicks from his one foot.

• • • •

He was not only misunderstood but unappreciated. "That incorrigible gaiety of yours!" my mother would exclaim, not in reproach but in astonishment. She thought he was gay because he sang. But I who whistle whenever I am sad, and turn the pulsations of fever, or the syllables of a name that torments me, into endless variations on a theme, could wish she had understood that pity is the supreme insult. My father and I have no use for pity; our nature rejects it. And now the thought of my father tortures me, because I know that he possessed a virtue more precious than any facile charms: that of knowing full well why he was sad, and never revealing it.

It is true that he often made us laugh, that he told a good tale, embroidering recklessly when he got into the swing of it, and that melody bubbled out of him; but did I ever see him gay? Wherever he went, his song preceded and protected him.

"Golden sunbeams, balmy breezes . . ." he would carol as he walked down our deserted street, so that "She" should not guess, when she heard him coming, that Laroche, the Lamberts' farmer, was impudently refusing to pay his rent, and that one of this same Lambert's creatures had advanced my father—at seven percent interest for six months—a sum he could not do without.

> By what enchantment, say, didst thou my heart beguile?
> When now I thee behold, methinks it was thy smile.

Who in the world could have believed that this baritone, still nimble with the aid of crutch and stick, is projecting his song like a smoke screen in front of him, so as to detract attention from himself? He sings in the hope that perhaps today "She" will forget to ask him if he has been able to borrow a hundred louis on the security of his disabled officer's pension. When he sings, Sido listens to him in spite of herself, and does not interrupt him.

> This is the trysting place of dames and knights,
> Who gather here within this charming glade,
> To pass their days in tasting the delights [*twice*]
> Of sparkling wine and love beneath the shade! [*three times*]

If, when he comes to the *grupetto,* the final long-drawn organ note with a few high staccato notes added for fun, he throws his voice right up against the walls of the rue de l'Hospice, my mother will appear on the doorstep, scandalized but laughing:

"Oh, Colette! In the street!" and after that he has only to fire off two or three everyday ribaldries at one of the neighboring young women, and Sido will pucker those sparse Mona Lisa eyebrows of hers and banish from her mind the painful refrain that never passes her lips: "We shall have to sell the Forge . . . sell the Forge . . . Heavens, must we sell the Forge, as well as the Mées, the Choslins and the Lamberts?"

Gay indeed, what real reason had he to be gay? Just as in his youth he had desired to die gloriously in public, now he needed to live surrounded by warm approval. Reduced now to his village and his family, his whole being absorbed by the great love that bounded his horizon, he was most himself with strangers and distant friends. One of his old comrades-in-arms, Colonel Godchot, who is still alive, has kept Captain Colette's letters and repeats sayings of his. For this man who talked so readily was strangely silent about one thing: he never related his military exploits. It was Captain Fournès and Private Lefèvre, both of the First Zouaves, who repeated to Colonel Godchot some of my father's "sayings" at the time of the war with Italy in 1859. My father, then twenty-nine years old, fell before Melegnano, his left thigh shot away. Fournès and Lefèvre dashed forward and carried him back, asking: "Where would you like us to put you, Captain?"

"In the middle of the square, under the colors!"

He never told any of his family of those words, never spoke of that hour when he hoped to die, in the midst of the tumult and surrounded by the love of his men. Nor did he ever tell any of us how he had lain alongside "his old Marshal" (Mac-Mahon). In talking to me, he never referred to the one long illness I had. But now, twenty years after his death, I find that his letters are full of my name and of the "little one's" illness.

Too late, too late! That is always the cry of children, of the negligent and the ungrateful. Not that I consider myself more guilty than any other "child"—on the contrary. But while he was alive, ought I not to have seen through his humorous dignity and his feigned frivolity? Were we not worthy, he and I, of a mutual effort to know each other better?

EMCC

When J was eight . . .

When I was eight, nine, ten years of age, my father turned his mind to politics. Born to please and to do battle, inventive and good at telling anecdotes, he might as easily have succeeded, I have thought since, in swaying a house as in charming a woman. But just as his boundless generosity ruined us all, so his childish confidence blinded him. He trusted in the sincerity of his partisans, in the honor of his opponent—in this case, Monsieur Merlou. It was Monsieur Pierre Merlou, later an ephemeral Minister, who ousted my father from the general council and from a candidature for the deputation. Blessings upon his deceased Excellency!

A small collectorship in the Yonne could hardly suffice to maintain, in wise quiescence, a captain of the Zouaves, lacking one leg, fiery-tempered, and afflicted with philanthropic views. No sooner did the word "politics" assail his ear with its pernicious tinkle, than he began to think:

"I shall conquer the people by educating them; I shall instruct young people and children in the sacred names of natural history, physics, and elementary chemistry. I shall go forth brandishing the magic lantern and the microscope and distributing throughout the village schools those amusing and instructive colored pictures in which the weevil, magnified twenty times, humiliates a vulture reduced to the proportions of a bee. I shall give popular lectures against alcoholism that will send forth Poyaudin and Forterrat, habitual drunkards though they be, converted and washed clean in the tears of their repentance!"

He suited the action to the word. The shabby victoria and the aged black mare were duly laden, when the time came, with the magic lantern, the painted diagrams, test tubes, bent pipes, and other paraphernalia, and the future candidate, his crutches, and myself. A cold and placid autumn drained the color from a cloudless sky, the mare slowed to a walk up every hill, and I leaped to the ground to pick blue sloes and coral spindle berries from the hedges, and to gather white mushrooms with shell-pink linings. As we passed by the denuded woods, there was borne to us a fragrance of fresh truffles and crushed leaves.

Then began for me a time of delight. In the villages the schoolroom, vacated an hour earlier, offered its worn benches for the audience; there I found again the blackboard, the weights and measures, and the depressing smell of unwashed children. An oil lamp, swinging from a chain, lit up the faces of those who came, suspicious and unsmiling, to hear the comfortable words. The effort of listening furrowed the brows of the martyrs and made their mouths gape. But far removed from them, on the platform, absorbed in important duties, I savored the arrogance that inflates the child assistant who supplies the conjurer with the plaster eggs, the silk scarf, or the blue-bladed daggers of his craft.

A disconcerted torpor followed by timid applause would greet the termination of the "instructive talk." A mayor in sabots would congratulate my father as though he had barely escaped a shameful conviction. On the threshold of the empty hall, children waited to see the departure of "the gentleman who has only one leg." The cold night air would strike my heated face like a damp handkerchief impregnated with the smell of steaming tillage, cowhouses, and oak bark. The harnessed mare, black against the darkness, whinnied at our coming, and turned the horned shadow of her head toward us in the halo of one of the carriage lamps. But my always openhanded father would never leave his melancholy flock without offering a drink to the municipal council at least. At the nearest tavern the hot wine would be steaming on the embers, with the flotsam and jetsam of lemon peel and cinnamon bubbling on its purple swell. The heady vapor, when I think of it, still moistens my nostrils. My father, as a good Southerner, would accept nothing but a bottle of lemonade, but his daughter . . .

"The little lady must warm herself with a thimbleful of hot wine!"

A thimbleful? My glass was held out, and if the drawer was too hasty in raising the spout of the jug, I knew well how to command, "To the brim!" and how to add, "Your health!" I would clink glasses and lift my elbow, tap on the table with my empty beaker, and, using the back of my hand to remove any mustaches of mulled Burgundy, I would push my glass a second time toward the jug, remarking: "That warms the cockles!" Oh! I knew how to behave!

My rustic courtesy reassured the drinkers, who would suddenly catch a glimpse in my father of a man much the same as themselves —save for his missing leg—and "well-spoken, if a bit daft." The dreary session would end in laughter, with slaps on the back and tall stories bellowed in voices like those of sheepdogs that sleep out in all seasons—and I would fall asleep, completely tipsy, my head on the table, lulled by the friendly tumult. Finally, laborers' brawny arms would pick me up and deposit me tenderly at the bottom of the carriage, well swaddled in the red tartan shawl that smelled of orris root and of my mother.

Ten miles, sometimes fifteen, a real expedition under the breathless stars of a winter sky, to the trot of the mare gorged on oats. Are there really people who remain unmoved and never feel their throats tighten with a childish sob when they hear the sound of a trotting horse upon a frozen road, the bark of a hunting fox, or the hoot of an owl struck by the light of the passing carriage lamps?

On the first few occasions, my return in a condition of beatific prostration rather surprised my mother, who put me quickly to bed, reproaching my father for my evident exhaustion. Then one night she discovered in my glance a hilarity unmistakably Burgundian, and in my breath, alas, the secret of my mirth!

Next day the victoria set forth without me and returned that evening, to set forth no more.

"Have you given up your lectures?" inquired my mother of my father a few days later.

He bestowed upon me a sidelong glance of melancholy flattery and shrugged his shoulders:

"Damn it all! You've robbed me of my best election agent!"

UVT/EMCC

My father, a born writer . . .

My father, a born writer, left few pages behind him. At the actual moment of writing, he dissipated his desire in material arrangements, setting out all the objects a writer needs and a number of superfluous ones as well. Because of him, I am not proof against this mania myself. As a result of having admired and coveted the perfect equipment of a writer's worktable, I am still exacting about the tools on my desk. Since adolescence does nothing by halves, I stole from my father's worktable, first a little mahogany set square that smelled like a cigar box, then a white metal ruler. Not to mention the scolding, I received full in my face the glare of a small, blazing gray eye, the eye of a rival, so fierce that I did not risk it a third time. I confined myself to prowling, hungrily, with my mind full of evil thoughts, around all these treasures of stationery. A pad of virgin blotting paper; an ebony ruler; one, two, four, six pencils, sharpened with a penknife and all of different colors; pens with medium nibs and fine nibs, pens with enormously broad nibs, drawing pens no thicker than a blackbird's quill; sealing wax, red, green and violet; a hand blotter, a bottle of liquid glue, not to mention slabs of transparent amber-colored stuff known as "mouth glue"; the minute remains of a spahi's cloak reduced to the dimensions of a pen wiper with scalloped edges; a big inkpot flanked by a small inkpot, both in bronze, and a lacquer bowl filled with a golden powder to dry the wet page; another bowl containing sealing wafers of all colors (I used to eat the white ones); to right and left of the table, reams of paper, cream-laid, ruled, watermarked, and, of course, that little stamping machine that bit into the white sheet and with one snap of its jaws adorned it with an embossed name: *J.-J. Colette.* There was also a glass of water for washing paint brushes, a box of water colors, an address book, the bottles of red, black and violet ink, the mahogany set square, a pocketcase of mathematical instruments, the tobacco jar, a pipe, the spirit lamp for melting the sealing wax.

A property owner tries to extend his domain; my father therefore tried to acclimatize adventitious subjects on his vast table. At one time there appeared on it a machine that could cut through a pile of a hundred sheets, and some frames filled with a white jelly on which you laid a written page face down and then, from this looking-glass original, pulled off blurred, sticky, anemic copies. But my father soon wearied of such gadgets, and the huge table returned to its serenity, to its classical style that was never disturbed by inspiration with its disorderly litter of crossed-out pages, cigarette ends, and "roughs" crumpled up into paper balls. I have forgotten, heaven forgive me, the paper-knife section, three or four boxwood ones, one of imitation silver, and the last of yellowed ivory, cracked from end to end.

From the age of ten I had never stopped coveting those material goods, invented for the glory and convenience of a mental power, which come under the general heading of "desk furniture." Children only delight in things they can hide. For a long time I secured possession of one wing, the left one, of the great four-doored double bookcase (it was eventually sold by order of the court). The doors of the upper part were glass-fronted, those of the lower, solid and made of beautiful figured mahogany. When you opened the lower left-hand door at a right angle, the flap touched the side of the chest of drawers, and, as the bookcase took up nearly the whole of one paneled wall, I would immure myself in a quadrangular nook formed by the side of the chest of drawers, the wall, the left section of the bookcase, and its wide-open door. Sitting on a little footstool, I could gaze at the three mahogany shelves in front of me, on which were displayed the objects of my worship, ranging from cream-laid paper to a little cup of the golden powder. "She's a chip off the old block," Sido would say teasingly to my father. It was ironical that, equipped with every conceivable tool for writing, my father rarely committed himself to putting pen to paper, whereas Sido—sitting at any old table, pushing aside an invading cat, a basket of plums, a pile of linen, or else just putting a dictionary on her lap by way of a desk—Sido really did write. A hundred enchanting letters prove that she did. To continue a letter or finish it off, she would tear a page out of her household account book or write on the back of a bill.

AW

He was a poet and a townsman . . .

He was a poet and a townsman. The country, where my mother seemed to draw sustenance from the sap of all growing things, and to take on new life whenever in stooping she touched the earth, blighted my father, who behaved as though he were in exile there.

We were sometimes scandalized by the sociability which urged him into village politics and local councils, made him stand for the district council, and attracted him to those assemblies and regional committees where the human voice provokes an answering human roar. Most unfairly, we felt vaguely vexed with him for not being sufficiently like the rest of us, whose joy it was to be far from the madding crowd.

I realize now that he was trying to please us when he used to organize "country picnics," as townsfolk do. The old blue victoria transported the family, with the dogs and eatables, to the banks of some pool—Moûtiers, Chassaing, or the lovely little forest lake of Guillemette, which belonged to us. My father was so much imbued with the "Sunday feeling," that urban need to celebrate one day out of seven, that he provided himself with fishing rods and campstools.

On arrival at the pool, he would adopt a jovial mood quite different from his weekday jovial mood. He uncorked the bottle of wine gaily, allowed himself an hour's fishing, read, and took a short nap, while the rest of us, light-footed woodlanders that we were, used to scouring the countryside without a carriage, were as bored as could be, sighing, as we ate cold chicken, for our accustomed snacks of new bread, garlic, and cheese. The open forest, the pool, and the wide sky filled my father with enthusiasm, but only as a noble spectacle. The more he called to mind *"the blue Titaresus and the silver gulf,"* the more taciturn did we become—the two boys and I, that is—for we were already accustomed to express our worship of the woods by silence alone.

Only my mother, sitting beside the pool, between her husband and her children, seemed to derive a melancholy pleasure from counting her dear ones as they lay about her on the fine, reedy grass, purple with heather. Far from the importunate sound of doorbells, from the anxious, unpaid tradesmen, and insinuating voices, there she was with her achievement and her torment—with the exception of her faithless elder daughter—enclosed within a perfect circle of birches and oaks. Flurries of wind in the treetops passed over the circular clearing, rarely rippling the water. Domes of pinky mushrooms broke through the light silver-gray soil where the heather thrived, and my mother talked about the things that she and I loved best.

She told of the wild boars of bygone winters, of the wolves still known to exist in Puysaie and Forterre, and of the lean summer wolf which once followed the victoria for five hours. "If only I had known what to give him to eat! I daresay he would have eaten bread. Every time we came to a slope he would sit down to let the carriage keep fifty yards ahead. The scent of him made the mare mad, so much so that it was nearly she who attacked him."

"Weren't you frightened?"

"Frightened? No, not of that poor, big, gray wolf, thirsty and famished under a leaden sun. Besides, I was with my first husband. It was my first husband, too, who saw the fox drowning its fleas one day when he was out shooting. Holding on to a bunch of weeds with its teeth, it lowered itself backward into the water very, very gradually until it was in right up to its muzzle."

Innocent tales and maternal instructions, such as the swallow, the mother hare, and the she-cat also impart to their young. Delightful stories, of which my father retained only the words "my first husband," at which he would bend on Sido that gray-blue gaze of his whose meaning no one could ever fathom. In any case, what did the fox and the lily of the valley, the ripe berry and the insect, matter to him? He liked them in books, and told us their learned names, but passed them by out of doors without recognizing them. He would praise any full-blown flower as a "rose," pronouncing the "o" short, in the Provençal way, and squeezing as he spoke an invisible "roz" between his thumb and forefinger.

Dusk descended at last on our Sunday-in-the-country. By then our number had often dropped from five to three: my father, my mother, and I. The circular rampart of darkling woods had swallowed up those two lanky, bony lads, my brothers.

"We shall catch up with them on the road home," my father would say.

But my mother shook her head: her boys never returned except by cross-country paths and swampy blue meadows; and then, cutting across sandpits and bramble patches, they would jump over the wall at the bottom of the garden. She was resigned to the prospect of finding them at home, bleeding a little and a little ragged. She gathered up from the grass the remains of the meal, a few freshly picked mushrooms, the empty tit's nest, the springy, cellular sponge made by a colony of wasps, the bunch of wild flowers, some pebbles bearing the imprint of fossilized ammonites, and the "little one's" wide-brimmed hat, while my father, still agile, jumped with a hop like a wader's back into the victoria.

It was my mother who patted the black mare, offering her yellowed teeth tender shoots, and wiped the paws of the paddling dog. I never saw my father touch a horse. No curiosity ever impelled him to look at a cat or give his attention to a dog. And no dog ever obeyed him.

"Go on, get in!" his beautiful voice would order Moffino. But the dog remained where he was by the step of the carriage, wagging his tail coldly and looking at my mother.

"Get in, you brute!" What are you waiting for?" my father repeated.

"I'm waiting for the *command*," the dog seemed to reply.

"Go on, jump!" I would call to him; and there was never any need to tell him twice.

"That's very odd," my mother would remark, to which my father retorted: "It merely proves what a stupid creature the dog is." But the rest of us did not believe a word of that, and at heart my father felt secretly humiliated.

Great bunches of yellow broom fanned out like a peacock's tail behind us in the hood of the old victoria. As we approached the village, my father would resume his defensive humming, and no doubt we looked very happy, since to look happy was the highest compliment we paid each other. But was not everything about us, the gathering dusk, the wisps of smoke trailing across the sky, and the first flickering star, as grave and restless as ourselves? And in our midst a man, banished from the elements that had once sustained him, brooded bitterly.

Yes, bitterly; I am sure of that now. It takes time for the absent to assume their true shape in our thoughts. After death they take on a firmer outline and then cease to change. "So that's the real you? Now I see, I never understood you." It is never too late, since now I have fathomed what formerly my youth hid from me: my brilliant, cheerful father harbored the profound sadness of those who have lost a limb. We were hardly aware that one of his legs was missing, amputated just below the hip. What should we have said if we had suddenly seen him walking like everyone else?

Even my mother had never known him other than supported by crutches, agile though he was and radiant with the arrogance of one in love. But she knew nothing, apart from his military exploits, of the man he was before he met her, the Saint-Cyr cadet who danced so well, the lieutenant tough as what in my native province we call a *bois-debout*—the ancient chopping block, made of a roundel of close-grained oak that defies the axe. When she followed him with her eyes, she had no idea that this cripple had once been able to run to meet every danger. And now, bitterly, his spirit still soared, while he remained sitting beside Sido with a sweet song on his lips.

Sido and his love for her were all that he had been able to keep. For him, all that surrounded them—the village, the fields, and the woods—was but a desert. He supposed that life went on for his distant friends and comrades. Once he returned from a trip to Paris with moist eyes because Davout d'Auerstaedt, Grand Chancellor of the Legion of Honor, had removed his red ribbon to replace it by a rosette.

"Couldn't you have asked me for it, old man?"

"I never asked for the ribbon either," my father answered lightly.

But his voice, when he described the scene to us, was husky. What was the source of his emotion? He wore the rosette, amply displayed in his buttonhole, as he sat up very straight in our old carriage with his arm lying on the crossbar of his crutch. He would start showing off on the outskirts of the village, for the benefit of the first passers-by at Gerbaude. Was he dreaming of his old comrades in the division who marched without crutches and rode by on horseback, of Février and Désandré, and Fournès, who had saved his life and still tactfully addressed him as "my captain"? Had he a vision of learned societies, of politics perhaps, and platforms, and all their dazzling symbols—a vision of masculine joys?

"You're so human!" my mother would sometimes say to him, with a note of indefinable suspicion in her voice. And so as not to wound him too much, she would add: "You know what I mean, you always put your hand out to see if it's raining."

EMCC

I never surprised them . . .

I never surprised them in a passionate embrace. Who had imposed such reserve on them? Sido, most assuredly. My father would have had no such scruples about it. Always on the alert where she was concerned, he used to listen for her quick step, and bar her way:

"Pay up, or I won't let you pass!" he would order, pointing to the smooth patch of cheek above his beard. Pausing in her flight, she would "pay" with a kiss as swift as a sting, and speed on her way, irritated if my brothers or I had seen her "paying."

Only once, on a summer day, when my mother was removing the coffee tray from the table, did I see my father, instead of exacting the familiar toll, bend his graying head and bearded lips over my mother's hand with a devotion so ardent and ageless that Sido, speechless and as crimson with confusion as I, turned away without a word. I was still a child and none too pure-minded, being exercised as one is at thirteen by all those matters concerning which ignorance is burden and discovery humiliating. It did me good to behold, and every now and again to remember afresh, that perfect picture of love: the head of a man already old, bent in a kiss of complete self-surrender on a graceful, wrinkled little hand, worn with work.

For a long time he was terrified lest she should die before he did. This is a thought common to lovers and truly devoted married people, a cruel hope that excludes any idea of pity. Before my father's death, Sido used to talk of him to me:

"I mustn't die before him, I simply must not. Can't you imagine how, if I let myself die, he'd try to kill himself, and fail? I know him," she said, with the air of a young girl. She mused for a while, her eyes on the little street of Châtillon-Coligny, or the enclosed square of our garden. "There's less chance of that with me, you see. I'm only a woman and, once past a certain age, a woman practically never dies of her own free will. Besides, I've got you as well and he hasn't."

For she knew everything, even to those preferences that one never mentions. Far from being any support to us, my father was merely one of the cluster that clung around her and hung on to her arms.

She fell ill and he sat often near the bed. "When are you going to get well? What day, what time do you think it will be? Don't you dare not recover! I should soon put an end to my life!" She could not bear this masculine attitude, so threatening and pitiless in its demands. In her effort to escape, she turned her head from side to side on her pillow, as she was to do later when she was shaking off the last ties.

"My goodness, Colette, you're making me so hot!" she complained. "You fill the whole room. A man's always out of place at a woman's bedside. Go out of doors! Go and see if the grocer's got any oranges for me. Go and ask Monsieur Rosimond to lend me the *Revue des Deux-Mondes.* But go slowly, because it's thundery; otherwise you'll come back in a sweat!"

Thrusting his crutch up under his armpit, he did as she bade.

"Do you see?" said my mother when he had gone. "Do you notice how all the stuffing goes out of him when I'm ill?"

As he passed beneath her window, he would clear his throat so that she could hear him:

"I think of thee, I see thee, I adore thee,
    At every moment, always, everywhere,
    My thoughts are of thee when the sun is rising,
    And when I close my eyes thy face is there."

"Do you hear him? Do you hear him?" she would ask feverishly. Then her sense of mischief got the upper hand, making her whole face suddenly younger; and leaning out of bed, she would say: "Would you like to know what your father is? I'll tell you. Your father is the modern Orpheus!"

She recovered, as she always did. But when they removed one of her breasts and, four years later, the other, my father became terribly mistrustful of her, even though each time she recovered again. When a fishbone stuck in her throat, making her cough so violently that her face turned scarlet and her eyes filled with tears, my father brought his fist down on the table, shivering his plate to fragments and bellowing: "Stop it, I say!"

She was not misled by this, and she soothed him with compassionate tact, and comic remarks, and fluttering glances. The words "fluttering glance" always come to my lips when I am thinking of her. Hesitation, the desire to say something tender, and the need to tell a lie, all made her flutter her eyelids while her gray eyes glanced rapidly in all directions. This confusion, and the vain attempt of those eyes to escape from a man's gaze, blue-gray as new-cut lead, was all that was revealed to me of the passion which bound Sido and the Captain throughout their lives.

EMCC

He died in his seventy-fourth year . . .

He died in his seventy-fourth year, holding the hands of his beloved and fixing on her weeping eyes a gaze that gradually lost its color, turned milky blue, and faded like a sky veiled in mist. He was given the handsomest of village funerals, a coffin of yellow wood covered only by an old tunic riddled with wounds—the tunic he had worn as a captain in the First Zouaves—and my mother accompanied him steadily to the grave's edge, very small and resolute beneath her widow's veil, and murmuring under her breath words of love that only he must hear.

We brought her back to the house, and there she promptly lost her temper with her new mourning, the cumbersome crepe that caught on the keys of doors and presses, the cashmere dress that stifled her. She sat resting in the drawing room, near the big green chair in which my father would never sit again and which the dog had already joyfully invaded. She was dry-eyed, flushed and feverish and kept on repeating:

"Oh, how hot it is! Heavens! The heat of this black stuff! Don't you think I might change now, into my blue sateen?"

"Well . . ."

"Why not? Because of my mourning? But I simply loathe black! For one thing, it's melancholy. Why should I present a sad and unpleasant sight to everyone I meet? What connection is there between this cashmere and crepe and my feelings? Don't let me ever see you in mourning for me! You know well enough that I only like you to wear pink, and some shades of blue."

She got up hastily, took several steps toward an empty room, and stopped abruptly:

"Ah! . . . Of course. . . ."

She came back and sat down again, admitting with a simple and humble gesture that she had, for the first time that day, forgotten that *he* was dead.

"Shall I get you something to drink, mother? Wouldn't you like to go to bed?"

"Of course not. Why should I? I'm not ill!"

She sat there and began to learn patience, staring at the floor, where a dusty track from the door of the sitting room to the door of the empty bedroom had been marked by rough, heavy shoes.

A kitten came in, circumspect and trustful, a common and irresistible little kitten four or five months old. He was acting a dignified part for his own edification, pacing grandly, his tail erect as a candle, in imitation of lordly males. But a sudden and unexpected somersault landed him head over heels at our feet, where he took fright at his own temerity, rolled himself into a ball, stood up on his hind legs, danced sideways, arched his back, and then spun around like a top.

"Look at him, oh, do look at him, Minet-Chéri! Goodness! Isn't he funny!"

And she laughed, sitting there in her mourning, laughed her shrill, young girl's laugh, clapping her hands with delight at the kitten. Then, of a sudden, searing memory stemmed that brilliant cascade and dried the tears of laughter in my mother's eyes. Yet she offered no excuse for having laughed, either on that day or on the days that followed; for though she had lost the man she passionately loved, in her kindness for us she remained among us just as she always had been, accepting her sorrow as she would have accepted the advent of a long and dreary season, but welcoming from every source the fleeting benediction of joy. So she lived on, swept by shadow and sunshine, bowed by bodily torments, resigned, unpredictable and generous, rich in children, flowers, and animals like a fruitful domain.

UVT/EMCC

"J've just been sorting . . ."
From "Sido," in a Letter

"I've just been sorting some papers in dear Papa's desk. I found there all the letters that I wrote to him from the Maison Dubois after my operation, and all the telegrams you sent him during the period when I couldn't write to him. He had kept everything; how moved I was! But, you'll say to me, it's quite natural that he should have kept all that. Not so natural, believe me; you'll see. When I returned from the two or three short trips I made to Paris to see you, before his death, I found my dear Colette a shadow of himself and hardly eating. Ah, what a child! What a pity he should have loved me so much! It was his love for me that destroyed, one after another, all those splendid abilities he had for literature and the sciences. He preferred to think only of me, to torment himself for me, and that was what I found inexcusable. So great a love! What frivolity! And as for my side of it, how can you expect me to get over the loss of so tender a friend?"

EMCC

J can still see . . .

I can still see, on one of the highest shelves of the library, a row of volumes bound in boards, with black linen spines. The firmness of the boards, so smoothly covered in marbled paper, bore witness to my father's manual dexterity. But the titles, handwritten in Gothic lettering, never tempted me, more especially since the black-rimmed labels bore no author's name. I quote from memory: *My Campaigns,*

The Lessons of '70, The Geodesy of Geodesies, Elegant Algebra, Marshal Mac-Mahon seen by a Fellow Soldier, From Village to Parliament, Zouave Songs (in verse) . . . I forget the rest.

When my father died, the library became a bedroom and the books left their shelves.

"Just come and see," my elder brother called one day. In his silent way, he was moving the books himself, sorting and opening them in search of a smell of damp-stained paper, of that embalmed mildew from which a vanished childhood rises up, or the pressed petal of a tulip still marbled like a tree agate.

"Just come and see!"

The dozen volumes bound in boards revealed to us their secret, a secret so long disdained by us, accessible though it was. Two hundred, three hundred, one hundred and fifty pages to a volume; beautiful, cream-laid paper, or thick "foolscap" carefully trimmed, hundreds and hundreds of blank pages. Imaginary works, the mirage of a writer's career.

There were so many of these virgin pages, spared through timidity or listlessness, that we never saw the end of them. My brother wrote his prescriptions on them, my mother covered her pots of jam with them, her granddaughters tore out the leaves for scribbling, but we never exhausted those cream-laid notebooks, his invisible "works." All the same, my mother exerted herself to that end with a sort of fever of destruction: "You don't mean to say there are still some left? I must have some for cutlet frills. I must have some to line my little drawers with . . ." And this, not in mockery, but out of piercing regret and the painful desire to blot out this proof of incapacity.

At the time when I was beginning to write, I too drew on this spiritual legacy. Was that where I got my extravagant taste for writing on smooth sheets of fine paper, without the least regard for economy? I dared to cover with my large round handwriting the invisible cursive script, perceptible to only one person in the world, like a shining tracery which carried to a triumphant conclusion the single page lovingly completed and signed, the page that bore the dedication:

TO MY DEAR SOUL,

HER FAITHFUL HUSBAND

JULES-JOSEPH COLETTE

EMCC

❧❧ The Children

The house was large . . .

The house was large, topped by a lofty garret. The steep gradient of the street compelled the coachhouses, stables, and poultry house, the laundry and the dairy, to huddle on a lower level all round a closed courtyard.

By leaning over the garden wall, I could scratch with my finger the poultry-house roof. The Upper Garden overlooked the Lower Garden—a warm, confined enclosure reserved for the cultivation of aubergines and pimentos—where the smell of tomato leaves mingled in July with that of the apricots ripening on the walls. In the Upper Garden were two twin firs, a walnut tree whose intolerant shade killed any flowers beneath it, some rosebushes, a neglected lawn, and a dilapidated arbor. At the bottom, along the rue des Vignes, a boundary wall reinforced with a strong iron railing ought to have ensured the privacy of the two gardens, but I never knew those railings other than twisted and torn from their cement foundations, and grappling in mid-air with the invincible arms of a hundred-year-old wistaria.

In the rue de l'Hospice, a two-way flight of steps led up to the front door in the gloomy façade with its large bare windows. It was the typical burgher's house in an old village, but its dignity was upset a little by the steep gradient of the street, the stone steps being lopsided, ten on one side and six on the other.

A large solemn house, rather forbidding, with its shrill bell and its carriage entrance with a huge bolt like an ancient dungeon, a house that smiled only on its garden side. The back, invisible to passers-by, was a sun trap, swathed in a mantle of wistaria and big-nonia too heavy for the trellis of worn ironwork, which sagged in the middle like a hammock and provided shade for the little flagged terrace and the threshold of the sitting room.

Is it worthwhile, I wonder, seeking for adequate words to de-scribe the rest? I shall never be able to conjure up the splendor that adorns, in my memory, the ruddy festoons of an autumn vine borne down by its own weight and clinging despairingly to some branch of the fir trees. And the massive lilacs, whose compact flowers—blue in the shade and purple in the sunshine—withered so soon, stifled by their own exuberance. The lilacs long since dead will not be revived at my bidding, any more than the terrifying moonlight—silver, quicksilver, leaden-gray, with facets of dazzling amethyst or scintil-lating points of sapphire—all depending on a certain pane in the blue glass window of the summerhouse at the bottom of the garden.

Both house and garden are living still, I know; but what of that, if the magic has deserted them? If the secret is lost that opened to me a whole world—light, scents, birds, and trees in perfect har-mony, the murmur of human voices now silent forever—a world of which I have ceased to be worthy?

It would happen sometimes, long ago, when this house and garden harbored a family, that a book lying open on the flagstones of the terrace or on the grass, a jump rope twisted like a snake across the path, or perhaps a miniature garden, pebble-edged and planted with decapitated flowers, revealed both the presence of children and their varying ages. But such evidence was hardly ever accompanied by childish shouts or laughter, and my home, though warm and full, bore an odd resemblance to those houses which, once the holidays have come to an end, are suddenly emptied of joy. The silence, the muted breeze of the enclosed garden, the pages of the book stirred only by invisible fingers, all seemed to be asking, "Where are the children?"

It was then, from beneath the ancient iron trellis sagging to the left under the wistaria, that my mother would make her appearance, small and plump in those days when age had not yet wasted her. She would scan the thick green clumps and, raising her head, fling her call into the air: "Children! Where are the children?"

Where, indeed? Nowhere. My mother's cry would ring through the garden, striking the great wall of the barn and returning to her as a faint, exhausted echo. "Where . . . ? Children . . . ?"

Nowhere. My mother would throw back her head and gaze heavenward, as though waiting for a flock of winged children to alight from the skies. After a moment she would repeat her call; then, grown tired of questioning the heavens, she would crack a dry poppy head with her fingernail, rub the greenfly from a rose shoot, fill her pockets with unripe walnuts, and return to the house shaking her head over the vanished children.

And all the while, from among the leaves of the walnut tree above her, gleamed the pale, pointed face of a child who lay stretched like a tomcat along a big branch and who never uttered a word. A less shortsighted mother might well have suspected that the spasmodic salutations exchanged by the twin tops of the two firs were due to some influence other than that of the sudden October squalls! And in the square dormer, above the pulley for hauling up fodder, would she not have perceived, if she had screwed up her eyes, two pale patches among the hay—the face of a young boy and the pages of his book?

But she had given up looking for us, had despaired of trying to reach us. Our uncanny turbulence was never accompanied by any sound. I do not believe there can ever have been children so active and so mute. Looking back at what we were, I am amazed. No one had imposed upon us either our cheerful silence or our limited sociability. My nineteen-year-old brother, engrossed in constructing some hydrotherapeutic apparatus out of linen bladders, strands of wire, and glass tubes, never prevented the younger, aged fourteen, from disemboweling a watch or from transposing on the piano, with never a false note, a melody or an air from a symphony heard at a concert in the county town. He did not even interfere with his junior's incomprehensible passion for decorating the garden with little tombstones cut out of cardboard and each inscribed, beneath the sign of the cross, with the names, epitaph, and genealogy of the imaginary person deceased.

My sister with the too long hair might read forever with never a pause; the two boys would brush past her as though they did not see the young girl sitting abstracted and entranced, and never bother her. When I was small, I was at liberty to keep up as best I could with my long-legged brothers as they ranged the woods in pursuit of swallow tails, white admirals, purple emperors, or hunted for grass snakes, or gathered armfuls of the tall July foxgloves which grew in the clearings already aglow with patches of purple heather. But I followed them in silence, picking blackberries, bird cherries, a chance wild flower, or roving the hedgerows and waterlogged meadows like an independent dog out hunting on its own.

"Where are the children?" She would suddenly appear like an oversolicitous mother bitch breathlessly pursuing her constant quest, head lifted and scenting the breeze. Sometimes her white linen sleeves bore witness that she had come from kneading dough for cakes or making the pudding that had a velvety hot sauce of rum and jam. If she had been washing the Havanese bitch, she would be enveloped in a long blue apron, and sometimes she would be waving a banner of rustling yellow paper, the paper used around the butcher's meat, which meant that she hoped to reassemble, at the same time as her elusive children, her carnivorous family of vagabond cats.

To her traditional cry she would add, in the same anxious and appealing key, a reminder of the time of day. "Four o'clock, and they

haven't come in to tea! Where are the children? . . ." "Half past
six! Will they come home to dinner? Where are the children?
. . ." That lovely voice; how I should weep for joy if I could hear
it now! Our only sin, our single misdeed, was silence, and a kind of
miraculous vanishing. For perfectly innocent reasons, for the sake of
a liberty that no one denied us, we clambered over the railing, leaving behind our shoes, and returned by way of an unnecessary ladder
or a neighbor's low wall.

Our anxious mother's keen sense of smell would discover on us
traces of wild garlic from a distant ravine or of marsh mint from a
treacherous bog. The dripping pocket of one of the boys would dis-
gorge the bathing slip worn in malarial ponds, and the "little one,"
cut about the knees and skinned at the elbows, would be bleeding
complacently under plasters of cobweb and wild pepper bound on
with rushes.

"Tomorrow I shall keep you locked up! All of you, do you
hear, every single one of you!"

Tomorrow! Next day the eldest, slipping on the slated roof
where he was fitting a tank, broke his collarbone and remained at
the foot of the wall waiting, politely silent and half unconscious,
until someone came to pick him up. Next day an eighteen-rung ladder crashed plumb on the forehead of the younger son, who never
uttered a cry, but brought home with becoming modesty a lump like
a purple egg between his eyes.

"Where are the children?"

Two are at rest. The others grow older day by day. If there be a
place of waiting after this life, then surely she who so often waited
for us has not ceased to tremble for those two who are yet alive.

For the eldest of us all, at any rate, she has done with looking
at the dark windowpane every evening and saying, "I feel that child
is not happy. I feel she is suffering." And for the elder of the boys
she no longer listens, breathlessly, to the wheels of a doctor's trap
coming over the snow at night, or to the hoofbeats of the gray mare.

But I know that for the two who remain she seeks and wanders still, invisible, tormented by her inability to watch over them enough.

"Where, oh where are the children? . . ."

UVT/EMCC

"Savages . . ."

"Savages, that's what they are," my mother used to say, "just savages. What can one do with such savages?" And she would shake her head.

Her discouragement was in part due to a deliberate and considered refusal to interfere, and in part perhaps to an awareness of her own responsibility. She gazed at her two boys, the half-brothers, and found them beautiful, especially the elder, the seventeen-year-old with his chestnut hair and clear blue eyes, and that crimson mouth which smiled only at us and a few pretty girls. But the dark one, at thirteen, was not bad either, with his hair that needed a cut falling into his lead-blue eyes, which were like our father's.

Two light-footed savages, lean and bony, frugal like their parents; instead of meat, preferring brown bread, hard cheese, salads, fresh eggs, and leek or pumpkin pies. Temperate and pure they were —true savages indeed.

"What shall I do with them?" sighed my mother. By their very gentleness, they evaded all attempts to interfere with them or separate them. The elder was the leader, while the younger mingled with his enthusiasm a sense of fantasy which cut him off from the world. But the elder knew he was soon to begin his medical studies, whereas the younger dumbly hoped that for him nothing ever would begin, except the next day, except the hour when he could escape from civilized constraint, except complete freedom to dream and remain silent. He is hoping still.

. . . .

That graying man has grown out of a little boy of six who used to follow mendicant musicians when they passed through our vi·

lage. Once he followed a one-eyed clarinetist as far as Saints, a distance of four miles, and by the time he got back my mother was having all the local wells dragged. He listened good-naturedly to her reproaches and complaints, for he rarely lost his temper. When he had heard the last of his mother's fears, he went to the piano and faithfully reproduced all the clarinetist's tunes, enriching them with simple but perfectly correct little harmonies. He did the same with the tunes of the merry-go-round at the Easter fair on Low Sunday, and indeed with any kind of music, which he would intercept as though it were a flying message.

"He must study technique and harmony," my mother would say. "He's even more gifted than his elder brother. He might become an artiste—who can tell?"

Every three months my mother used to go to Auxerre, and when she was setting out in the victoria at two in the morning, she nearly always gave in to the pleadings of the baby of the family. The good fortune of being born last allowed me to keep for a long time this privileged position of being the baby-of-the-family, and my place in the back seat of the victoria. But before me it had been occupied for ten years by that agile and elusive little boy. On arrival at the county town he always vanished, evading every attempt to keep an eye on him. He disappeared all over the place, in the cathedral, in the clock tower, and especially in a big grocer's shop while they were packing up the sugarloaf in its oblique wrapping of indigo paper, the ten pounds of chocolate, the vanilla, the cinnamon, the nutmeg, the rum for grog, the black pepper, and the white soap. My mother gave the shrill cry of a vixen: "Hi! Where is he?"

"Who, Madame Colette?"

"My little boy! Did anyone see him go out?"

No one had seen him go out, and since there were no wells, my mother was already peering into the vats of oil and the casks of pickled brine.

This time it did not take them long to find him. He was up near the ceiling, right at the top of one of the cast-iron spiral pillars. Gripping this between his thighs and feet, like a native up a coconut palm, he was fiddling with and listening to the works of a big hanging clock with a flat owl face which was screwed on the main beam.

When ordinary parents produce exceptional children, they are often so dazzled by them that they push them into careers they consider superior, even if it takes some lusty kicks on their behinds to achieve this result. My mother found it quite natural, and indeed obligatory, that the children she had produced should be miracles; but it was also her view that "God helps those who help themselves," and to reassure herself, she was given to asserting: "Achille will be a doctor. But Léo will never get away from music. As for the little one . . ." At that point she would raise her eyebrows, interrogate the clouds, and postpone me till later.

• • • •

We disappointed her, more than once. But she never lost heart; she merely supplied us with a fresh halo. All the same she could never admit that her second son had got away, as she put it, from music, for in many a letter dating from the end of her life I read: *"Do you know if Léo has any time to practice his piano? He ought not to neglect such an extraordinary gift; I shall never tire of insisting on that."* At the time when my mother was writing me these letters, my brother was forty-four years old.

Whatever she might say, he did get away from music, then from his pharmaceutical studies, and then successively from everything—from everything except his own elfin past. To my eyes he has not changed; he is an elf of sixty-three. He is attached to nothing but his native place, like an elf to some tutelary mushroom, or a leaf bent like a roof. Elves, we know, live on very little, and despise the coarse garments of mortals: mine sometimes wanders about without a tie and with flowing locks. From behind he looks not unlike an empty overcoat, straying bewitched.

He has deliberately chosen his humble clerical job because it keeps sitting at a table that part of himself that looks deceptively like a man. All the rest of him is free to sing, listen to orchestras, compose, and fly back to the past, to rejoin the small boy of six who opened every watch, haunted town clocks, collected epitaphs, never tired of stamping on spongy mosses, and played the piano from birth. He finds him again without difficulty, slips into the light and nimble little body that he never leaves long, and roams through a country of the mind, where all is to the measure and liking of one who for sixty years has triumphantly remained a child.

Alas, no child is invulnerable, and this one sometimes comes back to me badly hurt because he has tried to confront his well-remembered dream with a reality which betrays it.

One dripping evening, when every arcade of the Palais-Royal was hung with great draperies of water and shadow, he came to call on me. I had not seen him for months. He sat down, wet through, beside my fire, absent-mindedly took some of his curious nourishment—fondants, very sugary cakes, and syrup—opened my watch, then my alarm clock, listened to them for a long time, and said nothing.

I stole an occasional glance at his long face with its nearly white mustache, my father's blue eyes, and a coarser version of Sido's nose—inherited features connected by bony modeling and unfamiliar muscles whose origin I could not trace. A long and gentle face it was, in the firelight, gentle and distressed. But the habits and customs of childhood—reserve, discretion, and liberty—persist so strongly between us that I asked my brother no questions.

When he had finished drying the sad, rain-sodden wings that he calls his coat, he smoked with half-shut eyes, rubbed his hands, which were shriveled and red for lack of gloves and hot water in all weathers, and spoke:

"I say!"

"Yes?"

"I've been *back there,* did you know?"

"No! When?"

"I've just returned."

"Oh!" said I with admiration. "You've been to Saint-Sauveur? How?"

He gave me a conceited little look. "Charles Faroux took me in his auto."

"My dear! Was it looking lovely at this time of year?"

"Not bad," he said, shortly.

His nostrils dilated and he relapsed into silence and gloom. I went back to my writing.

"I say!"

"Yes?"

"*Back there,* I went to Roches—you remember?"

A steep path of yellow sand rose in my memory like a serpent against a windowpane. "Oh, how is it looking? And the wood at the summit? And the little pavilion? And the foxgloves . . . the heather . . ."

My brother whistled. "Gone. Cut down. Nothing left. A clean sweep. You can see the earth. You can see . . ." He scythed the air with the side of his hand and shrugged derisively, staring into the fire. I respected this derision and did not imitate it. But the old elf, quivering in his pain, could not longer keep silence. Profiting by the half light of the glowing fire, he whispered:

"And that's not all. I went to the Cour du Pâté too."

Back to my mind you rush, childish name for a warm terrace beside a ruined castle, arches of climbing roses spindly with age, shadow and scent of flowering ivy falling from the Saracen tower, and stubborn, rusty gates that close the Cour du Pâté . . .

"And then, my dear, and then?"

My brother gathered himself together.

"Just a moment," he ordered me. "We must begin at the beginning. I arrive at the castle. It's still a home for old people, since that was what Victor Gandrille decided. That's all right, I've nothing against that. I enter the park by the lower entrance, the one near Madame Billette's . . ."

"Surely not Madame Billette? Why, she's been dead, it must be for at least fifty years!"

"Maybe," said my brother with indifference. "Yes, I suppose that's why they told me another name . . . an impossible name. If *they* think I'm going to remember names I don't know! Well then, I enter by the lower entrance and go up the lime avenue. Now I come to think of it, the dogs didn't bark when I pushed the door open . . ." he remarked irritably.

"Come now, my dear, they couldn't have been the same dogs. Just think."

"All right, all right . . . it's a mere detail. I'll say nothing about the potatoes that *they*'ve planted in place of the bleeding hearts and poppies. I won't even mention," he went on in an intolerant voice, "the wiring round the lawns, a fence of wire netting . . . you can hardly believe your eyes. It appears it's for the cows. The cows!"

He rocked one of his knees between his clasped hands and whistled with a professional air that suited him about as well as a top hat.

"And was that all, my dear?"

"Just a moment!" he said again, fiercely. "As I said, I go up toward the canal,—if indeed," he added, with studied precision, "I dare call canal that filthy pond, that soup of mosquitoes and cow dung. But never mind. So on I go to the Cour du Pâté, and . . ."

"And?"

He turned toward me, without seeing me, with a vindictive smile.

"I'll admit that at first I wasn't particularly pleased that *they* should have turned the first court—the one before the gate and behind the stables—into a kind of drying ground for the washing. Yes, I'll admit that! But I didn't pay much attention to it because I was waiting for 'the moment of the gate.'"

"What moment of the gate?"

He snapped his fingers impatiently.

"Oh, come now! You see the knob of the gate?"

I could indeed see it—of shiny black cast iron—as though I were about to grasp it.

"Well, as long as I've known it, when you turn it like that"— he mimicked the gesture—"and let go of the gate, it opens through its own weight and as it swings it says . . ."

"Ee-ee-ee-ang," we sang in unison, on four notes.

"That's right," said my brother, frantically jiggling his left knee. "I turned it. I let the gate go. I listened. Do you know what *they*'ve done?"

"No."

"*They*'ve oiled the gate," he said coldly.

He left almost immediately. He had nothing else to say to me. He folded the damp membranes of his voluminous garment about him and took himself off, the poorer by four notes. Henceforth his musician's ear would strain in vain to catch that most delicate of offertories, composed by an ancient gate, a grain of sand, and a trace of rust, and dedicated to the one untamed child who was worthy of it.

EMCC

My half-sister . . .

My half-sister, the eldest of us all—the stranger in our midst—got engaged just when she seemed about to become an old maid. Plain though she was, with her Tibetan eyes she was not unpleasing. My mother did not dare to prevent this unfortunate marriage, but at least she made no secret of what she thought about it. From the rue de la Roche to Gerbaude, and from Bel-Air to Le Grand-Jeu, the talk was all of my sister's marriage.

"Is Juliette getting married?" a neighbor would ask my mother. "That's an event!"

"No, an accident," corrected Sido.

A few ventured, acidly: "So Juliette's getting married at last! How unexpected! It almost seemed hopeless!"

"I should rather say desperate," retorted Sido, belligerently. "But there's no holding a girl of twenty-five."

"And who is she marrying?"

"Oh, some wretched upstart or other."

At heart she was full of pity for her lonely daughter, who spent her days in a fever of reading, her head stuffed with dreams. My brothers considered the "event" entirely from their own detached point of view. A year of medical studies in Paris had by no means tamed the elder; magnificent and aloof, he resented the glances of such women as he did not desire. The words "bridal train," "dress clothes," "wedding breakfast," "procession" fell on the two savages like drops of boiling pitch.

"I won't go to the wedding!" protested the younger, his eyes pale with indignation under his hair cropped close as a convict's, as usual. "I won't offer anyone my arm! I won't wear tails!"

"But you're your sister's best man," my mother pointed out to him.

"Well then, all she's got to do is not to marry! And for what she's marrying! A fellow who stinks of vermouth! Besides, she's always got along without us, so I can't see why she needs us to help her get married!"

Our handsome elder brother was less vocal, but we recognized that look on his face that he always wore when he was planning to leap over a wall and was measuring the obstacles. There were difficult days and recriminations which my father, full of anxiety himself and eager to avoid the malodorous intruder, was unable to quell. Then all at once the two boys appeared to agree to everything. Better still, they suggested that they themselves should organize a choral Mass, and Sido was so delighted that for a few hours she forgot her "upstart" of a son-in-law.

Our Aucher piano was carted along to the church and mingled its sweet but slightly tinny tone with the bleating of the harmonium. Bolting themselves in the empty church, the savages rehearsed the Suite from *L'Arlésienne*, something of Stradella's, and a piece by Saint-Saëns especially arranged for the nuptial ceremony.

Only when it was too late did my mother realize that her sons, each chained to his keyboard as a performer, would not appear for more than a moment at their sister's side. They played, I remember, like angel musicians, making the village Mass, and the bare church, which lacked even a belfry, radiant with music. I swaggered about, very proud of my eleven years, my long locks that made me look like a little Eve, and my pink dress, highly delighted with everything except when I looked at my sister. Very small and pale, weighed down with white silk and tulle and trembling with nervous weakness, she was gazing up at that unknown man with a swooning look of such submission on her strange, Mongolian face that the sight filled me with shame.

The violins for dancing put an end to the long meal, and at the mere sound of them the two boys quivered like wild horses. The younger, slightly tipsy, stayed where he was. But the elder, unable to bear any more, disappeared. Jumping over the wall of the rue des Vignes, he got into our garden, wandered around the closed house, broke a windowpane, and went to bed, where my mother found him when she returned, sad and weary, after handing her bewildered and trembling daughter over to the care of a man.

Long afterward she described to me that dust-gray, early dawn of summer, her empty house that felt as though it had been pillaged, her joyless fatigue, her dress with its beaded front, and the uneasy cats summoned home by her voice and the night. She told me how she had found her elder boy asleep, his arms folded on his breast, and how his fresh mouth and closed eyes, his whole body was eloquent of that sternness of his, the sternness of the pure savage.

"Just think of it, it was so that he could be alone, far from those sweating people, and sleep caressed by the night wind, that he broke the windowpane. Was there ever a child so wise?"

I have seen him, that wise one, vault through a window on a hundred occasions, as though by a reflex action, every time there was a ring at the bell which he did not expect. When he was growing gray and prematurely aged by overwork, he could still recover the elasticity of his youth to leap into the garden, and his little girls would laugh to see him. Gradually his fits of misanthropy, although he struggled against them, turned his face haggard. Captive as he was, did he perhaps find his prison yard daily more confined, and remember those escapes which once upon a time used to lead him to a childish bed where he slept half naked, chaste, and voluptuously alone?

EMCC

❦❦ The Footwarmer

I search my memory in vain for any early signs of the sacred fire, childish poetry, vocation, predestination. Instead, I find a footwarmer. Yes, at the start of my career there was a footwarmer! A few years more, and in order to make myself understood I will have to describe an accessory that almost does not exist nowadays. Already the dictionary speaks of it in the past tense: "FOOTWARMER: a metal box in which live coals were put, mingled with ashes." So then, a footwarmer reigns over the earliest recollections of my intellectual life, which is to say, my schooldays.

In the vast, icy-cold country houses, drafty with the winter blasts, the footwarmer was a prime necessity. At home, I remember there was the cook's footwarmer, the footwarmer of the sewing woman, my mother's footwarmer, and finally mine, the one I carried to school, filled with hot poplar-wood cinders covered with fine ashes. I was given the handsomest one because it was the most solidly made: a magnificent wrought-iron object, indestructible, as heavy as a packed suitcase. In the playground during recess, can you imagine my wrought-iron footwarmer's potential as a weapon of defense or offense? I carry with me the ineradicable trace of one of those combats in which footwarmers dealt the blows: the broken cartilage of my left ear. Footwarmer, thou wert my shield, projectile, stove, every kind of comfort for so many years! Every little girl had hers, in the primary class—the six- to eight-year-olds—of the bare and poverty-stricken school. Massive emanations of carbon monoxide rose from all those braziers. Some children fell asleep, more or less asphyxiated . . .

During my first school winter, a severe one, I walked to school between two walls of snow that were taller than I. What's become of those tremendous winters of former times, white, solid, durable, embellished with snow, associated with fantastic tales of pine trees and wolves? After having been as real as my childhood, are they likewise lost? As lost as old Mlle Fanny, phantom schoolmistress, who subsisted on novels and privations? Sometimes Mlle Fanny emerged from her romantic reverie and uttered a whinny that announced the reading lesson. That year we learned to read in the New Testament. Why the New Testament? I believe, simply because it happened to be there. And the phantom old-maid schoolmistress punctuated with blows of the ruler on her desk the rhythm of the sacred syllables, singsonged in chorus: "In—that—time—Je—sus —said—to—his—dis—ci—ples . . ." Sometimes a baby pupil, who had tried to warm herself by sitting on her footwarmer, would let out a squeal, because she had burnt her little bottom. Or an odor would spread in the room from a chestnut, a potato, or a winter pear that one of us was trying to cook in her footwarmer . . . Surrounding us was the winter, a silence disturbed by crows, the moaning of the wind, the clatter of wooden shoes, winter, and the belt of woods encircling the village . . . Nothing else. Nothing more. A humble, rustic image.

I believe that if a little harmless magic could provide me all at once with the aroma of an apple melting on the hot coals, of chestnuts burning, and especially the smell of the extraordinary old volume of the New Testament, mildewed, worn to shreds, in which Mlle Fanny preserved between the pages petals of dried tulips, translucent as red onyx, some little gray corpses of violets, the square, bearded faces of spring pansies—I believe, yes, I believe that I would be content. In those combined scents I believe I would capture the very breath of that wizard's book of spells which unveils the past, that key to childhood, and I would have restored to me my sixth year, when I knew how to read but refused to learn to write.

No, I would not write, I did not want to write. When one can read, can penetrate the enchanted realm of books, why write? This repugnance which the act of writing inspired in me—was it not providential? It is rather late in the day for me to inquire into that. What is done is done. But in my youth I never, *never* wanted to write. No, I did not get up secretly in the night to scribble poems on the cover of a shoebox! No, I never flung inspired words to the West wind or to the moonlight! No, I never made good marks in composition between the ages of twelve and fifteen. For I felt, and felt it each day more intensely, that I was made exactly for *not* writing. I never sent to a famous writer some essays that showed promise; yet everyone does so nowadays; I never stop receiving manuscripts. Well, then, I was the only one of my kind, the only creature sent into the world for the purpose of not writing. And how I enjoyed such an absence of literary vocation! My childhood and my free and solitary adolescence were equally preserved from the urge to express myself, both periods being uniquely occupied in directing their subtle antennae toward what can be contemplated, heard, touched, breathed. O deserts, fenced in and without dangers, footprints of bird and hare on the snow, ponds covered with ice or veiled with the warm mists of summer, assuredly you gave me as many joys as I could hold. Should I call my school a school? Rather, it was a kind of rude paradise where disheveled angels chopped wood in the mornings to light the stove, and ate, instead of celestial manna, thick slices of plain farm bread on which they spread a paste of kidney beans that had been cooked in red wine. There was no railway in my part of the country, no electricity, no college or big city nearby. In my family there was no money, but there were books; no gifts, but there was tenderness; no comfort, but we had freedom. No voice borrowed the sound of the wind to whisper into my ear, along with a gust of cold air, the advice to write and write, to dim by writing about it my thrilling or tranquil perception of the living universe . . .

I had expected that the story of a writer who did not want to write would be amusing. Instead, as I finish the tale, I find it melancholy. For at seventeen, when love came into my life, despite love and despite my seventeen years, I still had no desire to write or to describe, and I thought that love could do without love letters, could withdraw within itself in silence and be satisfied with a sovereign presence, and so I did not write my own romance.

Yet my life has been spent in writing. Born into a family without wealth, I had learned no profession or craft. I knew how to climb, how to whistle and run—gifts useful to a squirrel or bird or doe. The day when necessity placed a pen in my hand and I was given a little money in exchange for the pages I had written, I realized that every day of my life I would have to write, slowly, submissively, patiently, would have to match the sound to the word, would have to rise early by preference and go to bed late by necessity. The young reader does not need to know more than this about the stay-at-home, sober-minded writer hidden beneath her voluptuous fiction . . .

HB

PART Two ❦❦ [1893-1910]

Marriage—Literary Apprenticeship—Masks

Rien d'alleurs ne rassure autant qu'un masque . . .

Nothing gives more assurance than a mask . . .

❦❦ Wedding Day

The white train of my dress draped over one arm, I went down, alone, into the garden. The weariness of a day that had begun early after a night given up to wakeful dreaming had at last overwhelmed me.

Mine had been a quiet and modest wedding. The witnesses had been a timber merchant of the locality, Monsieur N., and his wife and daughter; Adolphe Houdard and Pierre Veber were the groom's best men. No Mass, merely a benediction in the afternoon at four o'clock. At five, Sido took a short rest, very prim in her faille silk dress with jet trimmings. She was flushed, as always when she felt unhappy and was trying to conceal it. My father, in his armchair, was reading a paper, *La Revue Bleue*. Pierre Veber and Houdard, with my youngest brother, had gone out to play billiards in the back room of a nearby wineshop, dark and cool.

Did anyone ever see a quieter wedding? However, there was no lack of strange elements. To begin with, all photographers, even amateurs, had been barred. The bride had avoided the duchess-satin dress, the diadem of wax flowers. Instead the gown was of muslin patterned with tiny bouquets, gathered at the round neck and at the waist, and in lieu of a crown I wore a wide ribbon bandeau ("*à la Vigée-Lebrun,*" said my mother), my long braid lost in the folds of my long skirt. As for the rest, I can only say that I looked quite nice and was rather pale.

What the wedding procession lacked in number, it made up for in beards. How hairy men's faces were at that time! My father still wore his beard, as he had worn it since his army service, when he was in the Zouave infantry. My young physician brother, as well as the delightful Pierre Veber—both twenty-six, with golden-brown eyes and the charm of favorite sons—wore pointed beards, trimmed with scissors, as did also Houdard and my husband. Most extraordinary was my husband's mustache, an opulent blond roll with narrowed points—he had acquired it at Mans in the Thirty-first Artillery.

Teetering on the heels of my ready-made white satin slippers, I was soon glad to sit down on a step. From the house came the sound of men's voices. Despite the sacred occasion, my husband and my eldest brother had taken off their coats, the one a jacket, the other a morning coat, and in their shirt sleeves were at work drafting some short, rhymed fables.

"Yours is the best," my husband said. "Mine has less popular appeal. If only we could have two more by tomorrow, before train time . . . Reread what you've done?"

I heard my brother declaim:

"The chasm yawned; the field above was doomed to slide
And be engulfed, with a prolonged uproar.

MORAL

Throughout your life beware, think twice before
You perch a field above a chasm opened wide."

"Marvelous!" my husband commented. "And what do you have for my 'Literary Publicity'?"

"No less than these lines from the revered Victor Hugo:

" 'When the infant appears,
The family surrounds it
And raises loud cheers . . .'

And warmly congratulates Madame Lachapeigne, first-class Midwife who successfully supervised the labor of childbirth."

. . . .

"Haven't you two in there finished?" I called.

"No," my husband replied. "And I must say, this is a weird kind of hamlet where the mail goes out at five o'clock and wedding breakfasts are given at half past six in the evening! I'm still trying to find something for my 'Literary Publicity' section in a terribly dilapidated copy of Sully Prudhomme . . . I adore you!"

Exasperated by my train, I wrapped it around my white arms and waited patiently. A childhood and girlhood adapted to the life of my two elder brothers had accustomed me to taking a back seat, asserting myself very little, and tolerating bachelor amusements, among which I number irreverent parodies, rebuses, puns, and satirical acrostics.

In the village where my eldest brother practiced medicine I had my own circle of friends, but I formed a romantic admiration for a prestigious and very Parisian journalist, the son of a former classmate of my father, and fifteen years older than I. The admired friend had become my fiancé and had been my husband since about half past one that day.

I stood up, nibbled a mint leaf, then sat down again on the edge of a forcing frame which was incubating some seedlings—pulling up my skirt and exposing my lightly starched petticoat edged with lace.

The tricolor cat came out of the cold frame where she had been baking herself, and the strong scent of some tomato plants that had been crushed by her siesta came out along with her.

The infatuation of a girl in love is neither as constant nor as blind as she tries to believe. But her pride keeps her brave and self-contained, even in the moments when she will utter the inevitable and sincere great cry of awakening and fear. That cry had not risen to my lips, for two long years of engagement had settled my fate without altering anything in my life. After becoming my fiancé, the family friend came to see us rather infrequently, bringing books, magazines, sweets, and then leaving . . . The great event in our engagement as far as I was concerned had been our correspondence, the letters I received and the letters I freely wrote.

When he left us, I had always accompanied him to the station, which was only a whistle stop. Afterward, I covered the kilometer of road again, with the dog Patasson. I pretended not to hear the unflattering remarks of my brothers—are there any brothers who do not criticize a bit and make fun of the fiancé who is stealing a sister from them? My brothers, to exasperate me, never called him by name but referred to him merely as "he."

"Did you notice how he has grown since we last saw him?" Achille asked Léo.

"Grown? You're sure?"

"What? Am I sure? Didn't you notice how his cranium has grown above his hair?"

"Will you shut up?" said Sido. "Are you absolutely determined to hurt the poor girl?"

"It's very good for her," the eldest replied. "She'll get plenty of it when she's married. This is good training."

He spoke the truth. I bit the inside of my cheek and put on a show of disdain. My eldest brother, to make amends, threw out a suggestion as he left:

"I've got the devil of a list of calls to make. Have to go to Adon, Montcresson, Saint-Maurice . . ."

I took the hint. And when, as we set off, he threw his doctor's bag on the seat of the two-wheeled carriage, he found me, as he knew he would, already installed there with my book, my snack, my old coat, ready for a long journey with its steep parts of the road that we would climb on foot to rest the mare, prepared to endure the loud screams of women in labor, and to look after the mare, plucking handfuls of green oats or fine hay for her enjoyment—in short, to return to my childhood.

And now, limp and weary at the end of that fifteenth of May, 1893, the bride was occupying herself poking with a stick at the openings of an anthill. Pink sunlight climbed the wall of the house; the fatigue of that day excited me, and also the embarrassment of having spent the whole day, ever since morning, being stared at by eyes that were measuring me and estimating the risk I was taking. So little anguish? So little romance? But the romance of my young days had been my solitude and independence, my inherent unsociability, and from early morning everything had fought against all this. "Tomorrow I'll put on my everyday dress, the most becoming one, and I will go with my fiancé to the station, along with my brother . . . Tomorrow . . ."

"Can't you leave one end of the table clear for our papers?" my brother's voice was demanding.

I could hear the clatter of the knives and forks that were being laid out on the big table. The long evening was falling without modifying the unseasonable heat. With eyes and voice I sought for Sido, who gave no sign. Ever since morning she had avoided me as if I were the plague. "Tomorrow, on the way back from the station, we will follow the Croches, that's the prettiest route. We will take the milk can . . ."

I could still only think in terms of my family. Tomorrow the whistle-stop train, reached after an hour's journey in a hired carriage, would take me, a bride, to Paris.

Could it be that there, with the tomato seedlings and the calico cat, I glimpsed for a moment the mistake I had made and reassured myself as to my courage? There is no need to waste pity on young girls who are having their moments of disillusionment, for in another moment they will recover their illusion.

Mealtime assembled our guests, increased the hubbub of voices.

"To the table, to the table!" my father commanded.

"But-able, but-able!" echoed my second brother, who sounded a bit drunk. The one and only maid of honor appeared at the top of the flight of steps, all in dove-colored shot silk, and I stood up to go in, not without having decorated the bodice of my bridal gown with a cluster of dark red clove-scented carnations that had been forced in the cold frame.

"Oh, heavens!" the young girl in shot taffeta exclaimed. "Take that off, will you!"

"Why should I? It's pretty, and it smells nice."

"Very pretty," Sido agreed. "All that white is so insipid. And naturally my daughter isn't much to look at today. Girls usually have a papier mâché face on their wedding day."

"It's hard to avoid," Mme N. began.

"Very easy," Sido retorted. "All they have to do is not get married."

"Do as I say, and not . . ." murmured the entrancing voice of her son-in-law, brand new if not very young. For Sido had been twice married.

Many recollections of this bygone day have escaped me; all the people gathered around the festive board are now dead, except for the bride with the splash of red carnations on the bodice of her white wedding gown, and perhaps also the maid of honor in the shot silk dress. I believe the menu was quite simple and very good. But between the sea pike *sauce mousseline* and the sweets—*bastions de Savoie,* a molded almond pudding capped with quivering pink spun sugar—my memory has bequeathed nothing to me. For, thanks to a few draughts of champagne, I dropped off into the sudden kind of doze that overwhelms tired children at the table. Apparently my head leaned against the back of my chair and stayed there. Madame N. had her second fit of indignation over this, Sido having insisted, in a vindictive tone addressed to everyone and no one, that I be allowed a moment's sleep. I slept for a few minutes and heard, as I awoke, my husband speaking.

"She looks rather like the Beatrice Cenci of the Barberini Palace . . ."

"With her red carnations," said Pierre Veber, "she looks more like a dove stabbed to the heart."

Sido's voice rose, aggressive.

"Can't you think of something better than to compare her to a decapitated woman and a wounded bird?"

A minute later, her superstitious hand, as it slid a white shawl around my shoulders, plucked the carnations from my bodice and woke me up completely, just in time for me to be asked to perform the ritual of cutting the cake, deflating the nougat bastion, and ruining the molded pink and green ice cream with a silver spade . . .

Next day I felt separated from that evening by a thousand leagues, abysses, discoveries, irremediable metamorphoses.

An hour before the departure, next day, Pierre Veber performed a mock bullfight in the middle of the street, using Sido's venerable red shawl as a matador's cape. I traveled to Paris in an old railway carriage that rattled along like a stagecoach, accompanied by three men who were all complete strangers to me, although I had just been married to one of them.

The thrilling idea of seeing Paris again—and also, I think, the farewell champagne—made them a bit hilarious. Corpulent and agile, as always, my husband performed amazingly deft acrobatics on the luggage racks. Houdard sang a few songs from the depths of his Sadi-Carnot black beard, and Pierre Veber patiently demolished the mechanism of the alarm bell. Then they calmed down and incautiously went to sleep as the night closed in.

Now and then I pressed my face to the window for a glimpse, on the horizon, of the indefinite glimmer that would announce our approach to Paris. But I encountered nothing except my blurred reflection and behind me the reflection of the three unknown men, who, with lolling heads, were sleeping. I suffered from thirst, and my heart was swollen with pain over a mental impression that remained with me. My mother had stayed up all night and at daybreak was still wearing her grand outfit of black faille and jet. Standing at the blue-and-white tiled stove in the little kitchen, Sido was pensively stirring the morning chocolate, her features, unguarded, betraying a look of terrible sadness.

HB

❦❦ Monsieur Willy

His constant cry . . .

His constant cry—I know it only too well—was "Quick, dear, quick! There's not a sou in the house!" Quickly, indeed, his secretaries flew to the post office, laden with a copious correspondence—consisting entirely of express letter-cards—and quickly Pierre Veber, Jean de Tinan, Curnonsky, Boulestin, Passurf, Raymond Bouyer, Jean de la Hire, etc., knocked off chapters of this or that novel. Quickly, first Alfred Ernst, then Vuillermoz, André Hallays, Stan Gollestan, Claude Debussy, Vincent d'Indy himself, provided precious matter for the *Lettres de l'ouvreuse*.[1] Quickly Eugène de Solenières and Aussaresses rattled off *Le Mariage de Louis XV*. Quickly, quickly I wrote the *Claudines* in four volumes, *Minne, Les Égarements de Minne*. At the *Retraite sentimentale* I jibbed. And I don't think that anywhere in the course of these recollections, which I am setting down as they come, without deliberate order or plan—I don't think I shall be led into saying why. The names of his more recent collaborators are unknown to me. We, the veterans of the old gang —Pierre Veber, Vuillermoz, that excellent fellow "Cur," Prince of Gastronomes, Marcel Boulestin and myself—whenever we meet and talk of our duped and despoiled past, we always say: "In the days when we worked at *the factory*."

My life as a young woman began with this freebooter. A mo-

[1] The title of a weekly article of musical criticism.

mentous encounter for a village girl! Before that—except for my
parents' ruin, the money gone, the furniture sold by public auction
—it had been roses, roses all the way. But what would I have done
with everlasting roses?

The book that should be written is that man's life story. The
trouble is that no one ever really knew him. Three or four women
still shudder when they hear his name—three or four whom I know
personally. Now that he is dead, their terror is gradually subsiding.
While he was alive, I must admit, there were good reasons for it.

Quite a lot of us have our own little private picture of M.
Willy. The people who did not see much of him talk of "that good
fellow Willy." Those who had to do with him at all closely say
nothing. Because of the many tales, the direct and indirect allusions,
I am obliged to speak of him, although, as Tessa says, there are
"nicer subjects of conversation." But his name is linked with a certain moment of time, with a particular case in modern literature, and
with my name.

The personal appearance, the manner, a tone of voice, a turn of
mind, are enough to disguise a human being utterly in the eyes of
other human beings. How could we have guessed—I cannot do better than use the plural pronoun and take my place modestly in the
crowd—how could we have realized that figures, figures first and
foremost, haunted M. Willy and his fine mathematician's brow?
Most of us refused to believe it. Figures were his greatest entertainment, the source of his deepest pleasures and of his gravest guilt. To
count, to amass, to hoard—even in the flood of letters that have
survived him, these are his chief concerns. The handwriting slants
upward; it is extremely small, microscopic in fact, and the curious
reader soon becomes as weary deciphering it as he is bored with the
monotony of the text. The notes are as dull as the letters themselves!

"Sub. from *L'Echo*
53 marks 10 forwarded"

"Enter all this in the book, old man.
To expenses:

M.M. on account   200 francs
Hans Dichter   50 —
Félix Potin   17 —
August balance   30 —
Rates   20 francs 50
To Juliet for the housekeeping: 124 francs 50,
from which you must deduct the 94 francs she was
given by hand.
I have made a note of all this but had no time
to copy it into the book. Put it down! Put it down!
That postal order for a louis—have you entered it?
I can't trust that harebrained memory of yours!
I think I made a note of the 40 francs sent to
Eisenhardt, but make sure, old man."

But what *book?* I have had account books myself, like other people. The book that was constantly in M. Willy's mind, even, as you see, during his travels, was something very special, very private, indeed very secret. He was a tidy man and kept it with the utmost care, entrusting it, when he left home, to one only of his many secretaries. For all his love of order, the margins are sprinkled with minute calculations, figures as wee as midges, as grains of sand. One day, after my divorce, a yellowing sheet of paper covered with such figures slipped out of an old letter rack that had been sent to me. I picked it up. O wonder of wonders! It was a list of shares purchased by M. Willy, the soundest on the market.

I have hardly ever seen *the* book; it had fallen to pieces by the time I glanced through it—a very common, cheap kind of ledger, long and rather narrow, bound in black cloth.

Figures, figures. . . . Where did you take me—I who paid so little heed to you? We had been married a year or a year and a half when M. Willy said to me: "You ought to put down what you remember of your board-school days. Don't be shy of the spicy bits. I might make something of it. Money's short."

These last words, which were his daily leitmotiv—a theme developed with unfailing fantasy for thirteen years—alarmed me less than the first. For I had just recovered from a long and very serious illness that had left me sluggish in mind and body. But having found and bought, at a local paper shop, a number of copybooks similar to those I had used at school, I set to work. The heavy gray-ruled pages, the vertical red line of the margins, the black cover and its inset medallion and ornamental title, *Le Calligraphe,* reawakened the urge, a sort of itch in my fingers, to do an "imposition," to fulfill a prescribed task. A well-remembered watermark in the thick, laid paper took me back six years. Diligently, with complete indifference, perched at the corner of the desk, the window behind me, one shoulder hunched and my knees crossed, I wrote.

When I had finished, I gave my husband a manuscript that was closely written and did not go over into the margins. He read it through and said: "I was wrong. It's no use at all." ·

Relieved, I returned to the divan, to my cat, my books, my new friends, to the life I tried to make pleasant, which I did not know was unhealthy.

HBk

I have known people . . .

I have known people who were huge: Gaston Leroux is a case in point. M. Willy was not huge, he was bulbous. The powerful skull, the slightly protuberant eyes, the nose, which was short and had no visible bridge, the drooping cheeks—every one of his features approximated to the curve. His mouth, under the heavy gray-gold mustaches that he dyed for a long while, was narrow, dainty and agreeable-looking, and had something faintly English about its smile. As for his dimpled chin, which was small, weak, you might even say fragile, it seemed the best thing to hide it. Which M. Willy did, at first with a sort of glorified imperial, then with a short beard. It has been said that he bore a marked resemblance to Edward VII. To do justice to a less flattering but no less august truth, I would say that, in fact, the likeness was to Queen Victoria.

Curves and soft surfaces, a baldness that caught the light and held the eye, a modulated voice, a bland outline. Little as I could penetrate these many defensive convexities, I had enough to brood over, darkly. It is indeed a very strange moment, in any life, when fear is born, seeds and takes root, spreads.

The young and healthy-minded do not readily entertain fear. Even a child-victim (people talk of child-victims nowadays, just as they talk of land-surveyors or mothers-in-law, but I use the hyphen with reluctance; it is like the stripe, a symbol of some hideous rank) —even the victimized child is not in terror at every hour of the day; there are always occasions when its tormentors are cheerful and kindly. Perhaps the mouse, between one blow and the next, has respite enough to appreciate the softness of a cat's paw.

Among all the forms of absurd courage, the courage of girls is outstanding. Otherwise there would be fewer marriages and still less of the wild ventures that override everything, even marriage. All that can be said is that if so many girls put their hands into the hairy hand, give their lips to the exasperated convulsion of gluttonous lips, and watch without alarm the huge, unknown, male shadow on the wall, it is that the promptings of sexual curiosity are potent in their ears. In a few hours an unscrupulous man will transform an ignorant girl into a prodigy of licentiousness. Disgust will not deter her; disgust has never been a hindrance. Like morality, it comes later. I once wrote: "Dignity is a man's fault." I would have done better to write: "Squeamishness is not a woman's virtue."

A consuming sensual audacity drives too many impatient little beauties into the arms of Lotharios half spoiled by time, and it is with them that, remembering my own youth, I have my quarrel. The seducer does not even have to take trouble; his mettlesome prey is afraid of nothing—at first! In fact she is often surprised: "And is that all? Isn't there anything else people do? At least we can begin again, can't we?" As long as her compliance or her curiosity lasts, she does not see her instructor clearly. Ah! if only she would pay more heed to the shadow on the wall—Priapus! looming huge in the lamplight, the moonlight. The shadow dwindles and is presently revealed as the figure of an already aging man with bluish eyes, a veiled and impenetrable glance, a terrifying gift for tears, a marvelously husky voice, whose stout body is strangely light and quick, who is hard as an eiderdown stuffed with flints. Such a rich assortment of conflicting subtleties, such a variety of traps!

HBk

A third floor . . .

A third floor in the rue Jacob, between two courtyards. One of the courtyards faced the north and the rue Visconti, so that I had, at least, a glimpse of old tiled roofs to remind me of the tiles of Burgundy.

No sun. Three living rooms; a small, dark study; a kitchen on the other side of the landing—all this for fourteen hundred francs a year. In the square drawing room was a salamander stove, and in the recess where I had set out my tub, my basins, and my ewers, a gas fire. It was almost a poor man's flat, yet its white doors were early nineteenth century and still had their little carved wreaths and garlands, now half clogged with paint. I had not chosen it. On the day I saw it first it was empty, and I felt that I was only half awake. The last tenant had lived there for fifty years, long enough to complete a most singular form of decoration. The doors, the ornaments on the doors, the cornices, the skirtings, the niche for the porcelain stove in the dining room, the sham wood panels, the shelves of the cupboards, the window frames, and a large surface of the walls themselves, were covered with tiny diamond-shaped confetti of many colors, cut out and glued on by hand, one by one.

"I understood from the gentleman himself," the concierge confided to me in a low, reverent voice, "that there were more than 275,000 pieces. I call that work."

Work such as you do in nightmares. The thought of living in

these rooms, in the presence of walls that had witnessed so secret a madness, so evil a joy, appalled me. And then I forgot about it. I was only a young bride.

No light, no air, the dark enchantment that sometimes lingers in places that have crushed and stifled many souls. The little flat must, I think, have been profoundly melancholy. And yet, to me, it seemed agreeable. What it is to have known worse! I had gone to it from another lodging, M. Willy's bachelor establishment, a quaking, echoing garret, at the top of one of the houses on the quays, that shivered at every passing bus and truck. I have never been able to forget that attic and its murky, rattling double windows. Painted in bottle green and chocolate brown, filled with unspeakably sordid cardboard files, soaked in a sort of horrible office gloom, it looked uninhabited, utterly forsaken. The drafts crept over the creaking boards; their slightest breath brought forth out of the black shadows, from under the sagging springs of the bed, a gray snow, a drift of flakes born, as some frail nests are born, of a thread, a hair, woven with dust as light and soft as down. Heaps of yellowing newspapers occupied the chairs; German postcards were strewn more or less everywhere, celebrating the attractions of underclothes, socks, ribboned drawers and buttocks. The master of the house would have strongly objected to any attempt on my part to remedy the disorder.

It was a relief to get away, every morning, from these indecent surroundings. The place had been adapted solely to the use, the careless convenience of a dissolute bachelor, and I welcomed the daylight that took me from it. I welcomed the daylight also for its own sake, because it drew me out of bed and into the open air. And because I was hungry. By half past eight or thereabouts, M. Willy and I were crossing the bridge. Ten minutes' walk took us to the humble milkshop where the blue-smocked packers from La Belle Jardinière kept up their strength, as we did, on rolls dipped in pale mauve chocolate.

HBk

Judging from various . . .

Judging from various incidents that stand out sharply in a haze
of unhappy memories, it would appear that M. Willy and I lived
very poorly. It is quite possible, I may say probable. I remember that
Sido, my mother, came to Paris for a few days in the winter of 1894,
or 1895—she always stayed at the Hôtel du Palais-Royal—and
found that I had no outdoor coat of any kind against the bitter
weather. She said nothing. She gave her son-in-law a look out of her
keen wide eyes and took me off to the Magasins du Louvre to buy a
black topcoat, trimmed with "Mongolian" fur that cost 125 francs
and seemed to me sumptuous. The very young are not deeply
affected by certain forms of hardship. The incongruous, too, often
scarcely touches them. The picture comes back to me suddenly of a
heap of gold shining on the black-painted deal writing table and its
red baize cover—a mass of gold louis that M. Willy had spilled
there out of his pockets.

"Take as much of it," he said, "as you can hold in both hands.
You'll count up afterward."

I counted 820 francs. Coined gold is a pretty metal; it has a
fine, clear ring, and warms pleasantly to the touch.

"I hope," said M. Willy, "that you won't want any more housekeeping money now for at least two months."

It seemed quite natural to go about with an empty purse, as I
had done before my marriage; it never occurred to me, either, that I
might have lived more comfortably. After the morning's cup of lilac
chocolate, I would hurry back to my dark quarters. I did not realize
that in their strange gloom I was gradually losing strength, that the
life was ebbing from a vigorous country girl brought up on the
wealth that the countryside granted in those days to the poor: milk
at twenty centimes a quart, fruit and vegetables, butter at fourteen
centimes a pound, eggs at twenty-six centimes the dozen, chestnuts,
walnuts . . . In Paris I was never hungry. I hid in my corner,

chiefly because I did not wish to know Paris. The town filled me with dread, and after ten months of marriage I already had most excellent reasons for fearing it. A book, hundreds of books; low, airless rooms; sweets instead of meat; an oil lamp instead of sunshine—and always the persistent, absurd hope to which I clung: this great evil, this city life, could not last; it would be cured miraculously, by my death and resurrection, by a shock that would restore me to my mother's house, to the garden, and wipe out everything that marriage had taught me.

HBk

Is it hard to understand . . .

Is it hard to understand how to have gone from a village home to the life I led after 1894 was an adventure so serious that it could bring a child of twenty to despair? Despair or a wild intoxication. It is true that at first, ridden by youth and ignorance, I had known intoxication—a guilty rapture, an atrocious, impure, adolescent impulse. There are many scarcely nubile girls who dream of becoming the show, the plaything, the licentious masterpiece of some middle-aged man. It is an ugly dream that is punished by its fulfillment, a morbid thing, akin to the neuroses of puberty, the habit of eating chalk and coal, of drinking mouthwash, of reading dirty books and sticking pins into the palm of the hand.

So I was punished, quickly and thoroughly. One day, dressed in my handsome, 125-franc coat, my serpent of hair bound with a new ribbon, I took a cab to the rue Bochard-de-Saron and rang the bell of a minute, mezzanine-floor flat. Anonymous letters often tell the truth. There, in fact, were M. Willy and Mlle Charlotte Kinceler, not in bed but sitting in front of—yes!—an open account book. M. Willy was holding the pencil. I listened to the pulse beating in my tonsils, and the two lovers stared, astounded, at the pale young provincial with the long hair, her plait coiled around her neck, her fringe curling on her forehead. What could I say? A dark little woman—four foot ten, to be exact—was watching me, a pair of scissors grasped tightly in her hand; a word, a movement, and she would have flown at my face. Was I afraid? No, I wasn't afraid. Violence, catastrophe, the hope of disaster, blood, a sudden shriek— at twenty, if you look into yourself, you can see tragic landscapes any day that are far finer than that. I should say that neither Mlle Kinceler nor I seemed in the least put out, whereas M. Willy sat mopping his brow, which was vast, powerful, and pink.

"You've come to fetch me?" he said.

I glanced uncertainly at Mlle Kinceler and my husband, at my husband and Mlle Kinceler, and found nothing better than to say, in my politest drawing-room manner:

"Why yes. Don't you think . . . ?"

He rose, pushed me in front of him, hustled me out of the front door with almost magical celerity. In the street I felt a little proud of having shown no fear, uttered no threats. But I was sorry I had not heard Mlle Kinceler's voice. And above all I was taken up, bitterly absorbed, by what I had seen: the neat, tidy little flat, a sunny window, a general air of ease and familiarity, the half-folded table with its American-cloth cover, a cage of canaries, the corner of a large bed just showing in the next room, the shining brasses and enamels of a tiny kitchen, the rather corpulent man seated sideways on a cane chair, the little firebrand of a woman grasping her scissors—and the intruder, the girl with the long plait, silent and slender in her ready-made coat.

I could hear my husband's short, agitated breathing. From time to time he removed his flat-brimmed top hat and wiped his forehead. He could not make out what it all meant, my arrival, my silence, my oddly restrained behavior. Nor could I. Later I understood that through the strangeness and the shock, the depths of my amazement and indeed of my despair, I had been able to think quickly, to make up my mind at once that whatever happened I must hide the truth from Sido. I kept my word.

I was not able to deceive her completely; she had eyes that could see through walls. But for thirteen years I did my best to make her think me altogether happy. It was not easy, especially at first. When I went to stay with her at Châtillon-Coligny, there was always one moment that I looked forward to with dread. The early hours of my visit were simple enough. Although the house was small and poor, very different from the big house at Saint-Sauveur where I was born, merely to be in it, to live a country life again, gave me back my fondness for laughter, for chattering and asking questions, for driving in the wheezy De Dion with my doctor brother and waiting for him by the farmhouse gates. On the evening of my arrival I used to tell my mother of the new people I had met, describe Catulle Mendès and Gustave Charpentier, Judith Gautier's black cat and her green lizard, Courteline. . . . But soon the moment would come, I could feel it drawing near, when my brother's weariness, the exhaustion of fifteen hours' ceaseless rounds, must take his white face and tired limbs to rest, the moment when my father must enjoy the sleep that comes so swiftly to aging men, the moment, the beloved hour when I would be alone with my mother. Stretched out, the hot-water bottle at my feet, I had to watch her sit down in the dilapidated armchair beside my bed, her cheeks flushed with pleasure at the sight of me and exasperation at her own fatigue: "Oh, that back . . . that left leg . . . that neck of mine!"

She would have nothing of her ills. Her way of speaking of them was a rejection, a denial of their existence. She had a gesture, too, that seemed to cast them off, as though she were flinging back a cloak that was too hot, or a mane of long thick hair.

"Now tell me, tell me . . ."

Her questions, her eyes searched me with alarming penetration. But I was her daughter and already proficient at the game. So I chattered on of Paris, told her a hundred more tales of the hateful town I knew so little. I talked about plays and concerts, I kept a harsh grip on myself, in terror of that last, that greatest danger: "If she tucks me in, if, before tucking me in, she takes me in her arms, if I smell her soft hair and feel it on my cheek, if she chooses to call me her 'lovely sunshine,' then all is lost."

An hour later she called me her "lovely sunshine," pressed her thin, silky hair against my cheek, and tucked the bedclothes under the mattress. I lay stiff and attentive, making no movement, saying no word, allowing nothing, nothing to escape me except a mumble of feigned drowsiness, a pretense of half sleep. At the cost of such self-denial I got safely to the time when Sido would cry: "Eleven o'clock!," take the cat under her arm, pick up the oil lamp with her free hand, and leave me until the morrow.

I have never been able to cry with ease, decency, and fitting emotion. Tears are as grievous to me as vomiting; they swell my nostrils and distort my mouth into an ugly square shape; they leave me with stiffened, aching ribs and hideously puffed eyelids. I cry as badly, as painfully as a man. But you can do away with tears if you put your mind to it; after I had been through a thorough training, I scarcely ever indulged in them. I have friends of thirty years' standing who have never seen my eyes damp. "What? *You* cry?" they exclaim, and stare at me under or over their spectacles, scanning my face, trying to imagine the traces of weeping, there beside the nose, there by the corner of the mouth. "*You* cry! Why, how absurd!" They burst out laughing, and so do I, for after all to cry in public is a sort of incontinence that does not give you time, if it comes upon you suddenly, to run away and hide behind the nearest wall. I detest tears—perhaps because I have found them so very hard to conquer.

HBk

The memories of my first . . .

The memories of my first and second years of marriage are clear and fantastic, like the impressions that dwell in the mind after some confused dream in which every detail, beneath its apparent incoherence, is plainly and fatally symbolic. But I was twenty-one and kept forgetting the symbols.

The spells woven by a voluntary seclusion are not all evil. Before the Kinceler incident came to warn me of my danger and arouse a taste for survival and self-defense, I had found it very hard to accept that there should be so marked a difference between the condition of a maid and the condition of a wife, between life in the country and life in Paris, between happiness—or at all events, the illusion of happiness—and its absence, between love and the laborious, exhausting sexual pastime.

I had certain compensations. I enjoyed the prolonged, sheltered leisure that prisoners enjoy and the rest that is allowed to invalids. A child that is wounded, or in a cast, and is compelled to lie down, will soon become accustomed to its helplessness. It will arrange and furnish its bed and grow fond of it. My bed, my refuge, my worldly goods were my youth and my dislike of people, my hatred of the town all around me, and a desperate determination to suffer from love rather than renounce it or complain. I had books and the listless, unceasing poison of the salamander stove that burned without interruption from September till June. I had my new men friends but no woman friend. Girls like the company of mature men but, secretly, it depresses them. My husband was fifteen years older than I was. Pierre Veber, M. Willy's witness at our marriage ceremony, was twenty-eight, but he had gone off immediately after the wedding, to join the young people that his own fresh, slim, whispering, witty youth deserved, nay demanded. He used to come, sometimes, to the rue Jacob, and I would breathe the air he brought in with him, his well-groomed young man's scent; I would look at him with pleasure and surprise and never dream that I could possibly have desired him. Meanwhile M. Willy's bald head glistened under the lamp, and . . . every day, to beguile my ceaseless craving to be with her, to live by her side forever, I wrote a letter to Sido. I let myself sink back, sink down into a half dream, a half light, a vagueness, the habit of silence, the dim pleasure of being pale and a little breathless, of spreading my long, heavy hair—long, long as myself—over a trailing Renaissance tea gown.

I could brush and plait it, but in other ways I was awkward and could not dress the long hair that my mother's hands had never coiled and pinned about my head. If I felt cold, I unplaited it and grew warm, wrapped in its smooth cape. At night I plaited it again and dreamed of snakes when the ends of the braids caught between my toes.

In 1895—or was it 1894?—my father-in-law presided at the Polytechnique Annual Ball, and I went there on his arm, dressed in a grand, sea-green frock with a lace cape, the masterpiece of a Batignolles seamstress. People stared a good deal at the *jeune fille* in the green gown that was no greener than herself—I was extremely ill—with the ribbon knotted on her forehead and the great serpent of hair stirring in the folds of her train.

That wan *jeune fille* was near death, yet did not die. She gave a lot of trouble to Dr. Jullien, the great Saint-Lazare physician, who looked after her for two months and scolded her gently. "Get well, my dear! Help me a little! I am trying so hard to cure you and you do nothing!" There is always a moment in the lives of the very young when death seems as natural and as attractive as life, and I was hesitating. How could I, in any case, have complained of an illness that brought me back Sido?

For she came, bringing with her a light array of black satinette frocks for the daytime and white bed jackets for the night; she came when Dr. Jullien wrote to tell her that he would probably not save me. She hid everything from me and everybody else, nursed me with a laughing tenderness, slept in the black dining room. All I noticed was that she seemed flushed, from time to time, and out of breath. No doubt she toiled, day and night, dragging me away from the threshold she would not have me cross. And so I got well, and Sido hastened back to where my father waited and pined—though not without my having noticed the singular, invariable coolness she displayed toward the man she always called—am I not right to copy her?—Monsieur Willy.

Never having been through another serious illness, I have not known that astonishing state again, a weakness so great that it left me no strength for deep suffering. I remember that I was in bed for sixty days and that I was gay and laughed easily. I took care of my face and hands and confided my feet and hair to Sido.

But I needed water as a dry plant needs rain. I begged for

baths, which my merciful doctor allowed me, rather unwillingly, every five or six days. Once a week or so the bath was brought up, just as it would have been in the eighteenth century. A hairy and muscular herald appeared first, cowled in a red copper bath that must surely have been used by Marat. The steaming buckets came next; the inside of the bath was shrouded in a coarse linen sheet, and they were poured out. My mother's hands wound my plaits around my head, four arms lifted me up, I was deposited in the hot water. I lay there, shivering with fever, weakness, the wish to cry, the exhaustion of bodily misery. My teeth continued to chatter for a long while after I had been dried and put back to bed and could amuse myself watching the bath attendants taking out the water, first by the bucketful, finally in little saucepans. The copper sarcophagus went its way; Juliette, the little maid, mopped up the traces of its passage; and Paul Masson or Marcel Schwob would come in to pay me a visit . . .

Sitting faithfully beside my bed, Marcel Schwob would open a book of American or English tales, Mark Twain, Jerome K. Jerome, Dickens, or *Moll Flanders*—which he had not translated at that time—and would read to me, so that I should lie still, so that I should bear with my illness and the round, black blistering plasters that bit into my hollow belly, symmetrically, so many on each side. I took the wealth poured out by this excellent scholar—he was much greater than his work—as a matter of course. He was already weak and walked with difficulty, yet he climbed our three stories twice, three times a day, talked to me, translated for me, wasted his time on me with superb generosity. And I was not in the least astonished; I treated him as if he belonged to me. At twenty, you accept munificent gifts in the royal manner, as though they were your due.

Paul Masson, my other friend and daily visitor, was less striking in appearance and manner, if no less mysterious. He was gray of feature, inconspicuous and unforgettable; his little beard was like dry hay, his laugh thin and grating, his glance that of a bad priest. He was addicted to puns and hoaxes, which he worked out as elaborately as the subtlest crimes. The few crumbs of writing that he left were signed "Lemice-Térieux": the *Thoughts of a Yogi,* a Catalogue of the "Salon de la Nationale," composed with incredible ingenuity entirely of puns prodigiously contrived to include the name of the artist and the title of the picture.

His looks and general air made you think of the evil spirits who visit villages and whose business is to seduce the girls, turn the lord of the manor into a wolf and the virtuous attorney into a vampire. He sometimes gave his address but never opened his door. I believe that he had kept the habits of his colonial-magistrate days and still smoked opium, but I have no proof of this whatever. All I am sure of is the affection and probably the compassion that he felt for me when he understood the circumstances of my new life and saw me waste away so grievously. As for his passion for mystification, I believe that it was to him what to another man would be a vice, or an art.

When at last, and most surprisingly, I got almost well and went with M. Willy to Belle-Île-en-Mer, Paul Masson came with us, clad in the suit he invariably wore, which was of black cloth, bound with mohair braid. He did not seem strong, yet he was never tired, always ready to follow me and my lively young exuberance that every day of sunshine and salt water made livelier. The positively Mediterranean riches of the island amazed and enchanted us. Terraces and vines, fig trees as plentiful as in Italy, lizards in gray traceries upon the rocks, blue and pink sails upon the sea. The yearly tide of women had already come, the Bigoudines, bright as scarabs in their caps and glittering dresses, who were engaged to prepare and cook the season's catch of sardines. When the fish were delayed the girls waited, filling in time by a determined pursuit of every creature in trousers.

"Don't you want someone?" they used to call after my friend.

"What for?"

"To sleep with you . . ."

He made a forked sign at them with his fingers, and they fled in terror, their rich skirts wafting toward us, as they ran, a lingering smell of rotten fish. Together we wandered over the island, from

Kervilaouen to the wild Mer Sauvage, from Sauzon to the Poulains, leaving M. Willy respectfully to his writing, which was extraordinarily copious at least in its epistolary form, each long hour of solitude and quiet producing a huge volume of letters and telegrams that might well have alarmed a young wife. But I was already learning to look the other way.

I made Paul Masson come with me to the old fortress on the Pointe des Poulains that Sarah Bernhardt bought later on. At the Pointe the sands shone mauve in the sunlight, strewn with a dust of crumbled rubies; I collected the biggest I could find and lost them again. For the first time in my life I tasted, I touched the salt, the sand, the seaweed, the moist and fragrant bed of the ebbing tide, the glistening fish. The Atlantic air soothed, lulled the memories of my long illness and the habit of active thought.

To the west of the island the Mer Sauvage came racing in— "all the way from America!" I would say with deep consideration. The constant thunder of the waves, the galloping manes of foam that drove the wind, the stones and sands before them, made all talk between Paul Masson and myself impossible. From time to time squalls would come up over the restless water, bringing rain that could be as harsh as hail. When this happened, I would take shelter with my silent companion in the caves and hollows of the rocks. I was quite happy to wait there patiently and watch the sea grow pale on the horizon. On one such occasion I remember Paul Masson turning up the braided collar of his coat and sitting himself down on a stool of purple granite. The afternoon was blue with low clouds, milky with rain. He drew from his pocket a small writing case, a pen that had a cap on it, and a little bundle of cardboard dockets on each of which he proceeded to write a few words in a round, copperplate hand.

"What are you doing, Paul?"

His eyes, narrow between their creased lids, did not look up from the cards before him.

"I am working. I am working at my job. I am on the staff of the Library Catalogue. I am writing out titles."

I was already fairly credulous; I gasped with surprise and admiration.

"Oh! And you can do that from memory!"

He pointed his little clockmaker's beard at me.

"From memory? What would be the good of that? I am doing something much more useful. I have observed that the library is singularly lacking in Latin and Italian works of the fifteenth century. Also in German manuscripts. Also in the private correspondence of royalty. And there are many other small lacunae. No doubt, luck or scholarship will soon remedy the shortage, but until that occurs I propose to provide the titles of these extremely interesting works . . . they should, they ought to have been written. In this way I shall at least save the honor of the catalogue, of the Khatalogue. . . ."

"But why?" I objected naïvely, "if the books don't exist?"

He waved an airy hand. "Ah!" said he. "I can't do everything. . . ."

I have written a good deal about Paul Masson because he astonished me and because, when he died, I lost my first friend, the first friend of my young womanhood. Later it came into my mind that he had grown very fond of me. From that to supposing that I deserved his fondness was only a step: he was a solitary man, a prematurely aged bachelor who had traveled much, and his affection did something to restore the confidence of a child deceived, betrayed as soon as married, secluded in her semblance of a home and obstinately resolved to hide there and reign over two friends and a cat. Thanks to him, I came to value a little more highly what there was in me that was unusual, attractive, desolate, secret. Outwardly I was all silence and disquiet, a sovereign ruling and moving in the shadows, followed by her long tresses, fed on nuts and bananas like a monkey in a cage. If Paul Masson, in whom M. Willy sometimes confided, suffered from what he knew and was fearful for me, at least he never hinted at it by a single, dishonorable word.

HBk

Winter months . . .

Winter months, summer months. . . . How long it seemed for June to come around again when I was young! Winter months, drenched with rain and Sunday concerts, while I wilted and grew pale; summer months that restored me to life with the hope that they would last forever. It was Champagnolle in the Jura, I remember, that saved me for another spell—in 1896? 1897?—from the salamander stove, gloom, and resignation. At Champagnolle the inn cost five francs a day.

For five francs we were allowed a room disgraced by mildewed wallpaper, peeling off and dangling in liana-like strips, by two iron bedsteads and some nasty little curtains fit for wrapping up abortions. But from noon onward the common table was covered with crayfish, quails, hares, partridges, all poached in the neighborhood. The mountain streams ran between cyclamen and wild strawberries, and my cheeks grew fresh and pink again.

From Champagnolle we went to Lons-le-Saulnier to stay with my husband's family. Before my marriage I had never "lived in someone's house," as I always called it, and it took me a long time to break down the constraint that kept me, not from loving the people who welcomed us, but from yielding to the simple pleasure of letting them see me as I was. Fortunately, the children got the better of me. Three here, four there, not to mention the more distant offshoots of the same stock. They soon found out what I was worth as a maker of flutes, a weaver of grasses, a gatherer of berries. With them I recovered my lost childhood; I told them the names of plants, of stones, lit them a fire using the punt of a bottle as a burning glass, caught grass snakes and let them go again, drove the little horse Mignon with proper care and precision, sang the magic formula that bids the snail put out its horns. A chain of quiet, disciplined children closed about me. Were they fond of me? Wherever I went, they followed. I never let them know how beautifully behaved I thought them, how easy of manner, nimble of mind, and how astonished I felt when I considered the difference between their childhood and mine. I, who had been broken in to an outward show of obedience, was as much impressed by the smooth, prompt deference they could always display as by their tidy, well-brushed curls, their clean nails, their smell of English soap, their habit of crooking their little finger when eating a boiled egg. The sound of their voices calling along the paths of the cool little mountain, the name they chose to give me, the pleasure I felt at their taking to me so simply—something of all this comes back when I hear the voice, over the telephone, of Paule, who is a doctor, or her sister, the musician, or their cousin, the interior decorator: "Aunt Colette, tell me, Aunt Colette . . ." The children's company was very sweet to me. My stains and bruises were only superficial, and I was still very young. Perhaps what I needed, without knowing it, was a child born of my own body.

It was on our return from one of these visits to the Franche-Comté that M. Willy decided to tidy his writing desk. At least I think so, for the memory is linked in my mind with a sense of mourning for a lost, russet September, sweet with bunches of small, sugary grapes and hard, yellow peaches whose hearts were a deep, blood-stained purple. The odious piece of furniture, hideous in its red baize cover and sham ebony paint, was turned out; the white-wood drawers appeared, disgorging a compressed mass of papers; and there came to light the forgotten set of copybooks I had so industriously blackened: *Claudine à l'ecole.*

"Hello!" said M. Willy. "I thought I had chucked those away."

He opened one of the copybooks, turned the pages:

"It's rather nice."

He opened a second copybook and said no more. A third, a fourth.

"My God!" he muttered. "I am the bloodiest fool."

He swept up the scattered copybooks just as they were, grabbed his flat-brimmed top hat, and bolted to his publisher's. And that is how I became a writer.

HBk

❧❧ Literary Apprenticeship: "Claudine"

At first . . .

At first, I was conscious only of the boredom of having to set to work again under pressing and precise directions.

"Couldn't you add a little spice to these—er—childish affairs?" M. Willy said to me. "A tender and overintimate affection, for instance, between Claudine and one of her friends?" (His actual words were brief and clear.) "And dialect, lots of dialect. And rather more playfulness. . . . Do you see what I mean?"

I saw what he meant, I saw quite well. I also saw, later, that M. Willy was managing to surround my collaboration with something better than mere silence. He got into the habit of making me listen to the lavish compliments that were paid him, of laying his soft hand on my head, of saying: "But you know this child has been most precious to me. Oh! yes, she has! Most precious. She has told me quite delicious things about her board school."

Young women who write seldom have much sense of moderation (neither have old women, for that matter). And there is nothing that gives more assurance than a mask. The origin and anonymity of "Claudine" seemed a rather indelicate joke that amused me and that I obediently made broader and broader. I did not read the preface until it was in print; I roared with laughter at the cover: a little girl, disguised as a peasant, sits, an open book upon her knee, writing. On her stockinged feet she wears yellow, comic-opera clogs;

Little Red Ridinghood's basket lies beside her, and her curls tumble over her rough, hooded, red cloak.

"What are you laughing at?" M. Willy asked me.

"Why! that picture! And the preface! How can you expect anyone to believe it's true?"

Though I kept my word and remained strictly silent, I found nothing pleasant or natural about the circumstances of this book. Only the companionship of men like Curnonsky, Paul Barlet, Vuillermoz, and their apparent resignation allowed me to get used to it. I could give the names of many others, men who were gay and talented and full of the charming, wasteful good humor of the very young writer who imagines that his gifts and his energies can never be exhausted. Ernest Lajeunesse—as may be seen in a curious series of letters—made difficulties from the first, wanted to be paid, became quarrelsome, and finally, after an exchange of threats and abuse, refused, as he puts it, "to sign my work 'Willy' like everyone else." As for Pierre Veber, I shall leave the real author of *Une Passade* to give his own story of a novelist ousted and dispossessed. Jean de Tinan is no longer here to tell us about *Maîtresse d'esthètes* and *Un vilain monsieur*.

To form a habit does not mean to become blinded; I did not think very highly of my first book, or of its three sequels. Time has not changed my opinion, and my judgment on all the *Claudines* is still severe. They frisk and frolic and play the giddy girl altogether too freely. The work reveals, indeed, an irrepressible youthfulness, if only in its lack of technique. But I do not like to rediscover, glancing through these very old books, the suppleness of mood that understood so well what was required of it, the submission to every hint, and the already deft manner of avoiding difficulties. To kill off a character, for instance, whom I had come to detest, seems rather grossly casual. And I blame myself when I see how certain things in the *Claudines*—allusions, features that are caricatured yet recognizable, tales that come too near the truth—betray an utter disregard of doing harm. If I am mistaken, all the better! But I am not mistaken.

Claudine à l'école sold well from the start. After a while it sold even better. The series has gone through hundreds of editions and is, I am told, still selling. I only know of it by hearsay. At the time of my first divorce, the copyright already belonged to two publishers, who had bought it, out and out, from M. Willy. I had dutifully set my signature beside my husband's on the two contracts. I shall never forgive myself for having done so. The renunciation was indeed the most unpardonable act that fear ever made me commit.

HBk

I have often thought . . .

I have often thought that M. Willy suffered from a sort of agoraphobia, that he had a nervous horror of the blank page. His correspondence shows a preference for postcards, letter cards, half or quarter sheets of notepaper, the flaps of envelopes, triangles cut off and used just as they are, even newspaper wrappers. And again, on these scraps, the writing is huddled in the far corners. Sometimes he scribbles the answers in the margins of the letters he has received, and so posts them back.

I fancy he was frequently overcome by fits of weakness, a pathological shrinking, when he considered the courage, the grim fortitude that is needed to sit without disgust before the virgin field, the naked page, unscored by arabesques, headings, scratched-out words, the cold, indifferent paper, white and blinding, thankless, greedy. Or perhaps work bored him so intolerably—which can happen, does happen; boredom can kill—that he preferred to exchange the anguish of it for the perils and problems of the managerial chair, among which, alas! the question of quality was the least important.

Perhaps he enjoyed his acid, pedagogic prestige, the biting comments he used to let fall, drily, from the heights of his superiority, on to my bent head, or that he wrote in the margins of my manuscripts. Nothing will rid me of the conviction that he was a born critic, although even the opinions on which he based his judgments were borrowed from other people—a born monitor, incisive,

quick to find the sensitive spot, to give the faintly cruel thrust that
reawakens a drowsy self-esteem.

He must, in the old days, have often believed that he was on
the point of writing, that he was about to write, that he was, in fact,
writing. And then, as he felt the pen within his fingers, there would
come a slackening, a collapse of the will, and his illusion vanished:

> "Your *Maugis amoureux* is very very good. I like the tone of
> it immensely. A good dodge: Maugis, disappointed in his yearn-
> ings for sweet innocence, chucks loathly Bayreuth and basting
> back to Paris recounts how *passus est.* Hence, some moderation in
> the Bayreuth passages. Leave gaps.
>
> "All the same, as I shall have very little time, don't leave too
> much space for Bayreuth, just enough to rag the music and the
> town.
>
> "P.S. On second thoughts, no, don't leave any gaps. I'll insert
> a word or two here and there in your stuff—up to ten lines in all.
> At most . . ."

Between the first and the third paragraph, between the words:
"Leave gaps!" and the words: *"On second thoughts, no, don't leave
any gaps,"* a tragedy has taken place, a struggle, a sudden stiffening
of pride, followed by what Balzac calls in old French, in his *Contes
drolatiques,* a *"déflocquement,"* the ghastly state of prostration that
seems to turn the very bones to water, to unknit the fibers of the
will. Was his a case of that paralysis, that complete inability to act,
which some drug takers experience when faced with an effort? I
believe not. M. Willy was addicted to remedies but not, to my
knowledge, to poison. One of his letters refers to opium and P-J.
Toulet with a certain naïveté. He appears to confuse the morphino-
maniac with the opium smoker and describes Toulet as the simulta-
neous victim of the "dark vapor" and excessive drink.

But these are all conjectures and oddities for which I have
never found an explanation. Nor shall I ever know the reason for
his chronic haste: "As I shall have very little time . . . Quick, my
dear, quick! . . . Run along now, old man . . . Need I remind

you, my dear Colette, of the extreme urgency . . ." Sufferers from a
creeping illness who know their days are counted may say aloud: "I
am in a hurry." Under their breath, they whisper: "I am pursued.
. . ." M. Willy, although somewhat the worse for wear, was a
strong man; he died at seventy-five. He probably endured no such
tortures, so that his impatience was no more than a mental trick—
"trick" being, perhaps, a pet name for neurosis.

HBk

It must be acknowledged . . .

It must be acknowledged that, authorship apart, our fashionable
novelist was a most active man, orderly and methodical and with a
great power of inspiring others. I still believe that the job of editor
on a big daily would have suited him to perfection. He knew how
work should be distributed, how to assess exactly the capacities of
those about him, how to criticize in a manner that was apt and stim-
ulating, how to judge without praising too highly. These are rare
gifts, I feel, that were very ill-employed. Personally, the compliments I got were few and always commonplace. "Delightful, my
dear. Yes, yes, I assure you, that will do very well. Since I say so, you
can believe me!" His reproofs, on the other hand, written in the
margins of my manuscripts (which Paul Barlet preserved; he had
been given orders to destroy them), were sharp, brief, and to the
point: "Not clear." "Too soon." "Had they agreed on this? Well,
then, say so."

He saw to everything, neglected no opportunity; for a while he
never allowed a topical revue to appear at the end of the year without its caustic scene on Willy and Claudine. He would arrange and
talk over the sketches himself with the authors of the revue.

The immense size of his correspondence was always disconcerting—that is, his own contribution to it; no one was ever entrusted
with that formidable task. He never filed a letter without adding, in
his own hand, in the top left-hand corner: "Answered on the—"

When *Claudine* became well known, things got even worse. Letters, portraits of underage maidens in socks and white collars dripped from every pocket of the "Father of Claudine," as he liked to be called. The pernicious adolescents themselves flowed in at the very doors of a dwelling that I really can no longer refer to as conjugal.

A little more and there would have been nowhere for me to put my blotting pad and laid paper copybooks, if, now that the money was coming in, we had not moved. The rue de Courcelles gave us sunny accommodations, first at No. 93 and then at 177 *bis*.

My husband, by this time, had been able to estimate the value of my output, and it was he, as soon as we settled in our third flat, who saw to it that I had a good table, a lamp with a green globe, the comfort befitting a scribe. To reach my narrow domain, I had to go through the drawing room, which was a sort of stylized tavern furnished with tables and benches of polished wood. One day I found M. Willy there in close proximity to an unknown lady. With the ease that comes from long habit, with the free humor (which I was acquiring) of the indispensable employee, I paused a moment as I went by and whispered urgently in M. Willy's ear: "Hurry up! For God's sake, hurry up! The next one has been waiting for a quarter of an hour!" After all, what had I to lose? A year before, a joke of this kind would have cost me—yes, quite a lot! But on this occasion, if you please, M. Willy was flattered.

So there was no longer any need to protect or to shift a sphere of solitude that did not go beyond the edges of the table, the circle of light shed by the lamp, the dull green walls of my little drawing-room jail. Pens, "Flamant No. 2" nibs, ruled laid paper, scented glue, long, stork-shaped German scissors, unnecessary colored pencils, childish implements of a rather finicking worker. Since I could not like my life, I liked its setting, and every afternoon I sat and wrote with an indolent air while M. Willy's business activities took him out and about in a hired brougham. At that time a hired carriage and two horses a day cost less than six hundred francs a month, for Comoy, the liveryman, let us have them at especially reduced, "professional" prices. I and my dog used to go out on foot before lunch, thus avoiding the eccentricities of the morning horse, which was black, emphatic, superb to look upon, but somewhat difficult to manage, being ungelded and given, at every season of the year, to emitting cries of a sudden and savage nature.

Affluence! Luxury! I was dazzled by the grant of a three-hundred-francs-a-month bonus—except in the summer months, which did not count. Three hundred francs, if you please, for me to spend as I liked, three hundred francs that had nothing to do with the famous "Book." What a lot you could buy, in those days, for three hundred francs! It was my turn, now, to give Sido presents. She chose them herself, sticks of pure cocoa from Hédiard, a quilted bed jacket, fine wool stockings, books. But my supreme gift to her was a lie: my pretense of happiness. Hour by hour I fought my unutterable yearning to go back to her, to be with her, torn and bleeding, unknown and penniless, a burden on the last days of her life. And when I think of the person I was during those long years of stubborn self-control, of filial deceit, come, come, I don't believe I am as bad as all that.

HBk

What Polaire made . . .

What Polaire made of "Claudine" is quite unforgettable. Even where she went wrong, where she refused to obey the authors' and the producer's directions, to her audience she was invariably right and she never made a slip that was not happy. She asked for the part, claimed it for herself, with the inspired tenacity of a visionary: "No, Monsieur Vili, Caudine is not So-and-so; nor Mrs. Thingummy, or Miss This-and-that or Whatnot. . . . No, Monsieur Vili, *I* am Claudine."

On the day of our first meeting, Polaire was dressed like a well-brought-up young girl in navy blue or dark green. She was letting her famous short hair—which was not black but a natural shade of chestnut—grow longer and had tied it with a ribbon on the nape of her neck. She was not heavily made up. Except for the bister shadow on her lids, the mascara of her wonderful long lashes, a faintly purple rouge on her lips, she glowed with her own radiance that flashed and faded, flashed again, a shining that seemed near to tears in her eyes' sad infinity, a long-drawn, unhappy smile, all the pathetic appeals that contradicted her diabolic eyebrows, her dancing ankles, restless as a mountain goat's, the sudden jerks and snake twists of her tiny waist, and that proclaimed, luminous and moist and tender, that the soul of Polaire had got into the wrong body.

In the theater her approach to her art was unusual. She understood all the more delicate shades, the subtleties, the thoughts that were suggested, half concealed, and expressed them to perfection; but with the grossly obvious she became awkward, and humor often made her sad. But when did Polaire ever miss an opportunity of being sad?

She was forever sighing: "I'm *so* unhappy!" We used to laugh at her for it. She would breathe the words plaintively, her sensitive hands pressed in above her waist, squeezing her strong, rounded little body, her high, wide-set ribs. "I've got ribs like an empire bolero," she said. She sorrowed because the daylight faded or the rain fell; she was saddened by love, by her ambitions, her doubts, her thirst for everything that life could give, her simplicity. "And to think that I've got the lucky signs!" she would cry. "I've got the teeth that bring you happiness!" and she would display her healthy gums, her faultless white teeth and the little spaces between them. . . .

People still remember the success she made of the play. Against all likelihood, she dressed the sixteen-year-old heroine, for the first act, in socks and a black overall, like a Poulbot drawing, and for the second, in a foaming white dress that was equally impossible. But the public adored everything she did. As she played it, the scene in the second act, where Claudine drinks a mite too much, became a thing of delicate fantasy, deliciously chaste and gay; she sailed blissfully through the banalities of the last act, danced over its pitfalls without so much as seeing them. How passionately she loved, she still loves, the stage! A visionary, a soul possessed.

I often went to see her in her dressing room. If we did not go on to a tavern with M. Willy to eat her favorite supper, which was my favorite too—a big wedge of cheese with the knob of a round loaf and a glass of red wine—we would say goodbye at the stage door of the *"Bouffes."* Already she was no longer the carefree, happy Claudine; her mood had darkened.

"Goodbye, Colette. Good night."

"Sleep well, Polaire."

"Oh, I don't sleep much, you know. I lie and wait."

"Who for?"

"Nobody! I wait and wait for tomorrow's performance."

She was telling the truth. Every real passion has its ascetic side, and her passion for her art made Polaire neglectful of love. Her neglect was deeply mortifying to the handsome young man, the rich young "blood," who loved "Popo" in his simple, frank, sometimes rather brutal fashion.

She went so far as to banish Pierre L—— from "her" theatre, even forbidding him, except on rare occasions, to come there at midnight and fetch her away.

"What would people say," she cried indignantly, "if gentlemen called for me here? They'd say I wasn't serious, they'd say I was only thinking of having fun!"

So she often went home alone, springing lightly into her victoria, when the weather was fine, her tiny toy terrier clasped to her breast. Her carriage was drawn by two piebald horses, like something out of a fairy story or a traveling circus, and away she drove, a strange young woman who had no need of true beauty to put all other women in the shade, an inspired actress to whom training and study were equally unnecessary. The hem of her pale-colored dress swept like a curling wave about her ankles, hiding or curving up over her high white boots—boots such as a hunting nymph might have worn, or a lion tamer at a fair—and the passers-by turned to stare at "Claudine."

One night M. Willy was awakened by the violent ringing of

the telephone. He lifted the receiver and heard a confused noise of sobs and muffled cries: "Vili! Oh Vili! . . . Come quick! I'm dying."

A short outburst of curses, and M. Willy leapt from his bed, flung a topcoat over his Russian-embroidered nightgown and hurried off, calling a few brief orders to me over his shoulder:

"Dress. Get there as soon as you can. I don't know what's up at Polaire's, but it looks as if tonight's takings were bitched."

He found, we found, Polaire on the floor of her bedroom, half under the bed. Sitting on the bed, and most admirably lit by a pink-frilled table lamp, was a young man in pajamas, Pierre L———. His eyes glowered, and with arms folded on his chest, he was breathing quickly through his nostrils like a boxer at the end of a round.

Down for the count, Polaire lay prostrate, if indeed the word "prostrate" can be applied to the stricken serpent, the frantic panther, to every live creature that can writhe and toss and buckle madly, tear the ground with its claws, sob, roar. The young man looked down at her in silence, motionless, making no attempt to help or soothe.

"Good God!" gasped M. Willy. "Whatever is the matter with her?"

Pierre L———'s handsome mouth remained grimly closed, but an answer issued, panting and incoherent, from underneath the bed:

"Vili! He hit me! . . . The brute! The brute! . . . Here . . . and here . . . and here! . . . Vili! I want to die! . . . Oh! Oh! Oh! Oh! I'm *so* unhappy! . . . Get a policeman! Get a policeman! I'll have him sent to prison! I'll have him put in irons!"

M. Willy wiped his forehead and inquired anxiously (first things first):

"Is she badly hurt?"

Pierre L——— shrugged his shoulders.

"Hurt? Don't be funny! A couple of wallops . . ."

The prostrate victim sprang to her feet. Crowned with curl papers large as the largest Roman snails, puffed with tears, swollen with sighs and cries, she still glowed, in her long nightdress, like some fiery Eastern sorceress; nothing that was excessive or frenzied could ever make her ugly.

"A couple of wallops?" she repeated. "And what about this? . . . And this?"

She pointed to her arms, her neck, her shoulder, her thighs that were made to grip the bare flanks of a horse.

"The police!" she whispered childishly. "Call the police."

Tears of exhaustion and defeat overcame her, and she sank to the ground again. M. Willy, much relieved, sat down on the bed beside Pierre L——.

"My dear old fellow! This sort of thing isn't decent. You must forgive me if I tell you, as a friend, that a decent-hearted man, a man of feeling . . ."

The dear fellow laid a large, white, well-kept hand upon his unfeeling heart:

"In the first place I don't care a damn," he declared, "whether I'm decent or not. As for tonight—she said something I couldn't stand. No!" he suddenly shouted. "No! I can't and I won't stand it!"

He got up, scrabbling with his fingers in his thick, ash-gold hair.

"Can't you tell me what happened?" suggested M. Willy in a conciliatory tone. "You know you can trust me."

"She said—" began Pierre L—— at the top of his voice. "She said—that I wasn't gentle!"

Below him, on the carpet, Polaire stirred feebly, shook her cluster of monster snails, moaned.

"That—I—was—not—gentle!" Pierre L—— barked out. "When I heard that, I saw red. . . . Not gentle! I! I!"

He struck his fine chest with his fists.

"I—! Everybody knows it! I'm the mildest of men! *I*, not gentle! . . ."

Groans came from the carpet, broken and despairing. . . .

"No, you're not. You're not gentle. . . . You don't understand anything. . . . You don't know what gentleness and understanding are. . . . What a woman really wants from love isn't what you think it is. . . . It's . . ."

"Do you hear her?" Pierre L—— thundered. "She's at it again! My God!"

He threw off his pajama jacket, bent over the floor. M. Willy was about to intervene when two amber arms rose and closed about the smooth neck of the mildest of men.

"Pierre . . . I'm so unhappy. . . . Nobody loves me. . . . Pierre . . ."

"My little duck. . . . My lovey girl. . . . Popo, darling. . . . Who said nobody loved you?"

He picked her up, held her slung across his breast like a dark gazelle, carried her, humming softly, back and forth about the great Louis XV bed. M. Willy turned to me:

"I feel that our presence is no longer essential. But they did give me a turn! They're killing, don't you think?"

He wiped his forehead and laughed, but I could not do the same. Standing there, unwanted, almost in silence, I had had ample time to watch a strange, unknown sight—love in its youth and its violence, an outraged lover, naked to the waist, the silky woman's skin above the perfect muscles, the rippling play of light upon the proud, careless body, his easy assurance as he stepped over and then picked up the fallen body of Polaire.

I saw the back of his trim, well-shaped neck and the ash-gold hair falling like rain over Polaire's hidden face. Her arms about him, he rocked his victim gently, and she had forgotten we were there.

"Hey! Young Pierrot! Can you promise not to try our star's nerves too hard? Not to give her advice so—er—convincingly?"

The young head lifted and we saw the flushed, ferocious face, the mouth still moist from the interrupted kiss.

"Only when it's absolutely necessary, old man. I promise . . ."

I joined M. Willy, who, by the way of being funny, was tripping to the door on tiptoe, and we went out.

M. Willy, his mind now entirely at rest, seemed greatly amused by our night's adventure. I was not so entertained.

"Are you cold? You don't want to go home on foot, do you?"

No, I was not cold. Yes, I was cold. All the same, I would have liked to go home on foot. Or not to go home at all. Walking beside him, I looked back in my mind at the room we had just left. I can see something of it still—highlights of pale blue against a dim background, lamps that shone pink in their little embroidered shades, the tumbled, white expanse of a lovers' bed. I have kept the memory of a prolonged, uneasy sadness that I ought, perhaps, to call jealousy.

HBk

From the day . . .

From the day when, following M. Willy's instructions, I cut off my too long hair, a number of clever people discovered that I bore a strong likeness to Polaire. Unless twin sisters are dressed in identical clothes and do their hair in the same way, clever people seldom exclaim at their striking resemblance. It is true that Polaire's ears and mine were set very far from the nose and that our eyes were perfectly level. But indeed I envied the beauty of her eyes as much as I envied her ankles, her teeth, her delicate little ears.

To be strictly honest, I must admit I was not sorry to lose the great inconvenient rope of hair that was weighing me down, feeding on my strength. Once I was rid of it, the only thing that spoiled my pleasure was a letter from Sido. She rebuked me in strangely grave terms: "Your hair was not your own. It was mine, the work of twenty years of care and attention. You have disposed of a precious trust that I had confided to you."

But I shook a happy head, freed from its burdens and its pins, and cried joyfully to myself: "I can feel the air! I can feel the air tickling my scalp!" Beside me, someone infinitely more farseeing was otherwise concerned; M. Willy was busy inventing a pair of twins.

Under his direction, Polaire and I were fitted out with three precisely similar costumes—only three, but that was quite enough, that was altogether too much. There was a tartan suit in black and brown and green; there was a white dress and a hat of the sort known as a "Charlotte," in white tulle with bunches of cherries; there was a second coat and skirt in grayish blue with bands of grayish white and tabs and stitching and heaven knows what ribbed braidings that the tailor called "straps" and that led, during one of our early fittings, to a slight confusion. The cutter explained:

"This is where the straps tail off. They have got to be stitched."

Polaire, who had, as usual, been lost in her own thoughts, suddenly woke up:

"Oh! Poor little creatures! Oughtn't you to bandage them as well?"

Her mind and the situation having been cleared up, she apologized:

"I thought a 'straps' was a little dog. Rather like a fox terrier, but much smaller."

On the days when our manager took us out to restaurants in our "twins" disguise, she was constrained, sad as a dressed-up animal is sad, and her shrinking made people stare and smile more maliciously still. She could not hide it; Polaire always put her whole soul into her face. Mine was not so easily read; no signs of a decent embarrassment could be detected there! I was thirty; I had had ten years' training.

I am sure that Polaire remembers the night of a dress rehearsal at one of the music halls—Moulin Rouge? Casino de Paris? Folies Bergère?—at which we were "on duty."

"Put on your white frocks," said M. Willy. "I'll look as if I were trotting out my two kids."

As the three of us went into the stage box, the audience focused its attention on us with such intensity, a feeling so unanimous, so silent, so heavy, that Polaire's sensitive antennae caught it and quivered. She took a quick step back, as though a trap had opened.

"Well, Popo? What is it?" our manager asked.

She was clinging with both hands to the door of the box, trying to slip away: "No . . . no . . . I don't want to . . . Please, please . . . I can hear what they're thinking—it's ugly, it's horrible."

She gave in, of course. But as she presently sat beside me in the blazing lights, sighing out her "I'm *so* unhappy," I was very very sorry for her that night.

HBk

[*Meantime*] . . .

[Meantime,] surrounded by the evidence of an ever increasing success, M. Willy began to reverence, as well as to exploit, his own symbols. From the moment your Negro sorcerer starts to believe in the virtues of the noxious remedy he is concocting, you must fear for the sorcerer rather than for his patient. But perhaps I should put down to natural instability the excitement which robbed M. Willy of much of his caution, disclosed his craze for notoriety, any kind of notoriety, and which was at the root, maybe, of the feverish anxiety, the haste, "Quick, dear, quick!"—neither of which has ever been explained.

But since my sorcerer continued, in private life, to be exactly like himself—and I do not feel called upon to comment upon the subject—I had quite enough to do, dealing with my own ever present fears. You do not notice changes in what is always before you. Haunted by money to a perilous degree, imprudent and darkly secretive, weakly and plaintive when it served him, disarming when he chose, he never failed to provide me, throughout the years that I made prosperous, with my share of confused pleasure and clearly defined pain. Under this regime I acquired, I developed and shaped within me, the ways and temper of a china repairer. A prison is indeed one of the best workshops. I know what I am talking about: a real prison, the sound of the key turning in the lock, and four hours' claustration before I was free again. "Show your credentials!"

What I had to show were so many well-filled pages. I am aware that these details of a routine jailing do me little honor, and I do not enjoy looking like a shorn sheep. But their somewhat Gothic flavor and the respect due to freakish truths give them their place here. The window, after all, was not barred, and I had only to break my halter. And so—peace be upon the hand, now dead, that did not hesitate to turn the key! It taught me my most essential art, which is not that of writing but the domestic art of knowing how to wait, to conceal, to save up crumbs, to reglue, regild, change the worst into the not-so-bad, how to lose and recover in the same moment that frivolous thing, a taste for life. What I chiefly learned was how to enjoy, between four walls, almost every secret flight, and also to compromise, to bargain and finally, when the "Quick! My God! Quick!" fell upon me, to hint, "Perhaps I could work faster in the country."

HBk

At the faintest stir . . .

At the faintest stir of memory, the little estate of Monts-Boucons comes back to me. I see its roof of almost black tiles, its Directoire façade—which was probably no older than Charles X—painted in a yellowish monochrome, its copses, its arch of broken rocks in the best Hubert Robert manner. M. Willy appeared to give the place to me, the house and the little farm and the ten or twelve acres of land: "All this is yours." Three years later he took them away again: "Nothing of this is yours any longer, or mine."

The orchard was very old; it still yielded a meager crop of delicious fruit. Up there, from June till November, for three or four years running, I led a life as lonely as a shepherd's. Needless to say, M. Willy kept a watchful eye upon my loneliness and came to visit it himself from time to time. He used to arrive dead beat and go off overwhelmed, cursing the weight of his "labors" and the necessity of being "tied to Paris" in the middle of summer. He would leave behind him in my care ("These repulsive volumes are worth a very great deal of money") a number of small trunks full of obscene literature, English as well as French, some of it ancient; and then proceed to remove them.

My more acute distress went with him, and yet his sudden going still hurt something in me, the persistent normal dream: a couple living together in the country. But, away from his presence, I felt myself becoming once again a better person, that is to say, better fitted to live upon my own resources and as punctual and orderly as though I already knew that discipline is the cure for every ill.

At six o'clock in the summer, at seven in autumn, I was out of doors, aware of the rain-drenched roses, or the red leaves of the cherry trees quivering in the red November dawn. The silver-coated rats squatted at ease, eating their meal of grapes straight from the vine; the big snake, caught in the trellis of the hen run, could not escape the fowls' ferocity. The swallows ruled the cat with extreme rigor, driving it away with sharp blows of their beaks and shrill whistling war cries from the barn and the rows of nests that lined every rafter. I had a bulldog, Toby Dog, who lived in a turmoil or a swoon of emotion, and a long, luxurious, subtle angora cat, Kiki-the-Demure.

A *pégot* cat—the *pégot* cats of the Franche-Comté are those that follow like dogs—attached herself to me. Fond, familiar beasts, infinitely precious. I did not talk to them a great deal, since they were always with me. Another came to join our company, an elderly half-bred horse, slim-legged and light-footed, torn by a thousand lashes, covered with wounds, that I bought and cared for as best I could and presently rode. We were an odd sight, the two of us: he in his dressings, with pads of greased linen between his skin and the saddle girths, and bandages of soft rag about his fetlocks; I astride him in checked bicycle bloomers of the zouave type. To be on the safe side, I went to the military riding school at Saint-Claude and called upon the excellent help and advice of Calame, the riding master; for a week or so I went round and round, over the fences, at the tail of the last horse, behind four would-be pupils of the Saint-

Maizant academy. "Tuck in your buttocks! Tuck in your buttocks!" Calame shouted at me in his flat, Franche-Comté voice. "Upon my word! You do me more credit than all these bumpkins!"

I also bought, for two or three hundred francs, during the last year, a charming relic, an old *petit-duc* and its silver-buckled harness. The *petit-duc* is a carriage that is something between a fairy chariot and a child's pushcart. There is room for two people, but no coachman's box, and the body is set so low that your feet are almost level with the road. Without stopping or disturbing anybody, you can step out and gather hedge roses and mushrooms, scabious, oak apples, wild strawberries, and, when you please, step in again. The horse saunters, browses, dreams beside you. I used to fill the empty seat with flowers and fruit and chestnuts. One day I brought back my most splendid find, bottles of wine—Volnay, Chambertin, Corton, and a forty-year-old Frontignan, glowing with warmth and amber sunshine. They were all wines of a respectable age and vintage that I had picked up for a few francs at a wayside tavern that was changing hands.

Though many years have passed, the savor of those Franche-Comté days is still alive in me, nothing has been lost of the myriad sights and scents, the long hours of work and study, the sadness. I was, in fact, learning to live. Can you learn to live? Yes, if you are not happy. There is no virtue in felicity. To endure without happiness and not to droop, not to pine, is a pursuit in itself, you might almost say a profession. I was writing *La Retraite sentimentale* at the time, a book that tells of the light adventures of a young woman, Annie by name, who likes men very much, and of Marcel, who does not like women at all. As I wrote, a new strength was growing in me that had no connection with literature. But it gave way if I tried it too hard; I had not yet reached the point of wishing to leave the "domestic hearth," and the work that was even more domestic than the hearth. But I was changing. Slowly, if you like, but what matter? To change is the great thing.

I had become vaguely aware of a duty toward myself, which was to write something other than the *Claudines*. And so, drop by drop, I squeezed out the *Dialogues des bêtes*. In it I enjoyed the moderate but honorable satisfaction of not talking about love. I had a further reward, the best of all: Francis Jammes's fine preface. All my novels, after that, dwelt most persistently upon love, and I have not grown tired of the subject. But I brought it back into my books and found pleasure in it when I had recovered my respect for love—and for myself.

It is the image in the mind that binds us to our lost treasures, but it is the loss that shapes the image, gathers the flowers, weaves the garland. What would I have kept of the Monts-Boucons if M. Willy had not taken them from me? Less, perhaps, than I have now. I cried out, as we all cry out, losing a passion that is in its first sweetness: "How can I live without the Monts-Boucons?" And . . . And I laid to my breast, and later hung up before me, the garland of yellow leaves, intermingled with cherries half honeyed by the fierce Franche-Comté summers, with clusters of sleepy wasps, dug at dawn, basketful by basketful, from their potent subterranean nests. And the handful of speckled feathers, quills of my five goshawks that pursued the snakes and lizards so vigorously, that perched so insolently upon the smallest wild quince tree. They would let me draw quite close to them, staring at me as I stared into their eyes, and then would rise into the air in a spreading wheel of wings. That is my memory of the Monts-Boucons. Before that, nothing had been of real account but my own native Puisaye. My Puisaye garland is of flowering rushes, the great rose-colored butoma blossoms rising from the lake, bolt upright upon their own reflections in the water, and the berry of the rowan and the sorb apple of the service tree, and the medlar, ruddy and tough, that will not ripen in the summer sun but softens and yields to autumn. It is the water caltrops with its four sharp horns, its grayish flesh that tastes of tench and lentils; it is the red, the white, the purple heather, growing in a soil as light as birch ashes. It is the bulrush with its brown rat's fur and, to bind my wreath together, the snake that swims across the pool, its little chin just ruffling the water. Nothing, no hand, no storm, can take from me the marshes of my childhood, the fruitful, swampy places by the ponds, where the reeds grow. Every year the harvest of rushes is cut down and roughly plaited into mats, but it is never altogether dry before the plaiting. My bedroom had no other comfort than these rush carpets, spread over the cold red tiles, and no other scent. Green scent of earth and water, marsh fever that we brought into our homes like some gentle beast, wild and sweet of breath—it is with me still, I press it close, between my pillow and my cheek, and it breathes as I breathe.

HBk

Above the flat . . .

Above the flat in the rue de Courcelles, a narrow stairway led to a studio and a tiny bedroom. There were already many more studios in these days than there were painters, but the painters could find nowhere to paint in, the studios being all taken up by high-class lovers, eccentric ladies, and even quite ordinary people who fought for the privilege of furnishing them with garden benches, divan beds, Japanese umbrellas, church vessels, and choir stalls. Mine had no ornaments beyond the fittings of a gymnasium, the horizontal bar, trapeze, rings, and knotted rope. I used to swing and turn over the bar, suppling my muscles half secretly, without any particular zeal or brilliance. Yet, when I reflected on it later, it seemed to me that I was exercising my body much in the way that prisoners, although they have no clear idea of flight, nevertheless tear up their sheets and plait the strands together, sew gold coins into their coat linings, hide chocolate under the mattress.

For indeed I was not dreaming of flight. Where could I go? What could I live on? And Sido, Sido! The thought of her was always with me and the obstinate determination never to go back to her, never to admit. It must be understood that I had nothing that belonged to me personally. And it should be realized, too, that captives, animals or men, are not constantly absorbed by the notion of escape, for all their restless pacing behind the bars and the way they have of gazing far away into the distance, through the encircling walls. The long glance, the unquiet step are only reflexes, brought about by habit or the size of their prison. Open the door that the bird, the squirrel, the wild beast have been eyeing, besieging, imploring, and instead of the leap, the sudden flurry of wings you expected, the disconcerted creature will stiffen and draw back into the depths of its cage. I had plenty of time to think, and I was constantly hearing the same grand, contemptuous, sarcastic words, shining links of a fine-wrought chain: "After all, you are perfectly free . . ."

Flight? But how do you set about flight? To "desert the domestic hearth" was, to us provincial girls of 1900 or so, a formidable and unwieldy notion, encumbered with policemen and barrel-topped trunks and thick veils, not to mention railway timetables.

. . . .

Freya, the clairvoyant, who was young in those days and at the outset of her fame and her career, looked at my hands and was astonished.

"It's . . . Oh! it's very odd . . . I would never have thought it . . . You must get out!"

"Of what?"

"Of where you are."

"The house I'm in?"

"Yes, but that's only a detail. You must get right out of it. You've lost a lot of time already."

With which pronouncement, for all the cryptic aspect of her diagnosis, I entirely agreed. Later I changed my mind and came to the conclusion that we were both wrong and that I had not lost too much time. It is better not to haggle over ten years of your life—I gave good measure and spent thirteen—provided they are youthful years. Later it is well to be thrifty.

Was it love that kept me there, in defiance of the signs and omens, waiting, waiting? Any answer I might give to this question, whether yes or no, would seem to me suspect. When a passion is really the first, it is hard to say: at this hour, of this blow, love died. The dream that brings back to you in sleep the poignancy of a vanished first love is the only dream that can rival the tenacity of the nightmare that haunts schoolchildren and octogenarians—the dream of returning to school and facing the oral exam.

One thing is certain: the extraordinary man I had married possessed the gift and practiced the policy of occupying a woman's thoughts, several women's thoughts, at every hour of the day, of tracing, imprinting, maintaining a track that could never be confused with other tracks. The traces that happiness leaves are not necessarily permanent. I know women who, after they had done with him, had only happy lives before them. They came near, it seemed, to crying out, like the lover of great music translated by mistake into a Gounod paradise: "Nothing but harps! Nothing but harps! Merciful Father! Give us something on the triangle and the clarinet and a few sharp discords, for pity's sake!"

Flight would have meant thinking out, organizing a future. My improvident father had bequeathed me no sense of tomorrow, and Sido, the faithful, had done no more than cast a frightened glance at the narrow ways by which her children would travel toward death.

Like her, I was lacking in imagination, and also in the faith that upheld Polaire and inspired the apocalyptic formulas of which she was so fond: "It's when you're sunk under a hundred feet of muck that someone comes along and gets you out."

No one, so far, had come to get me out. It is true that mountains would not have been heavier or more difficult to move than I was, although you would not have thought so if you had seen me riding in the mornings on the hack at ten francs an hour which I hired twice a week. My horse cannot have found me much of a burden; I was growing thinner every day. I did not realize then that to lose weight without dieting, to suffer a mysterious volatilization of the body's substance, deserves serious attention. . . .

But the time always came when the portents faded and I returned to my well-concealed, unsettled life. No threats, no prayers were needed to urge me back or keep me there. Surely such obstinacy should have discouraged the shapers of my destiny and their dark messages? Already, as though they knew just how to please and excite me, they were making absurd and comical suggestions that carried auguries in doubtful taste, proposals smelling of the caravan and the big top. Without warning or preamble, I was asked:

"Will you take over a 'turn' with thirteen trained Russian greyhounds? The woman who trained them is dying in the hospital. It's a ready-made job, you can just step into it. Everything's fixed up, the tours, the contracts, everything. And it would be quite your style."

I have forgotten the name of the envoy who let fall this balm, this dew, this temptation, this breath of the highroad, this scent of the circus. I shrugged my shoulders and refused even to see the thirteen greyhounds. Thirteen greyhounds, their fabulous necks outstretched, the curve of their bellies drinking in the air. And thirteen hearts to conquer. Disquiet, anxiety. It was all very well for me to shrink back into my scribe's virtue; my familiar, faithful fear, anxiety remained, working within me, for me. Thirteen greyhounds, a rampart, a family, a home. How did I ever let them go? Sadly, my regrets followed them in their circuitous and glorious course: "Perhaps another time."

But thirteen greyhounds, made in the image of speed and flight —you cannot recover them once you have allowed them to slip by. They were adrift; my hand was worthy, I am sure, to gather them up. Not having found the courage to do so, I had to accept other allies—ridicule, for instance. It is a most potent adjunct! Without it, how could I ever have drawn attention to myself?

One fine afternoon, on a lawn at Neuilly, in the gardens of Miss Nathalie Clifford-Barney, I played one of the two parts in Pierre Louÿs's *Dialogue au soleil couchant*. The name of the other improvised actress was Miss Eva Palmer. She was an American and had the most miraculous long red hair. Only on my elder half-sister have I seen the wealth that poured from Eva's forehead to her feet. For the *Dialogue* she bound its amazing abundance in ropes about her head and put on a blue-green, more or less Greek tunic, while I felt I was the perfect Daphnis in terra-cotta crepe de Chine, cut very short, a pair of Roman buskins, and a wreath in the Tahiti style.

Eva Palmer, white as a sheet, stammered out her words. I was so stiff with stage fright that the rolling "r's" of my Burgundy accent became positively Russian. Pierre Louÿs, author and guest, listened. Or perhaps he did not listen, for we were undoubtedly pleasanter to look at than to hear. But we believed that the whole of Paris under its sunshades and its hats, which were immense that year, had its eyes upon us. After the performance I plucked up the courage to ask Louÿs if "it hadn't gone too badly."

He answered gravely: "I have experienced one of the greatest emotions of my life."

"Oh! dear Louÿs!"

"I assure you! The unforgettable experience of hearing my work spoken by Mark Twain and Tolstoy."

Eva Palmer reddened beneath the red splendor of her woven and interwoven tresses, and Pierre Louÿs murmured consolingly, adding his mild praises to the praise of Miss Barney and her friends. But the next moment everyone had forgotten the Boston shepherdess and the Moscow herdsman; from behind a screen of foliage a naked woman had appeared, riding on a white horse, its strappings studded with turquoises—a new dancer whose name was already known among the studio and drawing-room cliques: Mata Hari.

She was a dancer who did not dance much, yet at Emma Calvé's, before the portable altar that she used as a backdrop, supported by a little group of colored attendants and musicians and framed in the pillars of a vast, white hall, she had been sufficiently snakelike and enigmatic to produce a good effect. The people who fell into such dithyrambic raptures and wrote so ecstatically of Mata Hari's person and talents must be wondering now what collective delusion possessed them. Her dancing and the naïve legends surrounding her were of no better quality than the ordinary claptrap of the current "Indian numbers" in the music hall. The only pleasant certainties on which her drawing-room audiences could count were a slender waist below breasts that she prudently kept hidden, a fine, supple moving back, muscular loins, long thighs, and slim knees.

Her nose and mouth, which were both thick, and the rather oily brilliance of her eyes did nothing to alter—on the contrary—our established notions of the Oriental. It should be said that the finale of her dance, the moment when Mata Hari, freed of her last girdle, fell forward modestly upon her belly, carried the male—and a good proportion of the female—spectators to the extreme limit of decent attention.

In the May sunshine, at Neuilly, despite the turquoises, the drooping black mane of hair, the tinsel diadem, and especially the long thigh against the white flanks of her Arab horse, the color of her skin was disconcerting, no longer brown and luscious as it had been by artificial light, but a dubious, uneven purple. Having finished her equestrian parade, she alighted and wrapped herself in a sari. She bowed, talked, was faintly disappointing. It was much worse on the day Miss Barney invited her as an ordinary guest to a second garden party.

"Madame Colette Willy?"

A loud, strongly stressed voice, calling me by my fancy name, made me turn around. I found a lady in a black and white check suit, her breasts held high by a boned cuirass of stays, a veil with velvet chenille dots upon her nose, holding out a hand tightly gloved in white glacé kid stitched with black. I also remember a frilled shirt with a stiff collar and a pair of shoes of a bright egg color. I remember my amazement.

The lady laughed heartily, displaying a set of strong, white teeth, gave me her name, wrung my hand, expressed the hope that we might meet again, and did not move a muscle as the voice of Lady W—— rose beside us, saying in clear, plain words:

"She, an Oriental? Don't be silly! Hamburg or Rotterdam, or possibly Berlin."

The same summer another garden saw me, almost as shy and awkward as the first time, on another improvised stage. The spectators were scattered here and there beneath the trees, and I introduced myself to them, in verse, from the top of a platform:

I am a faun, so small and slim,
Lusty and shapely, light of limb,
My eye is soft, my smile has grace

I know, for when thirsty, if I look
In the clear mirror of the brook
Among the reeds I see my face.

The little play, which was attributed to Willy but had been written by the most expeditious of his henchmen (he has produced other, infinitely better poetry), was ordered, composed, delivered and rehearsed inside a week.

"If it amused you to act in a real theater," M. Willy said to me shortly after, "I have another sketch, in prose. In fact, I am sure that it would be easy for you to organize a series of performances, of pleasant little trips. Brussels, for instance, is always interested in certain forms of entertainment, in well-known people."

The formal, "newspaper-article" style of this communication, the cautious, neutral tone in which it was delivered, were enough to raise my alarm. I stiffened into utter silence, deepest attention to hear the remainder of the speech:

"And on the other hand it would provide an excellent opportunity of getting rid of these wearisome rooms and of finding an adequate arrangement better suited to a different kind of life—oh! just slightly different. There's no hurry."

I could not possibly be mistaken, what I had heard was a dismissal. While I had been dreaming of flight, close beside me someone else had been planning to turn me quietly out of the house—out of my own house. But this time I was not asked if I were willing. Hastily, confusedly I tried to think, to decide. . . . Could I leave it so, could I endure this quiet, these few words? In our heart of hearts we all love loud cries and gestures that hit the ceiling.

I remember the flush that crept over my cheeks, I remember my stupidity. Deprived by fraud of something I had wished to leave by stealth, I could only repeat to myself, again and again, the words of the Napoleonic Code: "to desert the domestic hearth"—words that did not seem to me unpleasant, yet were big with a vague sense of disorder in the field, suggestive of pickets abandoning their posts, of hurried first aid, words and actions that made me hesitate. The spirit of contradiction is as strong in a woman as her possessive instinct. If she has nothing in the world but her suffering, she will cleave to her suffering. She will bury a centime deep in the ground, she will grasp at walls that are crumbling, roofless.

"There's no hurry . . ." What I had heard was: "It is all over." I would have liked to have been the one to say, "It is all over." Since I had said nothing, I could only hold my peace. From the moment of that "there's no hurry," I distinctly saw the hours rush by. I clung to what I planned to disrupt. In ten years I had not waited so consciously or so shamefully. I waited another week, another fortnight; I waited for some final thing, knowing that it would not be I who would put an end to my abjection, but the man who had first had his way with me. And still the same mildness, the same absence of noise, a silence as of falling snow. Before that moment I could have pictured an elopment as well as anyone else—the white plume of the departing train, if not the galloping of splendid horses, a goodbye letter, breathing peace and good will, truly noble-hearted, a scarf fluttering in the wind, all the romantic glories of running away, alone or in company. But I could not make eviction lyrical. It can be so, however. I discovered that later, in the little ground-floor flat in the rue de Villejust.

It was there that I faced the first hours of a new life, between my dog and my cat. I had also brought away with me my old, faithful fear; it remained faithful for a long while. At every ring of the bell—a real bell with a real clapper and an intolerable, sharp voice, like an orphanage bell—I sprang to my feet, terrified. The sound often meant that a hand had slipped a letter under the door. I opened the letter, firmly resolving not to open the next one; yet I opened that too. What I read was irksome to me, tedious and as though dulled by excessive use, in spite of the words that stood out in capitals, underlined by a slashing flourish: "I am so made that, with me, SPITE is the active counterpart of gratitude." "Come, come, my dear Colette." "Your farcical diplomacy in refusing to return that manuscript." "We have been partners, don't let us become enemies. I assure you that you would gain nothing by it. Our agreement, which is still in operation and on which I am still reckoning . . ."

But none of the letters ever asked me to retrace the steps that had taken me with my trunk and my dog and my cat and a little furniture from the rue de Courcelles to the rue de Villejust. And so, in the small, ground-floor flat, I grew accustomed to the thought that here the flavor of my life must change, as the flavor of a wine changes according to the slope on which the vine is planted.

HBk

❧❧ Freedom

A fable: the tendrils of the vine

In bygone times the nightingale did not sing at night. He had a sweet little thread of voice that he skillfully employed from morn to night with the coming of spring. He awoke with his comrades in the blue-gray dawn, and their flustered awakening startled the cockchafers sleeping on the underside of the lilac leaves.

He went to bed promptly at seven o'clock or half past seven, no matter where, often in the flowering grapevines that smelled of mignonette, and slept solidly until morning.

One night in the springtime he went to sleep while perched on a young vine shoot, his jabot fluffed up and his head bowed, as if afflicted with a graceful torticollis. While he slept, the vine's gimlet feelers—those imperious and clinging tendrils whose sharp taste, like that of fresh sorrel, acts as a stimulant and slakes the thirst— began to grow so thickly during the night that the bird woke up to find himself bound fast, his feet hobbled in strong withes, his wings powerless . . .

He thought he would die, but by struggling he managed after a great effort to liberate himself, and throughout the spring he swore never to sleep again, not until the tendrils of the vine had stopped growing.

From the next night onward he sang, to keep himself awake:

As long as the vine shoots grow, grow, grow,
   I will sleep no more!

As long as the vine shoots grow, grow, grow,
   I will sleep no more!

He varied his theme, embellishing it with vocalizations, became infatuated with his voice, became that wildly passionate and palpitating songster that one listens to with the unbearable longing to *see* him sing.

I have seen a nightingale singing in the moonlight, a free nightingale that did not know he was being spied upon. He interrupts himself at times, his head inclined, as if listening within himself to the prolongation of a note that has died down . . . Then, swelling his throat, he takes up his song again with all his might, his head thrown back, the picture of amorous despair. He sings just to sing, he sings such lovely things that he does not know any more what they were meant to say. But I, I can still hear, through the golden notes, the melancholy piping of a flute, the quivering and crystalline trills, the clear and vigorous cries, I can still hear the first innocent and frightened song of the nightingale caught in the tendrils of the vine:

As long as the vine shoots grow, grow, grow . . .

Imperious, clinging, the tendrils of a bitter vine shackled me in my springtime while I slept a happy sleep, without misgivings. But with a frightened lunge I broke all those twisted threads that were already imbedded in my flesh, and I fled . . . When the torpor of a new night of honey weighed on my eyelids, I feared the tendrils of the vine and I uttered a loud lament that revealed my voice to me.

All alone, after a wakeful night, I now observe the morose and voluptuous morning star rise before me . . . And to keep from falling again into a happy sleep, in the treacherous springtime when blossoms the gnarled vine, I listen to the sound of my voice. Sometimes I feverishly cry out what one customarily suppresses or whispers very low—then my voice dies down to a murmur, because I dare not go on . . .

I want to tell, tell, tell everything I know, all my thoughts, all my surmises, everything that enchants or hurts or astounds me; but always, toward the dawn of this resonant night, a wise cool hand is laid across my mouth, and my cry, which had been passionately raised subsides into moderate verbiage, the loquacity of the child who talks aloud to reassure himself and allay his fears . . .

I no longer enjoy a happy sleep, but I no longer fear the tendrils of the vine . . .

HB

ALONE

During the loneliest years . . .

During the loneliest years of my life, I lived on ground floors. Beyond the net curtain and the windowpane passed my dear human beings to whom I would not for the world have been the first to speak or hold out my hand. In those days I dedicated to them my passionate unsociability, my experience of human creatures, and my fundamental shyness, which had no relation to cowardice . . .

AW

Behold me then . . .

Behold me then, just as I am! This evening I shall not be able to escape the meeting in the long mirror, the soliloquy which I have a hundred times avoided, accepted, fled from, taken up again, and broken off. I feel in advance, alas, the uselessness of trying to change the subject. This evening I shall not feel sleepy, and the spell of a book—even a brand-new book with that smell of printer's ink and paper fresh from the press that makes you think of coal and trains and departures!—even that spell will not be able to distract me from myself.

Behold me then, just as I am! Alone, alone, and for the rest of my life, no doubt. Already alone; it's early for that. When I turned thirty, I did not feel cast down because mine is a face that depends on the expression which animates it, the color of my eyes, and the defiant smile that plays over it—what Marinetti calls my *gaiezza volpina*. But if I look like a fox, it's a fox without guile, which a hen could catch! And a fox without rapacity, one that remembers only the trap and the cage. A gay-looking fox, if you like, but only because the corners of its mouth and eyes look as if they were smiling. A captive fox, tired of dancing to the sound of music.

It is true enough that I do look like a fox. But a slender, pretty fox is not an ugly thing, is it? Brague says, too, that I look like a rat when I purse my lips and blink my eyelids so as to see better. I see nothing to mind in that.

But how I dislike seeing myself with that drooping mouth and those slack shoulders, the weight of my whole sad body slumped on one leg! My hair hangs dank and lank and in a little while I shall have to brush it for a long time to give it back its shining beaver brown. My eyes are still faintly ringed with blue eye shadow and there's a wavering trace of red on my nails. It will take me at least fifty good minutes of bathing and grooming to get rid of all that.

It is one o'clock already. What am I waiting for? A smart little lash with the whip to make the obstinate creature go on again. But no one will give it me because . . . because I am alone. How clearly one sees, in that long frame which holds my reflection, that I'm used already to living alone!

No matter what visitor, for a mere tradesman, or even for my charwoman Blandine, I should raise this drooping neck, straighten that slouching hip, and clasp those empty hands. But tonight I am so alone.

Alone! Really, one might think I was pitying myself for it!

"If you live all alone," said Brague, "it's because you really want to, isn't it?"

Certainly I "really" want to, and in fact I *want* to, quite simply. Only, well . . . there are days when solitude, for someone my age, is a heady wine that intoxicates you with freedom, others when it is a bitter tonic, and still others when it is a poison that makes you beat your head against the wall.

This evening I would much prefer not to say which it is; all I want is to remain undecided, and not to be able to say whether the shiver that will seize me when I slip between the cold sheets comes from fear or contentment.

Alone . . . and for a long time past. The proof is that I am giving way to the habit of talking to myself and of holding conversations with my dog, and the fire, and my own reflection. It is an idiosyncrasy which recluses and old prisoners fall into; but I'm not like them, I'm free. And if I talk to myself it is because I have a writer's need to express my thoughts in rhythmical language.

Facing me from the other side of the looking glass, in that mysterious reflected room, is the image of "a woman of letters who has turned out badly." They also say of me that I'm "on the stage," but they never call me an actress. Why? The nuance is subtle, but there is certainly a polite refusal, on the part both of the public and of my friends themselves, to accord me any standing in this career which I have nevertheless adopted. A woman of letters who has turned out badly: that is what I must remain for everyone, I who no longer write, who deny myself the pleasure, the luxury of writing.

To write, to be able to write, what does it mean? It means spending long hours dreaming before a white page, scribbling unconsciously, letting your pen play around a blot of ink and nibble at a half-formed word, scratching it, making it bristle with darts, and adorning it with antennae and paws until it loses all resemblance to a legible word and turns into a fantastic insect or a fluttering creature half butterfly, half fairy.

To write is to sit and stare, hypnotized, at the reflection of the window in the silver inkstand, to feel the divine fever mounting to one's cheeks and forehead while the hand that writes grows blissfully numb upon the paper. It also means idle hours curled up in the hollow of the divan, and then the orgy of inspiration from which one emerges stupefied and aching all over, but already recompensed and laden with treasures that one unloads slowly on to the virgin page in the little round pool of light under the lamp.

To write is to pour one's innermost self passionately upon the tempting paper, at such frantic speed that sometimes one's hand struggles and rebels, overdriven by the impatient god who guides it—and to find, next day, in place of the golden bough that bloomed miraculously in that dazzling hour, a withered bramble and a stunted flower.

To write is the joy and torment of the idle. Oh, to write! From time to time I feel a need, sharp as thirst in summer, to note and to describe. And then I take up my pen again and attempt the perilous and elusive task of seizing and pinning down, under its flexible double-pointed nib, the many-hued, fugitive, thrilling adjective . . . The attack does not last long; it is but the itching of an old scar.

It takes up too much time to write. And the trouble is, I am no Balzac! The fragile story I am constructing crumbles away when the tradesman rings, or the shoemaker sends in his bill, when the solicitor, or one's counsel, telephones, or when the theatrical agent summons me to his office for "a social engagement at the house of some people of very good position but not in the habit of paying large fees."

The problem is, since I have been living alone, that I have had first to live, then to divorce, and then to go on living. To do all that demands incredible áctivity and ' persistence. And to 'get where? Is there, for me, no other haven than this commonplace room? Must I stay forever before this impenetrable mirror where I come up against myself, face to face?

EMCC

Having rescued . . .

Having rescued from among my earthly goods, paltry enough, my portrait by Ferdinand Humbert, a lithograph by Forain, in which I have only one eye, the photograph of the portrait of Renée Vivien by Lévy-Dhurmer, a fish platter which has never, at my table, found a turbot of its size, a small *gouache* in which my eighteen months shine out in full brilliance, my bag of glass marbles (I still have them), some books, and my mauve glass lamp, with its lilac blooms, I took my leave. A small Japanese dwarf tree, which did not like displacements, died as a result of being moved to a new address.

The house I occupied in the rue de Villejust has vanished. Where it once stood, you will now find a sumptuous apartment building, quite recently erected. The house it has replaced was pleasant in a modestly comfortable way, with a kind of suburban charm. Once you were past the porte-cochere, you found that its shady court communicated by an iron-grilled gate with the apartment house fronting on the avenue du Bois and bearing the number 23. The two shaded courts amounted to a garden: there were chestnut trees, clumps of Silene roses, and blue forget-me-nots. Lanka, the white cat belonging to Robert d'Humières, descended from her Persian heaven, sat down in the midst of the rosebushes, and rested the gaze of her supernaturally blue eyes on all surrounding things. Thus she exposed her whiteness to the loud admiration of the passers-by. A telegraph boy exclaimed: "A powder puff, a powder puff!"; the facetious concierge called her "Blackie"; and I hummed for Lanka some white song or other. This was more than could be endured by this creature of spun silver and sapphire. Beneath the too direct homage, she shuddered with all her fur and, by way of an open window almost opposite mine, she returned to her master, whom she loved with single-hearted devotion.

Never before in my life had I lived alone. From the very first night that I spent in this ground-floor flat, I left the key in the lock of my outside door. It was not mere negligence, but confidence in my safety. I have never felt as safe in any shelter as I did in that one, which cost 1,700 francs a year. Facing the street, one room opened upon full sunlight, since the Leroy-Beaulieu town house on the opposite side of the street was low and set back at the end of a courtyard, leaving me the entire benefit of the western sky. When I have told you that two other small rooms completed my domain, I will still not have explained or described its charm, and I would be very hard put to do it today. At times elated by a new happiness, at times sunk in a boundless and reasonless feeling of security, I know that I wanted to live and die there. In the morning I listened to the carriage horses, checked on the steep incline, as they slowed down their trot in front of my window before turning the corner of the avenue, and then the sunlight reached my bed. When I think about the jug of cold water and the jug of hot water set beside the rim of the shallow zinc tub placed in front of an open fire of wood and coal, I tell myself that this comfort could have satisfied me for years . . . I remember the spherical piece of English soap, black and smelling of tar and roses, and how the sunlight danced in the water . . .

Yes, I wanted to live and die there, wanted to pace the Bois up and down and in all weathers, wanted forever to open my window and watch the daily passage of horseback riders, men and women; every day I wanted to touch the ears of the horse that the "Millevoye boy" brought over to the curb to say good morning to me; I wanted to go on exclaiming over the pretty little she-mule ridden by Menabrea, admire the handsome bearing of Iza de Comminges and the smart looks of Arthème Fayard. Polaire sometimes went by, on her way to the stables of Mme Hensmann, who let her ride an astounding light-bay mare, almost rose-colored, its black mane and tail almost touching the ground. The first horsewomen to ride astride, of whom I was one, watched with astonishment that wasp in the saddle, her long skirt, her tortured smile, and the *cadogan* which, binding her short hair at the back of the neck, revealed—rare sight!—two perfect little ears. I wanted to assure myself for a long time my enjoyment of that window balustrade, that modest crow's nest above a sumptuous hurly-burly. From the center of this calm I saw, astonished, a distant shimmering and flickering of a mysterious and tranquil flame, a glory that was promised me, as I settled down comfortably beside my white marble fireplace. I wrote to Madame W., the invisible American owner, to tell her of my desire to grow old quietly in the rue de Villejust and to ask for a lease of twenty or thirty years. In her letter of reply she informed me that the entire building was doomed to be demolished and that a decent indemnification would be paid, three months later, to all its tenants.

I did not joyfully resign myself, for I knew the worth of what I was going to lose. I had thought I had arrived in port, safe and sound, and my longest stop had lasted only two and a half years. The devil take Madame W. and her real-estate operations! We were, in her house, a small batch of tenants, people of little fame and little money, content to breathe the air of the Bois, its scent of catalpa in the spring, its yellow aroma of fallen leaves in the autumn. And we could all of us have earnestly wished that this American lady would forget us there with our log fires, our zinc tubs, our Auer gas burners, and our pink-flowering horse-chestnut trees.

I flatter myself that in all those years of movings-out and movings-in I acquired at least ten kinds of wisdom and as much of unreasonableness. Unhygienic as it was said to be, I nonetheless entrusted myself to that ground floor, soundproof against the hurricanes of winter, with its illusory character of a place of refuge, always in the hope of secreting there, one day, a happiness that would at last be mine.

HB

❦❦❦

The Sémiramis bar

What has to happen happens . . . Accused of every sin, I appeared before my friend Valentine, after having received from her this enigmatic communication by *pneumatique:* "I have a lot of things to scold you for. You grieve me . . ."

How could I, unworthy person, have distressed that lithe young woman, so very elegant, without a doubt sewed into her woolen dress, for it looked as though she could neither quite sit down nor quite bend over nor quite walk in it . . . What in the world had I done? My pretty judge collected her thoughts, searched in the depths of herself for an exceptional amount of courage, and finally spoke.

"Well, then, this is it. You dined at the Sémiramis bar day before yesterday."

"That's true. But so what?"

"So what? That's all. Isn't it enough for you?"

"Yes, it's enough, since I dine there two or three times a week. One eats well there."

The aigrette—what material could it be in? steel wool?—on the top of the bonnet of woven wood and American cloth shuddered, danced, saluted:

"Why, you unhappy creature, that is a place . . . a place . . ."

"With a bad reputation. Heavens, yes."

My friend Valentine abandons declamatory means and looks at me with sudden gentleness, a superior solicitude.

"Really, my poor dear, it looks as though you wanted to make your friends' task of defending you impossible."

"Who imposed that task upon you? I certainly didn't."

"I mean, well, that . . . you know I'm very fond of you. What would you have me say when someone comes to tell me you were dining at the Sémiramis?"

"Tell them the plain truth—that it's none of your business."

My little judge blushes, hesitates. Dear me, how much easier is the role of the accused! I revel in the situation, I settle myself complacently, I sink into the most luxurious of my errors, and Valentine lacks the confidence needed to dislodge me from them.

"Of course, it's none of my business. It's in your interest. That sort of thing can do you harm. You seem to be doing it on purpose. And then, I will say, it's all right if you just drop in there by chance. But it's quite another thing to make a habit of it, to become as it were a subscriber to the place . . . If at least you went there with a group of people occasionally . . . But all alone in your corner there, with your newspaper and your dog, and all those people who speak to you, those odd little men in weird jackets, who wear rings and have bracelets on their ankles . . . And besides," she adds, plucking up courage, "they tell me that the suppers at that place are . . . frightful!"

"I don't know anything about that, my dear. I don't go there for supper."

"That's true, you don't take supper. But you surely know that the suppers . . ."

"I know all about it. Sémiramis tells me."

"She tells . . ."

"Why, yes. She's a great person, Sémiramis. You don't know her? Haven't you ever seen her little snub nose, like a bulldog's, and her auburn chignon, and her fringe like the visor of a helmet, and her bosom like a Spanish balcony?"

"I haven't had the pleasure."

"Too bad. She exudes an air of impudence, good nature, patience, and ridiculous good health. She charges very little for her leek-and-potato soup, her roast chicken with sausages, and her loin of veal—she even gives it away to a crowd of hard-ups in weird jackets, poor little paupers all dolled up, and they can get at her place their plate of food and *la thune*—a *thune,* Valentine, is a five-franc piece . . ."

"Oh, I know that, everyone knows that, for goodness' sake."

"Excuse me. Well, you see, in her 'ill-famed' bar, Sémiramis reigns, helmeted, armored in an apron with pockets. And ill-famed it is, according to your way of seeing things, which is the way of everyone, moreover."

"I certainly hope so."

"Me, too. She knows all her customers by name, and knows the names of their friends. She doesn't like strangers and will bark at the people who drop in just by chance. 'There's no chow here for you!' I've heard her tell them. She knows all the scandals, all the gossip of all the bars, but is discreet, for one day, after telling me the sad and scandalous story of a brave little woman sitting there, Sémiramis added, 'I'm the only one in the world who knows her story, she'd be terribly upset if anyone else in Paris knew it!' "

"Charming."

"And I'll bet you do the same every day! At any rate, with Sémiramis it's only thoughtlessness. Then, what can I do about it, my dear? I'm a homebody, I'm finicky, I like my quiet habits. I'm often obliged to dine out, before the theater, and I don't willingly go into a big restaurant in the boulevards or into a fashionable grill room where you hear the people at other tables being named in whispers and gossiped about, skinned alive. I go to the bar kept by Sémiramis, appropriately named—Sémiramis, warrior queen, helmeted in bronze, armed with the meat cleaver, who speaks a colorful language to her crowd of long-haired young lads and short-haired girls . . ."

"That's exactly what I reproach you for—associating with that low-class crowd!"

"Why?"

"Every night in that bar there are scenes: orgies, fistfights, even."

"I repeat, I know nothing about all that. What's it to me? The orgies at the Sémiramis bar must be, like all orgies, so banal they would convert the most far-gone to virtue. I'm only interested in the people who dine there. Valentine, it's about them I'd like to talk to you, since I goodheartedly consent to give you an explanation. True, you find there a majority of young men who are not at all interested in women. At dinnertime there they are, comfortably at home, enjoying a rest. They are recovering their strength for suppertime. They have no need to waggle their hips or cry out shrilly or flutter a handkerchief soaked in ether, or dance together, or call out their order in a loud voice: 'Sémiramis, another sherry for me, on Monsieur's bill!' They are gentle, weary, with their painted eyelids heavy with sleep. There's one who bestows upon himself the name of a genuine princess; he asks for Vittel mineral water, and a lot of leeks in the soup, because it's a depurative. Another one has the pathetic face of an anemic little girl, and he goes to the Sémiramis bar for his bouillon and his noodles, and the coarse ruler of the place fills his plate twice, crassly maternal. Then she exclaims, arms akimbo, standing in front of the lean and lanky young fellow with hallucinated blue eyes, who pushes aside his full plate: 'There you go! You've been hitting dope again, eh? What's your mother thinking about to let you destroy yourself like this? Doesn't she have a heart?' And there's another one who, with his dark blue eyes and his innocent little nose, looks like Suzanne Derval; he barely pecks at his food and says, 'Oh hell, don't give me any sauce, I don't want to ruin my stomach! And, waiter! Once and for all, take away these pickles and bring me some *benzonaphthol* tablets.'

"Yes, there they are, not posing, but gentle and indolent and melancholy, like out-of-work prostitutes, but laughing easily and playing with the dog that Sémiramis found one night in the street. But if a stranger manages to get inside the bar for dinner, they become uneasy, with the sulky manners of shopkeepers wakened up too early, exchanging from one table to another their shrill cries, forced laughs, obscene and trite remarks, the hanky-panky that attracts . . . Then, when the stranger or the group of thirsty and curious sightseers have emptied their beer steins, sipped their kummels on ice, and left, as the door shuts upon them there is a whoop of relief, and afterward a settled calm and the murmured gossip, the thin chests bedizened with loud cravats and bright pocket handkerchiefs lean once more against the tables, relaxed and slothful, like circus animals after the exercise."

Valentine is not very fond of having people talk to her at great length. The animation, the brightness of her face dims after a few minutes of attention and are replaced by a rigidity, a drowsy effort to keep the eyes wide open. I notice this now and fall silent. But decidedly she has not said all she has to say.

"Yes, yes, that's all very nice. When you want to exonerate something you adorn it with literature and you tell yourself, 'If I talk very fast and insert some fancy words, Valentine won't see the fire for the smoke!' It's easier than telling me to go to the devil, isn't it?"

This kind of gentle feminine trickery always disarms me, and Valentine, who often exasperates and sometimes astounds me, as if I suddenly glimpsed through her coils of false hair or through her cloche hats or extravagantly big and gauzy hats the pointed tip of a sly little animal's ear. I cannot help laughing.

"But I'm not defending myself, you little beast! Defend myself for what and against whom? Against you? Would I condescend to that, megalomaniac that you are?"

She puts on her most seductive expression, as if responding to a man's overtures.

"You see, you see? Now I'm the one that's being attacked! Now, really! Because I allowed myself to say that the Sémiramis bar is not exactly a provincial branch of a convent and lacked respect when I spoke of that Queen of Babylon and other such places!"

"Sémiramis doesn't ask for respect. What would she do with it? Respect can't be eaten, can't be sold, and it takes up room. But she allots to me a portion of her grumpy motherliness, which transforms her regular customers into a progeny pampered, knocked about, and submissive. Besides, her capricious humor, both grasping and spendthrift, renders her in my eyes worthy of an authentic scepter. For example, take this exchange I overheard one night. 'What do I owe you, Sémiramis?' asked in a low voice a wretched-looking regular customer with anxious eyes. 'No idea,' Sémiramis growled. 'I haven't made out your bill. Do you imagine I have no one but you to think about?' 'But I happen to have some money on me tonight, Sémiramis.' 'Money, money, money! You're not the only one who has money!' 'But, Sémiramis . . .' 'Oh, shut up, that's enough! I can always find money when I need it, you know. That yokel down there at the farthest table, he's just paid me a gold louis for his chicken-in-the-pot, that's one hundred sous more than he'd pay at Paillard's, just look at that bigmouth now, he's getting ready to leave. His lordship didn't want anything on my menu! His lordship had to order à la carte! His lordship thinks this is a restaurant!' As she spoke, she focused her brown eyes on the intimidated and fugitive back of the 'yokel' and if looks could kill he'd have dropped dead. Just imagine! He thought that by paying a golden louis he could eat *poulet cocotte* at Sémiramis's bar . . . Am I boring you, Valentine?"

"Not at all. On the contrary."

"I didn't hope for so much! This is success! Well now, I can tell you that while dining at Sémiramis's bar I enjoy watching the girls dancing together, they waltz well. They're not paid for this, but dance for pleasure between the cabbage soup and the beef stew. They are young models, young scapegraces of the neighborhood, girls who take bit parts at the music hall but who are out of work. Under their big umbrella hats or cloches pulled down to their eyes, their faces are hidden, I have no idea what the waltzers' faces are like, so I can forget their no doubt dubious little fizzes, their slightly prognathous little fizzes, blue-white with powder. I see only two graceful bodies united, sculptured beneath thin dresses by the wind of the waltz, two long adolescent bodies, skinny, with narrow feet in fragile slippers that have come without a carriage through the snow and the mud . . . They waltz like the habitués of cheap dance halls, lewdly, sensuously, with that delicious inclination of a tall sail of a yacht . . . I can't help it! I really find that prettier than any ballet . . .

"And that, dear Valentine, is when I leave the Sémiramis bar, with Sémiramis herself sometimes detaining me with a friendly hand as I reach the doorway. 'Hush! don't say a word,' she whispered the other night, slipping over my finger the string of a bumpy parcel. 'Not a word! These are apples dug out for you, some old pippins the way you like them, wrinkled like the hind end of a pauper . . .' That makes you laugh, doesn't it? I thought it was very nice of her. You see, she'd found out that I like old wrinkled apples with that musky smell of the cellar where I used to line them up when I was a child . . ."

HB

Renée Vivien

Born in London in 1877, of a British father and an American mother, Pauline Tarn spent most of her short life in France, where, under the pen name of Renée Vivien, she celebrated Lesbian love in a dozen volumes of fervent but not very original verse. She died in 1909, at thirty-two, and Colette's memoir was written two decades later.

I still have in my possession some thirty letters Pauline Tarn wrote to me. I had a great many more, but some of them were filched from me, and the shortest, the least attractive, I gave away to "fans" of Renée Vivien. A few of them, too, have been mislaid.

If I were to publish the correspondence of this poet who never ceased claiming kinship with Lesbos, it would astound only because of its childishness. I stress this very particular childish quality, which strikes a false note—dare I say a note of obvious insincerity? The charming face of Renée Vivien reflected only a part of that childlike quality, in the rounded cheek, soft and downy, in the innocent short upper lip, so typically English, curled up and revealing four little front teeth. A bright smile constantly lit up her eyes, a chestnut-brown which became greenish in sunlight. She wore her long, beautiful ash-blond hair, which was fine and straight, massed at the top of her head, from which stray locks came down now and then like wisps of fine straw.

There is not a single feature of her youthful face that I do not vividly recall. Everything in it bespoke childishness, roguishness, and the propensity to laughter. Impossible to find anywhere in that face, from the fair hair to the sweet dimple of the weak little chin, any line that was not a line of laughter, any sign of the hidden tragic melancholy that throbs in the poetry of Renée Vivien. I never saw Renée sad. She would exclaim, in her lisping English accent, "Oh, my dear little Colette, how disgusting this life is!" Then she would burst into laughter. In all too many of her notes, I find that same exclamation repeated, often spelled out frankly in the coarsest words: "Isn't this life sheer muck? Well, I hope it will soon be over!" This impatience of hers amused her friends, but her hope was not dashed, for she died in her thirtieth year.

Our friendship was in no way literary, it goes without saying— or rather, I should say, thanks to my respect for literature. I am sparing of words on that subject, except for occasional exclamations of admiration, and in Renée Vivien I found the same diffidence and well-bred restraint. She, too, refused to "talk shop." Whenever she gave me any of her books, she always hid them under a bouquet of violets or a basket of fruit or a length of Oriental silk. She was secretive with me on the two literary aspects of her brief existence: the cause of her sadness, and her method of work. Where did she work? And at what hours? The vast, dark, sumptuous, and ever changing flat in the avenue du Bois gave no hint of work. That ground-floor flat in the avenue du Bois has never been well described, by the way. Except for some gigantic Buddhas, all the furnishings moved mysteriously: after provoking surprise and admiration for a time, they had a way of disappearing . . .

Among the unstable marvels, Renée wandered, not so much clad as veiled in black or purple, almost invisible in the scented darkness of the immense rooms barricaded with leaded windows, the air heavy with curtains and incense. Three or four times I caught her curled up in a corner of a divan, scribbling with a pencil on a writing pad propped on her knees. On these occasions she always sprang up guiltily, excusing herself, murmuring, "It's nothing, I've finished now . . ." Her lithe body devoid of density languidly drooped, as if beneath the weight of her poppy-flower head with its pale golden hair, surmounted by immense and unsteady hats. She held her long and slender hands in front of her, gropingly. The dresses she wore were always long, covering her feet, and she was afflicted with an angelic clumsiness, was always losing as she went her gloves, handkerchief, sunshade, scarf . . .

She was constantly giving things away: the bracelets on her arms opened up, the necklace slipped from her martyr's throat. She was as if deciduous. It was as if her languorous body rejected anything that would give it a third dimension.

The first time I dined at her place, three brown tapers dripped waxen tears in tall candlesticks and did not dispel the gloom. A low table, from the Orient, offered a pell-mell assortment of *hors d'oeuvres*—strips of raw fish rolled upon glass wands, *foie gras,* shrimps, salad seasoned with sugar and pepper—and there was a well-chosen Piper-Heidsieck champagne *brut,* and very strong cocktails—Renée Vivien was ahead of her time. Suffocated with the obscurity, mistrustful of the unfamiliar fire of Russian, Greek, and Chinese alcohols, I scarcely touched the food. I remember that Renée's gay laughter, her liveliness, the faint halo of light trembling in her golden hair all combined to sadden me, as does the happiness of blind children who laugh and play without the help of light. I did not believe that this meeting in this luxurious flat submerged in darkness could result in any real friendship with this tall young woman who tossed off her drink with the obliviousness one sees in bridesmaids at a country wedding.

Among the beverages that she raised to her lips was a cloudy elixir in which floated a cherry harpooned on a toothpick. I laid a hand on her arm and cautioned her.

"Don't drink it."

She opened her eyes so wide that the lashes of her upper eyelids touched her eyebrows.

"Why not?"

"I've tasted it," I said, embarrassed. "It's . . . it's deadly. Be careful, it tastes like some kind of vitriol."

I dared not tell her that I suspected a practical joke. She laughed, flashing her white teeth.

"But these are my own cocktails, *ma pethith Coletthe.* They are excellent."

She emptied the glass at one gulp, neither gasping nor blinking, and her rounded cheek kept its floral pallor.

I did not notice that evening her almost total abstention from food, but later on I discovered that she subsisted mainly on a few spoonfuls of rice, some fruit or other, and alcohol—especially alcohol. During this first evening, nothing could dispel the uneasiness engendered by the strangeness of the place, bound to astonish a guest, the semi-darkness, the exotic foods on plates of jade, vermeil, or Chinese porcelain, foods that had come from countries too far away.

However, I was to see Renée Vivien many times afterward.

We discovered that her house and mine communicated, thanks to the two garden courts separated only by a grille, and that the concierge who had the keys was not incorruptible; I could therefore go from the rue de Villejust to the avenue du Bois to visit her without setting foot in the street. Occasionally I used this facility. On my way, I would rap on the windows of the garden flat where Robert d'Humières lived, and he would open his window and hold out an immaculate treasure, an armful of snow, that is to say, his blue-eyed white cat, Lanka, saying, "To you I entrust my most precious possession."

Twenty meters farther on, and I would confront, at Renée's, the air which, like stagnant water, slowed down my steps, the odor of incense, of flowers, of overripe apples. It is an understatement to say that I was stifled in that gloom. I became almost wickedly intolerant there, yet never wore out the patience of the gossamer angel who dedicated offerings of lady apples to the Buddhas. One day, when the spring wind was stripping the leaves from the Judas trees in the avenue, I was nauseated by the funereal perfumes and tried to open the window: it was nailed shut. What a contribution such a detail is, what a flourish it adds to a theme already rich! What a quantity of lurid gleams and glints of gold in the semi-darkness, of whispering voices behind the doors, of Chinese masks, of ancient instruments hanging on the walls, mute, only vaguely whimpering at the banging of a door beneath my heavy hand. At Renée Vivien's I could have wished to be younger, so I could be a little fearful. But impatience got the better of me and one evening I brought an offending, an inadmissible big oil lamp, and plumped it down, lit, in front of my plate. Renée wept big tears over this, like a child—it is only right to add that she consoled herself in like manner.

Try as she would to please me by inviting along with me two or three of my best friends, to make me happy, our intimacy did not seem to make any real progress. At the table in the darkness, or lounging comfortably and provided with exotic food and drink, Turkish cigarettes or Chinese blond tobacco in miniature silver pipes, we remained a bit stiff and uneasy, as if our young hostess and we ourselves apprehended the unexpected return of an absent and unknown "master."

This "master" was never referred to by the name of woman. We seemed to be waiting for some catastrophe to project her into our midst, but she merely kept sending invisible messengers laden with jades, enamels, lacquers, fabrics . . . A collection of ancient Persian gold coins came, glittered, disappeared, leaving in its place glass cabinets of exotic butterflies and other insects, which in their turn gave way to a colossal Buddha, a miniature garden of bushes having leaves of crystal and fruit of precious stones. From one marvel to another Renée moved, uncertainly, already detached, and showing the indifferent self-effacement of a guard in a museum.

When I recall the changes which gradually rendered Renée more understandable, I believe I can link these with certain gestures at first, then with some words that threw a different light on her. Some people become transformed by riches, others acquire a real life only by impoverishment, their very destitution giving them life.

When was I able to forget that Renée Vivien was a poet, I mean, when did I begin to feel a real interest in her? No doubt it was one evening when dining at her place, an evening of spicy foods and of disquieting drinks—I risked drinking only two glasses of a perfect and very dry champagne—a gay evening and yet inexplicably strained, when Renée's gaiety expressed itself in laughter, in an eagerness to applaud exaggeratedly any least droll word.

Exceptionally that evening she wore a white dress that bared her delicate and youthful throat and the nape of her neck, where wisps of her soft straight hair were always coming undone. Between two remarks and without warning, she suddenly leaned against the back of her chair, her head bowed, her chin on her thin chest, her eyes closed . . . I can still see her two slender hands resting open and lifeless on the tablecloth.

This fainting spell, or whatever it was, lasted less than ten seconds, and Renée came to without embarrassment.

"Forgive me, my dears, I must have gone to sleep," she murmured, and resumed the argument she had left for the fleeting death from which she had returned fired with a strange frenzy.

"Oh, that B.!" she exclaimed, "I don't want to hear any more about him or his verses tonight. He has *no* talent. He is—wait, I know what he is, he's a cunt, a cunt with a pen. Yes, a cunt with a pen!"

The word fell into our silence, coarse, blunt. Anyone of us would have been capable of pronouncing that word in an undertone and among ourselves, but as Renée repeated the indecent remark, there reigned on her childlike features a blank expression that set the words outside time, deprived of any significance, and revealed in the speaker a profound disorder.

The wily lunatic is lost if through the narrowest crack he allows a sane eye to peer into his locked universe and thus profane it. Afterward, it is the sane eye that changes, is affected, becomes fascinated with the mystery it has seen and can never cease to question. The more sensitive the lunatic, the less able is he to resist this prying interest of the normal human being. I felt that Renée's change of key—to myself, I compared Renée to a sweet melody, a little flat despite its laborious harmonies—was approaching.

At Pascaud's, where we had gone to hire costumes for the fancy-dress ball Robert d'Humières was giving at the Théâtre des Arts which he directed, Renée Vivien, as she dressed again after the fitting of her costume—she intended to go as Jane Grey on the executioner's block, exactly, alas, as Paul Delaroche painted her—put on by mistake my black coat instead of her own.

"It almost fits you," I said, laughing. "But for you to look your best in it, something is needed here, and here . . . Otherwise . . ."

"It almost fits me?" Renée repeated.

I can still see how her face clouded, how her mouth fell open in stunned surprise.

"It's a great misfortune," she stammered, "a great misfortune that you've just announced to me . . ."

She turned a gloomy and calculating look upon me—at that period I was a pleasant little cob pony of a person—then rapidly collected herself and we separated. That evening I was handed a letter she had addressed to me and my friends who were to figure in the *tableau vivant* of Jane Grey. It read:

> My dears, the worst possible thing has happened to me: I've carelessly put on weight—ten pounds. But there are still ten days before our ball, in which I can lose them—that's enough, it's got to be enough, for I must not, at any price, weigh more than fifty-two kilos. Don't try to find me, I'm going to a place none of you knows. Count on me, I'll be back in ten days, and all ready for the ball. Yours, Renée.

She kept her word. We heard later on that she had spent the ten days at the Pavillon Henri IV in Saint-Germain. In the mornings she drank a glass of tea, then walked in the forest until her strength gave out. Then she drank more tea, this time with alcohol added, and went to bed in an almost fainting condition. Next day it began all over again. She had the inexhaustible strength of unbalanced people. "We walked perhaps twenty kilometers every day," her companion confessed to us later on. "I don't know how Mademoiselle kept going. As for myself, I ate normally, yet was exhausted."

The ten days over with, Renée met us at eleven o'clock in the evening at the Théâtre des Arts. She looked very pretty in her costume, powdered and rouged, hollow-eyed, her hair loose on one shoulder, and she was gay in a distracted kind of way. She still had the strength to play the part of Jane Grey, her hands tied, her bowed head revealing a white nape, her fair hair flooding out on the block. But afterward she fainted backstage, the victim of the saddest and most violent case of alcohol poisoning, aggravated by starvation and some drug or other.

This was her very pathetic secret, the confession of a quite ordinary neurosis. Or was it? Yes, if one can be satisfied with a single fact, as I was for a time—a rather short time. Renée was dying when I was told how she had managed in a weirdly simple way to drink to excess without anyone in Paris or anyone in Nice in the little house in the Parc Cessole ever being able to catch her at it . . .

Adjoining the bathroom, in a small room that substituted as a linen closet, her docile chambermaid sat sewing. Quick, maladroit, stumbling against the furniture, Renée was constantly calling out for help to . . . let us call her Justine, for that was absolutely not her name.

"Justine, my dear, will you sew on this hook that's come off?" "Justine, dear, have you ironed my embroidered frock?" "Quick, my slipper ribbon is undone . . ." "Oh! These new gloves still have a price tag on, do take it off, Justine, will you?" "Please, Justine, tell the cook that tonight . . ."

Behind the sewing-room door, which remained open, you heard only a murmured reply: "Yes, mademoiselle. Very well, mademoiselle . . ." And the maid did not leave the chair where she sat at work. Every time Renée appeared, Justine had only to lean over to reach, under her chair, one of the filled wineglasses that her skirt concealed. She held it out in silence to Renée, who emptied it at a gulp and went from the linen closet to the bathroom, where she found waiting her, punctually renewed, a glass of milky-looking water clouded with perfumes. She would gargle this and hurriedly spit it out. People who had seen and smelled that glass of perfumed liquid believed and have affirmed that Renée Vivien drank toilet water. What she so foolishly imbibed was no better.

I sometimes met Renée in the mornings, when I led my memorable cat Prrou out on a leash for a walk along the grassy paths in the avenue du Bois, and I recall one such encounter. As usual when she ventured out into the streets, Renée was a bit overdressed. In getting into the carriage that morning, she stepped on the hem of her long skirt and caught the strap of her bag on the handle of the door.

"Where are you going this early in the day?" I asked.

"To buy my Buddha. I've decided to buy one every day. Don't you think that's a good idea?"

"Excellent. Enjoy yourself!"

She turned to wave goodbye and knocked her hat askew. To hold it on, she raised the hand she had passed through the strap of the bag and it, ill shut, fell open, scattering a quantitiy of crumpled bank notes. "Oh, *mon Dieu,*" she exclaimed, laughing softly. At last the fiacre, the big hat, the dress with the ripped hem went off in the distance, while, close to my cat hygienically scratching the grass, I stood, reflecting: "The alcohol . . . the thinness . . . the poetry, the daily Buddha . . . And that's not all. What is the dark origin of all this nonsense?"

May I be excused for having included as an element of "all this nonsense" the word "poetry." Renée Vivien has left a great many poems of unequal strength, force, merit, unequal as the human breath, as the pulsations of human suffering. The cult of which they sing arouses curiosity and then infatuation; today they have disarmed the indignation of even the lowest kind of moralists—and this is a fate I would not have dared to promise them if they had lauded only the love of Chloë for Daphnis, since the lowest kind of moralist follows the fashions and makes a display of broadmindedness. In addition, Renée's work inhabits a region of elevated melancholy, in which the *amies,* the female couple, daydream and weep as often as they embrace. Admirably acquainted with our language, broken to the strict rules of French meter, Renée Vivien betrays her foreignness—that is to say, her assimilation of French masterworks relatively late in life—by exuding her Baudelairism in the years 1900–9, which was rather late for us.

When I found out she was so fallible, so faddy, so enslaved to a ruinous habit that she hoped to keep secret, my instinctive attraction to Renée changed into friendship. Friendship is not always circumspect, and one day I went so far as to put a strange question:

"Tell me, Renée. Are you happy?"

Renée blushed, smiled, then abruptly stiffened.

"Why, of course, my dear Colette. Why would you want me to be unhappy?"

"I didn't say I wanted it," I retorted.

And I went off, dissatisfied with us both. But next day her embarrassed laugh was apologetic and she thrashed the air around me with her long arms, maladroit and affectionate, as if she were looking for a way into my confidence. I noticed her listlessness, the dark rings under her eyes, and I asked her if she was ill.

"Why, not at all," she protested emphatically.

She then yawned behind her hand and explained the reasons for her lassitude in terms so clear that I could not believe my ears. And she did not stop there . . . What new warmth had melted her reserve and encouraged such expansiveness? Unhindered by any ambiguity, she spoke openly, and what she spoke of was not love but sexual satisfaction, and this, of course, referred to the only sexual satisfaction she knew, the pleasure she took with a woman. Then it was a question of the satisfactions of another epoch, another woman, and regrets and comparisons. Her way of talking about physical love was rather like that of little girls brought up for a life of debauchery: both innocent and crude. The most curious thing about her calm and farfetched confessions, during the recital of which Renée never left off the tone of tranquil gossip, strangely in accord with the least ambiguous terms, was that they revealed an immodest consideration for "the senses" and the technique of obtaining physical satisfaction . . . And when, beyond the poet who praised the pallor of her Lesbian loves, their sobbing in the desolate dawns, I caught a glimpse of "Madame How-many-times," counting on her fingers, mentioning by name things and gestures, I put an end to the indiscretion of those young half-conscious lips, and not very tactfully. I believe I told Renée that certain frank remarks she had made were as suitable to her as a silk hat to a monkey . . . As a sequel to this incident, I still have the brief note she sent me, very imposing in its form:

> You gravely offended me last night, Colette, and I am not one who forgives. Adieu. Renée

However, the other Renée, the good and charming Renée, saw to it that I had a second note two hours after the first one. It read:

> Forgive me, dear little Colette, God only knows what I wrote to you. Eat these lovely peaches as a toast to my health and come to see me. Come dine with me as soon as you can, and bring along our friends.

I did not fail to do so, although I took exception to the odd, clandestine character of those feasts laid out among three candles, to which sometimes Renée invited a harpist, at other times a soloist. But on the threshold of her apartment, which I always said smelled like "a rich man's funeral," we met Renée in a black evening dress, ready to go out.

"No, my dears," she murmured agitatedly, "you've not made a mistake, I was expecting you tonight. Sit down at the table, I'll be back very soon, I swear it by Aphrodite! There are shrimps, *foie gras,* some Chios wine, and fruit from the Balearic Isles . . ."

In her haste, she stumbled on the steps. She turned her golden head toward me, the luminous heart of a great beehive of dark velvet, then came back to whisper in my ear:

"Hush, I'm requisitioned. *She* is terrible at present."

Constrained, mystified, we remained and we waited . . . And Renée did not return.

Another time she was gaily having dinner, I mean to say, she was watching us dine, and at the dessert she stood up, gathered together with a shaky hand her long gloves, a fan, a little silk purse, then excused herself:

"My dears, I have to go . . . *Voilà* . . ,"

She did not finish what she had to say but burst into tears and fled. A carriage waiting for her outside bore her away.

In spite of my old friend Hamel (called Hamond, in the *Vagabonde*), who had a paternal affection for Renée and who now interceded for her, I went home with dignity, swearing never to return. But I did return, because the friendship one has given to a human being who is already going to pieces, is already headed toward her downfall, does not obey the dictates of pride. When I went back, urged by Renée in a laconic note, I found her sitting on the rim of the tub in the cold, ugly, and rudimentary bathroom. Seeing her pallor, the trembling of her long hands, her absurd thinness encased in a black dress, I tried to cheer her by addressing her as the Muse of Lévy-Dhurmer. She paid no attention.

"I'm going away," she said.

"Yes? Where are you going?"

"I don't know. But I'm in danger. *She* will kill me. Or else *she* will take me to the other side of the world, to countries where I shall be at her mercy . . . She will kill me."

"Poison? Revolver?"

"No."

In four words she explained how she might perish. Four words of a frankness to make you blink. This would not be worth telling, except for what Renée said then.

"With her I dare not pretend or lie, because at that moment she lays her ear over my heart."

I prefer to believe that this detail and the "danger," which both, alike, seem to have been borrowed from P. J. Toulet's *Monsieur du Paur,* were conceived under the influence of alcohol. Perhaps, even, the exhausting Lesbian lover never existed. Perhaps, invisible, she owed her strength, her quasi-tangibility to the last effort, the last miracle of an imagination which, getting out of hand, brought forth ghouls instead of nymphs?

While I was on tour—the Baret Music Hall Tour—I was un-aware that Renée was very close to death. She kept losing weight, always refusing to eat. In her spells of giddiness, in the aurora bore-alis of starvation, she thought she saw the flames of the Catholic hell. Someone close to her perhaps fanned the flames, or described them to her? Mystery. Enfeebled, she became humble and was con-verted. Her paganism was so little rooted in her. Fever and coughing shook her hollow chest. I was by chance spared the sight of Renée dying, then dead. She carried off with her more than one secret, and beneath her purple veil, Renée Vivien, the poet, led away—her throat encircled with moonstones, beryls, aquamarines, and other anemic gems—the immodest child, the excited little girl who taught me, with unembarrassed competence: "There are fewer ways of mak-ing love than they say, and more than one believes . . ."

Blond, her cheek dimpled, with a tender, laughing mouth and great, soft eyes, she was, even so, drawn down beneath the earth, toward everything that is of no concern to the living. Like all those who never use their strength to the limit, I am hostile to those who let life burn them out. Voluntary consumption is, I always feel, a kind of alibi. I fear there is not much difference between the habit of obtaining sexual satisfaction and, for instance, the cigarette habit. Smokers, male and female, inject and excuse idleness in their lives every time they light a cigarette.

The habit of obtaining sexual satisfaction is less tyrannical than the tobacco habit, but it gains on one. O voluptuous pleasure, O lascivious ram, cracking your skull against all obstacles, time and again! Perhaps the only misplaced curiosity is that which persists in trying to find out here, on this side of death, what lies beyond the grave . . . Voluptuaries, consumed by their senses, always begin by flinging themselves with a great display of frenzy into an abyss. But they survive, they come to the surface again. And they develop a routine of the abyss: "It's four o'clock . . . At five I have my abyss . . ." It is possible that this young woman poet, who rejected the laws of ordinary love, led a sensible enough life until her personal abyss of half past eight in the evening. An abyss she imagined? Ghouls are rare.

HB

Letter to Léon Hamel

[*Paris, February 28, 1909*]

. . . I play for the last time, and without regret, tomorrow at the Comédie Royale. We do what we can to fight off the grippe, Missy and I, Missy especially, for she has caught a frightful cold. And this slushy snow, this sticky cold weather are atrocious. At least there where you are the snow must be cleaner?

I've also had some rather big troubles these days. Have no fear, they do not concern those most dear to me. It's Willy again . . . and putting it briefly, he has sold, without my knowledge, *all* the *Claudine* rights to the publishers for almost nothing, and those books which belonged to me so entirely (and morally) are forever lost to him and me. Really, given the conditions in which he has ceded the rights to those four *Claudines,* you would say that not only did he want to extract very little money from them but he wanted, in addition, to make sure that I would never recover possession of those books which are mine. I have been terribly upset over this and have written to tell him so. He answered my cry of despair with a cool and almost threatening letter, and I think that after the necessary explanation that will take place upon his return from Monte Carlo (day after tomorrow), everything will be ended between us.

Just imagine, after three years of separation I go on hearing all too often of other betrayals that I knew nothing about . . . Forgive me, I am letting myself be carried away by my "tale of woe."

We still have our dinners at Palmyre's [The Sémiramis bar], where she overwhelms us with motherly kindness. She is always giving us fruit or something, beefsteaks especially cooked for Missy, and yesterday she insisted that we go see the three little bulldog puppies that have just been born to Palmyre's bitch, Bellotte. Palmyre's maternal pride is now boundless, she raves about those puppies; I'm sure she'd not be more excited over a child she'd produced herself.

Did you know that we went to the Wagram fancy-dress ball? And dressed as Pierrots? We were accompanied by de Max and Sergine, neither of whom was masked or in costume. Sergine, in that festive atmosphere, exhibited an air of deep boredom, his face very pale and serious. The supper (also with them) at Palmyre's was worth the effort.

We heard from J. de Bellune that at the gala evening in Nice the Baroness Van Zuylen lorded it in a box, wearing white tie and tails—and a mustache! The Baroness Ricoy accompanied her, likewise in tails and looking quite emaciated beside that elephantine monster. They were recognized and were pestered by visitors to their box, although the Baroness Van Zuylen responded to the intruders with broadsides of very masculine oaths.

What do you say to this fountain pen I'm using? It's a lovely pen, Missy gave it to me, along with some exciting loose-leaf notebooks with ruled pages. I'll show you all this when you come back . . .

HB

Night without sleep

In our house there is only one bed, too big for you, a little narrow for us both. It is chaste, white, completely exposed; no drapery veils its honest candor in the light of day. People who come to see us survey it calmly and do not tactfully look aside, for it is marked, in the middle, with but one soft valley, like the bed of a young girl who sleeps alone.

They do not know, those who enter here, that every night the weight of our two united bodies hollows out a little more, beneath its voluptuous winding sheet, that valley no wider than a tomb.

O our bed, completely bare! A dazzling lamp, slanted above it, denudes it even more. We do not find there, at twilight, the well-devised shade of a lace canopy or the rosy shell-like glow of a night lamp. Fixed star, never rising or setting, our bed never ceases to gleam except when submerged in the velvety depths of night.

Rigid and white, like the body of a dear departed, it is haloed with a perfume, a complicated scent that astounds, that one inhales attentively, in an effort to distinguish the blond essence of your favorite tobacco from the still lighter aroma of your extraordinarily white skin, and the scent of sandalwood that I give off; but that wild odor of crushed grasses, who can tell if it is mine or thine?

Receive us tonight, O our bed, and let your fresh valley deepen a little more beneath the feverish torpor caused by a thrilling spring day spent in the garden and in the woods.

I lie motionless, my head on your gentle shoulder. Surely, until tomorrow, I will sink into the depths of a dark sleep, a sleep so stubborn, so shut off from the world, that the wings of dream will come to beat in vain. I am going to sleep . . . Wait only until I find, for the soles of my feet that are tingling and burning, a cool place . . . You have not budged. You draw in long drafts of air, but I feel your shoulder still awake and careful to provide a hollow for my cheek . . . Let us sleep. . . . The nights of May are so brief. Despite the blue obscurity that bathes us, my eyelids are still full of sunshine, and I contemplate the day that has passed with closed eyes, as one peers, from behind the shelter of a Persian blind, into a dazzling summer garden . . .

How my heart throbs! I can also hear yours throb beneath my ear. You're not asleep? I raise my head slightly and sense rather than see the pallor of your upturned face, the tawny shadow of your short hair. Your knees are like two cool oranges . . . Turn toward me, so that mine can steal some of that smooth freshness.

Oh! Let us sleep . . . My skin is tingling, there is a throbbing in the muscles of my calves and in my ears, and surely our soft bed, tonight, is strewn with pine needles! Let us sleep! I command sleep to come.

I cannot sleep. My insomnia is a kind of gay and lively palpitation, and I sense in your immobility the same quivering exhaustion. You do not budge. You hope I am asleep. Your arm tightens at times around me, out of tender habit, and your charming feet clasp mine between them . . . Sleep approaches, grazes me, and flees . . . I can see it! Sleep is exactly like that heavy velvety butterfly I pursued in the garden aflame with iris . . . Do you remember? What youthful impatience glorified this entire sunlit day! A keen and insistent breeze flung over the sun a smoke screen of rapid clouds and withered the too tender leaves of the linden trees; the flowers of the butternut tree fell like brownish caterpillars upon our hair, with the flowers of the catalpas, their color the rainy mauve of the Parisian sky. The shoots of the black-currant bush that you brushed against, the wild sorrel dotting the grass with its rosettes, the fresh young mint, still brown, the sage as downy as a hare's ear—everything overflowed with a powerful and spicy sap which became on my lips mingled with the taste of alcohol and citronella.

I could only shout and laugh, as I trod the long juicy grass that stained my frock . . . With tranquil pleasure you watchfully regarded my wild behavior, and when I stretched out my hand to reach those wild roses—you remember, the ones of such a tender pink—your hand broke the branch before I could, and you took off, one by one, the curved little thorns, coral-hued, claw-shaped . . . And then you gave me the flowers, disarmed . . .

You gave me the flowers, disarmed . . . You gave me, so I could rest my panting self, the best place in the shade, under the Persian lilacs with their ripe bunches of flowers. You picked the big cornflowers in the round flower beds, enchanted flowers whose hairy centers smell of apricot . . . You gave me the cream in the small jug of milk, at teatime, when my ravenous appetite made you smile . . . You gave me the bread with the most golden crust, and I can still see your translucent hand in the sunshine raised to shoo away the wasp that sizzled, entangled in my curls . . . You threw over my shoulders a light mantle when a cloud longer than usual slowly passed, toward the end of the day, when I shivered, in a cold sweat, intoxicated with the pleasure that is nameless among mankind, the innocent pleasure of happy animals in the springtime . . . You told me: "Come back . . . Stop . . . We must go in!" You told me . . .

Oh! If I think of you, then it's goodbye to sleep. What hour struck just then? Now the windows are growing blue. I hear a murmuring in my blood, or else it is the murmur of the gardens down there . . . Are you asleep? No. If I put my cheek against yours, I feel your eyelashes flutter like the wings of a captive fly . . . You are not asleep. You are spying upon my excitement. You protect me against bad dreams; you are thinking of me as I am thinking of you, and we both feign, out of a strange sentimental shyness, a peaceful sleep. All my body yields itself up to sleep, relaxed, and my neck weighs heavily on your gentle shoulder; but our thoughts unite in love discreetly across this blue dawn, so soon increasing.

In a short while the luminous bar between the curtains will brighten, redden . . . In a few more minutes I will be able to read, on your lovely forehead, your delicate chin, your sad mouth and closed eyelids, the determination to appear to be sleeping. . . . It is the hour when my fatigue, my nervous insomnia can no longer remain mute, when I will throw my arms outside this feverish bed, and my naughty heels are already preparing to give a mischievous kick.

Then you will pretend to wake up! Then I shall be able to take refuge in you, with confused and unjust complaints, exasperated sighs, with clenched hands cursing the daylight that has already come, the night so soon over, the noises in the street . . . For I know quite well that you will then tighten your arms about me and that, if the cradling of your arms is not enough to soothe me, your kiss will become more clinging, your hands more amorous, and that you will accord me the sensual satisfaction that is the surcease of love, like a sovereign exorcism that will drive out of me the demons of fever, anger, restlessness . . . You will accord me sensual pleasure, bending over me voluptuously, maternally, you who seek in your impassioned loved one the child you never had.

HB

PART Three ✿✿ [1910-1920]

Music Halls—Motherhood—World War I

Le bonheur, c'est changer d'ennuis

Happiness is a matter of changing troubles

❦❦ Music Halls

Was I, in those days . . .

Was I, in those days, too susceptible to the convention of work, glittering display, empty-headedness, punctuality, and rigid probity which reigns in the music hall? Did it inspire me to describe it over and over again with a violent and superficial love and with all its accompaniment of commonplace poetry? Very possibly. The fact remains that during six years of my past life I was still capable of finding relaxation among its monsters and its marvels. In that past there still gleams the head of Lise Damoiseau and the bottomless, radiant imbecility of Mlle d'Estouteville. I still remember with delight a certain Bouboule with beautiful breasts who wept offendedly if she had to play even a tiny part in a high dress, and the magnificent, long, shallow-grooved back of some Lola or Pepa or Concha . . . Looking back, I can rediscover some particular acrobat swinging high up from bar to bar of a nickeled trapeze or some particular juggler in the center of an orbit of balls. It was a world in which fantasy and bureaucracy were oddly interwoven. And I can still plunge at will into that dense, limited element which bore up my inexperience and happily limited my vision and my cares for six whole years.

Everything in it was by no means as gay and as innocent as I have described it elsewhere. Today I want to speak of my debut in that world, of a time when I had neither learned nor forgotten anything of a theatrical milieu in which I had not the faintest chance of succeeding, that of the big spectacular revue. What an astonishing milieu it was! One sex practically eclipsed the other, dominating it, not only by numbers but by its own particular smell and magnetic atmosphere. This crowd of women reacted like a barometer to any vagary of the weather. It needed only a change of wind or a wet day to send them all into the depths of depression; a depression which expressed itself in tears and curses, in talk of suicide and in irrational terrors and superstitions. I was not prey to it myself but, having known very few women and having been deeply hurt by one single man, I accepted it uncritically. I was even rather impressed by it, although it was only latent hysteria; a kind of schoolgirl neurosis that afflicts women who are arbitrarily and pointlessly segregated from the other sex.

My contribution to the program was entitled *Miaou-Ouah-Ouah. Sketch.* On the strength of my first Dialogues de Bêtes, the authors of the revue had commissioned me to bark and mew on the stage. The rest of my act consisted mainly of performing a few dance steps in bronze-colored tights. On my way to and from the stage I had to pass by the star's dressing room. The leading lady was a remote personage whose door was only open to her personal friends. She never appeared in the corridors except attended by two dressers whose job was to carry her headdresses, powder, comb, and hand mirror and to hold up her trailing flounces. She plays no part in my story, but I liked to follow her and smell the trail of amazingly strong scent she left in her wake. It was a sweet, somber scent; a scent for a beautiful Negress. I was fascinated by it, but I was never able to discover its name.

AW

Rehearsal

We are having a rehearsal in costume at the Théâtre X, a pantomime that the advance publicity predicts will be "sensational." Backstage there is the smell of plaster and ammonia, and in the depths of the dim abyss that is the auditorium, disquieting larvae move about hurriedly . . . Nothing is right. The scenery isn't finished, it's far too dark and swallows up the light and does not give it back; the spotlights are unfocused, they make haloes; and oh, that rustic window garlanded with russet grapevines which willingly opens but refuses to shut.

W., the overworked mime, does his *Dame-aux-Camélias* act, holding his stomach to repress a hoarse cough; his cough is frightening, it scares you to death, that dramatic working of the jaws. Upset, the Young Lover has applied poppy-red makeup to his nose, while his ears remain pallid, which earns him a string of epithets gasped out by the mime, W., who calls him, among other things, a blockhead, a duffer, a crackpot. Nothing is right, nothing will ever be right!

The manager of the theater is there, on stage, and also the big financial backer, who never shows up except for the expensive acts. The composer—a tall, limp fellow who looks boneless—has given up all hope and has shoved behind the scenery the tinny old rehearsal piano and is rinsing his ears, as he puts it, with some Debussy . . . "*Mes longs cheveux descendent jusqu'au bas de la tour* . . ." As for the men in the orchestra pit, surely they must be spending their time improving the breed of French race horses: handed about from the double brass to the flutist, the *Jockey* race sheet is being circulated . . .

"And Madame Loquette?" exclaims the nervous manager. "What's happened to her?"

"Her costume isn't ready," gasps the mime, W., in a stage whisper.

The manager bounds, and barks downstage, his chin jutting over the orchestra pit.

"What's that? What's that? Her costume not ready? A transformation costume, when we open tonight? Things like this are enough to drive a man insane!"

A shrug of helplessness from W., perhaps a gesture meaning farewell to life, with that cough of his! Suddenly the dying man leaps like a ballplayer and recovers his voice to yell:

"In the name of God, don't touch that! It's my knife for the red currant juice!"

With the hands of a hospital nurse he grabs his trick dagger, a special stage property which bleeds sirupy red drops.

"Well! Here at last is Madame Loquette!"

Everyone rushes forward with exclamations of relief, toward the star performer. The fat producer adjusts his monocle. Mme Loquette, who is chilly, rubs her elbows and hunches her shoulders beneath her costume, which is perhaps Montenegran, doubtless Croatian, surely Moldo-Wallachian, with a hint of Dalmatian in its general aspect . . . She is hungry, she has been standing exactly four hours at Landolff's, the costumer's, and is yawning with exasperation.

"Let's have a look at this famous costume!"

It is a disappointment. "Too plain!" grumbles the boss. "A bit dingy!" the big moneyman lets fall. The composer of the music, abandoning *Pelléas,* draws near, undulant and boneless, and says thickly, "Funny thing, I didn't imagine it like that. If I'd had my way, it would have been green, with gold, and, ah, with thingamabobs dangling, some . . . whatyoucallums, those gadgets, you know!"

But the mime, W., enchanted, declares that this rosy red marvelously shows off the dull brown and gray of his smuggler's tatters!

Mme Loquette, a vague look in her eyes, says nothing, having only one desire in the world, and that is for a ham sandwich or two . . . or three, with mustard . . .

Worried silence.

"Well now," the manager sighs, "let's see the underwear . . . Come on, W. Pick up the scene where you tear off her dress . . ."

The bronchitis patient, the pneumonia patient transforms himself, by screwing up his face, into a mountain outlaw and, with dagger drawn, rushes upon Mme Loquette, the hungry Loquette suddenly transformed into a pursued and panting little female, claws in evidence . . . They struggle for an instant, the dress rips at the collar and at the hem, Mme Loquette appears half naked, her head thrown back, her throat offered to the knife . . .

"Stop, stop, my dears! The effect is excellent. All the same, see here . . ."

The men gather around the star performer in studious silence. She, more indifferent than a filly up for sale, allows their eyes to linger on her bared shoulders and on the leg made visible by the torn tunic.

The director reflects, smacks his lips, mutters.

"Obviously, obviously . . . It's not, it's not sufficiently naked!"

The indifferent filly twitches, as if stung by a horsefly.

"Not sufficiently naked! What more do you want?"

"Ugh, it needs—well, something, I don't know what. The effect is good, but it's not startling enough. Not naked enough, I repeat the word. There, that muslin over the bosom. It's out of place, it's ridiculous, it muffles you . . . I think it needs . . ."

Inspired, the director steps back three paces, stretches out a hand, and in the voice of a balloonist taking off from the earth, exclaims:

"Let loose a breast!"

HB

Provincial tour

"For a successful theatrical tour, a really worthwhile tour . . ."

"Yes, I know. You need to have a big name, a talent recognized by Paris, City of Light, or even a star with some scandal about him."

"Who told you that? For a successful tour, you must have rugged health, unshakable good humor, nerves not worn to a frazzle, a well-regulated digestive system, and above all, the kind of easygoing optimism, the fatalism that turns a theatrical company on tour into a caravan of pilgrims in whom faith—latent, subdued—manifests itself rarely but is nevertheless sufficiently strong to lead them from station to station toward the goal never attained, toward repose . . ."

I'm not talking about the top actors but am limiting myself to the anonymous ones, the humble ones, the ones who "tour" all year long, who land at Baret's agency and say, "I've finished with Rose Syma, get me something interesting in Huguenet's company." They play an "interesting minor part"—three different roles in one play: the Footman in Act I, the Invited Guest in Act III, and the Doctor in the very last scene, the denouement.

For thirty-three days I lived their life, that singular life of the actor on tour, so special it isolates you from everything and everybody; I tasted its attraction, its bitterness, its fatigues and disappointments, and now, in the heart of my repose, I turn toward that past month which is still echoing within me, for I can't get out of my ears the incessant clickety-clack of trains, the whistling of locomotives, the hard, flinty sound of applause, and I still have before my mind's eye the rapid succession of landscapes intermingled like reflections of a subsiding wave in the sunlight.

They have barely three days to rehearse, to repair and launder their clothes, and off they go again, resigned, without even the hope of being dazzled by seeing their names in a provincial or foreign theatrical newspaper. What is it that sustains all those unknown actors, the badly paid, the ill fed, what is it that draws them on from town to town, from one cheap and disreputable hotel to another?

NEVERS. The first town on our tour. The first town . . .

> At the first town
> Her lover dressed her
> In a white satin gown . . .

I sing that old provincial song to myself as I face the brown and yellow wall of my first hotel room. I feel I have the craftiness, the docility, and the spitefulness of a soldier or a prisoner: "Good God, thirty-two days more of this life?" All the gross and desolate exclamations of sequestered people rise to my lips . . . I also remember that idiotic château of the Ducs de Nevers, with its sculptured stone draperies, puckered at each end.

AUXERRE. It's almost in my own part of the country. All along the way, I strained my eyes in the direction of Saint-Sauveur, hoping at every turn of the road to glimpse the tower armored in ivy, the crannied walls of the château, and on the side of the hill the terraced village that Claudine loved.

But I saw nothing except the dark, broken, tumbledown and dangerous wings of the little Auxerre theater and, next morning at five o'clock, a rising sun, tangerine-colored, in a sky barely blue, ash-gray, icy, fanned with the sound of bells and the flights of white pigeons . . .

A theatrical tour. I had expected it to be a pilgrimage of a close-knit fraternal troupe, a small group of people traveling together, eating together, sleeping together—I mean to say, sheltering at night in the same hotels. Instead, from the time we arrive at a station until we leave, each one indifferently goes his way as if in a hurry toward a lodging, without even mentioning its name. A superficial solidarity reassembles us only on stage, and I glimpse, during the inevitable meetings in the doorways of inns, the jealous looks, the sidelong glances of dogs that say, without words: "This is my bone. Keep off."

As we journey toward Besançon, springtime gushes ahead of us, more boldly from hour to hour, fresher, keener . . . Stirred, I recognize a land I had for a long time loved, a rustic domain adorned with flowers, a flourishing land intersected by rocky dells, naked and harsh like the winter, and valleys abounding in cherry trees, cherry trees, cherry trees with branches loaded with flowers. The light shade cast by these white trees on the ground, blue like the air, blue like the young wheat, blue like the horizon veiled in mist, blue like the impalpable cloud that scarcely dims the sun. Through the lowered window enters an odor of honey, waxy buds, of turpentine, also the scent of lilacs about to bloom, of lilacs before their flowering, their sharp-sweet perfume of bitter almonds . . . Here and there the first peach trees, rather feverishly pink, bloom in tufts that the first unseasonable frost will blacken and scatter . . .

DIJON. I do not recall much of Dijon, except that the landscape, first glimpsed from the heights of Talant, was almost too pretty under the April sky. I also see, in a corner of my memory, the glittering of the winding and wrinkled little river between two banks of green grass, of a green so aggravating, so edible . . .

BELFORT! I saw the Lion, the Lion in a granite that was wine-rose in the sunset, and I slept in "the bedroom of Brasseur"—what more could anyone ask?

Now, on the way to Nancy, we cross the landscapes of eastern France, blued with pine trees, where the spring still sleeps under the hard leaf buds of the oaks; the blossoms of the apple trees and the cherry trees have not yet opened. Cold and rushing waters, naked woods threaded with sunlight, strewn with mauve-veined anemonies, seas of violets . . . Running water separated into tumultuous streams, small islands of reeds and grasses, of willows covered with

silvery catkins, "Pride of India" trees with transparent leafage . . .
The river especially, the unknown river, greenish black and glittering in the morning sunshine, where men standing in the icy water
are fishing for trout . . .

NANCY. Oh, the handsome hotel, so well lighted, so comfortable!
Oh, the handsome white dining room! Oh, the handsome bug in the
soup! Oh, the handsome worm in the salad, a magnificent worm,
red, robust, very much alive, and revolted!

In the train that takes us from Chalon-sur-Saône to Avignon, I
drowse. When I wake up, I can believe that during a nap of two
hours I have aged by two months. It is the springtime, as one imagines it in fairy tales, the exuberant, ephemeral, irresistible springtime
of the Midi, fat, fresh, gushing out in deep foliage, in tall grass waving and shimmering like watered silk in the wind. Judas trees are
everywhere, mauve and red, and catalpas, their flowers like gray per-
iwinkles, and blue lilacs, the cross of their petals hemmed in a
nacreous purple, and laburnum, wisteria, roses . . . The first tea
roses! They come to meet me on the station platform of Avignon,
scarce half opened, transparent in the sun like an ear reddened by
racing blood, adorned with a leafage that resembles them, carmined
and brown, with curved thorns of polished coral . . . They smell
of apricot, vanilla, a very fine cigar, an exquisite brunette, everything
except a rose, and yet we exclaim, as we press the bouquet against
our lips: "Oh! How they do smell like tea roses!"

MARSEILLES is always Marseilles. It is the noise and crowd in La
Canebière—deafening, the noise; futile the haste of the people, who
for all their haste have the look of idlers; and flowers everywhere
and exotic fruits smelling of ether, and porous earthenware water
coolers that remind one of melons, and May lilies, and wet clams
and oysters, and those fan-shaped mollusks, the *praires,* purple-hued,
and sea urchins, and yellow and black bartenders, and fine ladies in
black silk and lace.

Our dressing rooms here smell of corpses and ammonia, but

outside there's the blue port, the white boats, the geometrical lace of masts and gear, the heat, the shouts, the animal happiness of a population that lives out-of-doors, a place of trading, of indolence, of carousing . . .

Actors on tour. A big strapping fellow, whom I will call Sylvain. Tall, young, with something of the loose-limbed aspect of a hunting dog, not yet full-grown. Indifferent, indefatigable, curious about everything, smart, he seemed to owe more to the Beaux-Arts than to the Conservatoire.

Upon getting off the train, he stows his valise anywhere at all, grasps his painter's kit and disappears. He returns in the evening, at dinnertime, bringing back a luminous water-color sketch, and some violets, or apple blossoms or a bird's nest, or even grass, fresh and juicy grass that he pulls out of his pockets by handfuls, raising it to his nostrils to smell avidly, faunlike . . .

SALON-DE-PROVENCE, where the awakening mistral murmurs, shady avenues of centenarian plane trees with their bark marbled like colossal serpents. In the small market square, the centuries have clothed with moss a fountain of graduated basins, and each fiber of moss, each tuft of green and gold silk, distills its drop of living water . . . At night, the mistral increases, little by little, beneath a black sky full of stars, and in the gardens the cats sing of love, in heart-rending voices. The fork of a plane tree holds a Siamese cat, enormous, masked with black velvet like a robber, gloved in velvet. He has come to make love and to fight, his sides are heaving, his wide-open eyes are the color of blue flame, his ears are torn, his face scratched . . . He rests, looking at us contemptuously, superb in his sand-colored coat.

NÎMES. At last, Nîmes and its gardens of La Fontaine! We push open the grilled-iron gate, gilded and black, and the world changes. We are in a springtime so fairylike that one trembles lest it sink and dissolve in a mist. The fountain, Diana's bath; deep avenues of stone where roars an imperious green water, transparent, dark, blue and brilliant like a serpent . . . I lean over this simmering water in which the Jadas trees are reflected, and I want to plunge into it, to reach that other garden where the pines and spindle trees, the trees with mauve blossoms, are mirrored and, decomposed by the aquamarine water, change color, become dark blue, violet, the violet of a bruised peach, the brown of dried blood . . .

With a loving hand I caress the warm stone of the baths of Diana, smooth and gilded, the broken capital of a pillar where appears, clear-cut and intact in its vegetal grace, the leaf of the acanthus.

A storm cloud that passes over us showers down drop by drop a slow and perfumed rain that rolls in heavy pearls, exhaling the scent of turpentine, pines, roses, and flowering thorn. One wants to stop, lie down with a sigh, sleep here and never wake up . . . A star of rain squashes at the corner of my lip and I drink it, warm, sweet, with a dust tasting of jonquils . . .

MONTPELLIER. Six hours of rain here have cloistered us in the hotel. We huddle together like chilly animals, we try to create something homelike, we risk an ephemeral arrangement of the dressing table, the writing table . . . The open blotter between the inkwell and the bouquet of narcissus in a glass of water; I pause, not knowing what melancholy words to cover this white page with . . . The wall opposite, the gray wall that I see through the window streams with water, and the rain pipe sobs. I wish for the hot tea, the golden loaf, my lamp and its milky shade . . . and the barking of my dogs, left behind in Paris, the friendly tinkling of the familiar doorbell . . .

We took the train at dawn, shivering with drowsiness and so tired! I was just settling down in a corner to resume my shattered sleep when a breath of salt air smelling of fresh clams and seaweed made me sit up: the sea! Sète and the sea! There it was, running alongside the train, exulting in a thousand tiny waves; it had put in an appearance quite unexpectedly. The seven o'clock sun, still low on the horizon, had not yet penetrated it; the sea was refusing to let herself be possessed and, hardly awake, kept her nocturnal color of ink-blue crested with white . . .

Salt pans filed past, edged with grass glittering with salt, and sleeping villas, white as the salt, among their lilacs. The desire to paint all this aroused in me a thirst of Tantalus, tense and impotent, which surrendered before the splendor of an April morning, at Sète, on the edge of the sea . . .

Types of actors. As I observe my companions, I realize that I am beginning to have a clearer view of them and to know them better. It isn't easy to know them, since they defend themselves well, for the most part using as weapons professional familiarity and obligatory surface intimacy. But to know them really, their private lives and worries that drive them on to an invisible goal jealously hidden is, I repeat, tempting but difficult. They call each other by their first names, but set up almost no friendships. A meal eaten together at a station lunchroom is merely a pretext for noisy laughter and trite jokes or on other occasions for a gloomy and silent indulgence in gluttony.

One of the kids of the company, a thin lad with a pinched face and staring dark eyes, suddenly began to talk to me backstage, during a performance. He talked volubly, feverishly, I have no idea why, for I had asked nothing.

"Can you believe it," he began, "we've been on the road more than eighteen days! How time flies! Next month, if I don't land something, I risk nothing less than having to sleep in a flophouse . . . If I don't clinch things with Monsieur Baret next month, then what? . . . I'm just talking, you think, but really I'm serious. I'm being paid fifteen francs a day on this tour. Well, at the end of every month, if I'm to meet all my bills, I've got to earn 220 francs. Naturally, this doesn't let me indulge in buying flowers for the girls, but I make do on 220 francs a month. I've got to earn that amount. Oh, if only a tour like this could last a whole year! That would be wonderful, wouldn't it? I could do an act at a Paris nightclub, but I'm not keen on nightclubs, you have to have a better stomach than I have. I lost my stomach during all that time I lived on twenty-five francs a month . . ."

"Twenty-five francs a month? Heavens! How did you manage?"

"I really don't know," he said, unconcernedly. "My God, I've forgotten how I did it. But I lived for six months on twenty-five francs a month. Funny I can't remember at all how I managed. I remember I had *one* suit, *one* shirt, *one* hat, nothing to change into. It's funny, I don't quite remember . . . Of course, it's hard, very hard. And so now I keep telling myself I've simply got to earn 220 francs every month!"

He hurries from station to hotel, from hotel to station, always on foot, nimble and graceful as a young skeleton. He wears a rose in his lapel . . .

Another type in our touring company: one of the young actresses. She is married. She brings to the theater the profoundly bourgeois temperament of "the honest working girl." I have never seen her idle. From the minute she arrives in a town she stows her valise in a very modest hotel and goes off to the theater to open her trunk, unfold, unpack, mend, and hang up her costumes. She inspects every corner of her dressing room, asks for some additional sweeping, looks over the light bulbs, then goes back to the hotel with the quick little steps of a working girl in a hurry.

On stage, that evening, she earns her living by saying her lines without a fault and without pleasure, goes off at a run, skirts tucked up, to her dressing room, where some sewing she has begun awaits her, and immediately there she is, sitting with her work, puting her needle in and out, singing softly to herself . . . She is a worker ant, an honest little ant. She is very pleased with the tour: "If this keeps up, I'll finish my six shirts before we reach Cherbourg. They would already be done if MY HUSBAND hadn't taken upon himself to wear out so many socks . . ."

:

And another little actress: the silhouette of this one amuses me. She has the lanky figure of a very young girl, without hips or bottom, she is elegantly and aggressively slender. A cheap hat well set on her dyed curls, a checked tailormade. A nice little face, but with irregular features; bright, mobile, but elusive. This is a spurious young girl, short-skirted, a typical dressmaker's errand girl whose diet is composed of raw apples and fried potatoes. It is as natural for her to travel as to breathe; she sleeps, lunches, dines, no matter where, substituting for the cutlet a cup of black coffee, for the sandwich a chocolate bar. I allowed myself to question an older member of the company about this sharp little creature whose frank gaiety and elusive liveliness intrigued me.

"Oh, she's a deserving little thing," said the worthy old woman I questioned. "I know her well. She's divorced, she has a son she's very fond of and she sees him on the sly. Just now, as it happens, she's all worked up over him."

"Why? Is he sick?"

"No, he's sitting for the entrance exams at Saint-Cyr."

From Montpellier to Pau, the route followed is an enchantment; the train is crossing a land that I am seeing for the first time, going toward the Pyrenees springtime. The first high mountain, dazzling with a snow the morning sun turns pale gold, has reared up there unexpectedly above hills that have the violet hue of a columbine, and for a long time it seems to follow us, now so near one wants to touch it, to lay one's hand on its glacial shoulder lined with black rocks, and then far off, austere, capped with clouds, lost in the melting blue of the sky. Behind it, the Pyrenees advance one by one and form a line shutting off the horizon that is coming toward us. Sparkling with a pure snow that makes one thirsty, slashed with vertiginous shadows, split into blue chasms, stained with bronze forests, there they are, the tempting mountains, the heroic giantesses of a book that delighted my childhood, the heroines of *Voyage aux Pyrénées!* As we pass the small stations, I read aloud to delight my ear the plain and rustic names ringing with Basque sunlight, the roar of slate-colored mountain torrents . . . The least fold of land covers itself here with Spanish grass, with rosy tufts of flowers, wild orchids the white of gardenias, anemonies, and soapwort. Yellow ranunculus, big starlike marguerites flourish as if it were June; but the beautiful undulating forest clinging to the sides of the mountains is still transparent and without mystery. Here and there a narrow pond gleams, the water made blue by the melting snows . . .

Lourdes goes rapidly by, but I had time to see, from the slowed train, the basilica and the grotto . . . It seemed to me to smack of the new style of chapel, a fantastic fairy tale, and a casino—all combined. Then a mountain torrent, frozen and at the same time foaming, full of an evil charm, clouded by the melting of the snows, transparent and milky like moonstones . . . It roars, it bounds and rushes ahead of the train that runs beside it, stops and frets itself against the rocks thrown across its bed . . .

Of Pau I shall see almost nothing except the moon at midnight shedding a green light that causes fever and drives off sleep . . . In the morning a veil of rain hides the valley, and I can find nothing more to say about this beautiful part of the country, where the traveler is fleeced, except that the sub-prefect of Oloron is a charming man with the beautiful eyes of a goat, who talks about Francis Jammes as both a friend and a poet . . .

BAYONNE: the massive old château, standing low and square like a bulldog, bordered by new grass . . . The main street and its low arcades buttressed by heavy pillars . . . Above the rampart, half-ruined windows from which hang tattered yellow wallflowers, trailing geraniums, stained cloths, torn quilts from which the feathers fly . . . The rococo gaiety of the Basque names: Etcheverry, Etchepare, Etchegoyen. The hot chocolate steams on the café terraces. The dark theater, and a certain terrifying spiral staircase carved out of the rock! I am thinking of the château where Pé de Puyane died, of the blood that dripped down through the ceilings . . . The sight of the dressers is not calculated to dispel this romantic impression, for they are ageless witches, with black silk kerchiefs on their heads, old hags who will perhaps sew into the hem of my costume a baleful white hair . . .

Let us forget them! Let us only remember that we are stopping at the Panier Fleuri and that the hotel chambermaid has a charming name and in her dark dress has the bearing of a Spanish Infanta, with long velvety lashes over her eyes, which are the color of a mountain torrent.

In the train that is running toward Bordeaux, the *petites* of the company have lowered the blue blinds and are sewing, bareheaded, in their white shirtwaists, unmindful of the lovely scenery. The sifted bluish light is kind to the tired young faces. A thin ray of bright sunshine turns, according to the curves of the road, inflaming in its passage a pale little hand, a lock of fair hair, a silver thimble. This shut railway carriage, where the free sunshine and the moving landscape do not enter, gives the girls the look of innocent and cheerful orphans in a needlework school.

BORDEAUX! Heat, fatigue, oh, the fatigue! Three performances in two days. Supposing I just sat down on this warm pavement and refused to budge, after all? Don't come near me, don't say a word to me or I'll bite! My one consolation is the Chapon Fin, and the proprietor of that tavern . . . So here I am, standing up again and seeking out the Cours de l'Intendance, warm, dusty, jammed with people glowing pink in the mingled illumination of electricity and a violet twilight, with flashy neckties, ruddy faces, dark and gleaming hair, the expressive eyes, both impertinent and flattering, of the true native of Bordeaux . . .

We are on our way to Nantes. The scene changes, the year becomes more youthful by the hour. As far as Lorient we see the springtime flee before us, the oaks become bare again, the grass short, the windmills turning on the horizon, and in the little stations the train runs through, there are white-starched Breton headdresses, the first white caps blooming like marguerites . . . Then we enter, dazzled, the yellow realm of broom and gorse. Gold, brass, and vermeil as well—for the pale colza is a part of all this—inflame these bleak moors. Leagues and leagues of flowering gorse, a desolate wealth that discourages the goats, even the butterflies—white pierids and greenish yellows zigzag here, wings torn . . .

LORIENT. What a melancholy arrival in this station that smells of fish! Some lads in big straw hats banded with black velvet stare contemptuously at a batch of young girls in long skirts, girls of thirteen to fifteen, wearing white-starched coifs, black dresses, and two-sided aprons, one in front, one at the back. They giggle and blow their noses on their sleeves . . .

BREST, RENNES, CAEN. I've forgotten, I can't remember, I forget . . . I'm sleepy. Where was it that I drank so meditatively that cup of smooth, incomparable cream? Where was it that I had the first strawberries, which I jealously hid and ate in my bed? Where, in what town, was that memorable dive that dared to call itself Le Théâtre des Folies?

Just as he is, with his defects and dullness, the property man interests me. Where did he come from? What did he do before manhandling our trunks like a gang of four men, accepting this destiny of a wandering stevedore and anonymous actor who is called in the town the property man but on the playbill figures as "A Laborer," "A Majordomo," "A Footman"?

Last night, a half hour past midnight, when we were leaving our dressing rooms, tired out and full of complaints, the property man, while waiting for the stagehands to carry down the last trunks, settled himself at a piano stored backstage in a dim corner, attacked a Chopin polonnaise, and played brilliantly, with an edginess, a kind of panting fury which brought us all to a standstill. At the end of the polonnaise, while still astounded, I thanked the lanky fellow who emerged from the shadows looking embarrassed and guilty, like an animal caught gobbling a stolen morsel.

"Yes," he replied, "at one time I didn't play at all badly; I won first prize at the Conservatoire in 19–. But what can you expect, graduating with honors doesn't pay the grocery bill, my family's too big . . . And so I became a sort of jack-of-all-trades . . ."

A brief scatological digression: On the boat that goes from Dieppe to Newhaven, I read, on the threshold of the first-class W.C., an inscription—blue enamel on white—making a courteous request: "Please do not drop *anything* except paper into the toilet." Since then, I have savored, if I may say so, on my travels the modest and good-natured restriction of the W.C. at Salon (Bouches-du-Rhône): "Toilets only for doing pipi"! How Jean Lorrain would have enjoyed this example of engaging meridional manners! I admired in the W.C.'s of Lorient the lewd liveliness of the pictorial decorations —how shall I say?—in the genre *cacamaïeu:* floral sprays, mosques, groves of palm trees; motifs suggesting fireworks and fountains: a boudoir for *Le Roi Ubu* . . . And shall I mention also *those* of the Théâtre des Folies in X? For the entire theatrical troupe, men and women, *they* are comprised of a bucket, *one* bucket without a lid. And shall I speak of *those* one wouldn't go into for anything on earth, dark and suffocating closets with treacherous floors, opening upon yawning black abysses, more frightful than a dungeon and enough to discourage an acrobat? Shall I recall the *in pace* with which one had to cross, without a light, the length of the room, to sit on . . . an iron bar, beneath which roared an invisible torrent?

CAEN, FLERS, CHERBOURG, and elsewhere: Nine hours of rail travel in ramshackle old trains that stop every ten minutes with a jolt that wrenches the brakes and the spine . . . The park at Flers hospitalizes our lagging troupe for an hour. Rhododendrons in flower, of a warm red and an orange-red; a blue-green and violet peacock twists its shimmering serpent's neck to look at us . . . "He is beautiful," my confrere Sylvain says, voluptuously chewing a blade of grass, "but it's mistaken of him to wear long, snuff-colored knitted underpants."

ÉVREUX. Oh, the delightful desert of a Sunday in the provinces, stretching itself out in the sun and shade of ill-paved streets! On the palings of the church that is being repaired, bills have been posted —*pro pudor!*—"Claudine" and some posters by Sem, which have nothing liturgical about them . . . In the hotel garden, seven puppies are being suckled by their mother, a cat plays lazily, chinchilla rabbits mutter vespers on leaves of lettuce, speckled chickens peck, and lo, I am overwhelmed with boundless discouragement, a disgust for any activity, any effort, fed up with the struggle to live.

After Rouen, the tour becomes more and more hectic. We sense the approach of home, and in every dressing room nervousness increases. With the ladies this explodes in shrill cries, tears, a small case of fainting, frequent breaking up on stage . . . With the men, terrible oaths follow songs bellowed *fortissimo,* or imitations of animals . . . The haggard lad ("I've got to make my two hundred francs per month") becomes even more white-faced. What will he find, when the tour is ended? He trembles, and yesterday his fear was revealed in this distressing remark: "The tour is going so well, maybe Monsieur Baret will extend it for a few days?"

AMIENS. Good food, and a garden enclosed in high walls where live at liberty a sea gull, a stork with clipped wings, and a young cat, a skinny cat that dances and crawls and twists itself like a beached eel, and some good friends who have come from Paris. Everything is good today! There is also, naturally, the cathedral, but one already knows it and one is so tired! We will not even pay it a polite visit. Grand-Rue, this sign: "Florentine Panamas, guaranteed exotic."

DOUAI. Everything is bad! The countryside fades out in flat cultivated fields bordered by ranks of poplars . . . And no hotels! We finally land God-knows-where, and I don't want to recall anything except a couple of servantmaids, two sisters who kept trotting up and down the stairs of the inn. The younger, a blonde out of a Jordaens painting, her hair pure gold, her complexion rose petal, the rosy tint of a not quite ripe strawberry. The elder, a brunette, but resembling the younger girl, with dark bronze-colored hair and the complexion of a ripe peach from an espaliered peach tree. I admire and envy her cheeks of warm velvet, the abundant down at the temples and lips, where the crude morning light steals.

LILLE. A sudden cold, a black cold. Disquieting news of a possible strike of postal workers, which will perhaps be followed by a railway strike? The company is in a fever of excitement and gossip, with each one outdoing the other in the wildest predictions. The least pessimistic predict a forced stop, and that terror of actors on tour, a complete breakdown that would leave them stranded . . .

We draw up futile plans of resistance and subsistence: an improvised performance that will pay our board and room; I will dance, our romantic lead will juggle knives, the first comedian will lift weights, the ingénue will sing ultra-naughty songs. "It's my speciality at parties," she says. The property man, ex-*prix du Conservatoire,* will play his Chopin polonnaise that won him the prize, and our young and serious stage manager, remembering that he was a lieutenant in a crack cavalry regiment the year before, will demonstrate some *haute-école* on the best hack from a nearby riding school . . .

Not for a month have I seen so much cordiality, so much solidarity in the troupe; it is a surprise, a revelation. Faces that were inscrutable light up, sparkle with the wish to serve, to employ forces and talents that are rusting and about which only yesterday there would almost have been cause to blush: "As for me, I can tell fortunes!" "For my part, I can walk on my hands, and I've had practice as a fire eater!" "Me, I was a 'promoter' at the Alcazar bar in Limoges." Tomorrow, if the postal strike is averted, all this will be forgotten, we will talk about something else, the *gommeuse* with experience at the Alcazar will recover her artlessness, and the acrobat

will reassume his stiff and formal "British look" in his greenish
overcoat . . .

BLANKENBERGHE. The tramway between two ridges of dunes,
undulating and bare except for the thin dune grass, acid, clean, dry
. . . The Villas Robida, a flat and pale landscape. Plantations:
leagues of poplars, still dwarf, planted with loving care and determination. Gigantic work of a patient king, Leopold II. The recompense
is already there: the trees have all taken root and are growing. A
small white house near Coq-sur-Mer, with the sign: *Café drama-
tique*(?).

LIÈGE. Neat, sleek, gourmand. Pastry shops, taverns, shop windows displaying laces, frills, and furbelows, everywhere a gaiety, a
cordiality that try to remain French . . . To arrive here, we followed the river Meuse, its banks mirrored in the clear water, with
their whitethorns, copper beeches, cliffs that call to mind a town in
ruins, their accessible caves, the whole comprising a rather facile
picturesqueness, a bit theatrical, but charming.

I can really think of nothing to say about the town of V.—
except that, directed to it by one of the troupe who was a practical
joker, we spent the night in a . . . in a . . . How to give a decent
name to that hostelry? Yes, how? A . . . house, an establishment
catering to modest purses, since they gave four bedrooms and a drawing room to our group of five, for the sum of ten francs! Dreadful
red hangings, the carved bedsteads painted a reddish brown, very
rich-looking, and the partitions between the rooms of a strange thinness beneath heavy and dusty draperies, as if contrived that way for a
purpose. My roommate, Barelli, asked for some cream in the morning at breakfast, and the intelligent and well-informed waiter replied, "Very good, madame. Simon's cold cream, I suppose?"

SAINT-QUENTIN. We leave the town after midnight, at 12:50, on
the return trip to Paris. Return to Paris! Can I believe it? I must

confess that the tour captured my imagination, with its lure of the unexpected, of hope, of irresponsibility, of curiosity constantly satisfied and constantly renewed . . . Even though tired, sun-tanned before summer, with hair dull and lifeless, the edge of my skirt hem frayed on hotel stairs and train steps, I breathe in the damp wind charged with the odor of rain and young leaves, wondering obscurely, "When will I go off again, when will I again take up this life of a salaried gypsy watching clock towers, forests, and rivers go by?"

I catch myself being sorry to part from my companions of a month . . . They behave in the carriages and corridors of the train like soldiers on leave, shouting and laughing, singing and exasperating the solitary passenger trying to sleep, a peace-loving person who had hoped to enjoy his solitude on a trip to Paris . . .

Arrival in the Gare du Nord, about four in the morning, beneath a green and rainy dawn . . .

Only a minute, in which I free myself from the embrace of two affectionate arms and reply to the barking of my little bulldog, who is almost bursting with excitement; then my companions have disappeared, each going his own way . . . Next month, next week, they will again go on tour, lucky they . . . And I am left behind. I fear I will never again find a place on their merry-go-round . . .

O Baret, prince of touring companies, take me again on your eternal wheel! And I shall consent to rise at five in the morning, do without a bed and sleep doubled up in a slow train, shall consent to eat twice a day the pale veal and the coffee served at railway-station restaurants, and to sleep in beds with mattresses as ravaged as the beds of mountain torrents. In addition, I will play my part in nightly performances, provided that spring, summer, and autumn ripen beneath my feet each day in an unknown countryside, and discover, length by length, the marvelous robe of Mother Earth, the changing robe, fringed with water . . .

HB

❧❧ Remarriage and Motherhood

Letter to Léon Hamel

[*Rozven, July 31, 1911*]

Dear Hamel,

I am absolutely full of chagrin and remorse over having worried you. Along with you, I have also worried Mamma and several people who love me, by leaving them in ignorance as to my fate.

Dear Hamel, such a lot of things have happened! I have had troubles—was it necessary to suffer in order to pay for the happiness (touch wood), yes, something very like happiness that I see glimmering quite near, within reach? (I am touching wood frantically!)

I arrived this morning in Rozven after a very exciting month spent almost entirely in Paris and during that ghastly hot weather. You must surely know that I played in Geneva and Lausanne. But do you know that the day after his duel Jouvenel dropped in at Lausanne, his arm badly wounded and in a sling, declaring that he could not and would not live any longer without me? Do you know that at the same time Hériot wanted to rejoin me in Switzerland and I prevented it by some panicky telegrams full of lies and contradictions? Do you know that upon returning to Paris, Jouvenel declared to La Panthère that he loved another woman? Thereupon she declares that she will kill that woman, no matter who she is. Alarmed, J. warns me of this threat, to which I reply: "I'll go to see her."

And I go, and I tell the Panther, "I'm the woman," whereupon she melts and implores. A passing weakness, for two days later she announces to J. that she intends to knife me. Realarmed, J. has me abducted by Sauerwein in a motorcar and accompanies me, still with S., to Rozven, where we find Missy, glacial and disgusted, who has just heard from La Panthère. Then my two guardians leave me and Paul Barlet stands guard, revolver in hand, to protect me. Missy, still glacial and disgusted, flies the coop and goes to Honfleur. A short time (three days) afterward, J. summons me back to him by telephone, and S. comes to fetch me in his car, because La Panthère is on the prowl to get me; she, too, armed with a revolver. At this point a period of semi-sequestration in Paris begins, during which I am guarded like a precious shrine by the Sûreté, as well as by Jouvenel, Sauerwein, and Sapène, those three pillars of *Le Matin*. And believe it or not, this period has only just come to an end, disposed of by an unexpected, providential, and magnificent event! Tired of carrying on, M. Hériot and Mme La Panthère have embarked on the yacht *Esmerald* for a cruise of six weeks at least, after having astonished Le Havre, the home port, by some remarkable drunken orgies. Is this good? Is it theater? A little too much so, isn't it?

Meanwhile, Jouvenel has distinguished himself by some very proper actions, which earned him the misesteem of Missy, since fundamentally she adores Hériot; she had arranged a room for him here and intended to inflict him upon me almost conjugally. I did not need this much to disgust me forever with that young man. What more can I tell you, dear Hamel! J. is having his house fitted up for me. He is without a fortune, but he has *Le Matin* (forty thousand or so francs), and since I earn a good living, we will manage. Need I tell you again that I love this man, who is tender, jealous, unsociable, and incurably honest? I would so like to see you. And I shall see you often, if it suits you, for J. has declared that he will allow me "only Hamel and Barlet" . . . Missy is still glacial and disgusted, and no matter what I do, I can't get a sensible word out of her. I assure you. It's not meanness on my part, and it troubles me a lot . . .

HB

My mother was twice a widow . . .

. . . My mother was twice a widow. Since she was faithful out of tenderness, duty, and pride, my first divorce upset her greatly and my second marriage still more. Her odd explanation of this was: "It's not so much the divorce I mind, it's the marriage. It seems to me that anything would be better than marriage—only it isn't done." I laughed and pointed out that on two occasions she had set me an example. "I had to," she answered. "After all, I belong to my village. But what are you going to do with so many husbands? It's a habit that grows, and soon you won't be able to do without it."

"But, Mother, what would you do in my place?"

"Something stupid, no doubt. The proof is that I married your father."

If she was afraid to say how great a place he had held in her heart, her letters, after he had left her forever, told me of it, as did also an outburst of tears on the day after my father was buried. That day she and I were tidying the drawers of the yellow thuja-wood desk, from which she took letters, the service records of Jules-Joseph Colette, Captain of the First Regiment of Zouaves, and six hundred gold francs—all that remained of a landed fortune, the fortune of Sidonie Landoy, frittered away. My mother, who had shown no signs of weakness as she moved about surrounded by relics, came across this handful of gold, gave a cry, melted into tears, and said: "Oh, dear Colette! He'd told me, eight days ago, when he could still speak to me, that he was only leaving me four hundred francs!" She sobbed with gratitude, and I began that day to doubt whether I had ever truly loved. No, certainly, a woman as great as that could not commit the same "stupidities" as I, and she was the first to discourage me from imitating her.

"So this Monsieur X. means a lot to you, does he?"

"But Mother, I love him!"

"Yes, yes, you love him. . . . All right then, you love him."

She thought again, refrained with an effort from saying what her celestial cruelty dictated, then burst out once more: "No, no, I'm not happy."

I pretended to be modest, dropped my eyes to shut in the image of a handsome, envied, intelligent man with a glowing future, and replied gently: "You're difficult."

"No, I'm not happy. I preferred, yes really I preferred the other one, the boy you now consider less than the dust."

"Oh Mother! He's an idiot!"

"Yes, yes, an idiot. . . . Exactly."

I still remember how she bent her head, half closing her gray eyes to dwell on the dazzling, flattering picture of the "idiot." And she added: "What beautiful things you'd write with the idiot, Minet-Chéri! With the other, you'll spend your time giving him all your most precious gifts. And what if on top of that he makes you unhappy? It's more than likely."

I laughed heartily: "Cassandra!"

"All right then, Cassandra. And if I were to say all I foresee . . ." The gray eyes, half closed, read the future: "Fortunately you're not in too much danger."

At the time I did not understand her. No doubt she would have explained herself later on. I know now what she meant when she said, "You're not in danger," an ambiguous phrase referring not only to the calamities I risked. To her mind I had already got over what she called "the worse thing in a woman's life: her first man." He is the only one you die of. After that, married life—or a semblance of it—becomes a career. . . .

EMCC

The always unexpected blast of air . . .

The always unexpected blast of air, the burning oxygen that gives life and color to women, shook my refuge . . . The days and nights crackled with telephone calls. A keen happiness and a blazing unhappiness threatened me all at once. Torn between the two, I hesitated, so eager was I to bestow upon the one the same respect and the same interest as upon the other. From this exceptional season of heartaches and heartthrobs dates the epoch of my exceptional dwelling places.

To begin with, I agreed to live in the 16ᵉ arrondissement, to occupy one of the "Swiss chalets" with which the first half of the nineteenth century dotted the village of Passy. It had the fragility of theatrical décor and the good Alpine style that included balconies and timberwork set against the brick. Virginia creeper took care of the rest, in draperies and garlands. This chalet filled one end of a garden surrounded by gardens, and its Helvetic romanticism benefited by a legend: it was to a jealous painter, in love with his model, that the small enclosure owed its porte-cochere and its lock, both of them of massive bronze.

The first time I went through the heavy door, it was a luminous June night with acacia flowers hanging in clusters, rosy lamplight behind closed curtains. A vast full moon, sitting on the ridge of the roof, looked ready to burst into song. The surrounding gardens hid the walls. I paused at the edge of this lure, this excess of charm, this snare. Perhaps there was still time to turn back? But already the proprietor was coming to greet me . . .

Inside the chalet, penury and superfluity combined to sustain my enchantment. The bathroom was situated under a lean-to and had been provided only for the use of the dogs of the place. The painter's former studio, isolated from the chalet, boasted Louis XV wood paneling, but rain leaked through its roof. A gallery library contained nothing but Latin works bound in full calf, and a few odd volumes of various memoirs—in short, the usual literary provender of provincial châteaux, where one goes to bed at nine o'clock . . . Jealous of the dogs, I too wanted a bathroom. Daring ambition! No sooner had the workmen set their hands to it than the chalet winced here and there, demanding its rights as a much worn piece of stage décor, its comedy of enchantment and illusion. The least intervention of the plumber produced an urgent need for a mason; the humidity and the fairy-tale moonlight short-circuited the electricity.

At the autumn equinox, large slabs of weather boarding with their clover-leaf openwork were blown off along with the leaves and the roof tiles . . .

[But] I owe a great deal to the chalet in Passy. Under its balconies and its clover-leaf cut-out woodwork, I led a life that was veritably feminine, glazed with ordinary and curable woes, with rebellions, laughter, and laziness. There I acquired the taste for ornamenting and destroying. There I worked, pursued by the need for money. There I had hours of indolence. . . . No other house ever encouraged me so assiduously to wait. Someone—perhaps the beautiful, sequestered artist's model—must have waited a long time in the same bedroom in front of a log fire, and I took up my sentry duty with patience.

HB

Letter to Christiane Mendelys

[Paris, December 27, 1912]

My dear little Croppy,

You were so sweet to write to me. What's new with me, you ask, and my answer is that I am getting bigger every day, slowly but surely. I'm especially pregnant in the evening—from eight o'clock on, there's not a dress or belt that fits, *he* must have room, or he'll break everything! You see how he already resembles his father! Aside from this . . . there has been a disgusting amount of celebrating. On the nineteenth the marriage took place, since when the *Matin* staff and friends have handed us about from one table to another, we bounced from lunch to dinner, from dinner to supper, until Christmas Eve, when we finished our week of excesses by going to bed at seven in the morning. If this child isn't the most ignoble roisterer, then I give up!

HB

I was forty . . .

I was forty, and I remember greeting the certitude of the be-lated child's presence with serious mistrust, while saying nothing about it. Physical apprehension had nothing to do with my behavior; I was simply afraid that at my age I would not know how to give a child the proper love and care, devotion and understanding. Love—so I believed—had already hurt me a great deal by monopolizing me for the past twenty years.

It is neither wise nor good to start a child with too much thought. Little used to worrying about the future, I found myself for the first time preparing for an exact date that it would have been quite enough to think about only four weeks beforehand. I medi-tated, I tried to think clearly and reasonably, but I was struck by the recollection that intelligent cats are usually bad mothers, sinning by inadvertence or by excess of zeal, constantly moving their kittens from place to place, holding them by the nape of the neck, pinched between their teeth, hesitating where to deposit them. What a com-fortable nest that sagging seat of an armchair! However, less so than under the down quilt, perhaps? But surely the acme of comfort would be the second drawer of the commode?

During the first three months I told almost no one of my condi-tion or my worries. I did tell Charles Sauerwein and was struck by his comment. "Do you know what you're doing?" he exclaimed. "You're behaving as a man would, you're having a masculine preg-nancy! You must take it more lightheartedly than this. Come, put on your hat, we'll go to the Poirée-Blanche and have some strawberry ice cream."

Fortunately I changed, without realizing it at first. Soon every-one around me began to exclaim how well I looked and how cheer-ful I was. The half-hidden and involuntary smile of pregnant women showed even through my makeup as the Optimistic Owl—for I was serenely continuing to play my part in *L'Oiseau de Nuit,* which involved some skillful pugilistics, mean uppercuts, and some rough and tumble clinches, on the table, under the table . . . A masculine pregnancy? Yes, and one might even say the pregnancy of a champion, for I had the taut, well-muscled body of an athlete . . .

Then, in the fourth month, one of the actors in the company, Georges Wague, reminded me of "the Geneva affair"—our plan to take our act to Geneva, and I realized that would be halfway between the fifth and sixth months . . . Hurriedly I confessed everything, and left behind me two dismayed friends, my two partners, Wague and Christine Kerf, contemplating the ruins of "the Geneva affair."

Insidiously, unhurriedly, the beatitude of pregnant females spread through me. I was no longer subjected to any discomfort, any unease. This purring contentment, this euphoria—how give a name either scientific or familiar to this state of preservation?—must certainly have penetrated me, since I have not forgotten it and am recalling it now, when life can never again bring me plenitude . . .

One gets tired of keeping to oneself all the unsaid things—in the present case my feeling of pride, of banal magnificence, as I ripened my fruit. My recollection of all this is linked with "the Geneva affair," for not long after breaking up our "turn," I summoned Wague and Christine Kerf and, strong in my newfound health and spirits, I reorganized our trio and our project for starting out on the road. Georges Wague hid his emotion by calling me an egg-laying hoot owl and predicting that my child would be day-blind. On the day settled upon, we left for Switzerland, and I celebrated my new importance by taking, at the hotel, the best room.

The lake cradled its swans on their reflection, the Alpine snows were softening, capped by mists, and I smiled at everything—the Swiss bread, the honey, the Swiss coffee . . .

"Beware of special cravings," said Wague. "What do you now have for breakfast, since you've gone astray?"

"Exactly what I had before the fault: *café au lait*."

"Good, I'll order your breakfast when I go down for mine. Is it for eight o'clock?"

"Yes, for eight o'clock . . ."

Next morning at eight there was a knock at my door and a frightfully affected little voice murmured: "It's the chambermaid!"

If you've never seen a strapping, dark-skinned young fellow, all seasoned muscle, half naked under a shirtwaist borrowed from Kerf, a red ribbon tying his black hair at the temples, and got up in a tailormade skirt, you cannot imagine how a pregnant and jolly woman can laugh. Serious, her dark hair draped on her shoulders —strange ornament for a female boy-impersonator—Kerf followed, bringing a little tin filter coffeepot and preceded by the aroma of fresh coffee.

What good comrades they were! In order that I might have a breakfast unlike the hotel slop, they had filtered fresh ground coffee and boiled a half liter of milk on a portable alcohol stove—and this they did every morning, buying the fresh rolls and butter at night and keeping them fresh by setting them out on the window sill. I was pleased and touched, but when I tried to thank them, Wague put on a refrigerated-Basque look. "We're not doing this for your sake," he said. "We're merely trying to keep down our expenses." And Kerf added: "It's not for your sake, it's for your baby's."

At night, on stage, during the well-regulated rough-and-tumble, I felt a careful arm being insinuated between my back and the table, helping my effort, which in appearance it was paralyzing.

Every night I bade farewell, more or less, to one of the happiest periods of my life, knowing well how I was going to regret it. But the cheerfulness, the purring contentment, the euphoria submerged everything and over me reigned the sweet animal innocence and unconcern arising from my added weight and the muffled appeals of the new life being formed within me.

The sixth month, the seventh month . . . Suitcases to pack, the departure for Limoges, a lightheartedness that disdained rest . . . But how heavy I became, especially at night! When climbing back up the road winding around the hill toward my lodgings, I let my two shepherd dogs, Bagheera and Son, haul me, by pulling on their two leashes. The first strawberries, the first roses . . . Can I regard my pregnancy as anything but one long festival? We forget the anguish of the labor pains but do not forget the long and singular festival; I have certainly not forgotten any detail. I especially remember how at odd hours sleep overwhelmed me and how I was seized again, as in my infancy, by the need to sleep on the ground, on the grass, on the sun-warmed hay. A unique and healthy craving.

When I had almost reached my term, I looked like a rat dragging a stolen egg. Feeling unwieldy, I sometimes was too tired out to lie down, and would sit in a comfortable armchair to exhaust the resources of a book or newspaper before going to bed. One night I had read a newspaper dry, skipping nothing, not even the racing forecasts or the name of the proprietor, and even going so far as to read the serial story. It was a high-class story, full of counts and marquises, and carriage horses that, noble beasts, only knew how to gallop and always seemed to be racing hell for leather:

Feverishly the Count paced up and down in his study. His black velvet smoking jacket accentuated his natural pallor. He pressed a bell; a footman appeared.

"Request Madame la Comtesse to rejoin me here," the Count commanded curtly.

After a short while, Yolande entered. She had lost none of her energy, but one guessed that she was feeling faint. The Count handed her the fatal letter which fluttered in his twitching fingers.

"Madame," he said through clenched teeth, "are you ready to reveal the name of the author of this letter?"

Yolande did not at once reply. Standing straight and white as a lily, she took a step forward and articulated, heroically:

"That goddamned swine, Ernest!"

I reread the last line to dispel the hallucination. Yes, I had read it correctly. Was it the vengeance of a printer who had been dismissed? A gross practical joke? The retort of the Countess gave me the strength to laugh and go to my bed, upon which the June wind had scattered, through the open french window, the flowers of an acacia.

Beneath the weight and beneath the fatigue, my long festival was not yet interrupted. I was borne on a shield of privileges and attentions. "Take this armchair! No, it's too low, take this other one instead." "I've made a strawberry tart for you." "Here is the pattern for the booties, you begin by casting on fifteen stitches . . ."

Neither fifteen nor ten. I would neither embroider a bib nor cut out a vest, nor gloat over white woolies. When I tried to visualize my little babe, I saw it naked, not all dressed up. It had to be content with a plain and practical English layette, without any frills or lace or smocking, and even that was bought—out of supersition —at the very last minute.

The "masculine pregnancy" did not lose all its rights; I was working on the last part of *L'Entrave*. The child and the novel were both rushing me, and the *Vie Parisienne*, which was serializing my unfinished novel, was catching up with me. The baby showed signs that it would win the race, and I screwed on the cap of my fountain pen.

My long festival came to an end on a cloudless day in July. The imperious child, on its way to its second life, maltreated a body no less eager than itself. In my little garden surrounded by other gardens, sheltered from the sun, provided with books and newspapers, I waited. I listened to the neighbors' cocks crowing and to the accelerated beating of my heart. When no one was looking, I took down the garden hose and gave the thirsty garden—which I would not be able to succor the next day or the following days—a token watering.

What followed . . .What followed doesn't matter, and I will give it no place here. What followed was the prolonged scream that issues from all women in childbed. If I like, this very day, to hear its echo, I need only open the window overlooking the Palais-Royal: from beneath the arcade rises the humble clamor of a neighbor woman who is pushing out into the world her sixth child. What followed was a restorative sleep and selfish appetite. But what followed was also, once, an effort to crawl toward me made by my bundled-up little larva that had been laid down for a moment on my bed. What animal perfection! The little creature guessed, she sensed the presence of my forbidden milk, and blindly struggled toward that blocked source. Never did I cry more brokenheartedly. Dreadful it is to ask in vain, but small is that hurt when compared with the pain of not giving . . .

What followed was the contemplation of a new person who had appeared in the house without coming from the outside. What followed, strange thing, was the proud and positive refusal of the Beauceron bitch ever to enter the room where the cradle stood. For a long time I tried to weaken this pensive enemy who wanted no rival in my heart. I even went so far as to hold out my sleeping baby girl, one little hand dangling, her naked feet pink as a rose, and say, "Look at her, lick her, take her, I give her to you," but the bitch consented only to a hurt silence and gazed at me briefly with golden eyes that were soon averted.

Did I bring sufficient love to my contemplation? I dare not state it with certainty. But I did have the habit—and still have—of marveling. I exercised it on the assemblage of wonders that constitute a newborn child. Her fingernails, transparent as the convex carapace of the pink prawn, and the tender soles of the feet that had come to us without touching the ground . . . The feathery lashes, lowered on the cheek, interposed between the terrestrial landscapes and the azure dream of the eye. . . . The little private parts, almond just barely incised, bivalve exactly shut, lip to lip . . .

But I did not call it love, this detailed admiration I devoted to my daughter, nor did I feel it so. I watched and waited. I studied the delightful authority of my young nurse, who treated the small body with its clenched fists as if it were a lump of dough, rolling and flouring it, holding it upside down with one hand . . . But such spectacles, which I had waited so many years to witness, did not stir me to emulation or give me a dazzled maternal feeling. I began to wonder when I would experience my second and most difficult metamorphosis. Finally I had to yield to the evidence: it would take more than one admonitory sign to change me into an ordinary mother. I would have to wait for the sum-total results of a series of admonitions and premonitions, both true and false: the secret and jealous rebellions, the feeling of pride at controlling a life of which I was the humble creditor, the sensation, rather treacherous, of giving a lesson in modesty to the other kind of love. As a matter of fact, I was not reassured on the score of my maternal endowments until language blossomed on the entrancing lips, until understanding, affection, and the spirit of mischief transformed a run-of-the-mill baby into a girl, and the girl into my girl, my daughter.

In the competition between the book and the birth, it was the novel, thank God, which got the worst of it. Conscientiously I went back to work on the unfinished *L'Entrave,* but it could not recover from the blows dealt by the weak and triumphant infant. Please note, O my hypothetical readers, how skimped is that ending, how insufficient the corridor through which I wanted my pared-down heroes to pass. Observe, too, the empty tone of a conclusion in which those heroes do not believe, an ending like a subdominant chord— the cadence a musician would call plagal—too hurriedly struck.

Since then, I have tried to rewrite the ending of *L'Entrave,* but have never succeeded. Between the interruption of the work and its resumption, I had performed the laborious delectation of procreating. My jot of virility saved me from the danger to which the writer promoted to the status of happy and loving parent is exposed, a danger that can turn him into a mediocre author, thenceforth preferring the rewards of a visible and material growth: the cult of children, of plants, of breeding life in some form or other. An old boy of forty under the surface of the still young woman that I was, kept a sharp watch on the safety of a perhaps precious part of me.

When I was a young girl, if I ever happened to occupy myself with some needlework, Sido always shook her soothsayer's head and commented, "You will never look like anything but a boy who is sewing." She would now have said, "You will never be anything but a writer who gave birth to a child," for she would not have failed to see the accidental character of my maternity.

HB

✿✿ Bel-Gazou

At the sea

I have watched and respected the solitude of a child sent to spend the whole summer by the sea, and the autumn and winter in a country of hills and chestnut woods. Both so entirely satisfied her that I was a little jealous of them, especially of the sea, which captivates all new creatures, who take to her as though they had known her before.

For a long time the child depended on me alone to contrive the necklace of chestnuts, the whistle of grass or bark, the pipe made out of an acorn cup, and the rattle that needs half a walnut shell, an elastic thread and a match, which I then put into her childish, still clumsy hands. But how could I compete with the first sea horse? And what, when it really came to it, did I know of the crab, and the edible crab, and the seaweed with floats? How could any treasure of knowledge that we might bring equal those which the wave casts at the feet of our child? He is already on familiar terms with the sea while we are still uneasy with her. He christens the eggs of the cuttlefish "grapes," calls the barbels of the sea dace "front paws," and laughs at the dab's tricks of mimicry: "There's another sole pretending to be sand and thinking I don't see him!" Before long it will be he who teaches us to look. If our aim is to guide his eyes and widen their field of vision, it is important not to be in a hurry and to make as few mistakes as possible. There are miracles enough, but we are not always worthy of revealing their splendors to a child.

I have not forgotten how I used to take a child every year to the sea, as to a maternal element better fitted than I to teach, ripen, and perfect the mind and body which I had merely rough-hewn.

EMCC

The lighted room

> "Not a drop of lamp oil,
> Not a drop of pet-rol,
> Not an inch of can-dle,
> Oh-what-mis-er-y!"

Hopping from one foot to the other and singing as loud as she can, Bel-Gazou is propagating the expression of the sad truth. It is a fact: there's a dearth of lamp oil at Brive and at Varets, petrol has vanished, candles cost four francs twenty-five the pound, and are becoming scarce . . .

> "Not a drop of lamp oil,
> Not a drop of pet-rol" . . .

Bel-Gazou, bathed in sunlight, ironically proclaims the general bereavement of artificial lights. June is ending, and she is tanned like a Breton fisherman. My nose, caught with a sunburn, is peeling, while her nose is syncretized with her cheeks by colors borrowed from bronzes, ceramics, glossy fruit, and I am envious. Her bare gypsy feet thud upon the flagstones and on the old parquet. A white canvas hat flops from an extended hand or is tossed and falls on the dog's head or sails off to perch in a tree; Bel-Gazou needs no covering other than her chestnut hair, cut straight above her brows and at the nape.

"Oh-what-mis-er-y!
  Oh-what-mis-er-y!"

She bounds off, a blaze of red and white in her striped sailor's jersey, and dives into the house, suddenly swallowed by the shadows.

Noon. A midday without a cloud or a breeze, a midday that swells the worm-eaten woodwork, fades the rose twining among the iron grillwork at the window, settles down the birds. Sunlight stabs the library from one wall to the other and nails on one panel the horned shadow of the araucaria tree. The bees nesting in the wall are working with innocent frenzy and weave a thread of gold as they fly about the room, thudding against a window, plundering the pink foxglove standing in a tall vase, whipping against my cheek and against Bel-Gazou's cheek, but without stinging anyone at all.

Until seven o'clock, the summer day will triumph over the thickness of the walls, the depth of the oblique embrasures. In declining, the sun will transform the plates hanging on the wall into so many mirrors to reflect his glory. But after seven o'clock the sun will leave this big piece of open sky stretched in front of us and will fall behind the poplars at first, then behind a tower . . . We will pull some furniture out on the balcony—the reading table, the armchair, and Bel-Gazou's campstool—and I will count on another good hour, still, of daylight. When a coolness rises from the valley, barely perceptible at first, felt only by the nostrils and the lips, ignored by the coarse surfaces of the skin, I will raise my head, astonished to find the page of the book that was pink awhile ago in the sunset light is now turning periwinkle blue.

It shall not yet be night, no, no, not yet!

Pulling up toward the french window the cloth-covered little table, Bel-Gazou and I will dine here together—"Bel-Gazou, one doesn't sketch alleys in the spinach with one's fork!" "Bel-Gazou, I saw you put the salt spoon in your pocket!"—we will dine without either lamp or candle. But when Bel-Gazou jumps down from her chair and says her good night, which begins so ceremoniously and ends so tenderly, I will really have to yield to the obvious: dark is the doorway of the salon, dark the vestibule; only Bel-Gazou, who goes everywhere like a young lynx, can unlatch the doors, elude the sculptured corners, find the box of matches in her bedroom. I hear her voice calling:

"Nursie-dear!"

And the banging of her door sequesters me in the shadows. Oh! I am well aware that, if I wished, I could allow myself the luxury of lighting the two double candlesticks, or even that wonderful lamp into which they pour, drop by drop, the small amount of paraffin available . . . The four candles are going to struggle against the darkness held captive beneath the painted beams, and will not win the battle. The flame of the low lamp and its halo will not be able to bore a hole into the walls through this dense cube of night. Phantoms are not what my weak eyes fear; what oppresses me is the certainty that no one wanders here, the certainty that neither tonight nor tomorrow night will the step of the master of this household weigh upon the thin old strips of the squeaky parquet flooring. To one who waits, no night is short.

But before capitulating to the night, I think about a certain bedroom, a room outside whose door I will sit, my head pressed against the wooden panel. Behind the door, Bel-Gazou is already in bed. Nursie-dear has taken away the only candle and is busying herself with her nightly chores before retiring. For a half hour, Bel-Gazou has permission to stay awake. And alone in her dark room, without even a night light, she raises her voice in imperious song, the song of a nightingale of darkness. Some chit-chat in English follows, some reprimands in the Limousin patois, then snatches of songs, improvisations on a theme she adores: *"Viens, Noël, viens!"* and "Where are you going, my pretty maid?" The voice is brilliant; the accent is now gentle, now despotic; between remarks and between songs, there is laughter . . . O cascades of silver on white gravel, O ascending rockets that light up in the instant of falling, ascending scales of which the highest note is like a torch, like spangles, like cornflowers of cut crystal—behind that door, in that dark room is my last treasure of light: the voice, the laughter of Bel-Gazou.

. . . .

Yesterday's storm has beaten down the green maize, gorged the river, and here and there has flattened the rye. At the late hour of my arrival, there remained nothing of the tempest but the gurgling rivulets in the park, the red and softened ruts of the road, and at the foot of the towers some fragments of slate and glass. A wind charged with perfumes had already dried the ragged cloak of the century-old jasmin against the wall of the terrace.

Now the morning promises us a cloudless Limousin summer day; the breeze of the upper air scarcely touches the treetops; the burning sun reddens Bel-Gazou's shoulders beneath the muslin sleeves, her bare arms and sandaled feet. The weather is fair, and I have Bel-Gazou's hand in mine.

Bel-Gazou, fruit of the Limousin land! Four summers, three winters have painted her with the colors of this part of France. She is as dark and glossy as an October apple, as a terra-cotta jar, her short straight hair is fine as corn silk, and in her eyes, neither green nor gray nor brown, lights play that are brown, green, gray, the silvery gray of the chestnut tree's trunk, or of a shaded spring . . .

I regard, in my pale hand that has come from Paris, the vigorous color of her childish hand. She has the hand of a laborer, and I considerately caress, in its palm, the small calluses that were earned from the spade and the rake, from the handles of the wheelbarrow. Oh, the pretty hand! With its skin dry and a bit cracked from the cold water and the wind, it suits this authoritative little girl who knows her realm and treads her land like a barefooted princess.

"Where are you taking me, Bel-Gazou? Are we going to the farm?"

Bel-Gazou, at times sparing of words, replies with a nod. Sometimes, in spite of the seriousness of her mission, she gives a sudden leap, as lambs do. She is dressed in a red bathing suit, faded and shrunken from laundering, which reveals—very touching on that sexless little body—the most graceful and rounded feminine shoulders in the world.

A blindworm, slow and swollen, crosses the road.

"Ay! Look out!" Bel-Gazou exclaims with the voice of a carter, giving it a nudge with her foot. Then she flashes me a sidelong glance. She knows that I am preoccupied with itemizing on her everything that six months have brought in my absence, everything of strength and beauty and novelty to a little four-year-old girl. She knows that I am containing my emotion, she knows that I admire her and will not tell her so. But I am truly afraid that, thanks to her fresh instinct and her savage-keen senses, Bel-Gazou must know me better than I know her. She parades for me—and oh, how soon I am dazzled! Last night she dragged my valise, punished a puppy that bared its teeth at me, and after dinner brought me a glass of cassis with a grace and an accent that were typically Limousin:

"Just a wee drop, eh?"

We enter the woods. The ancient trees, whose branches meet over the pathway, have imprisoned the heat, the dampness, and the obscurity of last night's storm. In the air protected from the wind hover the scents of mushrooms, of linden, of flowering chestnuts and of herb Robert, that dwarf geranium which breaks at the touch of a bird's wing and exudes, beneath the light foot of an insect, a sickening odor.

"Bel-Gazou, in your bathing suit here in the woods, you look like a goldfish at the bottom of some green water. Bel-Gazou, you also look like Little Red Ridinghood, you know, the Little Red Ridinghood who was taking a pot of butter and a pastry to her grandmother?"

"A pastry! What kind of pastry?"

"Oh, ah, a *millefeuille* . . ."

The hard little hand leaves mine and slaps a bare thigh.

"A *millefeuille* pastry! And didn't anyone tell the mayor?"

"The mayor? Why?"

"They should have told the mayor!"

Bel-Gazou points toward the brown roof tiles of a village visible through the branches.

"The mayor down there! Because pastry is forbidden, on account of the war!"

"But . . ."

"And the mayor, he'd have gone to Red Ridinghood and he'd have said: 'Monsieur, I am requisi . . . requisitioning your pastry! It's not allowed to use flour to make pastry during the war! And you must pay a thousand-sous fine! For that's the way it is!' "

"But see here, Bel-Gazou, the Red Ridinghood story is very old. At that time there was no war!"

"No war? Oh? Why was there no war?"

The charming nose lowers, then tilts up, the little hand catches mine again, but Bel-Gazou's slowed footsteps and a bound, two hesitant bounds of a young goat bespeak doubt and helplessness before a mystery: "No war?" It's true, she cannot imagine . . . In August, 1914, she was twelve months old . . .

HB

The hollow nut

Three shells like flower petals, white, nacreous, and transparent as the rosy snow that flutters down from the apple trees; two limpets, like Tonkinese hats with converging black rays on a yellow ground; something that looks like a lumpy, cartilaginous potato, inanimate but concealing a mysterious force that squirts, when it is squeezed, a crystal jet of salt water; a broken knife, a stump of pencil, a string of blue beads, and a book of transfers soaked by the sea; a small pink handkerchief, very dirty. . . . That is all. Bel-Gazou has completed the inventory of her left-hand pocket. She admires the mother-of-pearl petals, then drops them and crushes them under her *espadrille*. The hydraulic potato, the limpets, and the transfers earn no better fate. Bel-Gazou retains only the knife, the pencil, and the string of beads, all of which, like the handkerchief, are in constant use.

Her right-hand pocket contains fragments of that pinkish limestone that her parents, heaven knows why, name lithothamnium, when it is so simple to call it coral. "But it isn't coral, Bel-Gazou." Not coral? What do they know about it, poor wretches? Fragments, then, of lithothamnium, and a hollow nut, with a hole bored in it by the emerging maggot. There isn't a single nut tree within three miles along the coast. The hollow nut, found on the beach, came there on the crest of a wave, from where? "From the other side of the world," affirms Bel-Gazou. "And it's very ancient, you know. You can see that by its rare wood. It's a rosewood nut, like Mother's little desk."

With the nut glued to her ear, she listens. "It sings. It says: 'Hu-u-u . . .'"

She listens, her mouth slightly open, her lifted eyebrows touching her fringe of straight hair. Standing thus motionless, and as though alienated by her preoccupation, she seems almost ageless. She stares at the familiar horizon of her holidays without seeing it. From the ruins of a thatched hut, deserted by the customs officer, Bel-Gazou's view embraces, on her right hand the Pointe-du-Nez, yellow with lichens, streaked with the bluish purple of a belt of mussels which the low tide leaves exposed; in the center a wedge of sea, blue as new steel, thrust like an axehead into the coast. On the left, an untidy privet hedge in full bloom, whose oversweet almond scent fills the air, while the frenzied little feet of the bees destroy its flowers. The dry sea meadow runs up as far as the hut and its slope hides the shore where her parents and friends lie limply baking on the sand. Presently, the entire family will enquire of Bel-Gazou: "But where were you? Why didn't you come down to the shore?" Bel-Gazou cannot understand this bay mania. Why the shore, always the shore, and nothing but the shore? The hut is just as interesting as that insipid sand, and there is the damp spinney, and the soapy water of the washhouse, and the field of lucerne as well as the shade of the fig tree. Grown-up people are so constituted that one might spend a lifetime explaining to them—and all to no purpose. So it is with the hollow nut: "What's the use of that old nut?" Wiser far to hold one's tongue, and to hide, sometimes in a pocket and sometimes in an empty vase or knotted in a handkerchief, the nut which a moment, impossible to foresee, will divest of all its virtue, but which meanwhile sings in Bel-Gazou's ear the song that holds her motionless as though she had taken root.

"I can see it! I can see the song! It's as thin as a hair, as thin as a blade of grass!"

Next year, Bel-Gazou will be past nine years old. She will have ceased to proclaim those inspired truths that confound her pedagogues. Each day carries her further from that first stage of her life, so full, so wise, so perpetually mistrustful, so loftily disdainful of experience, of good advice, and humdrum wisdom. Next year, she will come back to the sands that gild her, to the salt butter and the foaming cider. She will find again her dilapidated hut, and her citified feet will once more acquire their natural horny soles, slowly toughened on the flints and ridges of the rough ground. But she may well fail to find again her childish subtlety and the keenness of her senses that can taste a scent, feel a color, and see—"thin as a hair, thin as a blade of grass"—the cadence of an imaginary song.

UVT/EMCC

The sempstress

"Do you mean to say your daughter is nine years old," said a friend, "and she doesn't know how to sew? She really must learn to sew. In bad weather sewing is a better occupation for a child of that age than reading storybooks."

"Nine years old? And she can't sew?" said another friend. "When she was eight, my daughter embroidered this tray cloth for me, look at it. . . . Oh! I don't say it's fine needlework, but it's nicely done all the same. Nowadays my daughter cuts out her own underclothes. I can't bear anyone in my house to mend holes with pins!"

I meekly poured all this domestic wisdom over Bel-Gazou.

"You're nine years old and you don't know how to sew? You really must learn to sew . . ."

Flouting truth, I even added: "When I was eight years old, I remember I embroidered a tray cloth. . . . Oh! It wasn't fine needlework, I daresay . . . And then, in bad weather . . ."

She has therefore learned to sew. And although—with one bare sunburned leg tucked beneath her, and her body at ease in its bathing suit—she looks more like a fisherboy mending a net than an industrious little girl, she seems to experience no boyish repugnance. Her hands, stained the color of tobacco juice by sun and sea, hem in a way that seems against nature; their version of the simple running stitch resembles the zigzag dotted lines of a road map, but she buttonholes and scallops with elegance and is severely critical of the embroidery of others.

She sews and kindly keeps me company if rain blurs the horizon of the sea. She also sews during the torrid hour when the spindle bushes gather their circles of shadow directly under them. Moreover, it sometimes happens that a quarter of an hour before dinner, black in her white dress—"Bel-Gazou! your hands and frock are clean, and don't forget it!"—she sits solemnly down with a square of material between her fingers. Then my friends applaud: "Just look at her! Isn't she good? That's right! Your mother must be pleased!"

He mother says nothing—great joys must be controlled. But ought one to feign them? I shall speak the truth: I don't much like my daughter sewing.

When she reads, she returns all bewildered and with flaming cheeks from the island where the chestful of precious stones is hidden, from the dismal castle where a fair-haired orphan child is persecuted. She is soaking up a tested and time-honored poison whose effects have long been familiar. If she draws, or colors pictures, a semi-articulate song issues from her, unceasing as the hum of bees around the privet. It is the same as the buzzing of flies as they work, the slow waltz of the house painter, the refrain of the spinner at her wheel. But Bel-Gazou is silent when she sews, silent for hours on end, with her mouth firmly closed, concealing her large, new-cut incisors that bite into the moist heart of a fruit like little saw-edged blades. She is silent, and she—why not write down the word that frightens me—she is thinking.

A new evil? A torment that I had not foreseen? Sitting in a grassy dell, or half buried in hot sand and gazing out to sea, she is thinking, as well I know. She thinks rapidly when she is listening, with a well-bred pretense of discretion, to remarks imprudently ex-changed above her head. But it would seem that with this needle play she has discovered the perfect means of adventuring, stitch by stitch, point by point, along a road of risks and temptations. Silence . . . the hand armed with the steel dart moves back and forth. Nothing will stop the unchecked little explorer. At what moment must I utter the "Halt!" that will brutally arrest her in full flight? Oh, for those young embroiderers of bygone days, sitting on a hard little stool in the shelter of their mother's ample skirts! Maternal authority kept them there for years and years, never rising except to change the skein of silk, or to elope with a stranger. Think of Philomène de Watteville and her canvas on which she embroidered the loss and the despair of Albert Savarus. . . .

"What are you thinking about, Bel-Gazou?"

"Nothing, Mother. I'm counting my stitches."

Silence. The needle pierces the material. A coarse trail of chain stitch follows very unevenly in its wake. Silence. . . .

"Mother?"

"Darling?"

"Is it only when people are married that a man can put his arm around a lady's waist?"

"Yes. . . . No. . . . It depends. If they are very good friends and have known each other a long time, you understand . . . As I said before: it depends. Why do you want to know?"

"For no particular reason, Mother."

Two stitches, ten misshapen chain stitches.

"Mother? Is Madame X. married?"

"She has been. She is divorced."

"I see. And Monsieur F., is he married?"

"Why, of course he is; you know that."

"Oh! Yes. . . . Then it's all right if one of the two is married?"

"What is all right?"

"To depend."

"One doesn't say 'to depend.' "

"But you said just now that it depended."

"But what has it got to do with you? Is it any concern of yours?"

"No, Mother."

I let it drop. I feel inadequate, self-conscious, displeased with myself. I should have answered differently and I could not think what to say.

Bel-Gazou also drops the subject; she sews. But she pays little attention to her sewing, overlaying it with pictures, associations of names and people, all the results of patient observation. A little later will come other curiosities, other questions, and especially other silences. Would to God that Bel-Gazou were the bewildered and simple child who questions crudely, open-eyed! But she is too near the truth, and too natural not to know, as a birthright, that all nature hesitates before that most majestic and most disturbing of instincts, and that it is wise to tremble, to be silent, and to lie when one draws near to it.

UVT/EMCC

The watchman

SUNDAY. This morning the children have an odd look on their faces. I've seen them look like this before, when they were organizing some theatrical production in the attic, with costumes, masks, shrouds, and dragging chains, that was their play, *Le Revenant de la commanderie*—a ghostly lucubration that cost them a week of fever, night frights, and furry tongues, so excited did they get with their own phantoms. But that is an old story. Bertrand is now eighteen and plans, as is suitable at his age, to reform the finances of Europe; Renaud, now over fourteen, has no other interest but to take apart and put together again motorcar engines; and Bel-Gazou, this year, asks me questions of desolating triteness: "When we go back to Paris, can I wear stockings? In Paris, can I have a hat? In Paris, will you curl my hair on Sundays?"

No matter, I find all three of them acting strange and disposed to go off in corners and talk in low voices.

MONDAY. The children don't look at all well this morning, and so I question them.

"I say, what's wrong with you youngsters?"

"Nothing at all, Tante Colette!" exclaim my stepsons.

"Nothing at all, Mamma!" exclaims Bel-Gazou.

A fine chorus—and certainly a well-organized fib. The thing is becoming serious, all the more so since I overheard the two boys, at dusk, behind the tennis court, engaged in this bit of dialogue:

"I tell you, old man, it didn't stop from midnight to three in the morning."

"Who are you telling that to, for goodness' sake! I didn't shut an eye, it kept it up from midnight to four this morning. It went 'poom . . . poom . . . poom!' Like that, slowly, as if with bare feet, but heavy, heavy . . ."

They glimpsed me and rushed down upon me like two male falcons, with laughter, with white and red balls, with a studied and noisy thoughtlessness. I will learn nothing today.

WEDNESDAY. When last night toward eleven o'clock I went through Bel-Gazou's bedroom to reach mine, she was not yet asleep. She was lying on her back, her arms at her side, and her dark eyes beneath the fringe of her hair were moving. A warm August moon, crescent, softly swayed the shadow of the magnolia on the parquet floor and the white bed gave off a bluish light.

"You're not asleep?"

"No, Mamma."

"What are you thinking about, all alone like this?"

"I'm listening."

"For goodness' sake, to what?"

"Nothing, Mamma."

At that very second I heard, distinctly, the sound of a heavy footstep, and not shod, on the upper floor. The upper floor is a long attic where no one sleeps, where no one, after nightfall, has occasion to go, and which leads to the top of the most ancient tower. My daughter's hand, which I squeezed, contracted in mine.

Two mice passed in the wall, playing and emitting birdlike cries.

"Are you afraid of mice now?"

"No, Mamma."

Above us, the footsteps sounded again, and in spite of myself I put the question, "Why, who can be walking up there?"

Bel-Gazou did not reply, and this stubborn silence was unpleasant.

"So you hear something?"

"Yes, Mamma."

" 'Yes, Mamma!' Is that all you can think of to say?"

The child suddenly burst into tears and sat up in bed.

"It's not my fault, Mamma. *He* walks like that every night."

"Who?"

"The footsteps."

"The footsteps of whom?"

"Of no one."

"Heavens, how stupid children are! Here you are again, making a fuss over nothing, you and your brothers! Is this the nonsense you hide in corners to discuss? Well now, I'm going upstairs. Yes, I'm going to let you hear some footsteps overhead!"

On the topmost landing, clusters of flies clinging to the beams whirred like a fire in the chimney as I passed with my lamp, which a gust of air put out the minute I opened the garret door. But there was no need of a lamp in these garret regions with their tall dormer windows where the moonlight entered by milky sheets spread out on the floor. The midnight countryside shimmered as far as the eye could see, the hills embossed with silver, the shallow valleys ashymauve, watered in the lowest of the meadows by a river of glittering fog which screened the moonlight . . . A little sparrow owl imitated the cat in a tree, and the cat replied to him. But nothing was walking in the garret beneath the forest of crisscrossed beams. I waited a long while, breathing in the fleeting nocturnal coolness, the odor of a granary which always hovers in a garret, then went downstairs again. Bel-Gazou, worn out, was sleeping.

SATURDAY. I have been listening every night since Wednesday. Someone does walk up there, sometimes at midnight, sometimes toward three o'clock. Tonight I climbed up and down the stairs four times. To no purpose. At lunchtime I forced the youngsters to speak out. Anyway, they have reached the limit with their hocus-pocus.

"Children, you must help me clear up a mystery. We're bound to be enormously amused—even Bertrand, who has lost all his illusions. Just imagine! I've been hearing, every night, someone walking above Bel-Gazou's room . . ."

They exploded, all at once.

"I know, I know!" Renaud exclaims. "It's the Commander in armor, who came back to earth once before, in Grandfather's time. Page told me all about it and . . ."

"What a farce!" said Bertrand laconically. "The truth is that isolated and collective instances of hallucination have occurred here, ever since the Holy Virgin, in a blue sash and drawn by four white horses, suddenly appeared in front of Guitras and told him . . ."

"She didn't *tell* him anything!" squealed Bel-Gazou. "She *wrote* to him!"

"And sent the letter by the post?" sneered Renaud. "That's childish!"

"And your Commander isn't childish?" said Bertrand.

"Excuse me!" retorted Renaud, flushing red. "The Commander is a family tradition. Your Virgin, that's a piece of village folklore, the kind you hear everywhere . . ."

"Now, now, children, have you finished? Can I put in a word? I know just one thing and it's this: in the garret there are sounds, unexplainable, of footsteps. I'm going to stand watch tomorrow night. Beast or man, we'll find out who is walking. And those who want to stand watch with me . . . Good. Adopted by a count of hands!"

SUNDAY. Sleepless night. Full moon. Nothing to report except the sound of footsteps heard behind the half-open door to the garret, but interrupted by Renaud, who, trigged out in a Henri II breastplate and a red bandana, dashed forward romantically shouting, "Stand back! Stand back!" We hoot at him and accuse him of having "spoiled everything."

"Strange," Bertrand remarks with crushing and reflective irony, "strange how anything fantastic can excite the mind of a boy, even though he grew up in British schools . . ."

"Eh, my lad," adds my girl in an unmistakably Limousin accent, "you must not say 'Stand back!' You must say, 'I'm going to give you a wallop!'"

TUESDAY. Last night the two boys and I stood watch, leaving Bel-Gazou asleep.

The moon at the full whitened from one end to the other a long track of light where the rats had left a few ears of nibbled maize. We kept ourselves in the darkness behind the half-open door and suffered boredom for a good half hour, watching the path of moonlight shift, become oblique, lick the lower part of the criss-crossed beams . . . Renaud touched my arm: someone was walking at the far end of the garret. A rat scampered off and climbed along a slanting beam, followed by its serpent tail. The footsteps, solemn-sounding, approached, and I tightened my arms around the necks of the two boys.

It approached, with a slow, muffled, yet incisive tread, which was echoed by the ancient floorboards. It entered, after a moment that seemed interminable, into the luminous path of moonlight. It was almost white, gigantic: the biggest nocturnal bird I have ever seen, a great horned owl, the kind we call "grand duke," taller than a wolfhound. He walked emphatically, lifting his feathered feet, his hard bird's talons, which gave off the sound of a human footstep. The top of his wings gave him the shoulders of a man, and two little feather horns that he raised or lowered trembled like grass in the gust of air from the dormer window. He stopped, puffed out his chest, and all the feathers of his magnificent face swelled out around a fine beak and the two golden pools of his eyes, bathed in moonlight. He turned away from us, showing his speckled white and pale yellow back. He must be quite old, I thought, this solitary and powerful creature. He resumed his parade march and interrupted it to do a kind of war dance, shaking his head from right to left, making fierce right-about turns, which no doubt threatened the rat that had eluded him. For a moment he apparently thought he had his prey, and he jostled the skeleton of a chair, shaking it as if it were a dead twig. He jumped with fury, fell back again, scraped the floor with his fanned-out tail. He had the mien of one used to command, and the majesty of a sorcerer.

No doubt he sensed our presence, for he turned toward us as if outraged. Unhurriedly he went to the window, half opened his angel wings, let out a kind of cooing sound, very low, a short incantation, pressed against the air, and melted into the night, taking on its color of snow and silver.

THURSDAY. The younger of the boys, at his desk, writes a long travel story. Title: "My experiences hunting the horned owl in eastern Africa." The elder boy has left on my worktable the beginning of "Stanzas":

A fluttering, a ponderous vision in the night,
Gray apparition, coming from the dark into the light.

Things have returned to normal.

HB

❧❧ World War I

Saint-Malo, August 1914

The war? Until the end of last month, it was nothing but a word, enormous, stretching across the pages of the lethargic newspapers of summer. The war? Yes, perhaps, very far away, on the other side of the world, but not here . . . How could anyone imagine that even the echo of a war could make its way through these rocky ramparts, forbiddingly wild, the wildness accentuating the quiet calm at the foot of the cliffs—the waves, the sparse dune grass, the sand embossed by the tiny claws of birds . . . ? This paradise was not made for war, but for our brief holidays, for our solitude. The reefs hidden beneath the sea are unfriendly to boats; the vigilant sparrow hawk has almost banished birds from these parts. Every day he climbs the sky and is slow to return to land; our field glasses discovered him on high, wings widespread and pressing against the wind, and his beautiful glowing eye did not gaze down at the earth . . .

Yet a war was on, there were signs of war. For instance, that Cancale fishwife who last month stopped gossiping with customers and no longer smiled but demanded her pay in silver and copper coins, refusing bank notes, and stood gazing out to sea as if expecting the arrival over that sea of a succession of days without bread or cider . . .

The war had come, and it was the grocery boy on a bicycle who relayed the news, to the merry tinkle of the bell, that food was getting scarce and that certain things should be stocked: sugar, salad oil, and paraffin.

The war was a fact. In Saint-Malo, where we ran to hear the news, a bolt fell from the blue just as we arrived: reserves had been called up.

How can I ever forget that hour? Four o'clock on a beautiful summer day at the seaside, the sky misted over, the golden-yellow ramparts of the old town facing the sea, which near the shore was green but on the horizon was blue—the children in red bathing suits leaving the beach for their teatime snack, and climbing the choked streets . . . And in the center of town, the uproar bursts forth all at once: alarm bell, drum, the shouts of the crowd, the crying of children . . . There is a press of people around the town drummer, who reads aloud the edict: no one listens to him because they know what he is announcing. Women leave the groups at a run, stopping short as if struck, then running again with a look on their faces that seems to say they have gone beyond some invisible boundary and have plunged into another world. A few of the women burst into tears, then as suddenly stop weeping and stand, openmouthed, to reflect. Some young lads grow pale and stare straight ahead like sleepwalkers. The car in which we are riding stops, wedged into the crowd, and the crowd congeals against the wheels. Some people climb up on it, the better to see and hear, then get down without even having noticed us, as if they had climbed a wall or a tree—in a few days, who will know whether this car is yours or mine? The details of that hour hurt me and are necessary, like the details of a dream that I would like both to leave and avidly to pursue. ·

A dream, a dream. More and more a dream, since the farther I go from town, the closer I come to the countryside, which is being swept by the startled wing of the tocsins. And these fields, these harvests, that drowsing sea are no more than a stage setting interposed between me and reality: the reality that is Paris, Paris where half of me lives, Paris which is perhaps blockaded now, Paris gray and suffocating beneath its August mist, full of shouts, fermenting with heat and fury, anguish and derring-do.

Will it be my longest evening of the war, the one I am spending here, waiting to leave, this evening when the dead calm drops the image of the purple cliffs down into the sea? All night long the sea is quiet, without a wrinkle, without a breath of life, imperceptibly swaying all the umbrellas of the crystal-blue jellyfish open in a milky phosphorescence . . .

HB

Paris: the wounded

Three o'clock . . . The beautiful glacial moon has left the sky, and two more hours will be needed to color the windows blue. It is the darkest time, and the quietest, in the college hospital ward. Beneath the dimmed electric lights the eight wounded men have gone to sleep. They are asleep, but not silent. Sleep liberates the moans they proudly repress during the day. The pleurisy patient whimpers regularly, in a sweet voice like a woman's. The man with the shattered jaw and eye says, from time to time, "Oh!" with an accent of dismay and disgust. A thin, fair-haired young man whose leg was amputated four days ago sprawls on his back, arms widespread, and his sleep seems to have renounced all signs of life. A bearded man with an arm in a plaster cast tries to find, sighing, the place in bed where he will suffer less. Is that a death rattle from that other man with the bandaged throat? No, he's snoring, half suffocated . . .

Since last night, they have only sampled crumbs of rest in the intervals of fever, thirst, lancing pain. One after another they have implored a glass of herb tea, hot grog or hot milk, a hypodermic, especially the hypodermic . . . And now there they are, these brave lads, vanquished by the long night. Miserable as they are, will they ever awake?

Yes, they will! When the sparrows cheep on the frozen white

lawn, the eight wounded men will also salute the red dawn with a sharper cry, a deeper sigh, a muffled oath in which life and laughter reappear. They are the scions of a stout race, which resuscitates and bounds up with the light. Sitting in his bed and smelling the aroma of coffee, the poor monster with the shattered, scarlet head will give me a wink with his single eye and will speak to me from his half mouth, banteringly:

"Admit it, I certainly have what could be called a ruddy mug!"

And he will demand his double ration of breakfast, alleging that liquid nourishment doesn't stick to the ribs.

Raising his heavy arm in plaster, the man in the next bed, a true Gaul whose humor is broad, will rejoice in Rabelaisian style, and the young fellow with the amputated leg, cadaverous, preoccupied with his stump, with the blond beard that is darkening his cheeks, with his future, poor handsome boy, will once more interrogate me.

"I say, tell me . . . Tell me how he was amputated, your father? Higher up than I am, wasn't it? And he could walk, couldn't he? And, I say, did he run? . . . Like a rabbit, you say? And it's true he found a girl who would marry him, all the same? Yes? A pretty girl? Is that so? What was she like, his wife? Tell me about her, will you?"

"How's The Head?"
"The Head is none the worse."

He is sitting on his bed, in one corner of the white room, and his eye follows us, bright and intelligent in the midst of the crisscrossed bandages, the miles and miles of bandages . . . He sighs hungrily at the passage of the odorous veal scallops and fried potatoes; his hearty countryman appetite despises the liquid nourishment which is the only nourishment his frightful wound will allow . . .

When he came to, after a long blackout, he had his face in a puddle of water. He told himself: "Well now, I'm not too badly hurt . . ." Then he noticed a quite big morsel of his tongue, all his teeth, and various other fragments of himself floating in the puddle.

And he told himself, "Yes, I'm not badly hurt." Slowly he got to his feet and began to suffer. Step after step he walked among the silent bodies and the groaning bodies, covering two kilometers, until he came to a village in ruins, where some of the inhabitants exclaimed in horror at sight of him:

"Oh, poor fellow! In what a state . . . But we can't give you first aid here, and our army is down there at X., twelve kilometers away!"

Mute, the wounded man walked the twelve kilometers. He could not say in how many hours. At X., he was led to the commanding officer, and he wrote on a piece of paper: "Sir, will you be so kind as to lend me your revolver." And he signed.

"Never! Not on your life!" the officer exclaimed. "They'll fix you up, my boy, they'll cure you, you'll be amazed! Where do you come from?"

The reply was written.

"Why, that's twelve kilometers from here! How does it happen you didn't meet any ambulances? Didn't you meet any?"

"Yes, several," wrote The Head.

"And they didn't see you?"

"Yes, sir," The Head wrote calmly. "But the ones they were picking up were so much worse off than I was, for I could still walk. And so *I didn't believe I ought to ask them to pick me up.*"

HB

Verdun, December–January 1915

It's ended, that beautiful terrified journey. Here I am—and I wonder for how long?—hidden in Verdun. A fake name, borrowed identity papers were not enough to protect me, during the thirteen hours of the trip, from the new-style gendarme that the war has made shrewd, jeering, indiscreet, or from the bossy railway superintendent at the Châlons station. En route, I ran into every possible peril. There was the volunteer nurse, appointed to meet the trainloads of wounded, she who happened to know me. "Imagine, you here!" she exclaimed. Then there was the ex-journalist in uniform who inquired: "Is your husband all right? Have you come to be with him?" Besides these, there was the army medical officer who "understood what was up," and gave me winks that would have been enough to alert a track watchman . . . The least troublesome hours were those of the "black train," when we ran with all lights out between Châlons and Verdun, going slowly, slowly, as if the train were groping its way, repressing its asthma and its whistle. Long hours? Yes, perhaps, because of my impatience to arrive, but full and anxious hours, alight with the aurora borealis of an incessant cannonading, a rosy glimmer palpitating on the horizon toward the northeast.

A magnificent thunder accompanied it, continuous, sustained, which did not hurt the ear but sounded throughout one's body, in the limbs, the stomach, the head; and sometimes on the horizon a flare sprayed its floral bouquet and splintered the night.

No one slept or talked until the wintry daybreak and our arrival at Verdun. And how I envied, in my disguise, those merchants of Verdun who passed the gendarme with a "How goes it?" and a handshake.

No matter. I have arrived, and I will try to remain here, a voluntary prisoner. The nearby cannonading does not roar alone: a coke fire crackles and flames, and my accomplices—a noncommissioned officer the color of ripe wheat, his young wife brown as a chestnut, who are letting me stay in their house—and their laughter, over our coffee with condensed milk. Provided that I don't go out of doors, that I don't approach the windows—"Beware of the medical officers billeted on the other side of the street!"—all will be well. The windowpanes emit a shrill "ee-eee" when the cannonading becomes more intense and obliges us to raise our voices, and a winter sunshine warns of freezing weather to come.

I am wild to hear about everything, to shudder, and to hope. I put questions.

"What's new?"

The noncommissioned officer, who is in the Quartermaster Department, frowns and pulls at his Vercingetorix mustache.

"New? Well, I can tell you the upholsterer is a swine!"

"The . . ."

"The upholsterer, that's right. The butter the upholsterer sells is margarine!"

"Yes . . . and what else?"

"Well, there's the piano merchant. He's just received a marvelous shipment of sardines. I'm hurrying over to his store on my way to look at our horses . . ."

"Yes, yes, and what else?"

"Why," exclaims the brown-haired young woman, "there's this shameful thing of making us pay three sous for one leek! But the sub-prefect is outraged, and he's going to get a stock of things put in the sub-prefecture—rice, macaroni, potatoes—and then we'll see if the grocers will still have the nerve to . . ."

"Yes, yes, yes! But please, what about the war?"

"The war?"

Vercingetorix looks at me reflectively, his innocent blue eyes wide open. I lose patience.

"The war, in the name of God, yes! What people are saying, what people are reading, what you are doing!"

The blue eyes narrow with laughter.

"Oh yes, of course, the war! Well, it still goes on, it keeps going, it's going very well, don't worry."

I deserved that reply from a calm and courageous man. It did not take me a week to realize that here in Verdun, chock-a-block full of troops, with the railway its unique supply line, war becomes a habit, the inseparable cataclysm of life, as natural as thunder and rainstorms; but the danger, the real danger, is that one may soon not be able to eat. Food comes first, everything else takes second place: the stationer sells sausages, the sewing woman sells potatoes. The piano merchant stacks a thousand tins of sardines and mackerel on his tired pianos that he used to rent out; but butter is a luxurious·

rarity, a can of condensed milk a precious object, and vegetables exist only for the fortunate of this world . . .

Eat, eat, eat. Well, yes, one must eat. The freezing weather nips, the East wind makes those who spend the nights out of doors ravenous. The important thing is to keep the blood hot in our veins, although it may at any time pour out in floods, immeasurable floods. Great courage goes with a great appetite, and the stomachs of the people in Verdun are not stomachs that are shrunken by fear.

Some German prisoners passed down the rue d'Antouard. I saw them, between the blades of my Persian blinds, which are always closed. Some civilians were standing in their doorways watching them go by, with a bored look. Their faces yellowed with fatigue and dirt, the prisoners marched in a slovenly way, many of them showing only unconcern and relief from tension, as though saying, "Good! It's over with, for us!" A German soldier, puny but high-spirited, stuck his tongue out at a woman as he passed.

Between seven and eight in the morning and between two and three in the afternoon, the German planes punctually come to drop bombs. They fall just about everywhere, without causing much damage or casualties. But the bombing and the response of our fighter planes and antiaircraft guns, my, what a din it makes! All the same, the neighbor across the street mourns her garden that was ravaged yesterday and her shed that was smashed. Also, a roof of the administration building quite near here, at the foot of the fortress, now yawns open to the sky. The noncommissioned officer, Vercingetorix, swears like a pagan against those *Aviatik,* as he calls them, "that try to keep us from taking care of our horses!"

His wife sets me an example of complete imprudence and comes home today under a veritable hail of shrapnel that didn't touch her.

"Oh, what a nuisance, what a nuisance!" she exclaims. "Just imagine, I had to take shelter under the porte-cochere of the X. family, and we're not on speaking terms!"

In the evening, toward nine or ten o'clock, I risk taking a furtive walk for my health, my legs trembling in fear of encountering a patrol. Not a street light, not a sound, not a glimmer behind the closed shutters or between the crisscrossed window curtains. But sometimes a muffled cry, the fleeing of slippered little feet, a panting: I have blindly bumped into one of those veiled and cloistered wives, one of the voluntary prisoners Verdun hides, she, too, out for a breath of night air. People know about these wives and mistresses, returned to an Oriental way of life; if you name them in a low voice, it is by no means a betrayal. People mention one of the women, they say she has not crossed the threshold of her jail for seven months or seen a human face except that of the man she loves. They say she is an occasional writer, and that she is the happiest of women . . .

A rather gloomy level pathway beside the canal. But a warm sun that is melting the frost and the cloudless sky give a rosy hue to the fortress and the archbishop's palace and make the water blue. We risk this walk in broad daylight, despite all marital interdictions and the dangers of what my hostess calls "the half-past-two airplanes."

The towpath is lined at intervals with sentinels and with bare poplars, and on the moored canal boats from Belgium, flaxen-haired children play. The spongy fields steam, and the thaw has swollen the streams. A regular peal of thunder scans our steps; it is one of those days when the people of Verdun say gravely, "They're getting a pounding in the Argonne."

"Do you see those dance halls stuck right in the fields?" asks my companion. "You can't imagine what fun we had in them last summer . . ."

A sharp detonation, a muffled din which comes down from the upper air, interrupts her.

"That's one of *theirs*," she says. "The .75's are firing at it . . . Look, there's the *Aviatik!*"

While I can still hear nothing but the humming of the engine, my Verdun hostess's sharp eyes have already found on the clear blue of the sky the minuscule pigeon which grows bigger and leaves the horizon; here it is, borne by two convex wings, new, gleaming; it circles the town, rises, seems to meditate, hesitates . . . Five white bouquets blossom in a wreath around it, five pompons of immaculate smoke which mark, suspended in the windless sky, the point where our antiaircraft shells are exploding—five, then seven, and their concerted blasts reach our ears later still . . .

"Oh, here come some of ours!" my companion exclaims.

And from a nearby post rise, with the buzzing of a furious wasp, two biplanes, two others rushing up from the town. They climb the sky in spirals, show their light bellies in the sunshine, the tricolor on their tails, their flat surfaces . . . They are buzzards, male falcons, slender swallows, and at a great distance, merely flies . . .

"Another German!"

"Yes! And another, and another!"

It took only a few seconds to fill that sky, vast and empty just now, with a flight of enemy wings. How many of them will the east, black with pines and rolling hills, hurl at us? One would say that the vertiginous blue space was barely big enough to hold them; they circle, return as suddenly as a bird striking the windowpane, and our guns fill the azure with white roses . . .

"Those over there are ours! There's going to be an air battle!"

"They are enemy planes. No. At this distance I can't distinguish . . ."

We shout, for the tumult has increased, necessary to the beauty of the aerial chase. The guns of the town and of the fortress bay like a pack of hounds, deep bass some of them; the others sharp, furious barks. The magnificent pursuit is right over our heads . . .

"He's hit, he's hit! No, no . . . Oh, he's getting away . . ."

"Farther ahead, farther ahead!" my companion shouts, as if the gunners could hear her. "Can't you see that all your shells are falling short?"

We run, unconsciously following the planes, screaming, and it took the shouts of a company of fusiliers and their emphatic advice to make us seek shelter under an iron bridge. Shelter . . . But why?

We soon know the reason: a weird hailstorm has begun to pepper the canal at our feet, a hot hail that makes the water hiss. Who is hurling this boiling shrapnel at us? We had not thought of this. Excitedly watching the fighter planes, we had forgotten the sparks, the burning cinders that would fall from a battle of demigods contesting the rights to the upper airs.

Under the narrow iron bridge, we tensely wait. We hope for and imagine the finest issue of the combat: the fall, the sudden stripping off of all the curved wings, the planes spiraling down, defeated, to crash on the grassy bank . . . Nothing falls there but a bomb, and the soaked field drinks it up, covers it over without its exploding. It was one of the last projectiles, a wicked tapered seed, thrown out by the German who is vanishing in the distance. The racing of a storm cloud is less rapid than his magical flight: the white smoke of the shells still floats up there where the enemy planes are now only a dotted line, far off, at the bottom of the sky swept clean. The baying of the guns is now intermittent; the fusiliers rejoice.

Returning toward the town, we find the first traces of the aerial bombardment: the trees along the promenade have undergone a brutal pruning, and in a freshly opened hole in the ground children are looking for shrapnel, babbling and scratching like chickens after a shower . . .

HB

Venice, 1915

Half past six on a morning in July. A pale sunshine forebodes a storm, and the level sea reflects some thunderheads, in gray, in oyster green. A day of the sirocco, then a starless night have warmed the flagstones of the Schiavoni and the marble balconies. The Church of the Redeemer appears to float, lifted above the sea like a mirage.

The night seemed long. Of her prewar night life Venice has kept only a whisper, a kind of breathing that one can distinguish by listening intently: a wave's lick of the tongue against a bridge, the creaking of a vessel's cable, the discreet departure toward dawn of a single gondola. The militarized *vaporetti* begin to drone later on, a little before that matutinal instant when, already swollen with heat, the air vibrates with the sudden roar of a cannon.

A second roar, and a third farther off. The magnificent echoes of the palaces fling back the sound toward the sea. Looking out of the window of the hotel, I search for the enemy plane: it is very high, it is crossing a narrow blue abyss between two clouds. A peaceable crowd of people, without making a sound, lean on the marble balustrade of the bridge; slender Venetian women point upward toward the plane, the black fringes of their shawls dangling like seaweed from their outstretched arms. To the delight of the eyes, these dark-clad women mingle with some sailors all in white. There is no haste, no fright, and no uproar other than the menacing miauling of the sirens. Some motorboats dart forth, streaking the sea.

A cannon booms quite near, fired from the Island of the Redeemer, shakes the air, the wall hangings, the glassware, strikes the lungs and the eardrums a blow that is almost agreeable. It is the "all clear" signal; the *Taube*[1] which threatened the statue of St. George on the church veers off, having dumped three bombs into the lagoon; it merely needed to see, high in the air, the French airplanes emerge from their hangars and spread their wings. One of them pursues it out to sea, and when it returns an hour later, the black Venetian women and the white sailors have gone back, the sailors to their post, the women to the cool damp shade of the narrow streets. The Sunday banners float above St. Mark's, fanning the burning and empty square. And the chambermaid who brings in the tea sums up the incident disdainfully in these brief and heroic terms:

"It's nothing. The enemy came. We drove him off."

HB

[1] A German war plane, from the word for pigeon.

Rome, 1915

Situated among palm trees, eternal oaks, and climbing roses, the hospital offered by the Queen Mother to the wounded Italians is a princely villa in a setting replete with pure air, bird song, bright sunlight, and leafy shadows. The gardens surrounding it shower down, even into the via Boncompagni, their palm leaves and magnolia petals. Nothing is lacking in this model hospital—nothing, except the wounded. Rome has not a single wounded man; until now, the war casualties have been kept away, the general desire being to keep Rome serene among her enclosed gardens plumed with fountains. How many able-bodied men there are in the streets, how many brand-new soldiers! Italy has not come to the end of her wealth of the living.

I had hoped to visit the first of the war wounded, but a necessary strictness forbids access to the front-line towns. No newspaper reporter, male or female, whether Italian, Allied, or neutral, can penetrate the zone of the armies. The same word, *Impossibile,* stops one and all alike, and nothing can shake a courtesy that does not leave room for argument. Therefore, I shall not see either Bologna bursting with troops, or Padua, or Mantua resuscitated and armed, like a warrior who has slept beneath his shield. Venice admits no traveler. And Rome knows nothing of the war other than the rumors its wall of steel cannot keep out.

I listen. I look at the men who tomorrow will leave for the front. They wear with ease the yellowish-green uniform. They do not have that look of being disguised, that self-consciousness—rather charming, moreover—of our own recruits. The reason is that here masculine beauty is in plentiful supply and these men could wear the toga as easily as the tunic with the colored collar and the kepi with its long, cambered visor.

A medical officer, in from the front, has seen some ambulances and feels nothing but joy over them, and patriotic pride.

"What a race ours is!" he says. "I examined a thousand sick or
wounded men, casualties of the war, and I didn't find a single trace
of enteritis or tuberculosis. And the wounded men we save get well
so rapidly."

Everywhere, along the alleyways of the Trastevere, in the
ditches of the Gianicolo, in the massive shadow of the Teatro Mar-
cello, which welds its enormous, smoke-blackened ruins to the low
houses of a piazza bright with lemons and tomatoes—everywhere a
younger generation swarms, adolescent sons and brothers of these
spirited soldiers. Often we feel like envying their exuberant poverty,
and their number gives pause. Impossible not to see them, for the
family custom, even among the well-to-do, is to make a place for the
child in a restaurant, at reunions, and on the afternoon strolls. Are
there many French husbands who would assume the responsibility,
as they do in Italy, of taking for a walk, of amusing and attending to
four or five youngsters throughout an entire Sunday, with the patience of a nurse, and when the youngest of the children is still unsteady on its feet? In Italy we are far from the French or English
custom of relegating the child to the nursery . . .

But it is in the poor streets that I like best to watch the swarms
of children in Rome. Sitting on the dark doorsteps, young mothers
are on display, covered and overrun with children, like tranquil
hound bitches who allow their progeniture to tumble and fight over
them even when they are already equipped with teeth. The loveliest
of the youngsters are the most serious, with their wealth of curly
hair and long lashes, their disdainful mouths above vivacious little
chins. As they grow older, these boys become the slender golden
fauns that have enchanted sculptors and painters; the little girls attain, at about fifteen, a perfection that draws all eyes. Moreover, they
submit to being admired, and it is the spectator who, embarrassed,
turns aside, unable to confront those calm faces that do not blush,
those downy lips that half smile and are prompt to put into words
what their rather unconcerned glance is reluctant to express. The
slender throat, the nape beneath the tresses are as pleasant to contemplate as a well-shaped vase, a polished column, a fruit perfected

in its form. The little girls are not unaware of it; they also know that five or six more years will metamorphose a slender nymph into a young matron. But they soon choose a love, a home, attach themselves and settle down like a plant, like an espaliered tree clinging to a wall, and all around them grow up other little fauns, other little nymphs whose number they do not think of restricting as we do in our avaricious bourgeoisie.

And so I return often to the streets and the city squares where flocks of squealing children fight over half-spoiled lemons, melons and tomatoes that have split open, the odds and ends of the morning market, and to the church squares where can be read, in that healthy, laughing, and poverty-stricken swarming, the magnificent destiny of a race that never tires of bringing forth young and can say to its sons, impatient and crowded in their native land hemmed in by water: "For you there is the whole world!" In spite of myself, I loiter here to enjoy a spectacle that is always rare with us in France, and that a war which has lasted twelve months has made impossible: the spectacle of pregnant women, opulent and massive as towers in the sunlight, who walk, carrying in front of them the future and the fortune of Italy.

HB

❦❦ Middle Age: A New Year Reverie

We came back powdered with snow, all three of us—the little bulldog, the Flemish sheepdog, and I . . . Snow had got into the folds of our coats, I had white epaulettes, an impalpable sugar was melting in the wrinkles of Poucette's blunt muzzle, and the Flemish sheepdog sparkled all over, from her pointed nose to her club of a tail.

We had gone out to look at the snow, the real snow and the real cold of the year's end, Parisian rarities, occasions almost never to be encountered . . . In my deserted neighborhood we ran like three lunatics and the vilified fortifications of Paris saw, from the avenue des Ternes to the boulevard Malesherbes, our panting joy of unleashed dogs. From the top of the slope we looked down upon the pit that was being filled with a purplish twilight, laced with white whirlwinds; we contemplated Levallois, dark, with openings of rosy fires behind a chenille screen of snowflakes like thousands and thousands of white flies, vibrant and cold as flowers being stripped of their petals, melting on lips and eyes, held a moment on our lashes, on the down of our cheeks . . . We scrambled with our ten feet over an intact and crumbling snow which collapsed under our weight with the soft rustling of taffeta silk. Far from all eyes we galloped, barked, snapped up the snow in our jaws, on the run, discovering that it tasted like a smooth sherbet, vanilla-flavored and a bit dusty . . .

Sitting now in front of the glowing grill, we three remain silent. The memory of the night, the snow, the wind let loose behind the door, sinks into our veins slowly and we are going to fall into that sudden sleep that is the recompense for long walks . . .

The sheepdog, steaming like a footbath, has recovered her dignity of a tamed she-wolf, her courteous pretense of seriousness. With one ear she listens to the whispering of the snow against the shut blinds, with the other she strains to hear the clinking of spoons in the pantry. Her slender nose quivers, and her copper-colored eyes, open directly upon the fire, move incessantly from right to left, from left to right, as if she were reading . . . A little mistrustfully, I study this new arrival, this feminine and complicated canine who is a good watchdog, laughs rarely, behaves like a sensible person and takes orders and reprimands without saying a word but with an impenetrable look that is full of mental reserve . . . She knows how to tell lies, how to steal—but when caught she cries out like a frightened young girl and almost gets sick with emotion. Where did this little she-wolf with a low back, this child of the Walloon fields get her hatred for ill-dressed people, her aristocratic reserve? I offer her a place at my fireside and in my life, and perhaps she will love me, she who already knows how to defend me . . .

Suddenly overwhelmed with drowsiness, my little bulldog, childlike soul, has fallen asleep, her muzzle and paws quivering feverishly. The gray cat is not unaware of the snowstorm and since breakfast I haven't seen the tip of her nose, which is buried in the fur of her belly. And once more here I am, confronting my fire and my solitude, confronting myself . . .

One more year . . . What good does it do to count them? This Parisian New Year's Day in no way recalls the festival as it was celebrated in my youth; and who can restore to me the childish solemnity of New Year's Day in bygone times? The form of the years has changed for me, while I too have changed. The year is now no more that undulating ribbon of a road that started to unwind in January, rose toward spring and mounted, mounted toward the summer, to spread out in a calm plain, in burning fields intersected with blue shadows, splashed with dazzling geraniums—then descended toward an odorous autumn, misty, redolent of marshlands, of ripe fruit and wild fowl—then sinking toward a winter that was dry, resonant, glimmering with frozen ponds, with snow rosy beneath the sun . . . Then the undulating ribbon in a vertiginous plunge reached a marvelous date, isolated, suspended between the two years like a frost flower: New Year's Day . . .

A child much loved, whose parents were not rich, who lived in the country among trees and books and never knew or wished for expensive toys: there, that is what I see again this evening as I reflect upon my past . . . A child superstitiously attached to the seasonal festivals, to the dates marked by a gift, a flower, a traditional cake . . . A child who instinctively ennobled the Christian festivals with paganism, mainly doting on the branch of boxwood that had been blessed, the red egg of Easter, the wilted roses of Corpus

Christi, and the flowers from the processional altars—syringas, aconites, camomiles—and with the nut-tree scion requisitioned for the contriving of a small cross blessed at the Mass of Holy Thursday and then planted at the edge of the field which it now shelters from hailstorms . . . A little girl infatuated with the five-horned cake, baked and eaten on Palm Sunday; with the pancake of Shrove Tuesday, with the stifling odor of the church during the month of Mary . . .

O you old guileless parish priest who gave me the holy communion, you supposed that silent little girl gazing open-eyed at the altar was awaiting the miracle, the elusive movement of the Virgin's blue sash? Yes, isn't it so? I was so well behaved! And it is quite true that I dreamed of miracles, but . . . not the same ones you thought of. Made drowsy by the incense and the warm flowers, enchanted with the mortuary perfume, with the musky decay of the roses, I inhabited, dear guileless man, a paradise of which you had no idea, peopled with my gods, with my talking animals, my nymphs, my goatish deities . . . And I listened to you talking about your inferno, while reflecting on the overweening pride of the man who, for his momentary crimes, invented an eternal hell . . . Oh, how long ago all this!

My solitude, this December snow, this threshold of another year do not give me the shiver of bygone days, when in the long night I listened for the faint roll of the distant municipal drum sounding above the beating of my heart, saluting the dawn of a January 1 in the sleeping village. That drum in the chilly night toward six o'clock, I dreaded it and summoned it from the depths of my childish bed, with a tense anguish close to tears, jaws set, stomach contracted . . . That drum alone, and not the striking of twelve at midnight, was for me the announcement of the dazzling opening of the new year, the mysterious advent the entire world panted for, listening with rapt attention to the first *rataplan* of the old drummer of my village.

He passed, invisible in the early morning darkness, making the walls echo with his brisk yet funereal little *aubade,* and behind him

a new life began, new and bounding toward twelve new months
. . . Released, I jumped from my bed to the candle, then ran toward the good wishes, the kisses, the candies, the gilt-edged books
. . . I opened the door to the bakers bringing the hundred pounds
of bread, and until noon, very serious and full of commercial importance, I handed out to all the poor, whether genuine or fake, the
hunch of bread and the ten-centime piece which they accepted without humility and without gratitude.

O winter mornings, red lamp in the night, motionless and keen
air before sunrise, garden guessed rather than seen in the dim dawn,
shrunken and choked with snow, O pine trees weighed down, hour
after hour letting fall in avalanches the burden of your dark arms—
wingbeats of the frightened sparrows and their anxious games in a
crystal powder more tenuous, more sparkling than the iridescent
mist of a fountain. O all the winters of my childhood, a winter day
has just restored you to me! It is my face of bygone days that I look
for in this oval mirror snatched up idly, and not my woman's face,
the face of a woman still young but whose youth is about to leave
her . . .

Still under the spell of my daydream, I am astounded to find I
have changed, have aged while I dreamed . . . I could repaint on
this face, with a tremulous brush, that fresh childish face, toasted
with sunlight, rosy with cold, the firm cheeks curving into a pointed
chin, the mobile eyebrows prompt to frown, a mouth whose sly corners belie the short, ingenuous upper lip . . . Alas, for only a moment. The adorable velours of the resuscitated pastel brushes off and
blows away . . . The dark water of the small mirror keeps only my
image, which is quite, quite like me, marked with light scratches,
finely lined at the eyelids, the corners of the lips, and between the
stubborn brows . . . An image which neither smiles nor becomes
sad, and which murmurs for me alone: "One must grow old. Do not
weep, do not join supplicating hands, do not revolt: one must grow
old. Repeat this word, not as a cry of despair, but as the signal for a
necessary departure. Look at yourself, look at your eyelids, your lips,
raise from your temples the curls of your hair: already you are be-

ginning to drift away from your life, don't forget it, one must grow old!

"Go away slowly, slowly, without tears; forget nothing! Take with you your health, your cheerfulness, your coquetry, the small amount of kindness and justice that rendered life less bitter for you; don't forget! Go away adorned, go gently, and do not stop on the irresistible way, you will try in vain to do so—because one must grow old! Follow the road, and do not stop for rest except to die! And when you do lie down across the vertiginous undulating ribbon of a road, if you have not left behind you one by one your curly locks, your teeth, your limbs one by one worn out, if the eternal dust has not, before your final hour, weaned your eyes from the marvelous light—if you have, to the very end, kept in your hand the friendly hand that guides you, then lie down smiling, sleep happy, sleep as one privileged . . ."

HB

PART Four ❧❧ [1920-1939]

Work—Appetites—La Grande Colette

Voilà que, légalement, littérairement et familièrement, je n'ai qu'un nom, qui est le mien.

So it came about that both legally and familiarly, as well as in my books, I now have only one name, which is my own.

✸✸ Lady of Letters

Origins of Chéri

Chéri? In the beginning he was just a little, gingery-haired fellow with one shoulder slightly lower than the other, pinkish eyelashes, a weak right eye, and a perpetually running nose. He had the appearance of a deprived child and 1,500,000 francs a year pocket money. Wherever Paris waited, a quarter of a century ago, for the dawn to paste up its blue and sadly tarnished tints against the windows of the place where they were drinking, he was to be seen allowing himself to be towed passively along behind his dark-haired mistress, a woman as hard and shiny as anthracite and habitually unfaithful to him. I should add that Chéri was at that time called Clouk, a name derived from the tiny, though intolerable clicking noise made by one of his blocked nostrils every time he took a breath. I think he must have been suffering from a polyp . . .

Such was the original, humiliating shape assumed by Chéri one day when I needed him very badly for my weekly stories in *Le Matin*. He openly admitted his feebleness of spirit and his morbid horror of being alone; he lived in complete subjection to the mineral malice of his mistress, and his friends used to touch him for money.

But one day when he was supping with his companion, sitting opposite the glitter of her jet, her savage features, her demands, her diamonds, and her pitiless pupils, he noticed four ladies of maturer years gathered at a nearby table. Together, without a man, they were drinking demi-sec champagne, eating prawns, *pâté de foie gras,* and rich desserts, and laughing as they talked about their pasts. Clouk caught a glimpse of his destiny, which was to die and to rise again beloved, by which I mean beautiful.

Like the coward he was, and as though I had administered to him some powerful narcotic from the South, Clouk slowly lost all consciousness and color, sank back into the void, and woke again in the arms of Léa, who called him "Chéri!"

I gave Chéri good measure from the start: twenty-five years old, dark hair, white skin, glossy as a six-month-old tomcat. Sometimes I stepped back to observe him. I never tired of adding to his beauty. Eyelashes and hair like the wings of a thrush, then slender hands, and a chest like a breastplate, and oh those teeth! And the curve of the lips . . . Not knowing what else to heap upon him, I made him the supreme and final gift: the majesty, the passion for honor, and the childlike pride of the great kept men. Nothing could have been more bracing for an idle young man with ample means. Chéri sighed with pleasure, stretched, and strolled off in the direction he thought suited him.

He went to join that band of cautious and dissolute young men, part of the generation in their twenties when I was in my forties, composed of the sons of spendthrift fathers. These strange children were casting off their parents' habit of automatically throwing money away, and some natural law, like the trajectory of the boomerang, always brought it back into their own hands. The expensive cars, the horses, the yachts, the priceless furs made into a lining for a cape, the rare pearls—all these were kept for their own personal use. A spirit of contradiction and rivalry then spurred them on to even greater lengths: they began to assume the role of heartless rogues and scandalmakers. One of these lost children deliberately allowed his woman friend to make off, one evening when they were at Maxim's, with a particularly beautiful ring he was wearing. But the following night, having a talent for such acrobatics, he shinnied up the ironwork on the façade of the young woman's apartment building and climbed in through her window as she lay asleep. He beat her, took back the ring, and, with a nice regard for his honor, stole a necklace belonging to her into the bargain. She herself told the story quite openly, and not without admiration.

Diseases produce their own remedies, or at least another disease which we accept as salutary. The ladybug kills the fruit beetle. Toward those ends which lay beyond the short patience of the furious younger women, their elder sisters employed personal methods that left the novice poachers openmouthed in amazement. Where, other than in the household of one of these heavyweight amazons, would I have encountered my "naughty babe-in-arms"? Blond in one case, dark in another, often rich, sometimes poor, he seemed to have come into being simply in order to confound me with astonishment, and would in fact have done so if I had not already learned earlier, with *Claudine,* that there is always room in any literary creation for a certain admixture of magic.

I have no habitual fear of the dangerous spells attendant on such materializations, and to begin with, I smiled at Chéri; I held out toward him a hand on which the ink spilled to bring him glory was still wet. Before he had begun to spring up everywhere, at the dictates of a somewhat contemptible snobbism, I first noticed him in the house of a friend, one of those women full of wise and imperfect lessons who, when their hour strikes, can occupy an ungrateful and prickly young heart without striking a single blow.

The first time I set myself to the task of observing Chéri, he was sitting on the edge of a chaise longue covered in sky-blue damask, and playing with this lady's little dog. The shadow of his eyelashes was flickering across his twenty-two-year-old cheek, warm and lustrous near the ear, as befits young flesh that the sun, from infancy, has constantly caressed. He had just arrived from a small country house and was intending to make a career for himself in Paris. He did in fact make a career for himself, but that is another story . . . On the face of the lady, his friend, so similar in its authority, its solid brilliance, its equable humor to the one that held sway over Chéri, I could read the leonine love, the happy suspicion, and the challenge that were stirring up the embers of that beautiful and womanly autumn in her.

"Do take Miki into the garden, it's such lovely weather," she said to the charming young man.

I thought that Irma, or Ida, or Léa, wanted to show me Chéri running in circles around the narrow, overgrown garden—as the horse dealer trots his horse around on a leading rein. I also thought she wanted to be alone with me.

But the blond lady following the frolics of the young man and the little dog with her eyes had too few illusions and too much self-restraint; she limited herself simply to making a few short comments on her feats as a mistress-tamer and her prowess as a keeper of the purse strings. She was smiling contentedly.

"Do you see him, hm? Do you hear that urchin's laugh? No, that one, not that one! . . . Such an appetite, I've never seen anything like it. And you realize he's only just arrived, that he still knows absolutely nothing . . . When I say nothing . . ."

She broke off and breathed in deeply, her eyes closed.

"Well, my dear, new as he is, he'd eat me alive if he could. He wants everything. With one hand he's at the *foie gras,* with the other he's stuffing my pearls in his pocket, and my big emerald into the bargain, you know, the famous one. 'But my poor boy,' I said to him, 'what are you thinking of? An emerald like that is more difficult to steal than an ocean liner! And the *foie gras* will give you pimples.' A child, in fact. Trésor!" she shouted as she leaned out into the garden, "don't throw pebbles for Miki to fetch, he might swallow them . . ."

She returned her smiling amazon's gaze, utterly without rancor, to my face.

"I have to start from the very beginning," she went on. "But I'm not averse to hard work. And he learns quickly. He already knows he's got someone to deal with who knows what's what. *Piano, piano* . . . After the cuff links comes the pearl tie pin, after the tie pin the platinum cigarette case . . . I can only be led as far as I want to go . . . Aren't you getting too hot, Trésor?"

Halted in the middle of his game, the treasure lifted up toward us a dark, disheveled, gilded head, somber blue eyes, and parted, panting lips . . .

"Why don't you go and play an hour's tennis at Mavrocordato's? The weather's so lovely, so . . ."

She fell silent and remained leaning out of the window, her breasts pressing against the sill as she watched him. She had been rendered speechless, not by a hectic surging of the blood, but by a purely contemplative and dreamy enchantment, like someone who has been singing as he walks, but halts his steps and abandons his song at the sudden appearance of a prospect too full of beauty . . .

I too remember having contemplated that young man, or another; and I remember speaking to him inside myself: "So there you are? You really are as I described you. But at that time, when I was still in the process of lavishing beauty on you beyond all the bounds of good taste, I could not see you as clearly as I do today. There was something cold in that black-and-white, enameled beauty of yours. The only living, human thing about you was the melancholy of your perfection as a work of art . . . After tailoring your caddish virtues and your orphan's charm myself to your exact measurements, must I now be made to fear them? . . ."

All those precautions I had taken did not enable me to avoid meeting him. In the depths, twenty-five years down, he lies in silence, evasive and fortunate. Even his gang of mediocre imitators can still flatter my pride, when I realize that they too are held in the spell of Chéri. Below the photographs—close-up, sports clothes, briefs, white tie and tails—they add their own commentary: Chéri

today would like to be a film star. He is full of youthful ardor.
Though inexperienced, he insists nevertheless that the part, large as
it is, will not be too much for him. I am ready to believe him . . .
But, beneath the gloss of the photograph, I detect with deliberate
malice the retouched nose, the heavy chin, the precocious wrinkle
scratched out by the technician. If needs be, I use a magnifying glass.
It is impossible to be too demanding when the object of one's scru-
tiny is an imaginary lover, once flatteringly disdained, and viewed in
retrospect.

DC

The poetry I love

I can tell you quite plainly now, either as a simple statement of
fact or in order to reassure you, that the few words I am about to
speak will at no point rise to the level of general ideas. Whatever a
woman's age, she never abandons coquetry; and as it happens, there
are three things in particular that suit me very ill: feathered hats,
general ideas, and earrings. I shall therefore avoid them now as I do
at all other times. And in any case, is it possible for poetry and poets
ever to accommodate themselves to general ideas?

You may well have thought, taking my title in good faith, that
I was in fact going to talk about the poetry and the poets that I love.
As for the latter, the poets, I have neither the competence nor the
presumption; as for the former, poetry itself, I am hampered by a
certain profound and obstinate form of dissimulation, which might
well turn out to be modesty. For you have before you a specimen of
an extremely rare species, a sort of monstrosity: a prose writer who
has never written a line of verse. A poet need not necessarily write
verses, or at least may write such a very small quantity that his reputation becomes rightly founded on his reticence, a minimum of text
going hand in hand with a maximum of quality. Such men have
been known in the past and are still seen today. But a writer of prose
who has never been driven, as an adolescent or during his maturer

years, either by an irresistible abandon or by an acquired taste for such things, either by love or by pain, to risk producing poetry in the form of verse is, I think you will agree, almost unheard of.

I beg, ladies and gentlemen, that you will all bear witness to the truth of this—all of you, that is, who still keep in your memories that secret, that dried rose, that scar, that sin: a poem in verse!

I appeal to all of you as my witnesses, all of you who have come to know by experience that there is no more an age for being a poet than there is for being in love. I am thinking of a poem made up by a little girl when she was three and a half. No, the little girl was not myself, she was one of my nieces. Since she had not yet learned to write, she used to recite her poem aloud, in an accent picked up from her German governess. I have given it the title *Hymn to Summer,* and I shall recite it to you just as the little girl herself recited it, with the accent:

> Heer iss the summer, it iss wery varm
> Ant the sun sheinz like a crate pig star
> Ant the moon iss lightink us up there
> All through the night.

Can you hear, beneath the simplicity of these words, can you already hear the little girl's submission to the rhythm? I am sure you sense that what you have just heard was not the revelation of a precocious genius, but a first song.

Beside this fledgling twittering, this nightingale's beginning, I should like to place a remark made by a woman in love, a woman who was at that time less than ten years old—she was to some extent the starting point of my novel *Le Blé en herbe.* She had loved the boy she shared her nursery with "since always," as she put it. And one day she said to this nine-year-old Don Juan, handsome and dark, like a fatally seductive little page:

"We're little. How sad it is to be little! We would have to be at least sixteen to belong to one another, and we shall never get there . . . No, you see, I'm disheartened . . ."

And the little girl really spoke that huge and somber word "disheartened" as though she were a woman who had drained the lees of bitterness from the very cup of love.

Here, I think, we are approaching the very heart of poetry . . .

In his *Memoirs,* which are by no means just a collection of frivolities, Casanova quotes a remark made by one of his friends, a writer: "My book is finished. All I have to do now is weed out the alexandrines."

Was the writer in question being overscrupulous? No, and there are few prose writers who do not share his scruples. Some, it is true, submit without a struggle. Michelet, in his *Histoire de France,* abandons himself to the yoke, to the seduction of those long, twelve-syllabled lines with sensuous pleasure. For my part, I keep as close a watch as I can for the intrusion of unintentional lines of verse; I watch for them and I weed them out. You may tell me that my severity is excessive, that the ideal sentence is the one in which every word is irreplaceable, whether it goes on twelve feet or thirteen. But you must allow me to do it my way; I know what I am about. If I were to relax the merciless control I inflict on my prose, I know perfectly well that I should soon cease to be the anxious and diligent prose writer that I am, and become nothing more than a bad poet, lacking in all restraint and as happy in my metronomic world as a tenor would be whose whole life was nothing but a pure and interminable high B flat! I am there. I am keeping watch. Not so efficiently, however, that a few offenders have not escaped me! In some of my earlier novels, written when I was still a young woman, there are some of these involuntary lines of verse, and not camouflaged at all. As many as three, following one after the other—I shall not tell you where.

During one of the too rare private conversations I enjoyed with Mme de Noailles, she once remarked that she could not understand why I had never tried out my talents on the poem. I replied that I had never felt myself worthy of the medium. Then I, in my turn, asked her if she had any intention (this was during the last four or five years of her life) of publishing any more works in prose. With a gesture of her magnificent little hand, she repulsed the very conjecture.

"Never!" she cried. "Why should I use a language in which I cannot say everything?"

DC

❧ LESSONS IN WRITING

To Marguerite Moreno

. . . By the way, I should like very much to see you so that we could talk about your articles. You haven't found the right way yet, your writing doesn't have the surface relaxation that alone produces the right journalistic tone; it's obvious that you've written about each one of your old codgers as though they'd been set as subjects for school compositions—I know you, you wretch, they gave you a lot of trouble, didn't they? For one that works (Jarry), there are two (Proust and Iturri) that don't, they don't *live* enough. And Sardou's opening on paper is as dry as *The Annals*. Verlaine is good. I'm telling you all this just as I'd tell myself, and with the same harshness. Houssaye has almost everything. But though you yourself are complete enchantment when you tell a story, you miss almost every one of your effects when you write; you omit them, or you make them dull. For example, the Proust, pages 3, 4, and 5. The setting of this scene would be breathtaking if you told me about it in person. You write it, and what do I find? "Mme A. was employing her critical wit, delivering judgments without indulgence, etc. . . . A chorus of flatterers backed her up—the conversation had taken on a bitter tone. —He forced his way between the closely packed groups. —People began to pass judgment on him. —Unleashing of human beastliness—mocking exclamations, derisive phrases, etc." Do you realize that there is not a word in all that which either *shows* or *makes one hear* the people you are talking about? If you were to tell me the same story, in fifteen lines you would have described old Mother A., old Papa France, the elder Caillavet, Victor du Bled, etc., etc. And if you were to change your "unleashed beastliness" into a scrap of *dialogue,* it would take on life along with the rest. No narration, for heaven's sake! Just separate brush strokes and splashes of color; and there is no need for a *conclusion,* I don't give a damn whether you ask Proust's pardon for having misunderstood him or not, and I don't give a damn about Sardou's being "one of the kings of the contemporary theater" either, do you understand? And the same-thing-likewise for Iturri . . . "A charming and delicate" dinner; "a conversation wandering from one subject to another"—what are you showing me when you write like that? Nothing! Stick me up a setting of some sort, some guests, even the food they eat, otherwise it just won't work! Liberate yourself. And dear heart, do try to conceal the fact that writing bores the hell out of you.

DC

From the preface to Renée Hamon's Aux Îles de lumière

"But I don't know what one ought to put in a book . . ."

"Neither do I, for heaven's sake. I have merely acquired a few glimmers of understanding as to what it's better not to put in one. Only describe what you have seen. Look long and hard at the things that please you, even longer and harder at what causes you pain. Try to be faithful to your first impressions. Set no store by "the unusual expression." Don't wear yourself out telling lies. Lying develops the imagination, and any gain for the imagination is the reporter's loss. Take notes . . . No, don't take notes. Beware of "embellishments," beware of obvious attempts at poetry. Don't write your accounts of things away from home, they might have become unrecognizable by the time you get back again. A novel about love cannot be written while making love . . .

DC

Fate has decreed . . .

Fate has decreed, where writing is concerned, that I should be incapable either of holding myself back or of giving instruction. What have I to teach, unless it be self-doubt, to those who since early youth have become secretly self-infatuated by self-love rather than by self-torture?

RS

❦❦❦

Making movies

The more I see of movie actors, locked up in their work like so many prisoners, the more esteem I feel for them. For the past two months I have been watching them at work quite often—though not as often as I should have liked. I am still at the stage of wondering where they find all their energy. I did extract a bitter reply from one of them on this subject, but it was too full of caustic modesty, too redolent of inverted pride to be of any use in answering the question.

Completely worn out, I was finally deserting the studio and one of those interminable working days that begin at dawn by the light of imitation suns, are oblivious of mealtimes, spurn the limits of human endurance, and often only come to an end—since the theaters insist on having their leading players back at eight o'clock—in order to begin again sometimes after midnight . . . And I confessed to X., who is both a movie actor and a theater actor, the various feelings inspired in me toward those who act in movies by my fatigue and their stoutheartedness. "Bah!" he replied, "no one is ever bushed if they're being paid enough."

Beneath that layer of makeup, renewed twice in the past twelve hours, he was putting on a front; he was playing the role of the embittered professional who is in it for the money. But I was not deceived. However much they may exceed the wages that theaters can agree to pay, the profits to be made from the movies cannot alone justify such extremes of heroism. Having approached the movies rather late, I am only now beginning to make a study of what it means to have a vocation for this medium, what its genuine essence, its aims, and its rewards really are when isolated from mere rapacity.

For, to the people of my generation, the movies will always be surrounded by a defensive aura that we find it difficult to pierce. My daughter, at the age of twenty-one, is already a director, passionate about her profession and impatient to show what she can do. She champs on her "Assistant's" bit, but she is also obviously humble. For the past four years she has been *inside* the movies. The length of this noviciate has made her unable to understand the astonishment I express. She shares the lot and the impassivity of the movie actors and the extras; like them she can rest standing up, and like them she can maintain interminable silences, for there is only one man who has the right to rage.

She is capable of discoursing with great subtlety on the agonies, the childishness, and the splendors of the movie industry; but she can never enlighten me as to the deep and underlying cause, the emotional wellspring of so marvelous an equality in the face of their work and the silence . . .

One day, during the coldest week of February, I was at the Billancourt studios watching fifty half-naked young women taking part in some music-hall scenes. For seven consecutive hours, working in a canvas-covered courtyard with no protection other than their special thick makeup, they were forced to undergo the extreme changes in temperature produced by an icy East wind occasionally and briefly interrupted by a cataclysm of lights. As Max Ophüls issued his terse orders, they walked up and down a set of unfinished wooden steps without handrails, ran hither and thither, and formed into patterns with inexhaustible grace. A terrible arrow of light transfixed Simone Berriau's golden eyes, and Gina Manès's phosphorous blue ones, in its flight. Philippe Hériat, naked and covered in silver paint, was standing, waiting with chattering teeth but refusing the robe someone was holding out to him because it would have dulled his body paint. Not one of the chorus girls, empty though all their stomachs were, would allow herself a moment's weakness. At a shout from Ophüls: "We can hear your feet on the steps! Take off your shoes!" fifty young women, Simone Berriau included, pulled off their dancing slippers without a word and ran about barefooted among the rubber-covered snakes, the sawdust, the gravel, and the nails.

That was also the day when its trainer was due to hang a python almost as heavy as a man around Simone Berriau's shoulders . . .

"What will he do?" I asked the snake's master a short while before the scene was shot.

He shrugged his shoulders to express his uncertainty.

"There's no telling . . . He's young, after all, and intelligent . . . Not savage, you understand, but he doesn't know this lady . . . The best thing is to let him do as he likes. If the worst comes to the worst, I always have this on me . . ."

With the utmost simplicity, he displayed a thick, double-edged knife. Then, from a suitcase that had been placed on top of a radiator to keep it warm, he drew out three yards of python, wound them around his neck like a muffler, and taught me how to scratch "Joseph" very gently under his chin and down that delicate throat, so extraordinarily slim in comparison with the thick, richly dappled body, in places almost pink.

As he deposited this fearful mute personage around "Divine's" shoulders, she sagged for a moment in her bayadere's costume, then pulled herself upright again. Then she was left there quite alone with "Joseph," and they were both flooded with a pitiless barrage of light. At first, the snake was around her hips. It tightened its coils and sent up its head to reconnoiter her breast and neck. It investigated the whole of her bosom, feeling its way with that long, forked tongue. A sort of anguished smile hovered over the bayadere's face, her lips pulled back slightly from her dazzling teeth. The snake's head disappeared behind her shoulder, and as it drew the heavy body after it in that indescribable, ophidian mode of progression, I thought the ordeal must be almost over . . . Then, above the actress's gold-decked hair, the python's head came back into view and reared up like the head of a lance. Another second and it was moving down toward the temple, halting at the outer edge of the eyebrow, licking the cheek . . . Simone Berriau's heavy eyelids sank in silence, covering her eyes, and Ophüls allowed the trainer to release her . . . But I honestly believe that he was more upset than the actress herself, for she was already shaking off the terrible spell and asking:

"Did it go all right? Did we look good together, Joseph and I?"

A vocation, a vocation—the need to reach the masses, the desire for unanimous judgment . . .

DC

On being elected to the Belgian Academy

I bring no feigned modesty with me to this place, Gentlemen. It is possible that I have brought no modesty at all. Humility has its origin in an awareness of unworthiness, and sometimes too in a dazzled awareness of saintliness. But where, in my career, could I have found cause for anything but astonishment? I became a writer without noticing the fact, and without anyone else's suspecting it. Having emerged from the shadows of anonymity, already the author of several books, some of them written under my own name, I was still astonished that people should refer to me as a writer, that I had not only a publisher but also a public, both of whom treated me as a writer, and I attributed these continued coincidences to a friendly chance, a chance which, moving upward from stage to stage, from meeting to miracle, has finally brought me here. You must not pity me because my sixtieth year finds me still astonished. To be astonished is one of the surest ways of not growing old too quickly.

As I listened to Valère Gille making his speech of welcome, I found myself thinking that it has been given only to the poet, the water-diviner, and God's chosen prophet—all of whom may be one and the same person—to summon up the invisible spring to the surface, and to draw out the flower from its unseeing seed. You have all witnessed how this poet has changed me into a poet also, and covered me from head to foot with flowers. Would you could see me here indeed as he has pictured me! Yet he has not intoxicated me so much that I have lost the only virtue in which I take any pride: self-criticism. Warier every day as I confront my work, and more and more uncertain as to whether I should go on with it, I find reassurance nowhere but in my fears themselves. The writer who loses his self-doubt, who gives way as he grows old to a sudden euphoria, to prolixity, should stop writing immediately: the time has come for him to lay aside his pen.

DC

❧❧ The South of France

In love

The "dark young man at the wheel" was Maurice Goudeket, whom Colette had met earlier in the year, and who was to become her third husband.

[June 11, 1925]

You ask where I am? Heavens, I'm in a whirl. And I use the phrase as a planet might use it. Yes, I am in a whirl. I have seen roses, honeysuckle, eighty degrees of blinding heat, the moon shining, the ancient wistaria clinging to the iron gate of my house at Saint-Sauveur, the night over Fontainebleau as I passed. I am in a whirl, I tell you. Beside me, there is a dark young man at the wheel. Here I am back in Paris, but am I really motionless? The dark young man beside me is still at the wheel. How strange everything is! How wise I am, how surprised I am, what sagacious unexpectedness in my every gesture! Yes, yes, I am in a whirl!

You see, you mustn't be worried about me. From time to time I begin to worry myself, I give a start, I prick up my ears, I cry: "But! . . ." and then I make myself stop thinking again . . .

Oh Marguerite! How strange everything is! I kiss you. When shall I see you? I don't know, but I shall see you. How could I not see you? I am beginning to feel that faith that is given to people who fall off towers; they stay hovering for a moment in the air, in some comfortable and magical region where they feel no pain at all. I kiss you, dear heart . . .

[June 21, 1925]

Ah, la la! And again, la la! And never enough la la's! A nice piece of work your girlfriend is, I must say. A nice kettle of fish she's in now too, and loving it, up to the eyes, up to the lips, and up to even further than that! Oh, these quiet ones have the very devil in them—and that remark is intended for that boyo Maurice. Do you want to know what he's like, my boyo Maurice? Well, he's a swine, and a this, and a that, and even a cute little fellow, and a skin like satin. That's how deep I am in. I kiss you, dear heart. And I kiss you again : . .

[August 5, 1925]

Dear heart, I've received a note from you at last. I was longing for one with all my heart, and it reached me in this place where I am so happy I am almost ready to start feeling guilty about it. I knew nothing at all about this part of France. I feel so much at home here;

I might be a salamander the way I wander through the crackling brazier of the pine woods, past the streaming resins, over the flagstones that burn your bare feet. I sleep out on the terrace—where else should one sleep on nights as pure as these? There are no mosquitoes, and the sparrow owl miaows because of the full moon. The water I swim in, the sand I walk on are my native element, and so is love. Am I not an abominable creature? I need your reassurance that I'm not. My charming companion is asleep, since it's three in the afternoon at the moment; but I don't need a siesta, I slept so well last night. One always feels a little guilty writing beside someone who's asleep, even when it's simply to confess, in a few brief words, that he is charming and that one is in love with him. Tell me, wasn't it last winter you warned me that I would get to know, in the *course of a journey,* a man who "would change my life"? I remember it was at your house, and it was cold that day.

DC

"La treille muscate"

To find it, I had to tear myself away from the little Mediterranean port, from the tunny boats, from the flat-roofed houses with their washes of faded candy pink and lavender blue and pale green, away from the streets filled with their hovering scents of sea urchins, of nougat, of disemboweled melons.

I found it by the side of a road that automobiles avoid, and behind the most ordinary-looking of iron gates—but a gate that was being choked by the oleander shrubs behind it, anxiously reaching out between the bars to offer the passer-by their posies sprinkled with the true dust of Provence, as white as flour and finer even than pollen . . .

Four acres, a vine, orange trees, fig trees with green fruit, fig trees with black fruit—and when I have said that the furrows of the vines, between the shoots, were brimming with garlic, with pimentos, with aubergines, have I not said everything?

There is also a house; but that counts less—it's small and low-ceilinged—than its open terrace covered with wistaria, for example, or the bignonier tree with its scarlet flames, or the old mimosas with their thick trunks lined up from the gate to the front door like a guard of honor. Behind the house . . . No, to be honest, I can see nothing behind the house to merit a description.

Behind the house, more vines, then a palisade of false bamboo, a flexible Provençal wall against which the mistral charges in vain, pauses to gather strength, and chants its angry battle song. The arborvitae shrubs enclosing the garden, behind the house, lean inwards over a half-rotten gate, and if you open the gate, which a child could break down, you walk, without climbing or going down a single step, straight into the sea.

I was forgetting, it is true, to tell you that the sea bounds, continues, prolongs, ennobles, and enchants this morsel of luminous seashore, the sea which is tinged with color or made wan again, according to the time of day, by the star that flings itself up, at dawn, out of a cold, blue East, only to perish when evening comes in the foam of the long, light, angrily smoldering clouds. It is the sea that provides the vineyard with that crumbling and salty soil in which the vines so mysteriously find their sustenance. It is the sea that summoned me here. In this place I am free now to live, if I wish, and to die, if I can . . . We have not got to that point yet. I have only just arrived, only just bought it. The musk-grape vine, which watches over the well with its name as well as with its branches, has not yet swelled out, for me, its grapes with their taut-skinned curves that reflect the daylight in blue glints. The "musk-vine arbor" I have bought is not yet mine.

My own contribution to it must be made respectfully and thriftily. A "musk-vine arbor" cannot be built in a single summer simply by the extravagant addition of a stucco tub, a load of saffron loam, and quantities of rustic earthenware. I shall get down immediately to the most urgent things, which is to say the garden, then—dare I write it?—the outside bedroom. The house is another matter, to be dealt with over an indefinite space of time. It has its own little past, its modest appearance, which one might wish more peasantlike, and household gods with the smile of old agricultural workers. It's very nice already as it is. If it finally comes to resemble me, it will only be little by little, and I shall make my nest in it like a dog in new straw, by turning round and round until I'm settled. The largest room will be for leisure hours, for chatting, for reading; the smallest will be for writing, and I must try and choose for this purpose the one that's rather dark, not very comfortable, facing away from the magic of the sea: a measure of austerest prudence.

The garden, the garden; quickly, the garden; but there is no "garden," a piece of luck for which I have chance to thank. There are the tall yellow feathers brushing the azure sky, the mimosa raining down their pollen and their scent; I mustn't touch those except on carefully spaced-out raids. The *gobéas* are already in their right place, decided for me by tradition, against the warm front wall.

I shall respect the wattle windbreak, leaning inwards in the middle, and I shall respect the old *olea fragrans* too . . .

But between the old mimosas, on either side of the path, are two low walls of openwork bricks keeping back the vines and narrowing the path . . . To the devil with brick walls! And away too with the sedate air of those vines! Oh no, vines, you are worthy of iron arches, delicately hooped, and certainly deserving enough for me to stick supports in for you here and there, as my fancy guides me, gibbets for you to hang yourselves from, sunshades on which you can spread yourselves and droop down . . . Vines, you shall rear yourselves into the sky, you shall breathe in the breeze that sometimes does not reach down to brush the earth, the rough undersides of your leaves shall taste the torrid mist that summer pumps up from the earth, and from your woody shoots, vines, I shall conjure myself a grove of trees!

Already lyrical, already in ecstasy? The shores of the Mediterranean have turned more than one steady head with their intoxication. Over the pine grove near the "musk-vine arbor" there blows a wind laden with resins; and the notched leaves crowding on the slope above the sea distill their camphor and their mint into the air. My garden will be no less quiet and sensible beneath the aerial transformation of its vines. The staked tomato plants will glow with a thousand berries turning red in June, and look how many love apples, how many purple aubergines and yellow peppers, all massed together into an old-fashioned, swelling clump, will enrich my neat, sedate enclosure . . . You must be calm, garden, calm and sensible! Don't forget that you are going to feed me . . . I want to see you adorned, yes, but with a fruitful beauty. I want to see you covered in flowers, but not in such tender blooms as a single summer day of sizzling crickets will scorch up. I want to see you green, but away with the relentless green of palm and cactus, desolation of a mock, Monaco Africa! Let the arbutus burst into its flames beside the orange tree, and let there be sheets of purple fire dripping down my walls: the bougainvillaea! And at their feet, let the mint plants, the tarragon, and the sage push up their spikes, just so high that a drooping hand, as it crushes their slender leaf stems, can set free their impatient scents. Tarragon, sage, mint, savory, and burnet opening your pink flowers at noon, then closing them again three hours later, I love you certainly for yourselves—but I shall not fail to demand your presence in my salads, my stewed lamb, my seasoned sauces; I shall exploit you. But all I have in me of disinterested botanical passion I shall keep for that other flower, over there, for her—honor of every climate favored by her presence—the queen, the Rose.

Don't ask me where I shall plant the white rose disheveled by a single gust of wind, the yellow rose which has a scent of fine cigars, the pink rose which has a scent of roses, the red rose which dies unceasingly from the pouring out of its odors and whose dry and weightless corpse still lavishes its balm upon the air. I shall not crucify my red rose against a wall; I shall not bind it to the edge of the water tank. It shall grow, if my good destiny allows it so, just beside the open bedroom, the room that will have only three walls instead of four, and stand open to the rising sun. I would not swear that such a room will even have a roof, unless it be of woven reeds.

Last summer I did without even that. Out of all the nature lovers in the world, how many love it enough to spend the whole night in its bosom, for love, solely for love? . . .

There are no mosquitoes here. Last summer I dragged my mattress out every night from a little rustic house and slept outside, with the mistral in my hair. Two faithful owls kept up their dialogue in the pines, till midnight came, and the crackling brazier of the crickets was never stilled till they fell silent. Clammy sleepers, stifled between your warm walls, envy me! For the nights in this dazzling country are cold, and they hold the bodies of all who yield themselves up beneath the stars balanced in a soft, cool region between dream and blissful insensibility. And what happy dream could ever outweigh the unsleeping hour that shared with me, with me alone, before the rise of day, the sleeping, washed-out Mediterranean, white with a premonition from beyond the sea—the sky bending to kiss it and press upon it, lively already and more awake than its companion —the sky and its sad, red seal being broken slowly at the edge of the world, and slowly unfolding as the moment came for me to fall back, satisfied, into an illusion made bright with colors by my vigil, much like the wind filling the sails of a ship, the bellying cloth, and the path out into the deep . . .

DC

The door leading to the vines . . .

The door leading to the vines from the enclosure walled with openwork bricks is straining slightly on its hinges; the wind must be rising. It will swiftly sweep a quarter of the horizon and fasten on the wintry purity of the greenish north. Thereupon the whole hollow of the bay will boom like a shell. Goodbye to my night in the open on the raffia mattress! If I had persisted in sleeping out of doors, that powerful mouth that breathes coldness and drought, deadens all scents and anesthetizes the earth, the enemy of work, voluptuousness and sleep, would have torn off me the sheets and blankets that it knows how to twist into long rolls. What a strange tormentor, as intent on man as any wild beast! Those who are highly strung know more about it than I do. My Provençal cook, when the wind strikes her near the well, puts down her buckets, holds her head and cries: "It's killing me!" On nights when the mistral blows she groans under it in her little hut among the vines, and perhaps she sees it.

Having retired to my bedroom, I wait with controlled impatience for the departure of this visitor for whom no sanctum is private, and who is already pushing under my door a strange tribute of withered petals, finely sifted seeds, sand, and battered butterflies. Be off with you, I've discouraged other tokens before now; and I'm no longer forty, to avert my eyes at the sight of a fading rose. Is that militant life over and done with then? There are three good times for thinking of it: the siesta, a short hour after dinner when the rustling of the newspaper, just arrived from Paris, seems oddly to fill the room, and then the irregular insomnia of the small hours, before dawn. Yes, it will soon be three o'clock. But even during these precarious small hours, which merge so quickly into day, where can I find that great cavern of bitterness promised me by my past griefs and joys, as well as my own books and those of others? Humble as I always am when I'm faced with anything I don't understand, I'm afraid of being mistaken when I imagine that this is the beginning of a long rest between myself and men. Come, Man, my friend, let us simply exist side by side! I have always liked your company. Just now you're looking at me so gently. What you see emerging from a confused heap of feminine cast-offs, still weighed down like a drowned woman by seaweed (for even if my head is saved, I cannot be sure that my struggling body will be), is your sister, your comrade: a woman who is escaping from the age when she is a woman. She has, like you, rather a thick neck, bodily strength that becomes less graceful as it weakens, and that authority which shows you that you can no longer make her despair, or only dispassionately. Let us remain together; you no longer have any reasons now for saying goodbye to me forever.

Love, one of the great commonplaces of existence, is slowly leaving mine. The maternal instinct is another great commonplace. Once we've left these behind, we find that all the rest is gay and varied, and that there is plenty of it. But one doesn't leave all that behind when or as one pleases. How wise one of my husbands was when he remonstrated: "But is it impossible for you to write a book that isn't about love, adultery, semi-incestuous relations and a final separation? Aren't there other things in life?" If he had not been in such a hurry to get to his amorous rendezvous—for he was handsome and charming—he might perhaps have taught me what can take the place of love, in a novel or out of it. But he went and I continued obstinately covering that same bluish paper, gleaming at this moment from the dark table to guide my hand, with chapters dedicated to love or regret for love, chapters blind with love. In them I called myself Renée Néré, or else, prophetically, I introduced a Léa. So it came about that both legally and familiarly, as well as in my books, I now have only one name, which is my own. Did it take only thirty years of my life to reach that point, or rather to get back to it? I shall end by thinking that it wasn't too high a price to pay. Can it be that chance has made me one of those women so immersed in one man that, whether they are barren or not, they carry with them to the grave the shriveled innocence of an old maid? At the thought of such a fate my plump double that I see in the sloping mirror, tanned by sun and sea, would tremble, if it could still tremble at a past danger.

A hawk moth from the oleanders is banging against the fine wire netting in front of the french window, returning to the charge again and again until the taut netting reverberates like the skin of a drum. It is cool. The generous dew trickles, the mistral has put off its offensive. The stars, magnified by the damp and salty air, twinkle broadly. Once again the most beautiful of all nights precedes the most beautiful of all days, and not being asleep, I can enjoy it. Let us hope tomorrow will find me equally sweet-tempered! In all sincerity I no longer ask for anything except what I can't have. Has someone broken my spirit, that I should be so gentle? Not at all: it's a very long time since I knew anyone really wicked—knew them face to face, bosom to bosom, and limb to limb. As for an authentic villain, the real thing, the absolute, the artist, one rarely meets him even once in a lifetime. The ordinary bad hat is always in part a decent fellow. It's true that the third hour of the morning encourages indulgence in those who enjoy it in the open and have an assignation with no one but themselves beneath the deepening blue of their window. The crystalline emptiness of the sky, the already conscious sleep of the animals, the chilly contraction that closes the calyxes up again, are so many antidotes to passion and iniquity. But I don't need to be feeling indulgent in order to say that in my past no one has broken my spirit. I was made to suffer, oh yes, certainly I learned how to suffer. But is suffering so very serious? I have come to doubt it. It may be quite childish, a sort of undignified pastime—I'm referring to the kind of suffering a man inflicts on a woman or a woman on a man. It's extremely painful. I agree that it's hardly bearable. But I very much fear that this sort of pain deserves no consideration at all. It's no more worthy of respect than old age or illness, for both of which I'm acquiring a great repulsion: both of them are anxious to get me in their clutches before long, and I'm holding my nose in advance. The lovesick, the betrayed, and the jealous all smell alike.

I remember very definitely that when I was wretched because I had been disappointed in love, my animals loved me less. They scented my grief, that great admission of failure. I have seen an unforgettable look in the eyes of a beautiful well-bred bitch, a look still generous but restrained and politely bored, because she no longer loved as much all that I stood for—a man's look, the look of a certain man. Shall we never have done with that cliché, so stupid that it could only be human, about the sympathy of animals for man when he is unhappy? Animals love happiness almost as much as we do. A fit of crying disturbs them, they'll sometimes imitate sobbing, and for a moment they'll reflect our sadness. But they flee unhappiness as they flee fever, and I believe that in the long run they are capable of boycotting it.

What a good use the two tomcats fighting outside are making of the July night! Those unearthly songs of the male cat have accompanied so many nocturnal hours in my life that they have become a symbol of wakefulness, of ritual insomnia. Yes, I know it is three o'clock and that I'm going to fall asleep again, and that when I wake I shall be sorry to have missed the moment when the milky blueness begins to rise up from the sea, reaches the sky, and flows over it until it stops at a red rift flush with the horizon.

The great voice of a baritone wild beast, long drawn out, persists through the sharp sounds of a tenor cat, clever at tremolos and at shrill chromatic scales interrupted by furious innuendoes growing more nasal the more insulting they become. The two tomcats do not hate each other, but the clear nights suggest battle and declamatory dialogues. Why sleep? They make their choice and in summer take only the best parts of the night and the day. They choose. All animals who are well treated choose whatever is best in us and in their surroundings. It was the realization of that which helped me to emerge from the period when their comparative coldness revealed to me my own lack of dignity. I chose the phrase "lack of dignity" advisedly. Surely I ought to have thrown off that sordid domination? It was all in such deplorable taste, those half-dried tears, that melodrama. What opinion of a woman like that could one expect from an animal, a bitch for instance, herself compact of hidden fire and secrets, a bitch who had never groaned under the whip or wept in public? She despised me, that goes without saying. And though I didn't hide my hurt from the eyes of my fellows, I blushed for it in her presence. It is true that she and I loved the same man. But, for all that, it was in her eyes that I read a thought that I've read in one of my mother's last letters: "Love is not a sentiment worthy of repect."

One of my husbands used to suggest to me: "When you're about fifty, you ought to write a sort of handbook to teach women how to live in peace with the man they love, a code for life as a couple." Perhaps I am writing it now. O Man, my former loves, how one gains and learns in your company! Yet the best of friends must part; but I pledge myself here to take my leave courteously. No, you have not broken me, perhaps you never meant me any harm. Farewell, dear Man, and welcome to you too. Across my bed which, since I am in good health, is better arranged for writing than a sick bed, a blue light creeps until it reaches the blue paper, my hand, and my bronze-colored arm; the smell of the sea warns me that the hour when air is colder than water is at hand. Shall I get up? To sleep is sweet.

BMCC

❦❦ Gastronomy

Recriminations

"Can we count on you next Sunday? Just a family dinner, but we eat well . . . I won't say any more . . . One of my grandmother's recipes . . ."

And the departing gastronome departed without my asking him to say any more. He had said rather too much for my taste already.

Always keep a wary eye on friends who suddenly develop a case of ancestor worship. Be wary of those old grandmothers who suddenly, after half a century of modest silence in their graves, assume an importance in the dining room which nothing up to that point had led you to expect, and spring to life again around a dish of hare and rutabagas. Do you yourself like hare cooked with beets? Do you set store by pike stuffed with salsify? And chocolate tart, secretly soaked in kirsch, do you rather like that too? Into the outer darkness with "Aunt Ludivine's tart"! A plague on all these "Mère this and Mère that" when all they ever give birth to is recipes! Beautiful France, smiling land of good food, shake all these false provincial frills from your skirts. Otherwise you run the risk of one day resembling those delightful young ladies stuck up on our walls who sing the praises of a biscuit from Limoges dressed in Normandy bonnets and Provençal skirts, not to mention their Basque fichus and their very Parisian smiles! An execrable form of snobbery is attempting to pervert the French people's appreciation of good food into a cult already dishonored by its own ridiculous antics. How can they make anyone believe that a mutton stew should only be eaten behind red-checked gingham curtains, or that red wine tastes any better in an earthenware pitcher with a motto on it? No, I am not comfortably seated on a "rustic" wooden bench. No, chopped onions, *fines herbes,* and vegetable macédoine do not constitute either a panacea or a basic diet. No, I do not accept that a glass of Calvados poured onto a piece of braised beef ten minutes before it is eaten earns it the title of "regional recipe"! And I also deny such a title to that grated, peppery, baked cheese which is used as an indiscriminate disguise for fried eggs, whiting, tomatoes, noodles, spinach, and a hundred other dishes which it simply reduces to banality by coating them all with the same sticky mess and depriving them of their original flavors.

And I rebel equally against the cultivated mushroom, that insipid creature born of darkness and hatched by damp. I've had enough of seeing it chopped up into fragments and swimming around in sauces which it merely dilutes; I forbid it to seek precedence over the agaric, I insist that it annul herewith its marriage with the truffle, and I hereby show them—the mushroom and its worthy companion the yellow rattle sold in tins—my kitchen door!

There is an ignorant and pretentious gang at work attempting to make the art of cooking in France, already the richest in the world, more rich and varied still. At the very moment when interior decoration, furniture—and woman, whom I was forgetting!—are aspiring to a strange nudity; I say strange for politeness' sake—the art of preparing and cooking food is being puffed up with all these romantic notions. These people "overload" their cooking in order to petrify the hordes of visiting foreigners with admiration. They go beyond the bounds, they clutter and break the line. The improviser is now ensconced in front of our kitchen stoves as firmly as he is everywhere else. His eyes on the heavens, instead of on his pots, he throws in here a pinch of curry powder, there a spoonful of cognac, and sometimes even worse: a few drops of Worcestershire sauce. He will stuff you no matter what with God knows what sort of stuffing. He will slip you in some evil-flavored essence, he will garnish you your meal with his spiced meats, he will fold you in his this and coat you something else with his that . . . The old words, the classical terms, the ancient rites, but abused by these improvised priests, and in no time at all we are a thousand miles from the discreet, measured, slow combinations which formed our French love of food, with its passion for certain "symphonies of the palate" in which the harmony took its source and its energy from a noble restraint.

Beneath the rustic sloping roofs of fine old farmhouses, in the depths of old beaten copper saucepans, there are "family recipes" now lurking in ambush that should be clapped under legal injunctions forthwith. For they are "embroideries," if I may use the expression, on fundamental articles of faith such as braised beef, Breton lamb, veal cooked in cream, jugged hare and chicken chasseur, which are immemorial, codified, venerated, and simple dishes. For these embroideries, by drawing attention to a particular condiment, by forcing one spice or garnish, tend to throw the original patient and mysterious edifices out of balance. Which of you, my readers, has any suspicion as you savor the authentic *lièvre à la royale,* melting, warm in the mouth, that sixty—yes, your eyes are not deceiving you, *sixty*—cloves of garlic have contributed to its perfection? A successful *lièvre à la royale* does not taste of garlic. Sacrificed to the collective triumph, consumed by a process of reduction without rival, the sixty cloves of garlic, though unrecognizable, are nevertheless present: undetectable caryatids supporting a light and climbing flora of simple, kitchen-garden savors . . .

Would you ever have imagined, as you ate the mutton or veal

stew prepared in a saucepan by Annie de Pène's admirable hands, that both these dishes contained two large lumps of sugar? Assuredly not. Each time she made one of these stews, Annie de Pène slipped the two cubes of sugar into the black cast-iron pot almost furtively.

"Why two pieces of sugar, Annie?" I asked.

"Because my mother always put them in," she replied.

"But why, why did she put sugar in those two dishes?"

"Not only those. In a lot of others too, if they had to cook a long time."

"But have you never tried leaving the sugar out?"

She laughed and shook her head.

"How easy it is to see you have no faith, Colette . . ."

Beside this reply I should like to set one or two simple and almost mystical phrases I heard from the lips of Mme Yvon, a thoroughbred *cordon bleu*. One day at her house, after I had eaten a *boeuf à l'ancienne* which completely gratified at least three senses out of the five—for apart from its dark, velvety savor and its half-melting consistency, it shone with an amber-colored, caramel-like sauce, ringed at its circumference with a light shimmer of fat the color of fine gold—I cried:

"Madame Yvon, it's a masterpiece! What do you put in it?"

"Beef," Mme Yvon replied.

"Heavens, I can tell that . . . But all the same, there must be a mystery, some sort of magic in the way the ingredients are combined . . . With a marvel like this, it should surely be possible to give it a name? . . ."

"Of course," Mme Yvon replied. "It's a beef casserole."

All it would take to preserve, to rescue, and to justify France's pride in her gastronomy would be a few more Mme Yvons. But she is a rare species in an age that is bent on making silk without silk, gold without gold, pearls without oysters, and Venus without flesh . . .

DC

Wines

I was very well brought up. As a first proof of so categorical a statement, I shall simply say that I was no more than three years old when my father poured out my first full liqueur glass of an amber-colored wine which was sent up to him from the Midi, where he was born: the muscat of Frontignan.

The sun breaking from behind clouds, a shock of sensuous pleasure, an illumination of my newborn tastebuds! This initiation ceremony rendered me worthy of wine for all time. A little later I learned to empty my goblet of mulled wine, scented with cinnamon and lemon, as I ate a dinner of boiled chestnuts. At an age when I could still scarcely read, I was spelling out, drop by drop, old light clarets and dazzling Yquems. Champagne appeared in its turn, a murmur of foam, leaping pearls of air providing an accompaniment to birthday and First Communion banquets, complementing the gray truffles from La Puisaye . . . Good lessons, from which I graduated to a familiar and discreet use of wine, not gulped down greedily but measured out into narrow glasses, assimilated mouthful by spaced-out, meditative mouthful.

It was between my eleventh and fifteenth years that this admirable educational program was perfected. My mother was afraid that I was outgrowing my strength and was in danger of a "decline." One by one, she unearthed, from their bed of dry sand, certain bottles that had been aging beneath our house in a cellar—which is, thanks be to God, still intact—hewn out of fine, solid granite. I feel envious, when I think back, of the privileged little urchin I was in those days. As an accompaniment to my modest, fill-in meals—a chop, a leg of cold chicken, or one of those hard cheeses, "baked" in the embers of a wood fire and so brittle that one blow of the fist would shatter them into pieces like a pane of glass—I drank Château Lafites, Chambertins, and Cortons which had escaped capture by the "Prussians" in 1870. Certain of these wines were already fading, pale and scented still like a dead rose; they lay on a sediment of tannin that darkened their bottles, but most of them retained their aristocratic ardor and their invigorating powers. The good old days!

I drained that paternal cellar, goblet by goblet, delicately . . . My mother would recork the opened bottle and contemplate the glory of the great French vineyards in my cheeks.

Happy those children who are not made to blow out their stomachs with great glasses of red-tinted water during their meals! Wise those parents who measure out to their progeny a tiny glass of pure wine—and I mean "pure" in the noble sense of the word—and teach them: "Away from the meal table, you have the pump, the faucet, the spring, and the filter at your disposal. Water is for quenching the thirst. Wine, according to its quality and the soil where it was grown, is a necessary tonic, a luxury, and a fitting tribute to good food." And is it not also a source of nourishment in itself? Yes, those were the days, when a few true natives of my Burgundy village, gathered around a flagon swathed in dust and spiders' webs, kissing the tips of their fingers from their lips, exclaimed—already—"a nectar!" Don't you agree that in talking to you about wine I am describing a province I know something about? It is no small thing to conceive a contempt, so early in life, not only for those who drink no wine at all but also for those who drink too much.

The vine and the wine it produces are two great mysteries. Alone in the vegetable kingdom, the vine makes the true savor of the earth intelligible to man. With what fidelity it makes the translation! It senses, then expresses, in its clusters of fruit the secrets of the soil. The flint, through the vine, tells us that it is living, fusible, a giver of nourishment. Only in wine does the ungrateful chalk pour out its golden tears. A vine, transported across mountains and over seas, will struggle to keep its personality, and sometimes triumphs over the powerful chemistries of the mineral world. Harvested near Algiers, a white wine will still remember without fail, year after year, the noble Bordeaux graft that gave it exactly the right hint of sweetness, lightened its body, and endowed it with gaiety. And it is far-off Jerez that gives its warmth and color to the dry and cordial wine that ripens at Château Chalon, on the summit of a narrow, rocky plateau.

From the ripened cluster brandished by its tormented stem, heavy with transparent but deeply troubled agate, or dusted with silver-blue, the eye moves upward to contemplate the naked wood, the ligneous serpent wedged between two rocks: on what, in heaven's name, does it feed, this young tree growing here in the South, unaware that such a thing as rain exists, clinging to the rock by a single hank of hemplike roots? The dews by night and the sun by day suffice for it—the fire of one heavenly body, the essence sweated by another—these miracles . . .

What cloudless day, what gentle and belated rain decides that a year, one year among all the others, shall be a great year for wine? Human solicitude can do almost nothing, it is a matter in which celestial sorcery is everything, the course the planets take, the spots on the sun.

Simply to recite our provinces and their towns by name is to sing the praises of our venerated vineyards. It is profitable both to the spirit and the body—believe me—to taste a wine in its own home, in the landscape that it enriches. Such a pilgrimage, well understood, has surprises in store for you that you little suspect. A very young wine, tasted in the blue light of its storage shed—a half bottle of Anjou, opened under a barrel vault dusted with pale light by a violent and stormy summer afternoon—moving relics discovered in an old stillroom unaware of the treasures it contains, or else forgetful of them . . . I once fled from such a stillroom, in the Franche-Comté, as though I had been stealing from a museum . . . Another time, among the furniture being auctioned off on a tiny village square, between the commode, the iron bedstead, and some empty bottles, there were six full bottles being sold: it was then, as an adolescent, that I had my first encounter with an ardent and imperious prince, and a treacherous one, like all great seducers: the wine of Jurançon. Those six bottles made me more curious about the region that produced them than any geography teacher ever could have done. Though I admit that at such a price geography lessons would not be within the reach of everyone. And that triumphant wine, another day, drunk in an inn so dark that we never knew the color of the liquid they poured into our glasses . . . Just so does a woman keep the memory of a journey, of how she was surprised one night, of an unknown man, a man without a face, who made himself known to her only by his kiss . . .

The present snobbery about food is producing a crop of hostelries and country inns the like of which has never been seen before. Wine is revered in these places. Can wisdom be born again from a faith so unenlightened, a faith professed by mouths already, alas, armored with cocktails, with venomous apéritifs, with harsh and numbing spirits? Let us hope that it can. As old age approaches, I offer, as my contribution, the example of a stomach without remorse or damage, a very well-disposed liver, and a still sensitive palate, all preserved by good and honest wine. Therefore, wine, fill up this glass I now hold out to you! A delicate and simple glass, a light bubble in which there play the sanguine fires of a great Burgundian ancestor, the topaz of Yquem, and the balas ruby, sometimes with a paler purple tinge, of the Bordeaux with its scent of violets . . .

There comes a time of life when one begins to prize young wine. On a Southern shore there is a string of round, wicker-covered demijohns always kept in store for me. One grape harvest fills them to the brim, then the next grape harvest, finding them empty once more, in its turn fills them up again. Perhaps you have a hoard of fine old wines in your cellar, but do not disdain these wines because they give such quick returns: they are clear, dry, various, they flow easily from the throat down to the kidneys and scarcely pause a moment there. Even when it is of a warmer constitution, down there, if the day is a really hot one, we think nothing of drinking down a good pint of this particular wine, for it refreshes you and leaves a double taste behind, of muscat and of cedarwood. . . .

DC

Cheese

Perhaps because of the ponds, whose often sinking waters and reedy banks I was given to frequenting, there was never a year during my childhood when I did not suffer from a strong attack of fever, which always rose and then fell again without doing me any permanent harm. In our family we fed fevers, and from time to time I was approached with creamed rice pudding, breasts of chicken, or consommé . . . But I pushed all these things away from me with a hot hand, and sighed:

"I'd like some Camembert . . ."

To a person as natural, as lively and full of caprices as my mother, Camembert seemed no more suspect than baked apples, and so she gave me my Camembert. If there was no Camembert in the house, I would see a generously veined Roquefort being brought in to me, or else one of those flat cheeses "baked" in the embers of a wood fire, dry and transparent as old amber. This is what I call, when I think back to my early years, having a good education:

> Cheeses, your poetry!
> Of each meal the essence.
> What would our life be
> Lacking your presence?

Such was the anxious cry of gratitude that escaped from the lips of Monselet. What would become of France's gastronomy without the number and variety of her cheeses, without the perfection of her cheesemakers' art? The great wheels of Brie, the Pont-l'Évêque, the Gournay, the Lisieux, the cheese from the Marquisat de Sassenage, and many more besides, were both celebrated and also prime necessities as early as the Middle Ages. A diversity of wines is the fitting accompaniment to a diversity of cheeses. Under Louis XIII,

Paris also insisted on importing Parmesan and the cheeses of Switzerland and Holland: the latter a great resource for the poor people! Other days . . .

In Lower Burgundy, the milk at a few centimes the quart, the abundance of curds and whey and fresh cream cheeses ensured, once upon a time, that the children were well fed and the workers temperate with meat. There was no phase in the cheese's life from which we did not derive advantage: the quivering, scarcely set jelly, then the big, pressed masses of curd, cooked in thick layers on great, salted, open tart crusts. Then the finished cheese, generally hewn out in triangles, firmly held onto its slice of bread beneath the field worker's thumb . . . To follow, a dandelion salad bathed in walnut oil, a glass of wine . . . The idea of such a rustic meal still makes my mouth water today, because of the Treigny wine, because of the salad and its clove of garlic—above all, because of the cheese.

Not far from my village there were farms where they made Soumaintrains, and the red Saint-Florentins, which came to our market decked out in beetroot leaves. And I remember how the butter alone had the right to wear the long, the elegant chestnut leaf, delicately toothed along the edges . . .

To travel through France is first of all to travel through the most beautiful country in the world, and the most individualistic too. An individualism in all things to do with food, local pride, attachment to a particular and delicate nuance of taste. Oh, may they never leave us! I find them still almost everywhere, as delightful to happen on suddenly as button mushrooms hiding in the grass . . . Near Paris, less than twenty-five miles from the city, I have been astonished by little, round cheeses, almost cream cheeses, wrapped in dry plane-tree leaves.

"What do you call them?"

"They're the cheeses from around here," the woman selling them replied.

Paris has all the cheeses there are. Rough, sweet, appetite-creating, rich in fermenting juices, refined in cellars all over France, or else ripened in far-off countries, none of them has to wait long for buyers. It is the genuine connoisseur who is rare. Though they love cheese, women have been depriving themselves of it in recent years, ever since the terrible slimming neurosis has had them in its clutches. Time was, when a woman was better at choosing cheese than a man was. Feeling the rind, gauging the elasticity of the inside, *divining* a cheese, is to some extent a question of possessing a special X-ray sense. Studying the way in which a Camembert, a Reblochon, or a Maroilles had developed fissures in its rind, the way the center of a Pont-l'Évêque has become either a little cushion or a little saucer, being able to decide whether the pearly distillation from a Munster is too liquid and holds a promise of premature bitterness, of sharpness rather than smoothness, all such fine attention to detail is now being lost. When I am in Brussol's, where I investigate the top, then the bottom of my cheeses, I am ashamed as I watch the procession of other women filing past: "Have you got a nice, runny Camembert? . . . I'd like a Pont-l'Évêque, the best you have . . ." Not a single glance of interest at the cheeses themselves, bound in their gilded leather, lying mysteriously beneath thick coats of lichen. Not a single gesture of personal inquiry. They pay, and they leave. Unless they stand there, hesitating for a moment, musing undecidedly, hoping to give themselves the air of connoisseurs . . .

If I had a son of marriageable age, I should say to him: "Beware of young women who love neither wine nor truffles nor cheese nor music."

If my daughter were to ask my advice about the contribution she should make to a picnic, I should say to her: "If you bring the desserts, the guests will be satisfied. If you choose the cheeses, they will repay you with gratitude." But my daughter doesn't ask my advice. One day, when we were both invited to the same improvised meal, I saw that she had brought not only the desserts but the cheeses as well. And I blushed with pride. Whereupon I gave my daughter a little lecture on the subject of thoughtless extravagance. She replied: "Yes, Mummy," with great deference, all the while thinking about something quite different. And we both felt, with equal satisfaction, that we had each discharged our respective duties.

DC

Truffles

We only do well the things we like doing. Neither knowledge nor diligence can create a great chef. Of what use is conscientiousness as a substitute for inspiration? I was born in the country, in a region where people still treasured recipes, which I have never found in any cooking guide, as they would the secret of a perfume or some miraculous balm. They were passed on by word of mouth alone, on the occasion of some feast accompanied by the sound of bells, the christening of a first-born, or a confirmation. They escaped, during lengthy wedding feasts, from lips unlocked by vintage wines: this was how my mother came to receive, in strictest confidence, the secret of how to make a certain chicken "ball," an ovoid missile sewn into the skin of a boned chicken. How could one reconstitute now the secret of that "ball," set out, on the table, in large, round slices studded with the glittering black eye of the truffle and the bright green of the pistachio nut?

At least I did learn—in the truffle country of Puisaye, whose soil produces a gray truffle with a good smell but no taste whatever —how to treat the true truffle, the black truffle, the truffle of Périgord. The most capricious, the most revered of all those black princesses. People will pay its own weight in gold for the truffle of Périgord, for the most part in order to put it to some paltry use. They insert it in glutinous masses of *foie gras,* they bury it in poultry overlarded with grease, they submerge it, chopped to pieces, in brown sauce, they combine it with vegetables covered in mayonnaise . . . Away with all this slicing, this dicing, this grating, this peeling of truffles! Can they not love it for itself? If you do love it, then pay its ransom royally—or keep away from it altogether. But once having bought it, eat it on its own, scented and grainy-skinned, eat it like the vegetable it is, hot, and served in munificent quantities. Once scraped, it won't give you much trouble; its sovereign flavor disdains all complications and complicities. Bathed in a good, very dry white wine—keep the champagne for your banquets, the truffle can do without it—salted without extravagance, peppered with discretion, they can then be cooked in a simple, black, cast-iron stewpan with the lid on. For twenty-five minutes, they must dance in the constant flow of bubbles, drawing with them through the eddies and the foam—like tritons playing around some darker Amphitrite—a score or so of smallish strips of bacon, fat, but not too fat, which will give body to the stock. No other herbs or spices! And a pestilence upon your rolled napkin, with its taste and odor of lye, last resting place of the cooked truffle! Your truffles must come to the table in their own stock. Do not stint when you serve yourself: the truffle is an appetite creator, an aid to digestion. And as you break open this jewel sprung from a poverty-stricken soil, imagine—if you have never visited it—the desolate kingdom where it rules. For it kills the dog rose, drains life from the oak, and ripens beneath an ungrateful bed of pebbles. Imagine the harsh winter of Périgord, the rough frost whitening the grass, the pink pig trained for its delicate prospector's task . . .

I have hunted truffles near Martel, in the Lot district, holding the leash of a little sow, an artist in her own way, who sniffed out the truffle in its earthy bed, then dug for it with an inspired snout, with squeals, with sudden thrusts, with every outward appearance, on my honor, of a sleepwalker. And each time she unearthed another treasure, the intelligent little sow lifted up her head and begged for her reward, a handful of corn.

Do not eat the truffle without wine. If you have no great Burgundy of impeccable ancestry to hand, then drink some wine from Mercurey, full-bodied and velvety at the same time. And drink only a little, if you please. In the region where I was born, we always say that during a good meal one is not thirsty but "hungry" for wine.

DC

❧❧ Portraits and Tributes

Honoré de Balzac

I once, almost, owned Balzac's tie pin. It came into my mother's hands as a gift from my godmother, General Désandré's wife, and stayed in our family for a very long time. General Désandré's wife, who was related to the Mallet family through the Survilles, had a deep affection for my mother, Sido, and my godfather's military career had made him a close friend of my father's. After the latter's death, once the noise of his two crutches and his single leg was no longer to be heard there, our house was invaded by a sort of malign disorder that caused rare books to go astray and scattered everywhere a quantity of white, ruled paper, once earmarked for some mysterious task, but still virgin at his death. Balzac's tie pin disappeared. Possibly some base soul assumed that the cornelian ball with the serpent's slender, golden head resting on its summit had some intrinsic value. It was a little bauble the color of burnt topaz, and we never saw it again. I felt regret that it had gone, but without bothering to wonder how or why. A family free enough in its ideas to set its children loose in the very heart of the Balzacian jungle, children free in their turn to dredge up, from those mahogany-fitted libraries, a miscellaneous treasure trove of novels, travel books, and poems, did not waste its time in vain and vague embargoes, even less on fruitless surveillance. I did not take long to choose. At an age when children are usually immersed in fairy stories, I tumbled into Balzac, drowned myself in him, and stayed there. I am there still, but with the difference that I no longer read Balzac for the therapeutic qualities I used to find in him when I was young. Nowadays I am daring enough to be bored in his company. I can forgive him now that taste he had for italics, that ingenuous way he had of underlining the things he liked. I prefer twenty lines describing a street that has lost its "reputation," to the portrait of Armand de Montriveau. Today, I am an old lover who fondles and kisses, in memory, the ugly little birthmark that a beautiful mistress used once to hide beneath a lock of hair. I correct the errors committed by passionate Balzac lovers . . . "What a memory!" people exclaim. I have only one reply to that, always the same: "No. But one has to start very young."

And very young indeed I was. Flat on my stomach on a garden seat, a volume of the Houssiaux edition open in front of my nose, the book spread flat, the pages hanging by their threads, but not yet loose. This first Houssiaux was succeeded, after my first marriage, by Houssiaux II. That was at a time in my life when some mysterious hand was in the habit of stealing books, drawings, and the smaller framed pictures from my house. Volume by volume, Houssiaux II grew sparser and sparser; and though it never dared to disappear completely, I ceased to love it when it became incomplete. Much later, during a music-hall tour, my love was kindled anew in Lyons, where I chanced upon a second-hand Houssiaux in one of Flammarion's stores. A Houssiaux that might have been made for me, marbled in red and black, just worn enough, just yellow enough at the edges, but not too dirty, and with those frightful Bertalls and sooty Henri Monniers . . . I still have it. It has grown no older since it came to live with me, because I take good care of it. And it repays my care: an excellent remedy for fevers, sovereign against certain "recently published" novels, especially those which seem to be clamoring for a prize. With me, it is well protected from breadcrumbs and pieces of cheese rind, but not always safe from an old rose petal or a dried, stiff pansy, like a portrait of Henry VIII . . .

I am well aware that I supply his genius with my own gift for rereading, which is worthy of mention and provides me, in the case of Balzac's works, with an elasticity and an ability to bounce straight back that are quite exceptional. I am Balzac's *pelotari*. On my first bounce, I run smack into what is for me one of his greatest attractions: the admiration he lavishes on the individual human being, whether it be loaded down with crimes or, by his grace, innocent of them all. When you know Balzac as well as I do, you are not far from believing that he grants a special allegiance to the hero on whom nature has bestowed a head of black hair and two azure blue eyes. In any case, Lucien de Rubempré's physical beauty is sufficient to cast a spell over Vautrin. It is also sufficient for the great writer himself to speak of it without embarrassment and affectation. What a meeting is that of the pseudo-Canon of Toledo and the young candidate for suicide—the stream, the posy of wild flowers in the wilting fingers . . . Not one explicit word is exchanged between the two men, one of whom ought to have chosen death, if he had not been weaker than any woman . . .

Extravagant overwork, magnificent self-satisfaction, contempt for anything that might conduce to good health—I like to muse over that life of penal servitude in which Balzac could still find room for a love story, which later became a tale of married life. What would he have thought of the caution—whether instinctive or acquired—that we temperate writers, we tentative lovers display? I find a gentle pleasure now in accepting a world-sized, enormous Balzac, hewn out in great blocks, enriched with delicately carved arabesques. But I refuse to accept, I thrust away from my vision of the great man that Slav lady of his . . . About her I have learned the absolute minimum, merely what historians of the Balzac-Hanska couple have offered me. I find it easy to neglect a woman who, after being chosen by a great and imprudent man, succeeded in making him neither happy nor desperate enough.

DC

Marcel Proust

When I was a very young woman, he was a very good-looking young man. Trust the portrait of him by Jacques-Émile Blanche. That narrow mouth, that mist around the eyes, that tired freshness, both the features and the expression really are those of the young

Marcel Proust. Pierre de Guingand looked very much like him later on. The appearance of Marcel Proust's eyes on Jacques Blanche's canvas and the picture they have left in my memory are exceedingly alike: opened very wide, more anxious than astonished, and wearing a deceptively naïve expression.

I was a regular visitor at Mme Arman de Caillavet's Wednesdays, and knew Marcel Proust at a time when he still had the appearance of an adolescent, as well as the bearing and the courtesy, which ought to have surprised no one but did surprise some people, of a young man taking his First Communion. Anatole France, under cover of a condescendingly goodhearted manner, displayed a very lively interest in him, whereas "that goodhearted Madame Arman" (Anatole France never used the "de" when referring to his friend) was rather harsh in her treatment of the very young man with the gentle face.

One evening, Proust came to the avenue Hoch with a companion scarcely older than himself and, like himself, graceful and soft-voiced. They arrived together, took their leave together, and left the room together walking with an identical gait. As soon as they had gone, Mme Arman de Caillavet, wheeling like a storm cloud, exploded.

"Ah no! This has become impossible," she cried. "Did you see them? Behaving like two doting twins! Billing like a pair of parakeets who can't be parted! That young man is really going too far! He's deliberately flaunting himself . . . And even if he's determined to shock people, at least he needn't make himself ridiculous! What do you think, Monsieur France? I ask you, do you really . . . Monsieur France! I am addressing you! Why are you looking at me like that?"

Our unanimous silence finally warned her, and she turned around. Behind her, Marcel Proust, in the frame of the door he had just opened, was leaning against one jamb, losing the delicate colors from his lips and cheeks.

"I came . . . I wanted to collect . . ." he stammered.

"What? What? You wanted what?" Mme Arman bayed.

"A book that Schwob gave me . . . Did I leave it here? There in the armchair . . . I'm sorry to have disturbed you . . ."

He managed to summon up just sufficient strength to pick up the book and make his escape.

The ensuing silence was not pleasant for any of us. But it did not take our intrepid hostess long to dismiss the matter with a shrug of her solid, bared, and diamond-hung shoulders:

"Ah well! It couldn't be helped . . ."

When I saw him again in the Ritz Hotel, where he lived during the war, his illness and the passing years had already done their swift work on him. His agitation and his pallor seemed to be the result of some terrible inner force. Dressed in tails, standing in his timidly lighted hallway, at the heart of a darkened Paris, Marcel Proust greeted me with faltering gaiety. Over his evening dress he was wearing an unfastened cape. The expression of the white, crumpled shirt front, and the convulsions of his tie terrified me as much as the black marks under his eyes and around his mouth, the sooty, telltale traces that an absent-minded malady had smeared haphazardly across his face. The same solicitude and the same courteous manner, both of which he retained throughout his life, still accompanied all his gestures and all his words, like morbid relics of his early youth. He offered one a drink or held out a delicacy with the eager hesitancy of a sixteen-year-old boy. Like many exceptionally delicate people, he ceased to be conscious of fatigue at an hour when his healthy companions were all beginning to admit how tired they were—I remember certain evenings spent in the company of Mme de Noailles, later on, when I found myself thinking of Marcel Proust as I looked at her, as she sat, half reclining, pale, glittering, her nose pinched, her little shoulders melting away beneath a shawl, casting until the dawn, in that voice of bronze, to those present and those absent alike, a just tribute of flowers and darts, of wreaths and judgments without appeal . . .

At two in the morning, when Proust's guests left him, it was he who wanted to go with them. There was an old cab, a brougham, standing dreaming in the Place Vendôme, and Marcel Proust wanted to pay the driver to take us all home, for there were only four or five of us. Then he insisted that he ought to accompany us to our respective homes. But I lived in the heart of Auteuil, and neither the driver nor the horse was of an age to travel so far through a dark, wartime night. I prevented Proust from blaming himself and lamenting over my lot by telling him that since my eyes were not of the best, it sometimes happened, when I was returning home late, that I slipped off my footwear under one of the blue street lamps in the Place de la Concorde, and then, having knotted my shoes and stockings into a bundle, I would entrust myself, between the Cours-la-Reine and the boulevard Suchet, to my bare and path-divining feet.

Our host stood listening to me, in front of the Ritz colonnade. The silence of the night, and the mist cutting off our view of the square, surrounded Proust with a halo exactly suited to his decline and his prestige. With his top hat pushed back, a great lock of hair covering his brow, ceremonious and disheveled, he looked like a young and drunken wedding guest. The stifled light emerging from the entrance hall, and a white, theatrical reflection striking up from the cracked shirt front, highlighted his chin and the curving lines of his eyebrows. He greatly enjoyed my little barefoot-beggar-girl story, and when he exclaimed: "No, really, do you?" a smile I could not describe, a sort of youthful astonishment, remodeled all his features. As we finally took our leave of him, he stepped back, waved goodbye with one hand, and the darkness once more hollowed out the deep sockets of his eyes and filled with ashes the black oval of his mouth, gaping in its quest for air.

DC

Eleonora Duse

In Rome, during the war, the motion pictures twice presented her to my admiring eyes. The first time she was acting, in a movie, the role of an old peasant woman. Beneath the knotted headscarf, beneath the cheap cotton dress and the dark apron, she displayed a luminously white head of hair, a stiff and delicate body, and a pair of moving hands that took upon themselves the task of conveying to us all that the slightly constrained, almost intimidated face was still refusing to yield up to the screen. In her most beautiful scene, those hands, lifted toward a high-set window, called out to a much loved child. La Duse had her back to the audience, who could gaze only at the calico blouse, at the kerchief knotted over the hair, and at the hands terminating her outstretched arms; and those hands were such —loving, beating wings, prolonged, extended by their shadows right up to the window sill—that the emotional Italian crowd by which I was surrounded suddenly burst forth into a mist of tears and sighs, all at the same moment.

The second time, only a few days afterward, was in another cool and darkened movie auditorium where I had taken refuge from the Roman spring which was then bursting out on every side with wistaria, iris, and lilac and had arrived at such a pitch of ardor that not even the *ponentino* could cool it down. A woman friend whispered very quietly in my ear: "Behind us, that lady in black: it's Eleanora Duse." I recognized the luminous hair combed into an oblique flame across the brow, its ardor dimmed by a large black hat, and the huge, deep eye sockets in which the eyes were swimming in shadows that merely added to their luster. Only the little nose was still that of a young woman, an imperious, ironic nose, a nose prompt to betray anger or disgust.

The celebrated face, inclining first to the right, then to the left, as it followed the sequences of a wretchedly melodramatic movie, permitted me to read, printed on all its features, a vast and melting naïveté, wholly without suspicion. But at intermission, as light returned to the house, the sight of la Duse drew a fairly large crowd of admirers clustering around her. Standing up, she accepted their homage and shook a few hands. She did not smile, but presented her brow to them as though it were a defensive wall; and the little nose, offended now, was quivering with disdain. "Look," the Italian woman with me whispered, "look what a *lady* she is!"

DC

Sarah Bernhardt

. . . I received an invitation from her that read like a command: "Madame Sarah Bernhardt expects you, on such and such a day, for lunch."

I had never seen her so close before. At the far end of a long gallery, she was the term and the *raison d'être* of a somewhat funereal museum of palms, dried sheaves of rushes, plaques, and commemorative tributes. Her body, with its missing leg, no longer counted; it was hidden in a sack of dark fabric that fell around her in great folds. But the white face, the tiny hands still shone like crumpled flowers. I could have gazed forever into the blue of her eyes as they changed their tint in accordance with all the movements, still so full of life, of that tiny and imperious head.

Just before lunch was served, Sarah disappeared, whisked away by some theatrical machine or perhaps simply by a set of faithful arms, and we rejoined her in a short while on the floor above, where she was sitting at the table in her Gothic palanquin. She ate, or appeared to eat. And she grew animated whenever the conversation turned toward the theater. One felt the presence of her extraordinary critical ability in every opinion she gave, in every word she spoke. She was gaily severe toward an artist who had recently assayed the leading role in *l'Aiglon:* "That poor creature who is neither man enough to make us forget she is a woman in a man's clothes nor woman enough to make them attractive . . ."

She ceased talking about the theater only in order to give all her attention to a large, brown earthenware coffeepot. She measured out the ground-up coffee, poured in the boiling water, filled our cups, and waited for the praises she had so justly earned:

"Do I make coffee as well as Catulle Mendès?"

She leaned down toward me from the height of her palanquin
. . . I record here, with respect, one of the last poses of this great
tragic actress, then about to reach her eightieth year: the delicate
and withered hand offering the brimming cup, the flowery azure of
the eyes, so young still in their network of fine lines, the questioning
and mocking coquetry of the tilted head, and that indestructible desire to charm, to charm still, to charm right up to the gates of death
itself.

DC

Claude Debussy

All my meetings with Claude Debussy took place in the sonor-
ous warmth, the delicate fever of an exclusively musical atmosphere.
A composer at the piano, a singer leaning back with his elbows
resting on its bare top, or a woman singer, not leaving her armchair,
but singing, exhaling the melody like a cloud of unconsidered
smoke, head tilted back. If Louis de Serres left the keyboard, Pierre
de Bréville replaced him, or Charles Bordes, or Déodat de Séverac.
Vincent d'Indy amused himself timidly, improvising a waltz for barrel organ, then suddenly broke off as though he had been burned by
his own shame as he sat on the revolving piano stool. Gabriel Fauré
and André Messager, in the grip of a sudden rivalry, sat down in his
stead to play four-hand improvisations. The rhythm gathered break-
neck speed beneath their fingers, and every modulation became an
ambush.

At such times, Debussy seemed to become intoxicated by the
music. His ambered satyr's face, his spiraling locks of hair, in which
the eye instinctively sought for a glimpse of vine leaves and grapes,
would quiver with an inner delirium. In moments of fixed intensity,
his pupils would cross their sight lines slightly, after the fashion of
hunting animals hypnotized by their own watchfulness. It seemed to
me that he loved music in the way a crystal tulip loves the shock
that draws a pure note tingling from its bowl. One Sunday evening,

after hearing *Antar* played for the first time in France, unless perhaps it was *Scheherazade,* we both chanced to go on to the same party, and Debussy, obsessed, overcome, was singing his symphonic memories of the work inside himself. He was giving out a sort of bee-swarm buzzing, something like the sound you hear from telegraph poles, a groping and hesitant murmur. Then the memory grew more precise, and his closed face suddenly opened.

"Wait! Wait!" he said very loudly. "Like that . . . mmmmm . . . and like this: mmmmm . . ."

One of us caught at this remembered shred of melody before it could fly away again, then drew it out a little further.

"Yes, yes," Debussy cried. "And then at the same time there are the cellos lower down, saying: mmm . . . And the kettledrums, oh heavens, the kettledrums, just the faintest murmur to tell us there's that explosion coming from the brass, and . . . and . . ."

Lips pursed, then miaowing as he went on to imitate the violins, he panted on, torn apart by all the different timbers vying for places in his memory. With the poker clenched firmly in one hand, he hammered on the rosewood of the piano. With the other he made a zzzzzzzzzzing! sound against the windowpane, then plopped his lips together drily to re-create the xylophone, and made a sound of "duk, duk" in a voice like crystal, to recall for us the liquid notes of the celesta.

He stood up, using his voice, his arms, and his feet all at once, while two black spirals of hair danced on his forehead. His faun's laugh rang out in reply, not to our laughter, but to some inner solicitation, and I engraved at that moment in my memory this image of the great master of French music in the process of inventing, before our very eyes, the jazz band.

DC

Maurice Ravel

Can I say that I ever really knew him, my illustrious collaborator, the composer of *L'Enfant et les sortilèges?* I met Maurice Ravel for the first time at the house of Mme de Saint-Marceaux, who received guests every Wednesday evening after dinner. Those receptions in the Saint-Marceaux town house, forty years ago now, were not merely a diversion for the worldly and the curious; they were a reward granted to faithful music lovers, a higher form of recreation, the bastion of an intimate artistic world. Those two, not particularly large drawing rooms opening into one another were for a long time the place which set a final seal on the reputations of composers and virtuoso performers alike, for their mistress was a woman of great musical culture. In truth, Mme de Saint-Marceaux was far from being a celebrity hunter, yet the honor of being a regular at her Wednesdays was very much sought after.

A dinner, invariably excellent, always preceded these musical evenings, during which the mistress of the house achieved an atmosphere of "supervised freedom." She never forced anyone to listen to the music, but she would immediately suppress the slightest hint of whispering. Everyone was at liberty to arrive at whatever time best suited him, provided only that the men were dressed in jackets and the women in day dresses. "My Wednesdays," Mme de Saint-Marceaux would explain, "are given for the benefit of hard-working friends who are tired after a hard day's labor, for neighbors who have decided at the last moment to leave their own firesides to come and sit by mine, and for painters who set great store by the casualness of their attire. It has taken me twenty years to dispel any feelings of unease they may have had, and to accustom them to this unostentatious comfort. If Fauré were to come on from his duchesses in evening dress and play the dandy in my house, then Messager, who is coquetry itself, would feel humiliated and start wearing that dismal, put-upon look of his. No, no, I will have no fine feathers here!"

The Princess Edmond de Polignac always made her appearances in a high-necked dress. I used to admire the indestructible character which was able to harmonize the definitive blue of her eyes with that conqueror's chin, but always from a little way off, for the sight intimidated me. Her husband was never seen at these

Wednesdays without his beige vicuña shawl; sometimes it was draped over his chill-prone shoulders, sometimes he used it to warm his knees. He was charming, young in spirit, and in appearance like a great, ironic bird. To listen to Fauré or Édouard Risler playing the piano, or Bagès singing Schumann, or Pierre de Bréville's brief melodies, the Prince de Polignac would settle himself in the depths of one of the sofas, take out his pencil, and doodle . . .

Big, well-shaded lamps; easily accessible tables piled high with magazines, newspapers, and cigarettes; warmth in winter; cool drinks and petits fours in the nearby dining room . . .

It was in this place, filled with sound but also sympathetic to meditation, that I first met Maurice Ravel, still very jealous of his prerogatives at that time, but capable of great gentleness nevertheless. He was young, not yet at the age when one acquires simplicity. In 1907, Jules Renard noted that Ravel was "dark, rich and delicate." His side whiskers—yes, side whiskers!—and his vast quantities of hair accentuated the contrast between his imposing head and his slight body. He loved startling neckties and frilled shirts. Though constantly seeking for attention, he was very apprehensive of criticism; and that of Henri Gauthier-Villars was savage. Perhaps because he was secretly shy, Ravel always maintained an aloof air, a clipped manner of speech. Except that I listened to his music, that I conceived a certain curiosity about it, then an attachment, to which the slight shock of uneasiness it used to cause me, its seductively sensuous irony, and its artistic orginality all added fresh charms, for a great many years that was all I knew of Maurice Ravel. I cannot recall sharing a single private conversation with him, not a single friendly confidence, during all that time.

The day came when M. Rouché asked me to write the libretto of a fairy-tale ballet for the Opéra. I still cannot explain to myself how I managed to produce *l'Enfant et les sortilèges* for him—I who write so slowly and with such difficulty—in less than a week . . . He liked my little poem, and suggested the names of several composers, all of which I received with as much politeness as I could muster.

"But," Rouché said after a pause, "what if I were to suggest Ravel?"

My politeness was immediately forgotten in my excitement, and my expressions of hope threw diplomacy to the winds.

"But we mustn't forget that it might take a long time," Rouché added, "even supposing that Ravel should accept . . ."

He accepted. And it took a long time. He disappeared with my libretto, and we heard nothing more about Ravel, or about *l'Enfant* . . . Where was Ravel working? Was he working? I was not then aware of all that the creation of a work demanded from him, the slow frenzy that would take hold of him and make him its solitary prisoner, careless of the days and hours. The war claimed Ravel, created a hermetic silence about his name, and I lost the habit of thinking about *l'Enfant et les sortilèges.*

Five years passed. The finished work, and its creator, emerged from the silence, escaping from the blue and nyctalopic eyes of the Siamese cats, his confidants. But the composer did not treat me as a privileged person; he allowed me no comments, no premature audition of the score. His only concern seemed to be the "miaow duet" between the two Cats, and he asked me with great seriousness if I saw any objection to his replacing *mouao* with *mouain,*" or it may have been the other way around . . .

The years had stripped him by then, not only of his frilled shirt front and his side whiskers, but also of his short man's hauteur. The white hair and the black hair on his head had mingled to form a sort of plumage, and he would cross his delicate little rodent's hands as he spoke, flicking every nearby object with his squirrel's eyes . . .

The score of *l'Enfant et les sortilèges*—I had thoughtlessly entitled it *Divertissement pour ma fille* until the day Ravel, with icy gravity, said to me: "But I have no daughter"—is now famous. How can I convey to you my emotion at the first throb of the tambourines accompanying the procession of the shepherd boys, the moonlit dazzle of the garden, the flight of the dragonflies and the bats . . . "It's quite amusing, don't you think?" Ravel said. But my throat was knotted tight with tears: the animals, with swift whispering sounds scarcely distinguishable as syllables, were leaning down, in reconciliation, over the Child . . . I had not foreseen that a wave of orchestrated sound, starred with nightingales and fireflies, would raise my modest work up to such heights.

DC

Jean Cocteau

Jean Cocteau came in, and I looked, with astonishment, at the time on my watch: half past eleven . . . in the morning? If it were the evening, then there would be no cause for astonishment. And in fact he answered my question before I had asked it.

"Yes . . . Just imagine, my technicians, my electricians, my carpenters, they've all just informed me that they're on strike."

He insinuated his long body onto the poop of my raft, folded up his legs and arms, then hunched up his torso with a view to accommodating the whole within the boundaries of my ray of sunshine, which was about to touch midday.

"And so?"

"And so nothing. I left the studio."

"A vacation! Rest. It's always the answer."

His nose glanced at me sideways with a perplexed expression.

"But the whole point is that it isn't the answer any more. I've been working like a madman for years now. At night, through the day, on Sundays. On the floor, on restaurant tables, on pieces of paper. Once upon a time the work used to leap out on me suddenly, then go away and leave me for dead. But now I no longer know how to stop myself working, unless my time off is arranged a long while in advance. They're taking my poison away from me again too. My joints hurt. It's a quarter of twelve. I'm not hungry yet. I'm not hungry any more. What does one do, at a quarter of twelve, when one isn't working? I've forgotten."

"Stay here with me."

"I can't. One just simply doesn't stay here with you at a quarter of twelve."

"Where do you intend to go?"

"That's just it, I don't know. I shall try to go home . . ."

From the tone in which he said this, it sounded as though he were about to embark on some perilous adventure.

He unfolded himself. His angular grace disturbed nothing, upset nothing on the piled-up bed, or so much as brushed against any of the obstacles filling the crowded little room. He walked to the door, then turned around:

"Watch me as I cross the garden, I'm sure I'm going to walk sideways."

DC

La Belle Otéro

As it happens, I remember Mme Otéro with pleasure. I might have been able to garner perhaps, from lips more august than hers, words of wisdom rich in echoes that would have led to my greater profit and enlightenment! But august lips are not so prodigal. I have asked for compensations from the unknown and the come-by-chance, and they have sometimes given them to me, rather in the way the coconut tree bestows its nuts—plump on the head! Mme Otéro, upright in the middle of that period in my life when I was exploring the possibilities of earning my own living, had not the faintest resemblance to a coconut tree. She was purely ornamental. Like all luxuries, she was curiously and variously instructive, and merely to hear her made me rejoice that the early stages in one of my careers should have set her in my way.

"You look a bit green, my girl," she once said to me. "Don't forget that there is always a moment in a man's life, even if he's a miser, when he opens his hand *wide*. . . ."

"The moment of passion?"

"No. The moment when you twist his wrist."

She added: "like this," and made a twisting movement with her two clenched hands. You seemed to see the blood flow, the juice of fruits, the gold, and goodness knows what else: to hear the bones crack. Can you picture me twisting the miser's wrist? I laughed, I admired; there was nothing else for me to do. Magnificent creature! She was, at the time of our first meeting, reaching the age when the women of today consider it necessary to practice sad, gymnastic, restrictive measures to disguise and preserve their precious forty-fifth year. Mme Otéro did not dream of any self-denying ordinances. I may have learned nothing from her rare remarks—she was not a great talker, at least not in French—but I had the good luck of being with her behind the scenes, away from the public ceremonies, the suppers and dress rehearsals of the music-hall stage that held her rigid in her gala corsets, her huge breastplate of jewels plastered to her chest. A motionless icon—alive as a tree laden with hoarfrost is alive, only in its glittering. I infinitely preferred another Lina, no less full of condescension, who used to call out to me, familiarly: "Coming to eat my *puchero* on Zaturday? Come early and I'll play you a game of bezique before dinner."

· · · ·

No men were invited, and no rivals. The official lover was bandaging his damaged wrist elsewhere. We took our places beside Lina, one or two aging friends and I, who was not old but colorless.

A true feast for the hearty eater is never the regular dinner of hors d'oeuvres, followed by entree and roast. On that point, Mme Otéro and I were entirely agreed. A *puchero,* with its beef, its knuckle of ham and fat gammon, its boiled fowl, its *longanizas,* its *chorizos,* all the vegetables of the *pot-au-feu,* its mountains of *garbanzos* and sweet corn, that is the dish for people who enjoy food. I have always enjoyed food, but what was my appetite compared with Lina's? Her queenliness melted, and a gentle bliss, an air of happy innocence took its place. Her teeth, her eyes, her glossy lips shone like a girl's. There are few beautiful women who can guzzle without loss of prestige. Lina did not push away her plate until she had emptied it four, five times. A little strawberry ice, a cup of coffee, and up she sprang, fastening a pair of castanets to her thumbs.

"Maria, to the piano with you. You others, zhove ziz table out of my way into zat corner!"

It would be hardly ten o'clock. Until two in the morning Carolina Otéro would dance and sing—for her own enjoyment, she cared little for ours. From a handsome forty she became a lively seventeen. The bathwrap tossed aside, she danced in her petticoat, which was of brocaded silk with a flounce five meters around, the only garment essential to Spanish dancing. Soaked with sweat, her fine lawn chemise clung to her loins. Her moist skin gave off a delicate scent, a dusty scent, predominantly of sandalwood, that was more subtle than herself. There was nothing base in her violent and wholly selfish pleasure; it was born of a true passion for rhythm and music. She would snatch up her sauce-stained table napkin and wipe herself vigorously, face, neck, and damp armpits, then dance again, sing again: "Ziz one? Do you know it?" Her feet were not very light, but her face, tilted backward over her shoulders, the muscles of her waist rippling above the powerful loins, the savage, swaying furrow of her naked back could defy the harshest glare. A body that had defied sickness, ill-usage, and the passage of time—a well-nourished body, sleek of sinew, bright of skin, amber by day, white by night—I have always told myself that I would, some day, with due care and detachment, describe it and its arrogant decline. We cannot paint a beloved face without passionately distorting it—and who speaks willingly of the things that belong to real love? But we can catch and hold—with words or with the brush—the crimson flush of dying leaves, the green of a meteor against the blue night, a moment of dawn, a catastrophe. Pictures which of themselves have no sense or depth, but which we invest with meaning or sharp foreboding—they bear forever the stamp of a particular year, mark the end of a run of bad luck, or the culmination of a spell of prosperity. For that reason, no one of us can ever swear that he has painted, contemplated, described in vain.

HBk

❧ Human Nature

❧ BEAUTY SALON

Colette's Institut de Beauté was accorded a Tout-Paris opening on June 1, 1932. With a salon in the rue de Miromesnil, and with Colette herself as star makeup specialist, it flourished for over a year and was then disbanded.

. . . The first time . . .

. . . The first time André Maginot came back, after his serious war wound, walking painfully, to have lunch with me on the boulevard Suchet, I settled him into the very largest armchair and slipped a low stool under his injured leg. He made fun of me, embarrassed at having to accept these attentions. The garden, small but thickly planted, then the cat and the tortoise, furnished us with subjects of conversation as we sat there together. Then Maginot asked abruptly if I still thought of starting my "luxury business."

"Not often," I replied, with truth.

"You're wrong. This is the moment to think about it. I'm talking seriously. We're on the threshold of a strange age. The people who try something new will be running no risk, except that of making a mistake. And even then, they need only start over again. The important thing is to make the attempt. The nice thing about it would be always having one activity to help you escape from another, not allowing yourself to be caught in a rut . . . We should never allow ourselves to be caught in a rut . . . If I were you, I'd

go about this thing quite openly. I can see so clearly how it should
be launched. On the door of the boutique, I would put up a
sign . . .

He opened his arms wide. His right hand went out toward the
wall and brushed a Moustier plate, which tinkled; his left forearm
left the drawing room, by way of the french window, and threw a
shadow across the gravel:

"I would put up a sign: 'My name is Colette and I sell perfumes here!'"

In all the time . . .

In all the time since I began making up and giving beauty
treatments to so many women of my own age, I have never yet encountered a fifty-year-old woman who has lost heart, or a sixty-year-
old suffering from nerves. It is among these lady champions that it
does one good to attempt—and to bring to fruition—cosmetic miracles. Where are those rouges of yesteryear, with their harsh red-
currant tints, those ungrateful whites, those Virgin Mary blues? We
now have a range of tints at our disposal that would go to the head
of a painter. The art of improving faces, and its ally, the cosmetic
industry, now have a yearly turnover almost as large as that of the
motion-picture industry. The harder the times are for women, the
more determined women become, and proudly so, to hide the suffering it inflicts on them. The creatures once known as "the weaker
sex" are now torn from their brief repose, before the dawn, by bone-
crushing jobs. Heroically concealed behind her mandarin mask, her
eyes enlarged, a tiny red mouth painted over the pale mouth beneath, the woman of today, thanks to this daily lie, can salvage a
daily measure of endurance, and the inner pride never to admit . . .

I have never felt so much esteem for woman, or so much admiration, as in the time I have been seeing her at such close quarters,
since I have been holding, tilted back beneath my blue metallic rays,
her face stripped of its secrets, rich with expression, so various be-

neath its agile wrinkles, or new once more and refreshed for having for a moment relinquished its added tints. Oh, brave fighters! It is the fight itself that keeps you young. I do my best, but how you help me! When some among you whisper your real ages in my ear, I stand there dazzled. There is one who hurls herself at my little laboratory as though it were a barricade. She is sharp-tongued, sprung from the people, superb.

"To work! To work!" she cries. "I've got a difficult sale coming up. Got to look thirty today—and the whole day, mind!"

It sometimes happens that I pass, in the time it takes to lift a curtain, from her courageous optimism to one of those tentative young women who have bellies as hollow as greyhounds, eyes full of a velvet reticence, few words to say, and a virtuoso's command of the cosmetic keyboard.

"That one . . . And that one . . . And then the eyelash thing . . . And the dark powder . . . Ah! And now . . ."

It is I who attempt to restrain them: "But what will there be left when you're as old as I am?"

One of them raised her eyes and fixed me with a long and disillusioned gaze: "Nothing . . . I don't do it for my own amusement, you know . . . My dream is to be made up once and for all, for life; I make up heavily so that I shall look exactly the same in twenty years' time. That way, I hope no one will see that I've changed."

One of my greatest pleasures is a new discovery. You would never believe how many women's faces in Paris stay exactly as God created them until their owners reach fairly advanced years. But then comes the dangerous moment, and with it a sort of panic—the desire not only to last but to be reborn; there comes the bitter, tardy spring that flowers in women's hearts, and its strength can move mountains . . .

"Do you think that . . . Oh, there's no question of making me into a young woman again, of course . . . But all the same, I'd like to try . . ."

I listen, but above all I look. A wide, brown eyelid, an eye unaware of its possibilities, a Roman cheek, rather wide but still firm, all that lovely territory to be explored, to be exploited . . . I am to be envied, I reap such fine rewards when the makeup is at last applied: the sigh of hope, the astonishment, the budding pride, and that impatient glance toward the door into the street, toward "the effect it will make," toward the risks to come . . .

DC

❦❦❦

Nudity

When the daughter of one of my women friends married the son of one of my men friends, people exclaimed: "They were made for one another!" I made no exclamations at all, for the engaged couple had also known each other since childhood, and I considered in my heart of hearts that there was something altogether too friendly about this love match. Though I did also think that certain half-concealed feelings of timidity I detected in the young woman were a good augury for the future, and likewise a certain air of authority in the young man, who was no more than twenty-one years old.

When it became evident, after they had been married a few weeks, that "all was not going as it should" with the newlyweds, the usual unpleasant family rumors began to raise their heads. It was impossible, for a time, to make out either who had started them or whether they were true or false. Who was the first to speak? The young husband? Ah no, it couldn't be the young husband. The young wife? But it was only yesterday that she was still an adolescent. You're dreaming. It would be more sensible to investigate the two mothers, perhaps? Ah yes, of course, that's it! Naturally, it's the two mothers-in-law! Not at all. The mothers-in-law were both gazing at the two young people with the stupefied astonishment of hens who have just broken the eggs they were hatching; and furthermore, though it was a thing that could not have been less expected at such a time, they were in complete agreement on the subject. "The poor things, there are too many people around them all the time," they decreed. "They must go away together, somewhere quiet."

They went away, and the somewhere quiet was just next door to a little house I was then occupying on the shores of the Mediterranean. Instead of retiring together into a scantily clad and savage solitude, they were pushing open my gate at every minute of the day, I found, and politely offering me their services: "Would you like us to go into the village to get something for you, to collect your mail? Wouldn't you like a pound or two of nice peaches? Would you like us to water the garden? Or to collect some pine cones for you?"

I accepted all their offers. Eager to please, those two children sallied forth on their bicycles, took turns at the wheel of their little car, leaped into the sea, dried themselves, and always with linked arms or a hand on each other's shoulders. Only as night fell did they begin to lose their gaiety, and for a young couple so newly wed they stayed out rather too long in the evenings, dancing in the "dives" of the nearby fishing village. I noticed too, on the tanned and pleasant face of the young girl, a frequent expression of uncertainty, a vague plea that boded no good. But one does not interrogate, no matter how tactfully, a couple so newly formed. They were at an age, after all, when everything looms larger than it is, when nothing can ever, as we say, simply arrange itself. I would have been quite willing to wager that the young woman was going to be the first to open her heart to me, and I should have lost the wager. For, of course, a very young woman naturally mistrusts the acquired experience of an older woman, whereas a young man who has recently been saddled with the responsibilities and difficulties involved in running a household, a young man who is a little tyrannical on the one hand, but with a touch of the orphan on the other, will allow himself to slip quite easily into a confidential mood, which is to say, an indiscreet mood, if he can be sure that the woman who receives his confidences will offer him nothing but her ear. Furthermore, this particular young man found himself forced one day into justifying himself to me, after having reprimanded his wife in my presence, rather as though he were an elder brother speaking to his younger sister, and even worse, an elder brother speaking to his younger brother.

Her only visible reaction was to fall silent, biting the inside of her cheek; then, taking her bicycle, she rode off to the Sainte-Anne fair, saying: "I'll see you in a while, I'm just going to buy some green pitchers."

After she had disappeared, her husband returned to his newspaper, I to my book, and for ten minutes we did not exchange a single word, unless I am to count as conversation the single "Damn!" of fury that escaped from the youthful lips of—let us say Didier—at the moment when he found he had burned a hole with his lighted cigarette in his lovely white pants. He added: "I beg your pardon," and then, since I did not reply, he said unexpectedly:

"You know, you mustn't think just because of that . . ."

And there he stopped, so that I could reply, in urbane tones, that I didn't realize I had given him any reason to think that I was thinking anything at all . . .

"You mustn't think I'm just simply a brute."

Naturally I replied that simplicity was not something often thought of in connection with young people. Instead of laughing, he seemed disturbed, and then, moved by the need he had been controlling for several weeks, of "saying something to someone," he disburdened himself, chaotically, grandiloquently, and childishly, of what had been weighing on him. At some points, always the wrong ones, he was reserved in his expression, at others chastely immodest. Since the use of either reserve or immodesty would be an embarrassment to me here, I shall simply provide a resume of what he said to me.

His extreme youth made of him, on his wedding night, a mentor proud of his knowledge. Try to understand by this that he neglected no means of dazzling his completely inexperienced wife. And to begin with, he taught her that the state of nudity is natural, desirable, exalting, and convenient.

He demonstrated to her, both by deed and gesture, that everything is permitted, he made fun of her final expressions of resistance, and at last, after it had been toasted with a little champagne, sleep lowered the curtain of his triumph.

From the next morning on, the surprise was all on his side. For the little wife, convinced by his arguments, was already to be seen walking around the house completely unveiled; and unveiled still, she sat down at the breakfast table to confront her foaming chocolate and her slices of bread and butter. Didier postponed the task of explaining to her that there are different modes of dress appropriate to different times of day, and contented himself with throwing her a pajama jacket. Taking this to be a game, she hurled back missile for missile as much at ease as if she had been in an athletics stadium. Whereupon they fell, wholeheartedly, to wrestling with one another, and when, that evening, the hour of solitude, of privacy, came round again, Janine—let us say that she was named Janine—made it clear that she found the state of complete nudity, and also the frolics authorized by such a state, natural, exalting, and convenient indeed . . .

"You do understand," Didier went on, "that it was less than forty-eight hours since we . . . since we had got to know one another and . . . I was almost at the point of being forced to say to her: 'I say, hey! not so fast . . . Go easy there, for heaven's sake! . . .' It got to the stage where I was shocked by it, where I would have been quite happy to have her back again as she was during those first few hours, young and disconcerted. I still went on hoping that she would pull away from me, tremble, put up a bent arm to hide her eyes . . . but there never came a time again when she hid her eyes with her arm, or bit her lip, or felt frightened of me . . . When I tried to point all this out to her, she simply opened her eyes very wide and said: 'But we are married, darling, after all!' So that in comparison, I was the one who looked like a greenhorn. People are always talking about the advice you should give brides *before* their wedding night . . . Dammit all, what they need more, it seems to me, is advice *afterward,* on how to be embarrassed . . ."

He was pouting as he talked, like a very sulky schoolboy. I would have liked to tell him, among many other excellent pieces of advice, that for the role of, if I may so express it, posthumous counselor, the institution of marriage has already designated the husband himself; that it is dangerous to give young fillies too loose a rein; that the more difficult task is not to produce paroxyms but to induce symptoms of regression; and that many young girls, once they have been awakened as women, immediately discard all expressions of modesty on the grounds that such things, as they believe, are simply obstacles to pleasure . . .

But I remained silent, thinking to myself that I was really too old to be playing the schoolteacher, and that there was, in any case, a god, friend to lovers and drunkards alike, who would no doubt bring Janine an awareness of how to blush one day, a day when beauty, in its fading, must have recourse to grace, when it begins to doubt the power of nudity and the ardor it inspires, and moves with fresh uncertainty to meet your hidden wishes, oh shadowy, delicate, modesty of the male . . .

DC

Landru (1921)

It was his entrance, not that of the black and red gowns, that finally brought a little gravity into that tiny room, so lacking in majesty until then, packed as it was with people talking at the tops of their voices and growing restless because the court was making them wait. It was he who attracted and held every eye, he alone, familiar from a hundred photographs and newspaper cartoons, recognized by all and yet different from what one knew of him. There was the beard, the bald head we had all expected, the frizzy eyebrows that looked as though they'd been stuck on. And yet there was a certain indefinable something in this thin man's face that made us all grow suddenly circumspect, even, I might say, deferential.

Why should I not use the language of polite society in writing of him? The innate courtesy of the man was immediately apparent. And I have no desire to take the same tone as the public prosecutor, who opened the proceedings by deluging the accused, for four long hours by the clock, with a steady downpour of the least ambiguous turns of phrase imaginable: "Murderer . . . Woman dissecter . . . Sinister wooer . . ." All that before the proofs? What words would there be left, should the truth finally emerge and the polygamist be overwhelmed by it, with which to blast him further, and more finally? Such a speech—if that is what it was—must inevitably drain every source of invective dry at one fell swoop.

Meanwhile, Landru, neither impudent nor humble, gazed at the crowd without insistence, bowed to the bench both before and after speaking, was restrained in his use of words and gesture, and we began little by little to gain the impression—strengthened by the venomous threats of the attorney general, the abusive cries of the civil prosecutor, the insulting snickers of the defending counsel, and the smutty murmurs of the public—the scandalous impression that there was only one person in that court who had any regard for good manners or any idea of "how to behave": the man in the prisoner's dock.

When meting out its punishments, society always lacks good manners, and sometimes even common decency. On the morning of an execution, we see a guillotine, a square fouled by laughter, by booze, by the frenzied excitement of monomaniacs and curious bystanders, and in its center a man, pale-faced, who walks forward without flinching, and almost always dies properly. It becomes easy for the condemned man to put on, if only for a moment, that greatness of spirit which is so lacking in our judges and in our penalties. A hint of good bearing, a display of haughty patience, a little determined courtesy, and he is already well on the way to becoming sympathetic by comparison.

A woman behind me, hatless, whispered: "He really does look like a gentleman."

What praise! . . . One journalist declared that Landru had "the beard of a drugstore dispenser."

A cartoonist said: "He looks so respectable you'd swear he was the head of a department in a big store."

The crowd will never produce a unanimous opinion on Landru. Even without moving, even before he spoke a single word, this man with fifty names, with 283 love affairs, was Proteus.

Was he seductive, this seducer? Was he attractive? Correct, certainly. But like a satyr? Like Verlaine, as he has been described? No. Nothing of either the genius or the monster. Above the thinly fleshed vertebrae of the neck, the skull was a fine one; it could have been harboring intelligence, who knows, even love . . . As to the face, its obvious resemblance to that of the former deputy Ceccaldi was indeed striking and disturbed one at first, but one quickly forgot it. One forgot it as soon as one had looked at Landru's eyes.

I searched those deeply socketed eyes in vain for a trace of human cruelty, for they were not human. They were the eyes of a bird. When Landru stared straight in front of him, they had not only the peculiar brilliance of a bird's eyes but also the same fixed length of gaze. But when he half lowered his eyelids, then his gaze took on the languor, the unfathomable disdain that one observes in the eyes of a caged wild beast.

I went on searching, behind the features of that regular head, for some sign of the monster, but without success. The face is bony but normal, and if it is frightening in any way it is because it seems to be giving a perfect imitation of humanity, like those motionless tailor's dummies used to display men's clothing in store windows.

Did he kill? Didn't he kill? We were nowhere near the answer to those questions. We watched as he listened, or appeared to listen, to the interminable case made out by the prosecution, delivered like some dismal litany, freezing the hearts of all who heard it.

I observed his breathing: it was slow and regular. He took some papers from the pocket of his brown topcoat. As he read through them and made notes, the sheets did not tremble in his hand.

"Sinister wooer . . . She was stripped of her possessions and then murdered . . . Mme Guillin's murderer . . ."

Landru took notes, attentive and distant at the same time, or else allowed those eyes, which had made so many victims fall in love with him, to move, without bravado, around the room. He made it evident that he disliked noise. He blew his nose with deliberate care, folded his handkerchief back into a square, then pulled out the little flap of his side pocket. What neatness!

Did he kill? If he did kill, then I would swear that it was with that same bureaucratic, slightly maniacal, admirably lucid attention to detail that he brought to the arrangement of his notes and the compilation of his files. Did he kill? If he did, then it was while humming a little tune, and only after he had tied on an apron, for fear of dirtying his clothes. A sadistic madman, Landru? Oh no. He is much more difficult to fathom than that, for us at least. We can imagine what an insane fury must be like, whether lubricous or not, but we remain dully uncomprehending when faced with the quiet and gentle murderer who keeps a notebook of his victims, and who perhaps rested a moment from his task, leaning out the window to throw breadcrumbs to the birds.

I believe we shall never understand the first thing about Landru, even if he wasn't a killer.

His serenity has scarcely any connection with the human race. During the trial of skills, the swift and menacing skirmish between Maître de Moro-Giafferi, a tiger cat whose claws glitter for an instant, slash, then disappear from view, and Godefroy, the attorney general, wrapped in his cloak of bearlike cunning, Landru seemed to be dreaming somewhere above them both, withdrawn from us all, back once more, perhaps, in a very ancient world, a time when blood was neither more sacred nor more horrible than milk or wine, a time when a man who has just made sacrifice, sitting on a streaming, blood-warmed stone, forgot himself for a moment as he smelled a flower . . .

If he were guilty, one wondered, could Landru be compared to these suave, Oriental assassins? But I was forgetting the "money argument." And Maître Moro-Giafferi was not of my opinion. He found the lucidity, the relentlessly logical and categorical memory of his client quite enchanting.

"Acquit him," he exclaimed yesterday in the vestibule, "and I'll take him on as my secretary!"

DC

Stavisky (*1934*)

And why should he not have committed suicide? Despite myself, I cannot get him out of my mind, this man for whom all Europe, by its preoccupation with his death, is providing a slanderous and international funeral. False information is winning the day. A dazzling variety of certitudes is crowding the streets, the restaurants, the stores . . .

"And you know, it was an English policeman who shot Stavisky!"

"But I tell you he isn't dead at all! The photographs are genuine enough, but he was only wounded. They've got him in a clinic somewhere and put someone else in his place, someone who died in a hospital or something . . ."

"Do you really think a man like that would have killed himself before his trial!"

Yes, I do think so. I am trying to find my way beyond the treacherous region of logic. I am looking back, in memory, at the features, soon to be erased, of the man I used to meet. The evening before his departure, he was chatting in the hall of his hotel with several other men. As he stood there, slender and bareheaded, he was laughing.

He had a particular talent for suppressing his face when he so wished, for existing only as a silhouette. But he never lost an opportunity of displaying the remarkable slimness of his waist, his supple movements, his enduring and cultivated youth of body. I must insist on this point: Stavisky was not *really* a young man. His delicate

complexion, and perhaps a fragile mental balance too, required constant care and precise attentions. He was reaching what, in a woman,
is the age of the menopause. And the "change of life" does not spare
the stronger sex. Men, too, experience the nervous afflictions, the
sudden feelings of hopelessness, and all the inner uncertainties it
brings in its train. Ten years earlier, Stavisky would have faced the
trial. But by 1934, Stavisky, behind his astonishing façade, was
without doubt a finished man.

I can state categorically that he wore a light, though detectable,
layer of makeup—cream and powder—in an attempt to retain his
youthful appearance. I attach extreme importance to this detail.

It reveals to me, at one glance, the long periods spent in front
of the mirror, the lucid study of a declining face, the secret struggle
against advancing age, all the effects of a despairing coquetry. I cannot forget that the "hunted man" practiced that time-honored precaution, observed by so many threatened but determined beauties:
an *escalope* of raw veal laid on each cheek. After the *escalope* came
the eurythmics, the masseur, the manicurist, the barber . . . And
these people's usefulness was not limited simply to defending Stavisky against the approach of his fiftieth birthday; their real role—
did Stavisky ever admit this to himself?—was to create a barrier
between him and solitude. When had he ever been seen alone? A
wife, another wife, children, friends, accomplices, enemies, innumerable voices on the telephone, crowded restaurants, casinos, gambling
rooms, his office, the noise of a crowd, muffled orchestras, suppers,
the gypsy violinists of the Poisson d'Or dances, beaches . . . Was
all that noise, were all those presences enough to make Stavisky forget the pitiless hour when, in the morning light, Stavisky was forced
to face his mirror?

Some hearts, female hearts, will understand me. Stavisky,
hunted till he was at his last gasp, had without doubt been panting
toward his end for a long time. For a young adventurer, a trial, a
prison sentence are a sort of sport. But Stavisky, soon to reach his
fiftieth year, would have run the risk of disclosing to the world a
man whom nobody, not even his wife, had ever seen. And besides,

he had looked further ahead still, he had looked into the future and seen the exhausted Stavisky who, after the mud had been struggled through, stroke after weary stroke, would be waiting on the farther, barren shore, waiting *to begin again* . . .

Alone with a serf, with the snow, with a pack of cards and a little bottle of ink bought at the village stationery store, submerged in silence, he knew that he was lost. And yet he waited a little longer . . . "Just a moment, executioner . . ." His little hand, holding the revolver, did not dare.

"When midnight strikes . . . When I hear the Angelus from the village . . . When I've smoked the last cigarette in this box . . ."

What suicide is ever without its romanticism, and its childishness? He waited until a fist smashed through his bedroom window, but I think that everything was all over for him already. And the proof, the proof is that this dandy had a three days' growth of beard on his chin—like a corpse.

DC

Temptations

"There's gold here, piled up as high as this," Paquita says to her lover in *La Fille aux yeux d'or.*

"It doesn't belong to us."

"Belong!" she echoed. "It'll belong to us all right when we've taken it."

"Poor innocent child . . ."

It is possible that this untamed "innocence" of Balzac's heroine would be to the taste of the man who has made himself, for a short while only no doubt, the new owner of *L'Indifférent.* One can envisage how so unreasoning a thief must have felt no desire for the money involved, how his gestures were guided by passion, how he was enmeshed by that graceful little pink and blue personage, with one foot so delicately turned out, and a light cape thrown over one shoulder. If the theft was committed by a frenzied art lover, who passed straight from contemplation to the act of robbery, then they must be alone now somewhere, face to face, the thief and the object of his mad passion, and their romance is very near its end.

For a masterpiece does not submit so easily to a chance master. And the one now missing from the Louvre will always, like any other prisoner, be looking for escape: that small canvas will continue to yearn toward the abundant light it knew in the museum, to which it owed its patina, its blues, even bluer when it rained, and the pinks that took on an added hint of gold when the sun shone. Now, it is visited only by sparse and timid rays; it may even be living in total darkness . . .

We know very little about the obsession that leads people to steal objects consecrated to public worship. It has been christened with various names, and psychoanalysis has had a great deal to say on the subject. I am not far from the opinion that once the act has been accomplished, the stolen treasure withers, like wild flowers, like those bunches of wayside blooms which marauding children gather and which we see, as soon as they begin to droop, left lying in faded heaps along a path. A masterpiece violated by an act of theft does not always submit so easily. Even before the curse begins to work, it seems to lose its color in hands that have not earned it. There is, besides, something a little fateful in the harsh-sounding name of the donor associated with the Schliechting Room. It so happens that I knew Baron de Schliechting. I cannot state with any degree of certainty that he was Polish, for there are those who say that he was Russian; others, that he was German; and yet others, that he was Austrian . . . But though his nationality in those days—1905, or thereabouts—was somewhat uncertain, there was no uncertainty whatever about this haughty art lover's private life. His very tall body, very bent and as thin as a sheet of metal, seemed always to be trying to efface itself in favor of the bizarre head, the strongly marked features, the misty halo of thinning hair, and above all the extraordinary side whiskers, not dense and disciplined after the style of Franz-Josef, but long, fleecy, pearl-gray ones that the wind blew around his neck like a necktie or sent streaming back over his shoulders. Above these strange adornments, there dreamed a pair of gray-blue, icy, wandering eyes containing not one trace of cordiality. The concave torso and the hands composed entirely of delicate little bones made it evident that the Baron de Schliechting, in about the year 1904, had reached an advanced age.

When the *Gioconda* disappeared, this wealthy collector, who had accumulated a large quantity of disparate works of art in his house on the rue de Prony, received a visit from the police. An anonymous letter had been sent to them disclosing the fact that Schliechting was in the habit of shutting himself up in his room to contemplate a painting that was kept in a metal-plated box with a combination lock . . . He protested but was finally prevailed upon to open the box, which did in fact contain a portrait, but one whose attractions had nothing feminine about them whatever. He harbored no grudge and after his death made a sizable donation to the Louvre.

I do not know what then became of the admirable pearl necklace which Schliechting would, in certain circumstances, fasten around his neck, and the usual grapevine of malicious gossip did not say whether or no the pearls were stolen from him during the course of some festivity or other. Who was not mad for pearls at that time? Women in those days were in a perpetual fever at the tales of pearls just stolen or pearls recently bought. Liane de Pougy's seven strands, Carolina Otéro's five strands, Polaire's enormous necklace—made up of thirty-seven huge pearls—the pearl *sautoir* belonging to the Vanderbilt family, unique, painted by Boldoni . . . *Sautoirs*, black pearls and white pearls on rings, long, pear-shaped pearls worn as pendants . . . No one wanted to wear anything, no one wanted to steal anything but pearls. Thefts and restitutions had a romantic and titillating character in those days. One night, having wound her *sautoir* around the neck of an angora cat in play, Suzanne Derval cried out, then swooned in anguish as the animal fled away across the roofs, still garlanded with pearls. But next morning, when the errant cat came home, far different cries were heard, for some unknown hand had rearranged on the Angora's neck, tying them firmly on again with scarlet ribbon, all six of the necklace's long strands.

Doubtless so that I should not appear conspicuous, I too used to wear a modest pearl necklace in those days. Its modesty seemed to me even greater when I was forced to part with it during the war . . . Before the war, I had no cause for complaint against it other than a habit it had of disappearing suddenly, then reappearing in the most unlikely places. The fourth time it disappeared, I displayed a certain amount of ill humor toward the honest woman who came in to clean for me. She took offense and maintained a stiff silence until the day when . . .

"Madame must come and look, without making a noise . . ."

Poised on the mantel shelf, my Persian cat, reflected in the mirror, doubly beautiful, was drawing my little necklace up out of the goblet where it was kept. She seized it between her teeth, laid it down, picked it up again by the middle, so that the two ends, now almost exactly equal in length, should hang down as little as possible, then leaped to the floor and walked off, head held high, with the proud gait of a mother cat carrying her kitten. I found the necklace again under an armchair, in the room I didn't use.

Two weeks later the cat did the same thing again, and I followed her. Then, later still, the same thing happened yet again. She would relinquish her prize, sometimes under an armchair, sometimes in the dark shadow made by two steps that led down to the scullery. But by then she knew she was discovered, and her inexplicable temptation flickered out. She never touched either the slender gold bar or the ring which always lay in the same goblet. What did this inedible and fruitless object represent to her feline mind that she should steal it? What is the meaning of the magpie's continual thefts, of the glittering treasures it hoards? My familiar, the squirrel, used to hoard away reserves of sugar, nuts, and potassium-chlorate tablets for himself in twenty different hiding places; but why, on twenty different occasions, with warlike cries, did he carry off a little comb with a silver mounting?

No temptation can ever be measured by the value of its object.

Perhaps we shall discover one day that the man who stole *l'Indifférent* had never even heard of Watteau's name. It is not impossible. Though the knowledge would make us start a little all the same, as at some unexpected breach of the conventions. Stealing in order to sell, all right. Why else should anyone steal? But what are those three silver dice, that spoon, that gilt button doing in the magpie's hiding place under a roof tile? Man's weakness when dazzled by beauty, the animal's weakness when hypnotized by a glittering dot on a convex surface, the recognition of a color—the pink of the stockings, the blue of the coat, there on the little, stolen canvas— vainly pursued, as necessary as water is, or bread . . . For Jean Lorrain, the yearned-for color was always green, green mingled with blue in the depths of eyes . . . When we consider the hidden moles that darken a being's nature, then everything is possible.

"I pinched some mints from a candy jar while you were buying your oranges," a young woman told me one day.

"Do you like mints as much as all that?"

"No, I just like taking them."

Another time when I spoke to her outside the store, it was licorice all-sorts, squashed into a sticky mass on her right palm. Finally, there was the last time. Turning around, I saw the young woman with a strange, rather ugly expression playing around her mouth. One hand stretched behind her back, she was stealing a fistful of dried beans . . .

DC

Desert flower

We caught sight of her as we drove into Bou-Saâda, at that moment when the setting sun lays a sudden sheet of purple on the nearest mountain, and on the farthest peaks a pink as pale as the pink of red-hot iron in bright sunlight. Our fatigue, our wonderment, the two hundred miles of desert we had just seen unfolded before our unprepared eyes, the sirocco, and the shimmering rain-

bow space behind a hanging curtain of sand had left us completely
dazzled, entirely credulous. The same exclamation, bursting from
our salt-dusted lips, greeted the short-lived dusk and the quivering
pink light that an almost night-filled sky drew up so violently from
sands that were themselves pink-tinted, and more luminous than the
space above them, the rockets of the flowering laurels, the burning
green of the palm grove, and the soothing, cooling forms, like
spreading fountains, of the palms themselves—the clumsy but
powerful flight of an enormous vulture, the threadlike trickle of a
spring emerging from a sun-scorched hill, the gauzy wings of a
grasshopper seeming to sparkle with water drops as it sped by, swift
as a swooping swallow . . .

The little girl we had caught sight of was sitting motionless
against a collapsing wall made of unbaked clay, a few cube-shaped
bricks molded by hand, half crumbled and melted away, all that
remained of a native dwelling after a short rainstorm and a long
drought. She might have been about five years old, resplendent with
melancholy coquetry. Her doe's ankles, one crossed over the other,
were fidgeting inside crude silver anklets; there were twisted wire
bracelets tinkling on her arms, and we bent down, with barbarian
curiosity, to touch her tiny feet, encrusted with the mud of the gutter, and her delicate hands, never washed, darkened with henna. She
had enormously wide eyebrows painted in bright black across her
forehead, a proud, fleshy mouth full of tiny fissures, a beautiful set of
teeth, and ageless eyes, heavy with languor between their heavily
blackened lashes. Each cheekbone was marked with a bright blue
star, and a blue arrow ran down the center of her chin. There were
also tiny constellations of blue characters extending the line of the
eyebrows between her eyes. A reddish scrap of cloth, twisted over
her hair, allowed us to glimpse two tiny, dust-covered braids coiled
into ram's horns over the ears; more cotton rags, hanging over the
body, permitted us a sight, here of a slender knee, there of a tiny,
hollowed flank like a whippet's. The crumbling bank behind her
exactly echoed the tone of her skin, a light yellow mysteriously
tinted with pink, and the motionless little girl seemed to have been

born just the moment before, freshly kneaded out of the blond clay, molded out of a handful of desert.

She stretched out a hand and began to beg in a high-pitched voice, speaking in Arabic. We had very little change on us, but Daurces did manage to find a twenty-five centime piece without a hole in the middle, around which the henna-tinted fingers immediately closed.

"Saha! Saha!"

After these words of thanks, the little girl leaped up and ran off, raising two wings of sunlit dust with her heels as she went. She turned back just once, pausing to express her thanks again with an imperious and graceful wave of the hand.

Next day, in the garden of the Petit-Sahara, we sat waiting for our meal, sapped and disheveled by the obligatory outings to the inferior mosque, to the fetid and weed-filled river, where the men wash their linen upstream, the women downstream from the men, and the Jews downstream from the women; to watch the makers of the local high boots, whose embroidered tops grip tight to the calf; to visit Ben-Grada, who sells carpets, bracelets, and beef tendons sheathed in orange leather, but who gives away his flowers, his scented cigarettes, and the coffee he serves in porcelain shells; to watch Zorah, who dances naked but who never takes off her head veils or her jewels . . .

A little brown hand made its way between the bars of the hotel railings and held out a twenty-five centime piece without a hole in the middle. A childish voice gurgled out some words in Arabic, and there were the eyes and the teeth of our little *Saha! Saha!* girl glittering on the other side of the fence . . .

"Oh, it's that lovely little girl again! What is it you want? Ahmed, what does she want?"

"She has brought back your coin," said Ahmed, our burnoosed guide. "She wants Algerian money instead."

"And quite right too," Daurces said.

He took back the original coin and gave the desert flower a beautiful Algerian one, as big around as a marigold, and with two palm trees stamped on it, a new ten-centime piece just made to dazzle the eyes of a little, desert child.

The tiny, tinted fingers did not close on the metal disk, and *Saha! Saha!* began once more to make those soft cooing noises in her throat . . .

"How pretty it sounds; rather like a slightly hoarse pigeon! No, Ahmed, don't drive her away. Leave her alone so that we can listen . . . What is she saying? Is she thanking us?"

"She says," Ahmed explained placidly, "that you still owe her fifteen centimes . . ."

DC

The bliss of confession

I also knew a little girl of eight years old who let her mother call her for a long while, far away in the park. Closely hidden, she listened to the voice that drew near, that receded, wandered, changed its tone, became strange and hoarse by the well and by the pond. She was a very gentle little girl, yet she already knew too much, as you can see, of the various terrible ways of giving oneself pleasure. She would come out of her hiding place at last and run wildly forward, flinging herself into her mother's arms, panting as though out of breath: "I was at the farm—I—I— was at the bottom of the kitchen garden—with Anna—I—I—"

"What will you do worse," I asked her once, reproachfully, "when you are twenty?"

She half closed her delicious blue eyes, stared away into the distance. "Oh, I'll find something," she said.

But I fancy she was boasting. I was surprised to see her play her game twice in front of me. She asked for no promise, no complicity on my part, she seemed to be quite sure of me, as other sinners were in later years, overcome by the bliss of confession and the need to mature under the eye of a human being.

HBk

❧❧ Animal Nature

The heart of animals

I am no more than half dozing through my siesta, but my bitch is asleep. She is sleeping the way French bulldogs sleep, which means that she is all twitches, imagined hunts, delicate convulsions of the jowls, and efforts to escape, to bark, perhaps to speak. At the darkest point of a dream her eyelids part. But her great irises, brown and spangled like a fragment of schist, see nothing but the dramatic underside of her own sleep. My cheek, lying near her flank, can sense the irregular fluctuations of her breath and the disordered beating of her heart, five little beats, swift as the tock-tock, tock-tock-tock of that percussive insect, frequenter of ancient woodwork, the death-watch beetle. Then a single shock suspended between two interminable silences, just one, the last? . . . No, just at the moment when I myself was about to suffocate, by contagion, three madly racing palpitations followed, then four. Then a mortal silence, then a resumption of life, expressed in a series of seven beats . . .

Such is the normal rate of a bulldog bitch's heart. How many times will this one survive her emotions? A little French bulldog, as I am beginning to know, wears itself out in ten years. Even then, it requires special treatment. My long silences, my immobility while writing protect her from herself, from her passionate curiosity, from her fear, present at every instant of the day, of feeling herself an orphan, and from her morbid need to listen to and remember human words . . .

She is asleep, the bulldog-bitch-entirely-beautiful. That was what the man I bought her from called her. He showed me a dirty pedigree, worn through at the folds, which must have served as an identification paper for more than one French bulldog bitch. For though I quickly saw that she followed him, that she was constantly at heel, as the trainers say, that she stood up when he did, lay down when he sat, still the heart—always the heart, or the viscera, or the feelings—was not in it. And I saw that even while she remained glued to his every movement, she was still waiting . . . for whom? Her gaze, the nervous tremor in her left foreleg when the doorbell rang, a sort of absent fixity in her manner, all these things betrayed the animal that feels lost, that has been stolen; would anyone leave such a bitch in a kennel for fourteen months?

That was how Cessy von Heschfurth—give or take a consonant or two—made her appearance in my home, where she is now known as Souci. She is sleeping, she abandons herself to her jolted slumber. "One, two . . . one, two . . . one, two, three, four, five . . . one . . . one . . . one . . ." counts out her heart beside my cheek. She is warm, she exhales a good smell of sleeping dog: milk and grass spiced with a hint of iodine and rosemary, because of her swim in the sea and then the hedge we walk along on the way back from the beach—that friendly consoling smell under whose influence human beings secretly flatter themselves: "Here is the spot where it would be good to find rest once and for all, where it would be good to shed at last those old, those serene tears kept back for so many years . . ." I must allow myself no such foolish hopes. This bitch could not bear my tears. The most that was allowed me, without her dying, was to break a leg . . . Her heart again. Once the first moment of shock had passed—a broken leg does not cause one a great deal of pain—I had the leisure to concern myself with her as I lay on my stretcher: "Take care of the dog . . . Take care of her . . ." For my bulldog bitch, unable to speak or moan, was in the grip of a nightmarish agitation, gasping for breath and displaying a chalky, mauve-colored tongue. "Give her some cold water. Squeeze a lemon into her mouth, can't you see she's going to faint?" And all the time they were pouring eau de cologne on my temples, when there was no further danger for me . . .

Yes, I mean it! She was going to faint, as I once saw a Persian cat do, one day when she caught her son fastened to the nipple of a common, black farmyard cat, as full of milk as a nanny goat . . . The Angora cat sensed this betrayal from afar and shrieked for all the doors to be opened for her: "Let me out, let me out!" Then she hurled herself down the stairs like a maddened bunch of feathers caught in a whirlwind, and did not stop until she finally collapsed with weakness, lying on her side, three paces from the child stealer and her gorged child.

"One, two, three . . . one, two . . . one . . . one . . ." counts out the sleeping bitch's heart. The hearts of animals are always there, palpitating, swelling, and breaking in our shadow. Despite all anatomy, I always envisage the hearts of animals as having the simple shape made traditional by religious pictures. An animal's heart curves to a slender point at the bottom, and the rounded curves at the top are like two breasts squeezed together; it is pierced by an arrow, it is flaming, crowned with roses, lying on lilies, wounded, with three little gems of fresh blood decorating the edge of its wound. Or else it's a fruit, such as the "pigeon's heart," a pale kind of cherry. Crimson-black is the color of the greyhound's heart, the greyhound "great-hearted" in the hunt, so much so that he sometimes dies of his own courage. The gray mare was "great-hearted" too, the mare that belonged to my elder brother, the country doctor. Mare and doctor both exercised a thankless profession. Both were lacking in placidity of soul, neither could feel indifference. Through the winter nights, through blazing dog days, they still kept going, upheld by the same faith, bound together by the same friendship. Standing outside, the mare would lean her intelligent head, her charming and feminine head with its short ears, against the farmhouse doors. She was listening to a man's voice mingling with the childish sobs, with the long cries of women in labor. When the final, "Well, I'll be back to see you again soon!" sounded near the door, the gray roan mare would shake herself, inch back coquettishly into her harness, make herself beautiful despite the darkness, the lateness of the hour and her fatigue, and then, off she went at a trot! . . .

Off at a trot without a flick of the whip, without so much as a click of the tongue. She pulled away to the sound of an air from the *Roi d'Ys*, to Rozen's air: *Why that grief in silence bear?*, for her master was a good musician and full of an ironic awareness of his harsh destiny. A mare among mares, who would accept neither the retirement nor the green meadow offered her. Bereft of her master, of her nighttime journeys and her long dozes standing on three legs, one haunch up in the air and the other sagging, she pined and preferred to die. It is a choice I cannot find it in me to be astonished by.

They set great store by us, all those frightened brothers with eyes on the sides of their heads, pricked-up ears, beaks, long dog teeth, and shoes. They resemble one another only in the terror and the love that we inspire in them. Nothing deflects the hope they place in us. What was it you wanted from me, little shadow in the garden who would never cross an open space? Muscat was your name, a timid and beautiful cat, always hidden as you kept watch for me. You waited for me to go out and snip off the dead blooms, to pull up the couch grass from my two tiered and densely blooming borders. So as not to spoil things, I had to walk out with bare feet, advancing cautiously as though through virgin forest. Then, suddenly, I felt the two melting paws and the fevered nose kissing my ankles, my bare toes. At the end of the flower bed, the caresses ceased. But so that the timid sprite should know we were still bound to one another, I sang him songs of my own making, mingling his name among the words. Trailing and uncertain airs they were, drawn out of me by the rasping ears of millet, interrupted by the thorny caper bushes, revived by the convolvulus and the plumbago fern. I have never known a lover more silent or attentive than that cat . . . Perhaps there are readers who think I have already talked too much and too often about cats? So much the worse for them: my song of praise to the Cat is not finished yet. I do not object, in tender moments, to praising dogs; or to looking out for those other, fleeting moments when a warm gust carries into my gaze, then wafts away again, the dappled wings, the faceted eyes, the nocturnal and noise-less pinions, and also the proboscis of the great hawk moth.

Why should I not paint the portrait of Baptiste himself, Baptiste the tame rabbit with a lion's heart? For years and years he mounted guard over his mistress, the fruitwoman in the rue de la Tour. Huge, with ears in tatters and eyes that never missed a thing, he sat in state on her doorstep, among the crates. Woe betide any passing dog! And woe to the intruder who ventured to squeeze the fruitwoman's arm or waist. My own bitch has had a taste of those piercing teeth, of wounds inflicted by this champion, who would fling all restraints aside and charge at full speed across the street, in among the taxis, when pursuing the flight of some terrified dog . . .

For the dog is a creature that believes in order. The slightest breach in the established scheme of things is enough to make man's best friend lose countenance. He has very precise but rudimentary ideas about dogs and game. He says to the game: "You are the game, and I am the dog." And I still laugh when I remember a morning long ago when, having spent the night in a hunting lodge, I awoke with 124 hounds dreaming aloud nearby in voices like distant bells . . . Beneath my window they let loose a Russian greyhound bitch, whose coat shone like spun glass, and her friend, a little boar sow. Then they released a terrible Angora rabbit, and though the little sow, young as she was, did not come out of the encounter too badly, the borzoi shrieked like a fox and fled. The mischievous owner of both the land and the hounds had amused himself by raising the rabbit as a bloodhound, and shouted "Tallyho! Tallyho!" to him when he was shown the dogs. But he had in no way modified the principles of the borzoi, which, faced with the rabbit's ferocity, lost face completely every time.

Those big puppies that suck at their mother's teats standing up—Romulus and Remus—beneath the stalactites of an arena full of milk, I have had them in my household too, in the past. I have known, I have loved the heady scent of phosphorus and fresh milk that they continue to give off as long as their food remains wholly pure. Well licked and well fed, a kitten smells of hay. Perhaps the good smell associated with young animals still at the nipple is a function of their contentment? The scent of her lavendar water apart, my daughter, before she weaned her child, always gave off an intangible odor of newly threshed corn. I thought, oh Francis Jammes, of the odor of warm bread that surrounds la Lucie with its fragrance as she sleeps in the arms of Jean de Noarrieu . . .

To the little Danish dogs that float about in skins cut so generously that they would do for a dog and a half, I myself prefer the little *bas-rouges* of Beauce, a sensible breed, thoughtful sheepdogs whose characters are already evident at six weeks. Though they are identical in appearance, wrapped in their black and flame coats, all with double dewclaws on their hind legs and the same pronounced ridge on their skulls, they cease to resemble one another cerebrally much sooner than human twins. Out of the litter of five presented to me by my beautiful bitch, I would be forced to give four away . . . Which one was I to keep? After the seventh week, my choice fell on a little female puppy less playful than the other four; she would gaze in front of her very seriously now and then, twitch her still unclipped ears at every sound, accept her brothers' and sisters' bites without flinching or yelping, and was already making attempts at threatening grimaces. When I lifted her up by the loose skin of her neck, she recognized my hand and hung there trustfully, as though dead. A little later, one day when I reprimanded her, instead of running away she sat down and listened. "So you are to be my dog," I told her, "and you shall be named Belle-Aude, after the fashion of the shepherds in the place where I was born."

I had the pride and the joy of seeing that the bitch her mother had made the same choice as myself, and that Belle-Aude's education was conducted according to the dictates of a stern and somewhat dissimulated maternal love. When dealing with Belle-Aude, the bitch did not allow any fond weakness to temper the warnings, or even the decisively delivered little nips with the incisors, that form the character and the manners of a *bas-rouge* puppy in its first weeks of life. It was Belle-Aude, too, who suffered most from those scrupulous attentions dictated by the need for cleanliness, those rough treatments administered by a tongue sponge, turning eyelids and ears inside out, drowning fleas, and giving a shine to the childish, naked belly! But it was Belle-Aude, too, who was the recipient of a hidden and thoughtful smile, a profound contemplative reverie, and the best place to sleep along the maternal flank . . .

Between her mother and myself, Belle-Aude grew up, passed through her perilous adolescence, all legs and clumsiness, and avoided the "distemper." She profited from the lessons imposed by a strange, aloof, and attentive maternal rule which forbade all play-fulness and familiarity the moment the daughter was fully grown. But when the bitch, Belle-Aude's mother, died suddenly of a heart attack—ah, that heart again—she bequeathed me her elegant double, her perfect likeness, one of those rare companions who re-main silent at the right time, respect our work and our sleep, howl for our own tears, and close their eyes with a bitter discretion in the face of anything—the kiss of a lover, the tender hug of a child—that deprives them of our fickle human friendship.

At any time it wishes to place itself within my reach, I shall always feast the free-flying bird, in memory of the time two tame swallows would separate themselves, at the sound of my voice, from a twittering cloud of their fellows and fly down to settle on my head. And I am still waiting for another opportunity to be the protector of a mother mouse like the one, no bigger than a hornet, who would rear up when I fed her and stand on her hind legs over the four little ones she was giving suck to. Can our crimes against them never free us from the trust of animals? No, it still holds firm. And no, I haven't finished singing the praises of the cat, of the heart of the cat. I have still to celebrate the cat which twice swam the torrent of the Doubs, just so that it could be with its masters. And the cat which overcame its horror of noise and movement to ride with me in an automobile. And the African panther, a female, which lost its will to live when its master went away. The master, in another country, heard that the beast was refusing to eat, and failing fast. He came back, for her sake. At the sight of him she revived for a moment, then those inner eyelids finally closed over the most beautiful eyes in the world . . .

It seems to me both just and necessary that I should also tell how a tabby cat, which I had been forced to give to my mother, followed my tracks in the snow, spent five days and four nights looking for me, returned exhausted to my mother's, and showed scarcely any concern for the newborn kitten she had left to die . . . I need hardly say that the death of the kitten gives me no cause for pride. But I am puzzled to know why she let it die, and why, having already resigned herself to living for a year without me, for I had been traveling abroad, she nevertheless betrayed her race and breeding after merely a glimpse of me . . .

Since there can be no love without loss, I accept being, in the feline heart, a favorite who is led, through a narrow and burning strait, to the very heart of a cat. When I return from that place, it sometimes happens that I am received back in this world as a somewhat suspect explorer. Have I not, perhaps, eaten the flesh of my fellow men in that far-off place? Or entered into some illicit pact? If so, then it is time the strictly human race began to show concern . . . And indeed it is showing concern. Lying here on my table, there is a newspaper article gravely entitled: *Has Madame Colette a soul?*

DC

A lizard

"The cat has caught a green lizard! She's caught a green lizard in the vines. Everyone come and look!"

Can one say that she had caught it? The cat was lying on the ground. Suddenly, she turned into a dragon, into a flame, into a flying fish, and under her belly, between her silver paws, I saw a green lizard appear as though she had just that moment invented it. She did not take the risk of biting it, for the tiny, exasperated, snakelike head, closely sheathed in its plaques of juxtaposed enamel, was taking aim at her delicate feline nose. But she had him fast, and her eyes were swimming with delirious delight.

"*Chatte!* Let it go!"

"Do you think I'm mad enough to let go of a lizard?" growled back the cat.

She tightened her delicate, powerful paws. The lizard's throat quivered as though it were about to burst, and a long, resplendent tail threshed beneath the furry body; I saw the red, suffocating throat of the *verdelle* begin to gape. I hurled myself to its rescue just in time.

"Give it back! It's mine!" cried the cat.

A black pistil, forked and agile, was reaching out blindly for air from inside the half-swooning lizard's throat. Drop by drop, I moistened the red flower inside its mouth with water, and the lizard opened its topaz eyes again.

"Give it back!" the cat miaowed. "If you want one as well, there are plenty more in the vines. That one's mine because I caught it! And what's more, it's going to bite you, which will be a good thing . . ."

"*Chatte,*" I replied, "go and find something else to do. I am old enough to know how to hold a lizard so that it can't bite me, or a crab so that it can't nip me. And it is a long while now since the spiky fans on the gurnard's back have held any terror for me. Off with you, cat, and capture yourself a few fat, harmless moths. And make sure you avoid the horse-faced locust, with his spring-hinged mandibles!"

"Oh, very well then," the cat answered, "I'll go. I'm not down to my last lizard yet! And you already know what I think about all those long speeches and lectures and tittle-tattle about our tribe that you think its your business to come out with all the time."

For my cat does not talk as respectfully to me as I do to her. But we've both found a way of putting up with each other's defects.

The lizard, still a little faint, allowed me to inspect it and discover two pink and penetrating wounds, the color of balas rubies, at the base of its tail. Apart from those, it was simply suffering from nervous shock. I decided to give it board and lodging in my clinic cage while it convalesced. Its plump belly and the lack of turquoise-blue markings on its temples informed me that I had been wrong in thinking of it as a he. The *verdelle* took its place in the cage clinic as successor to the tortoise-dying-of-thirst, a tortoise from the Provençal woods, yellow and black, which the long drought had brought, empty, weighing almost nothing, scarcely alive, to my inexhaustible well and my generous watering cans. Before giving him my kitchen garden and its daily sprinkling of dew, its green salads and its slugs, I had given him a room to live in and prescribed a course of overfeeding. To each day, its different needs.

My lizard, once in its cage, was given fresh water, a leafy branch, some dry sand, a few drops of milk, a strip of woolen cloth folded in two for it to sleep and meditate upon, and then I went off in quest of some meal worms. A miracle! I found some. At the mere sight of them, the lizard resumed its grand, dragonish, dress uniform. Swollen, embossed, drawn up onto its stilted front toes, every muscle taut beneath its breastplate of chrysoprase, enamelwork, and melted opal, it arched its back into a hoop and brought its nose down at the whitish worm with all the power of a striking snake. Though it was already caught, already disemboweled, it killed its worm and then rekilled it—just as my French bulldog bitch does with a slipper—and I could hear its horny nose, tock-tock, knocking against the cage floor like a finger in a thimble.

She ate well, and her pink wounds soon healed. She also learned to recognize me, and I was simply flattered by this, rather than surprised. She never hesitated to climb up onto my outstretched hand, and in the hot noons that boil the blood of lizards lying on their dry flints, she played with me at being a very fierce male lizard. Haughtily perched on the tips of her delicate toes, her belly like the span of a bridge and her scarlet throat full of mock menaces, she took aim at my nose or my cheek and nipped my fingers hard enough to leave her mark on me. From there, we progressed to lunching together. She would lie in all her green and golden brilliance on my tablecloth as the sun stood at its zenith and counseled her to immobility. By this means she reassured the flies, and then snapped one up from time to time in an electric arabesque. I discovered a passion in her for fresh cream, certain raw fruits, and the syrup of my compotes. She ate too much, smacking her horny lips like a badly brought up child, then lay prostrate and suffering from her gormandizing. We never know how to set a limit to the favors we receive, we country hicks.

I was afraid of seeing her turn purple and die one day, as a tree frog had once done, before my very eyes, after swallowing an enormous gray fly covered in bristles. I was afraid above all of weakening in the resolution I had made, the best, that no animal should ever in my home forfeit its liberty, its normal chances of life and death, and even that trembling that seizes an untamed creature when it feels that we are watching it.

So I took my plump little lizard, perched on my index finger and confronting the universe around her with an air of defiance, back to the vines. "If she doesn't run away when I release her," I thought, "that will mean that I must keep her and take her back to Paris, where she will lie and meditate on the warm stones of the hearth and gaze with reverence at the basket of hot coals. She will lie on the roof of the phonograph and listen to the music vibrating in her belly; she will run vertically up the length of the curtains, and keep me company clinging to the warmth of my lampshade . . ."

As I was thinking these thoughts, I laid her down in the hollow of a tiny track among the vines. The same sand, in that spot, nourishes the vines and forms a filter for the sea. Cold in the dawn, at noon it will burn the sole of an unshod foot. It sends the lizard into ecstasy, and the tortoise, when the sun is at its height, cannot contain itself. Because I have always remained naïve in my relationships with the animal world, I thought at first that the lizard had already made its choice, between me and . . . all the rest. For she remained quite calm, her tail held in a resplendent curve against her flank. I scratched her head and her throat swelled up in friendship, then I stopped scratching her head, so as to leave her free to make her choice. And then . . . And then nothing more happened. The spot where the lizard lay glittering was suddenly void. I had, it is true, perceived a green flash, the beginning of a tremendous feat of speed. But our senses are slow, and the fine, floury, shifting sand had retained no imprint. But at least that lizard carries with it, symmetrically positioned on each side of the plump tail, and perhaps suspect to all other members of that tribe arrayed in quartzy green, opal, and gold, the traces of a human solicitude that supposed itself to be disinterested.

DC

Bitterness

There has been only one occasion in my life when I applied for a job. It was refused me. I had asked to be put in charge of the Jardin d'Acclimatation at a time when it was abandoned and consisted entirely of rotting stalls, smashed glass houses, and disheveled thatch. It still housed a few remaining animals: a last, magnificent lioness, some gnawed-looking rodents, various deer, perhaps some birds, I can't say for sure . . .

My request didn't even have time to go through the usual bureaucratic channels, and I was advised that nothing would come of it. My only, and foolish, aim was to ensure a better life for the captive creatures there, and I had asked for no remuneration. Since that time, the zoo at Vincennes has done far more in this respect than I could ever have done, so that all has turned out for the best— always supposing that there can be a best when it is a question of making wild free creatures into captives and prolonging that captivity, in a country and a climate not their own, until their deaths. To any animal that has been given paws for running on, wings to soar on, claws or horns to use in battle, and sexual organs with which to make love and carry on its race, even the best that we can offer must seem a mockery . . . In the famous Antwerp zoo I have seen how man provides, for instance, for an ocelot, a wild animal with no spite in its nature, the perfect cat, a lover of the sun and comfort, a creature which at the time of my last visit was languishing in a sort of pigsty, bare, black, and on a level with the ground. I wanted to write to Her Majesty Queen Elizabeth, but then I lost heart and failed to do so. Perhaps I was wrong. And equally wrong not to try and lodge a complaint with the administration of the zoo at Vincennes when they instituted a series of nocturnal parades, exhibitions of wild animals maddened by spotlights . . . Can we not leave these creatures, dispossessed of everything else, at least one refuge: the darkness of their nights, the absence of men? And why do their jailers not allow them at least a screen in the daytime, a place to hide, some small protection against the blinding light that contracts the pupils of the great cats? Why! I still keep in my memory a frightful image of a tigress with her newborn cub. There was nothing in her rectangular cage to protect her from our offensive gaze. No shade, no recess, no straw, no place into which she could retire to give suck and care for her young. From right to left, from left to right, she paced to and fro without rest, her cub, his eyes not yet opened, hanging from her jaws, and in the end he died of it . . .

I don't think I shall ever go again into a zoological garden or a menagerie. It is in vain that my friend Thétard, a born animal tamer, an interpreter between wild animals and man, still attempts to make me go with him to see the innumerable efforts they are making now at Vincennes—like pirate captains wooing the princesses they have snatched aboard their vessels—to transform their captives into friends.

And yet Thétard knows what he is talking about when he speaks or takes up his pen on behalf of the kings of the wild. He has scarcely an equal when it comes to seizing hold of a heavy, scimitar-clawed paw hanging between two bars of a cage, when it comes to gripping it just tightly enough, spreading the beautiful sheathed toes just the right amount, feeling the retractile claws, opposing the animal force of the paw with another, more fluid force, and loosing hold on his prize just in time, before the sleeping paw awakes, slashes the air and his flesh, and becomes bright with blood . . .

Yes, I think I shall never stand in front of a cage again. I find even the circus hard to take, because of what they call the animals' "work." At the very most, I can bear to watch the horses. Having been domesticated for such a long time, the horse is a survival, it has by some miracle escaped the law which is removing all the larger animals from our planet. Perhaps it has only persisted because the food it requires is more or less the same as that of the indispensable cow. It has been deformed by the demands we have made upon it, it has developed defects from overbreeding, a brain that can create ghosts, and a taste for music as well as personal adornment. Possibly our tyranny, and the *haute école* training we have given it, bring contentment to the least equine part of its nature; perhaps it prefers being in a circus to sharing its life with the last of our wagoners . . .

Certainly as far as wild animals and all the other inhabitants of the wide-open spaces are concerned, including birds, I have reached one unshakable and funereal conclusion: we have brought them nothing but despair. And for this reason I no longer wish to see the creatures I love with so strong an attachment in the enclosures that have now replaced their cages. I shall live henceforth on the memories I still have of them. I shall read about what men call their crimes: a tiger has torn a piece off his tamer; a lion, in love with his despotic and booted mistress, has killed the handsome boy who was his successful rival; a bear, maddened at being more narrowly confined in his cage than Cardinal Balue in his, has torn his keeper to pieces . . . I shall dream, far from these wild creatures, that we could do without them, that we could leave them to live where they were born. We should forget their true shapes then, and our imagination would flourish again. Our great-nephews would once more invent an indestructible fauna, which they would describe as they beheld it in their dreams, with dazzling intrepidity, as our forefathers used to do. I have in my possession a few big pages torn from an old natural-history book, and their colors are vivid, if not exact. On one of these pages there glows a fruit in the shape of a heart, reproduced life-size, which is to say, slightly larger than an ox heart.

It seems to have a very porous skin, and from each pore there springs a large hair. A caption at the foot of the page informs us that the name of this fruit is the *lickie,* and that it grows in abundance on certain trees, thirty feet high, which are providentially distributed here and there across desert regions made desolate by the prevailing hunger and thirst. "A true gift of providence for the traveler, the lickie has the taste and consistency of veal, which makes it an ideal family dish . . ." After a single perusal of those lines, are you not perfectly delighted and dazzled? And so we should be always if we were to meditate upon documents describing distant fauna that originated, not in the austere file indexes of explorers, but in the exaltation of an artist. If some commandment of an all-powerful apostle could contain once more within the limits of their jungles, their savannas, and their polar regions all those beasts that now languish here with us, then I would willingly pledge myself to describe the animals thus placed beyond our reach, and to provide you with matter for your dreams. "The Pempek, an animal already known in Ancient Times, haunts the solitudes of the Matto Grosso. It has big, flat feet which produce a musical sound as it walks, and a trunk with which it sucks in butterflies on the wing. Its mane is very thick, and it always runs away from the color blue . . ."

The reality is otherwise, and we are no longer free even to remain ignorant of how a boa constrictor chokes a gazelle, or how a panther, deliberately starved, rips open the throat of a goat which— since the combat must be spiced somehow and the cinema has no use for passive victims—has a kid to defend. It is high time I said good-bye to reality, to such supposedly ferocious animals and such indubitably guilty men, to motionless birds standing upright on talons embedded in dung, to kangaroos yielding little by little to paralysis, and to lion cubs crippled by rickets. Where shall I find my place of solitude? There is no beautiful human face, no snowy fur, no azure pinions that can enchant me if they are branded with the intolerable and parallel shadows cast by bars . . .

DC

Leopards

There are two of them, two brothers. Their keeper told me that they are two years old—God defend me from learning more. I do not wish to know whether they were born in a distant country, whether they were brought here, blind and trusting, in the black cage of a boat, or whether they were given suck by a rubber nipple, just sufficient to prevent them from dying. Let us go no further along that path, let us console ourselves, cruelly, with this fact: they play together. Their games are virile, faithful imitations of real battles, and silent. They wrestle with one another like two naked amazons and crumple to the floor like heaps of snow. What dresses! A meadow in May is not more decked with flowers. A flight of black corollas across a yellow field, flowers with four, three, two petals, some even with five . . . A companion of the nomadic period in my life once taught me, in a music hall, how they imitate, on fur or velvet, the leopard's spots: "You dip the fingers of one hand in Indian ink, you squeeze the tips together, then press them down onto the fabric. In some places you use all five fingers, to make a flower shape, in others four, in others just two, side by side . . . Of course," he added, "if you don't have the right feeling for leopards, you just end up ruining the cloth."

They play together. During the truces, they pull leopardish faces at one another, flattening their ears, furrowing their foreheads, and blinking their eyes affectedly. They swell up their necks, breathe in through their noses with a sudden swallow, and put on a show of nausea, while each alternately stretches out toward the other a soft front paw devoid of all expression—the tentative hand of the wrestler meditating a fresh hold. The embrace that follows is so swift that both contestants have a grunting "hunh!" forced out of them. Then one of them treacherously yields, falling on his back to drag his brother with him and enlace him the more firmly. The spread-eagled thighs reveal the white fur of the belly and its immutably disordered array of spots, the almost hidden sexual organs, chastely enveloped in close-cut velvet, and the undersides of the paws, the spreading beauty of the claw-tipped toes . . .

Their keeper, a man instinctively at home with animals, manages them as if they were two kids. For him, their harsh and raucous language softens till it is no more than a miaow; for him, a ray of complicity enriches those four pupils, those four vertical slits, with a golden light, and the two heads slide benignly beneath his palms. I envied that man as he walked, on an equal footing, into the great cats' lair, and brushed their coats.

"What if I were to go in behind you, and scratch their heads the way you do . . ."

"They can tell by the hand," the man replied. "It's not that they're savage, but . . ."

I pleaded with him to such effect that he at last allowed me to enter the leopards' house with him. Being preoccupied with their beloved keeper, they did not scent me immediately and I placed my palms on a beautiful spotted brow . . . The sudden awareness, and the gesture that followed, were swifter than thought: a paw, a lightning flash, tore through the dress over my breasts, just breaking the skin, and then the man had thrust me back outside the cage. There was no uproar, no battle cries. The two leopards gazed at me, in silence, breathing heavily through their nostrils. They were threatening me, they were excluding me. The man, put out by what had happened, inquired about my scratch and tugged, with feigned Napoleonic severity at one of the offending leopard's ears. I reassured him and walked away, without his becoming aware that I was leaving him there, weak and defenseless as he was, the prisoner of an alliance whose conditions I perhaps knew better than even he himself—between his two keepers.

DC

Snakes

A hundred and thirty, a hundred and fifty pounds of snake, there on the lowest fork of the dead tree. There appears to be nothing living inside the cage. Will it be a dead branch that moves first? Smoothed, polished, oiled by generations of reptiles, cylindrical, undulating, thicker in some places than in others . . . Perhaps it was the branch that ate the rabbit a week ago?

In the upper fork there is a further two hundred pounds of python lying asleep, or apparently asleep. Having first coiled itself into a spiral, it has then secured its balance by a series of hanked figures of eight. But what to do with that ten feet still hanging down? It has hauled up this remainder at a venture, subjected it to various half hitches and sheet bends, then tucked in the end. Two transparent tatters, two coarse skeins of tulle the color of spiders' webs, bear witness to the fact that spring has unsheathed the two great snakes from themselves. They are brand new. A stream, a chased steel blade could not rival them in brilliance. But which is flank, which neck, which head? These cylinders, oppressed by their own weight, are all armored with enamel. The back and the flanks —if it is the back, if they are the flanks—display the blue of the swallow, the yellow-green of the willow, two or three browns taken from freshly glazed earthenware, as many different tints of beige, all disposed in the manner of the simplest mosaic. And I say, naïvely: "The naïveté of those designs . . ." at the very moment when I notice that at one point the tiny, scaly, four-sided figures, in some places square, in others drawn out into lozenges or squashed into trapeziums, form a sort of eye, an orb almost endowed with a lifeless gaze, and I recoil . . . This animal, which is hiding both its end and its beginning, which is looking at me, which can create terror with its back alone, this animal and I have come neither from the same country nor from the same womb . . .

I must take hold of myself. There is a sickliness in the air of this place, as of half-dried puddles and strange excrements, a green-ish, sweetish something that seems to sap away the strength from one's heart. Were it not for the rainstorm outside, darkening the daylight, I should have sought refuge with the giraffe, or with the parrots in their sociable pavilion. But as I was saying, some of these coiling arabesques stand out like letters of the alphabet—an O, a U, a big C, a little G—along the monstrous and motionless coils of cable . . . Scarcely had the idea of "motionless" formed in my mind than the walls of the cage, its murky pool, and the ground support-ing me were all sliding away together in one smooth surge, continu-ing for the space of several seconds, or the time it takes to dream a dream—the duration of a cataclysm is unmeasurable . . . I should like to leave this stifled place, to climb a wind-battered hill, to eat a lemon, or some raw vegetable in vinegar. Fortunately, everything is now motionless again . . . Stop! Once again everything is yielding, moving in an appalling slide—I feel no shock, only a gentle down-ward trend, accompanied by convex coilings . . . It is the python which has shifted, the python I had supposed to be lying motionless —I must beware of that word, I must beware of it; I'll just step around it, I'll avoid it—and which has now begun to set itself in motion, drawing my shocked senses after it, amazing my blinked eyes, accustomed only to paws, to leaps, to movements governed by the logic of the stride . . .

It is moving: just so does the tide advance over the flat sands, dependent from the moon. Just so does a poison steal along the veins, or evil make its way into the mind. I should still hope that it was not moving, if the oily sheen adhering to its surface were not rippling across its coils with such mellifluous and alarming grace. It is moving, yet it is not progressing. Neither its head nor its tail has as yet been set free. It is melting into itself, starting at its own begin-ning again, progressing and yet staying in the selfsame place, draw-ing itself into itself and dilating without unknotting its coils.

It moves, and it is the sole solid collapsing in my sight. Is it possible that man, since the first serpent was created, has been wav-ering and staggering forever under a serpent's weight? It moves, it

aggravates the confusion of its coils, swells and deforms its mono-
grams, abusing me: The O is a C, the G is a Z. It liquefies, flows
along the branch, and on the other side retracts itself, becomes rigid
—it is creating a tension within itself, presaging some emergence I
cannot guess at—at the thickest part of its spirals as they wrestle and
grind on one another, and at last there gapes a narrow abyss, which
extrudes a head, a tiny, flat head, as though beaten thin by its own
efforts, not even hideous, but gay, adorned with two unchanging,
golden eyes, two hard and horny nostrils, and a horizontal mouth. I
breathe again: the python is only an animal after all, not a kind of
concentric hell, not a sickening chaos without beginning and without end. It is an animal like you and me. It has a slender neck,
replete with grace, which it darts toward me in a flowing thrust of
such velocity, and such enmity, that I am reassured. But then it stops,
hampered by its coils, and the head begins the rhythmic sway, the
sideways dance common to all wild beasts, to all prisoners: slender
neck, tongue of flame; perhaps that is the punishment this head
must undergo, to drag behind it, forever, those twenty yards, those
two hundred pounds of snake . . .

DC

Fame

My guests gone, the cats creep out of their lairs, yawn, stretch
as they do when they come out of their traveling baskets, and sniff
the traces of the intruders. The sleepy tomcat glides down from the
mulberry tree like a liana. His ravishing companion, on the terrace,
which is given over to her again, displays her belly, where there
appears, in a cloud of bluish fur, a single rosy teat, for this season she
has suckled only one kitten. The departure of the visitors in no way
changes the habits of the Brabançon bitch who watches over me,
doesn't stop and never has stopped watching over me, and will only
at death cease to give me her whole attention. Her death alone can

put an end to the drama of her life: to live with me or without me. She, too, is aging sturdily.

Grouped around these three specimens of the ruling caste of animals, the second-rate creatures keep the place assigned them by a protocol not so much human as animal: the scrawny she-cats from the neighboring farms, my caretaker's dogs transformed by a bath of white dust. "In summer here all the dogs belong to the eighteenth century," says Vial.

The swallows were already drinking in the washhouse and snapping up the May flies when my "company" took itself off. The air had its stale afternoon flavor and it was very hot in the sun, which sets late. But it cannot deceive me, I decline with the day. And toward the end of each day the cat, winding herself about my ankles in a figure eight, invites me to celebrate the approach of night. She is the third cat in my life, if I count only the cats of real character, memorable among both cats and she-cats.

Shall I ever marvel enough at animals? This one is exceptional, like a friend one will never replace, or a perfect lover. What is the source of the love she bears me? Of her own accord she adapted her pace to mine, and the invisible bond that links her to me gave me the idea of a collar and a leash. She got both and she wore them as though she were sighing: "At last!" Her narrow little lean face, rain-blue, with eyes of pure gold, looks older and seems to get paler when the slightest thing worries her. She has the modesty that belongs to perfect lovers, and their dread of too insistent contacts. I shall not say much more about her. All the rest is silence, faithfulness, impacts of soul, the shadow of an azure shape on the blue paper that receives everything I write, the silent passage of paws silvered with moisture.

After her, but a long way after, I have the tomcat, her magnificent husband, all slumberous with beauty and power, and as timid as a professional strong man. Then come all the creatures that fly, crawl, and creak, the hedgehog of the vines, the innumerable lizards that the grass snakes eat, the nocturnal toad which, when I gather it into the palm of my hand and hold it up toward the lantern, lets two crystal cries fall into the grass. The crab under the seaweed too, and the blue gurnard with martlet's wings that rises in flight from the waves. If it falls on the sand, I pick it up stunned, encrusted with grit, and then put it back in the water and swim beside it, supporting its head. But I no longer like describing the appearance or writing stories of animals. The passage of the centuries never bridges the chasm which yawns between them and man. I shall end by hiding my own creatures, except from a few friends, whom they shall choose. I shall show the cats to Philippe Berthelot, himself full of feline power, and to Vial, who is in love with the she-cat and pretends, as does Alfred Savoir, that I can conjure up a cat in a place where no cat exists. One doesn't love beasts and men at the same time. I am becoming daily more suspect to my fellows. But if they were my fellows, I should not be suspect to them.

"When I enter a room where you're alone with your animals," my second husband used to say, "I feel I'm being indiscreet. One of these days you'll retire to a jungle." I keep toying with the agreeable picture of the future this prophecy offers me, though I've no wish to try and fathom what insidious—or impatient—suggestion may have lain behind it; but I dwell on it to remind myself of the deep, logical mistrust which it reveals in a very civilized man. I dwell on it as on a sentence written by the finger of a man on a forehead which, if one pushes aside the foliage of hair that covers it, probably smells, to a human sense of smell, of a lair, the blood of a hare, the belly of a squirrel, a bitch's milk. Any man who remains on the side of men has reason to shrink from a creature who opts for beasts and who smiles, strong in her dreadful innocence. "Your monstrous simplicity. . . . Your sweetness full of dark places. . . ." How true all those phrases were! From the human point of view, monstrosity begins where there arises connivance with animals. Did not Marcel Schwob dub "sadistic monsters" those withered old bird charmers one used to see in the Tuileries covered with birds? Connivance alone would be one thing, but there is preference too, and at this point I shall keep silent. I stop short also when it comes to arenas and menageries. For if I see no objection to putting into the hands of the public, in print, rearranged fragments of my emotional life, it's understandable that I should tie up tight in the same sack, strictly private, all that concerns a *preference* for animals and—it's a question of partiality too—the child whom I brought into the world. How charming she is, that child, when she scratches, in a thoughtful, friendly way, the granular head of a huge toad. . . . Ssh! Once upon a time I took upon myself to make a girl of fourteen or fifteen the heroine of a novel. May I be forgiven, for I did not then know what I was doing.

"You'll retire to a jungle. . . ." So be it. And I mustn't wait too long. I mustn't wait until I notice the first waverings in the graph of my relation and exchanges with animals. The wish to captivate, in other words to dominate, the different ways of wrapping up a wish or an order and directing them to their end, these I feel are still flexible in me—but for how long?

A poor lioness, a beautiful creature, recently picked me out from the bunch of gapers massed before her bars. Having chosen me, she came out of her long despair as out of a sleep, and not knowing how to show that she had recognized me, that she wanted to confront me, to question me, perhaps to love me to the point where she could accept only me as a victim, she threatened, sparked, and roared like a captive fire, hurled herself against the bars, and then suddenly, wearied, grew drowsy, still looking at me.

The mental hearing that I can project toward the Beast still functions. The tragedies of birds in the air, the subterranean combats of rodents, the suddenly increased sound of a swarm on the warpath, the hopeless look of horses and donkeys are so many messages addressed to me. I no longer want to marry anyone, but I still dream that I am marrying a very big cat. No doubt Montherlant would be delighted to learn it.

Love and respect for living creatures could be read in my mother's letters and in her heart. So I know where the spring of my vocation lay, a spring which I muddied as soon as I was born, through my passion for touching and stirring up the depths lying beneath the pure stream. I accuse myself of having from an early age, not content with loving them, wanted to shine in the eyes of these, my kin and my accomplices. It is an ambition I still have.

"So you don't like fame?" Mme de Noailles once asked me.

But I do. I would like to have a great reputation among those creatures who having kept, on their fur and in their souls, the trace of my passage, madly hoped for a single moment that I belonged to them.

EMCC

❧❧ The Palais-Royal

The moving men have gone. The stepladder has been folded away. And my friends, climbing one by one up the old staircase, beautiful in its nudity, dreaming each in turn as they look out at the sunlit mist that casts a morning spell over the gardens of the Palais-Royal, say to me: "Ah! So you've found another country home."

Upon which I assume a look of false modesty, the self-satisfied double chin of the collector . . . Yes, I have found still another country home, in Paris, where there are enough, if not for everybody, at least for those who take the trouble to look for them. Found? Why not rediscovered? The heart can begin again. Forty-five years in Paris have still not made me into anything but a provincial in quest, throughout its twenty arrondissements and on both banks of its river, of the country home I have lost.

The last but one country home I had was at the time I lived near the Champs-Élysées. Beautiful though it is, such a neighborhood is assuredly barren soil for any person who is cultivating a certain dream, has regular habits, and must drag a houseful of furniture around with her, stubbornly clinging to her mahogany, her chintz seat covers, and her constellations of brightly colored, massive, and completely useless glassware. But being patched together out of bits and pieces, my Country Seat was easily reborn in the VIIIe arrondissement. A curtain was lowered to shut out the wall opposite, which was too white, and also scarcely set. The low arm-chair and the austere bookcase immediately entered into the most harmonious of agreements. And when my desk lamp was switched on, its arena of light spread just so far as to include within its circle all the objects I needed to see, all the objects which had existed even longer than myself, and had as many memories. With so little, I had managed so well that when the great wind that blows from the Parisian peaks pushed open my window, it would bring to me in the month of May, and set down on my blue page, a wistaria flower, a golden butterfly, or a bee. For the flora and fauna of Parisian balconies put a great deal of determination into their refusal to die. At a time when my country home, at the Claridge, consisted of a sloping slate roof, two narrow, flower-filled balconies, and two tiny rooms, all up on the seventh floor, I saw passing successively beneath me in the deep gutter a singular, almost yellow rat, a green frog, and an escaped monkey; and on gala nights I gazed out, as they swam in the illuminated air below me, on the backs of nocturnal birds.

Wistaria in a box, red geraniums, hairy mint, balm, and the tendrils of a young vine changing the reinforced concrete into a convent wall—graceful and precarious country home abusing a Parisian captive, you were a part, and not the least part, of the nourishment that fed my heart.

It's because I'm so demanding . . . If I don't have the top of a tree in front of my eyes, then I must have a length of *moiré* sky. Or else some not too timid wings. Or else silence. Or else some human sound as dense, as chattery as a congregation coming out of the village church after Mass. And the smell of warm bread. And a voice, clear and sharp, thrown out of a window onto the head of a little girl running . . . I must be able to put a name to familiar faces, even if the names, at a pinch, are of my own invention. I need to be able to mingle miraculously, as I sleep, the country places I have loved, the one where I was born and the others. I must be able to reach out gropingly and feel them if I wake up in the middle of the night, to interrogate the chimes of a big watch—and yet I know quite well it is in Provence—the catch of a window that no longer exists except in my memory, a bedside table held captive in Brittany, a copper knob that used to shine, some half century ago, on the door of my childhood bedroom . . . A smooth wall, a rough-textured drapery, a glass of water, destroyed now, broken, banished, live again for the time it takes me to come to myself. But my meeting with them is a moment without price, as fleeting as hoarfrost in the brightening sunlight, the only moment when I can sense beneath my hand, almost tangible, the flower of the past now turned to dust, a gift granted to me by this memory residing in the senses, as inveterate in me as if it were a congenital limp or stutter . . .

Yes, I have found another country home in Paris. Every time, I think it is the last. I like the idea that I shall have to face my end watched over by some clock tower, some antique piece of paneling, a colonnade, the remains of an arbor that once gave shade to nuns . . .

But the country is faithful only to those who know, if the need arises, how to create it. It is a task that teaches you to be nimble-fingered and stubborn in your habits. I have brought them with me from a long way in the past, these habits that you would find slightly ridiculous. Not that I inherited them all from my mother Sido; far from it, for she was inwardly a romantic and disliked all rules. For though she was a countrywoman, she was not at all provincial. The unexpected always delighted to make forays into her life, which even the humdrum of a village could never succeed in making narrow, and she, in her turn, always leaped up to meet it. What would she say if she saw me walking past every morning? She would say: "Aren't you sick and tired of that brown knitted suit? You remind me of old père Pinoulle, who used to go out to his garden outside the walls every morning. Just seeing him go by at exactly the same time every day used to give me the nervous yawns . . ."

I remember père Pinoulle very well. I knew him for seventeen years. I saw him when he was quite old, older still, then very old. My way of going about things is in fact the same, more or less, as his. Who trained me to make such modest use of my leisure hours, or to return with such daily punctuality to the home awaiting me? I think it was provincial life, and its naïve belief that repetition has some votive power . . . It is not that it smiles at me every day, my little garden—the table, the unfinished page, the lamp—or that it gives me what I require from it every day. In that respect I am less fortunate than père Pinoulle with his garden outside the walls. For every day, as he came home, he would be holding a sprig of violet in his mouth, a sweet honeysuckle flower, a double cherry blossom, and then, on all high summer days, a rose.

DC

PART Five ❧❧ [1932]

The Pure and the Impure

On s'apercevra peut-être un jour que c'est là mon meilleur livre . . .

Perhaps some day this will be seen to be my best book . . .

❧❧ Don Juan

I have not had to go out of my way to be let in on masculine secrets. The average man overflows with confidential talk when he is with a woman whose frigidity or sophistication sets his mind at rest. And it strikes me that at a time of life when a woman will go on and on exulting, misty-eyed with enduring gratitude, over the riches that have slipped through her fingers, over the cruelty, the infamy, the arrogance of the donor, a man at the same age will nurse a rancor that time does not heal.

My friend X., a celebrity, never leaves off his good humor and natural reserve except when calling to mind, in intimate conversation with me, his past as a celebrated lover. "Oh, the bitches!" he exclaimed one evening. "I was never spared a single embrace by any of them." (He did not say "embrace," but used a blunter term that refers to the terrible paroxysm of male sexual satisfaction.)

Rarely have I encountered in a woman the kind of hostility with which a man regards the mistresses who have exploited him sexually. The woman, on the contrary, knows herself to be an almost inexhaustible store of plenty for the man . . . Am I, then, going to find myself, in the first pages of a book, declaring that men are of less use to women than women are to men? We shall see.

But let me return to the famous lover I have just quoted. Like most men capable of servicing (if I may put it that way) a great many women, possession, which is lightning quick, provoked in him a wretched feeling of hopelessness—the neurasthenia of the Danaïds. If I understood him rightly, he could have wished to find at long last a woman who would love him enough to refuse herself to him. But it is hard for a woman to refuse herself. And besides, at the moment when our conqueror glimpsed the veritable purpose of love and the pure and burning space that unites, better than the bonds of flesh, two perfect lovers, he was seized by desire so strongly that he flung the object of his love to the floor and possessed her on the spot.

"Ah, what a life!" he sometimes sighed.

I have always greatly appreciated his confiding in me and I hope our confidential talks are not ended. As a rule, we choose for our rendezvous a quiet, private dining room in a first-class restaurant in the center of town, the building an ancient one with thick walls that do not vibrate. We dine like gourmands, after which my friend X. paces up and down, smokes, and talks. Occasionally he raises the ball-fringed curtain and looks out. On the other side of the glass appears a strip of Paris, animated and silent, calling to mind a swarm of fireflies on a lake of asphalt, and I am enveloped in the facile illusion of danger lurking in the night outside, of safety within the old walls warm with secrets. That feeling of security increases as I listen to the man who is talking, for mine is the very human pleasure of witnessing catastrophes. I am fond of this man who from time to time reveals himself to me, but I am also very fond of seeing him denuded and stewing in his boiling caldron; besides, he refrains from calling out for help.

With the passing years, he shows signs of the neurosis that dishonors the voluptuary: the obsession with statistics: "There's no arguing the fact," says he, "my average is lower. But after all, no one could care less than I do." And then he rages once more against "those little bitches that keep score on a man." I talk to him, then, about Don Juan and tell him I'm surprised that he has not yet written a Don Juan novel or play, and he gives me a compassionate look, shrugs, and charitably informs me that "period plays" are as out of fashion as cape-and-sword romances. And suddenly he exposes the child hidden in the heart of every professional writer, a child obstinately infatuated with technique, flaunting the tricks and wiles of his trade. His pretended cynicism marvelously rejuvenates him, and I let him run on.

Once I confessed to him that I was thinking of writing a play on the subject of Don Juan grown old, a part designed for the aging actor Édouard de Max.

"Don't do it, my dear," he urgently advised.

"Why not?"

"You aren't sufficiently Parisian. Your concept of Don Juan, my dear—why, I can just see it. What would it add to the other concepts of Don Juan? A pleasant acrimony, a great show of gravity on licentious subjects, and to end up with, you'd find some way or other of inserting a dash of rustic poetics . . . Don Juan is a hackneyed type, but no one has ever understood him at all. Fundamentally, Don Juan . . ."

At this point, of course, my famous colleague expounded his own concept of Don Juan, who, to hear him talk, was a serious-minded tempter, a kind of diplomat of annexation, who seduced a woman tactfully and was soon bored.

"Don Juan, believe me, my dear, was another one of those men who think only of taking, another one of those grasping men whose way of giving is no better than what they give. Of course, I'm speaking from the voluptuary's point of view."

"Of course."

"Why 'of course'?"

"Because when you talk about Don Juan you never talk about love. The business of numbers gets in your way. That's not your fault, but . . ."

He gave me a sharp look.

". . . but such is your tendency."

The hour was late and the cold of a streaming wet night seeped between the curtains, which were fastened together with a safety pin. Otherwise, I would have talked to my friend about my own concept of Don Juan. But X. was already gloomy at the thought of the next day, worrying about his work and his pleasures, especially the latter, because there comes a time in life when one feels on safer ground alone than when trying to find pleasures with another.

The rain had stopped when we parted and I announced that I wanted to go home alone and on foot. My friend the seducer went off with the characteristic stride of a long-legged man, and looking very handsome, I thought. A Don Juan? If you like. If the ladies like . . . But this Don Juan is obsessed with his reputation and pays the price of his vanity with the punctuality of a timid debtor.

We saw each other again not long afterward. He was looking tense, high-strung: his features can age in a quarter of an hour and be rejuvenated in five minutes. Youth and old age come to him from the same source: the eyes, the mouth, the body of a woman. In thirty-five years of orderly work and disorderly pleasures, he has never found time to be rejuvenated by rest. When he allows himself a vacation, he takes his poisons along with him.

"I'm going away," he said.

"That's good."

He glanced at his reflection mirrored in a shop window.

"You think I look tired? I am."

"Tired of whom?"

"Oh, all of them, the she-devils . . . Let's have some orange-ade. Here, or farther on . . . wherever you like."

When we were seated, he put up his hand to smooth his silver-gray hair.

" 'The she-devils,' " I repeated. "How many are there, for good-ness' sake?"

"Two. That sounds like nothing, two . . ."

He brazened it out, laughing and wrinkling his big classic nose, the typical nose of a woman's man.

"Do I know them?"

"You know one of them, the one I call Ancient History. The other is new."

"Pretty?"

"Oh, indeed!" he exclaimed, tossing his head and rolling up his eyes so you could see only the whites. This facial exhibitionism is one of his traits that I dislike.

"She's a Tahitian kind of beauty," he went on. "At home, she goes about with her hair hanging loose down her back, hair as long as that, a mane of hair flowing down over that length of red silk she wraps around her body . . ."

His expression changed, he stopped rolling his eyes.

"It's all humbug, sham, a fiction, of course," he added savagely. "I'm not taken in. But she's quite sweet. I'm not dissatisfied with her. It's the other one . . ."

"She's jealous?"

He gave me a hesitant look.

"Jealous? Oh, that one is a real demon. Do you know what she's done? Have you any notion what she's done?"

"You're going to tell me."

"She's taken up with the new one, they're bosom friends. Ancient History talks about me to the new one. That disgusting way they have of telling each other everything! She describes our love-making, our 'amours' as she calls it, and of course burlesques it into an orgy. She recalls everything and makes up the rest. After which the Tahitian beauty . . ."

". . . expects to get as much out of you . . ."

He looked at me with a new and sad humility.

"Yes."

"My dear man, allow me to ask a question. With the Tahitian girl, is it real sensuality or merely athletic prowess and a spirit of competition?"

My celebrated friend changed countenance. I had the pleasure of seeing a whole series of expressions appear on his features—defiance, cunning, every nuance of primordial hostility. He fixed his eyes upon the distant and invisible adversary and blew out his cheeks.

"Pooh!" he scoffed. "That's an old story, I can handle it. A question of dog eat dog. And as for her sensuality, I'm cultivating it. She's young, she's reckless, you know. It's rather amusing . . ."

He threw out his chest and was again a man of distinction.

"Anyway, the girl is, when excited and disheveled, a marvelous sight. What splendor . . ."

There is a short scene in the play *Célimare le bien-aimé* where the lover, hurriedly shut into an adjoining room by his mistress as her husband appears, kicks and pounds the locked door. "What's that?" the husband asks. "Nothing . . . Some workmen are repairing the chimney next door," stammers the trembling wife. "But this is intolerable! Pitois," he says to the old diplomatic footman, "will you please go and tell those fellows to make a little less noise!" Pitois hesitates, then says, in embarrassment, "Sir, those fellows don't look very accommodating." "Oh yes?" says the husband. "So you've got cold feet? Well then, I'll attend to it myself." He approaches the locked door and shouts with all his might: "A little less noise you there! We can't hear ourselves think!" A horrified silence. "That's the way, Pitois," says the husband, "that's the way to talk to workmen. I can do it myself." Upon which Pitois goes out, after this aside: "I'm going. I really feel sorry for him."

I was mischievously recalling these lines of Pitois as I sat there facing my friend X., who was claiming victory over a silly girl, insatiable and reckless. I smiled to myself and changed, or at least appeared to change, the subject.

"I understand that you are preparing a warm reception for your colleague from the North?"

X. brightened up, for he is by nature enthusiastic and for some time now has left behind him all professional jealousies.

"You mean Maasen? Yes, indeed. A great man! I intend to have a front-page piece on him in the *Journal*. There will be a banquet and speeches, all very high-flown and humbug. I would like to see the Académie mobilize the best it has for him. A great man, very great. And you'll see, his political career has just started. He has everything. He's one of those men I call 'the well-endowed.' He has an extraordinary animal magnetism, a handsome head, silver threads among the gold now, of course, but there's still a look of youth about him . . ."

"Yes, I know. I even know . . . They say that . . ."

"They say what? Affairs with women?"

"Naturally. They say . . . Lean over, I can't shout this sort of thing!"

I whispered a few words in my friend's ear. He replied with a long whistle.

"By Jove! But what documentation, my dear! Those *are* impressive figures. Who gave them to you?"

"On this kind of information, all sources are suspect."

"Well said."

He straightened up and buttoned his coat like an offended man about to challenge another to a duel. His brown-gold eyes held a wicked gleam.

"Oh, those Nordics!" he joked. "I'd just like to see them . . ."

Suddenly conscious of betraying ill humor, he tried to cover up.

"All the same, I don't see how this . . . ornamental detail can be of interest. When we are concerned with a man like Maasen, that magnificent human edifice," he added, with gross irritation, "I don't care whether or not the edifice includes a room with mirrors and the appurtenances of a brothel . . ."

"Of course," I said.

He paid for our two orangeades and picked up his gloves and stick.

"At any rate," I said, "you'll let me know, I hope."

"Let you know what?"

"Why, of Maasen's arrival. I'd like to talk to him."

"Oh! Yes. Quite. A rather keen little wind this, isn't it?"

"A wind from the North . . ."

He acknowledged this mediocre thrust, giving me a piercing look.

"Heavens," he said, "you think I'm a little more than jealous of Maasen, don't you! All the same, I've not yet sunk so low as to indulge in physical jealousies!"

I shook my head in denial and affectionately patted his bristly six-o'clock cheek. "My dear man," I felt like saying, "is there such a thing as nonphysical jealousy?"

He went off, and it was to his swinging back, his exaggeratedly long stride, and to his hat that I addressed myself mentally. Especially the hat, the significant, informative, inconstant, perplexing hat! For a boyish look, he sets it too much on one side; for a bohemian look, it's tilted too far back; and when it's tilted too far forward, that means, "Watch out, we're sensitive and can be tough, let no one tread on our toes." In sum, a hat that refuses to grow old.

Thus once again X. and I played at awaking the echoes of that fulgurant climax of possession, the paroxysm waggishly called *le plaisir* or, euphemistically, "satisfaction"—nomenclatures I must adopt, though unwillingly. We can talk about it, perhaps, because it has never threatened us together, never pinned one upon the other; or perhaps because my friend lets me see, in his fine "courtship plumage" which he so frequently dons, the bald spots and the clipped quills . . . We have our habits. We begin by talking a little about our work, about the people passing by, about the dead, about yesterday and today, and we compete with each other in pleasant incompatibility: "No, the way I see it, not at all. On the contrary, I . . ." "How strange, I hold a diametrically opposite opinion . . ." It needs a word or a name and we fall again into our habitual pile of cinders, black for the most part, but glowing red here and there. Except for the fact that he is the one who talks and more often than not I am the one who listens, I feel as responsible as he, since, from the minute he first sets his feet in the ignited traces, I follow him and even goad him on. Having gone beyond the limit one day, he expostulated.

"Too much has been said and too much written about this. I gag at all the literature that deals with the consummation of love, do you hear me, it makes me vomit!"

With my fist held in his fist, he pounded the table.

"It's time you did," I said. "You should have vomited on it before writing your share."

"And what about you?"

"Oh, that's something else again. I do myself this justice: I've always waited, before describing the conflagration, to be a little at a distance, cool and in a safe spot. Whereas you . . . In the very midst of suffering, in the very midst of joy, oh dear, it's indecent."

He nodded soberly in agreement, flattered.

"Yes, yes," he murmured. "What an aberration!"

He smiled as if he were twenty-five, with a feigned sadness and a feigned humility that were charming.

"I have behaved like those shipwrecked voyagers who pitch into the cargo and gorge themselves until they can eat no more. And they eat no more, for nothing is left, and what will they eat tomorrow?"

"Exactly, my dear man, exactly. But invariably something will be found when the need is felt—a barrel of anchovies at the bottom of the hold, or a case of dried beef, or a quantity of grapefruit and coconuts . . ."

He shrugs. He meditates. He talks. He talks about *it*. I learn how he overwhelms women with letters, telegrams, telephone calls. He laments, he waits at a spa, he hides on a Swiss mountaintop, he makes and endures innumerable scenes, emerging from it all steaming, as if from a hot bath, thinner, and regenerated. There is nothing of Byronic gloom about him. Rather, he's a war horse, he rears and charges against what he does not comprehend. He is full of voices that are the echo of his own voice. He is too important for the women not to feel the need to imitate him, too masculine to elude the girl who puts on a show of being terribly naïve. The girl would never be able to fool you, Don Juan, my Don Juan as I see you!

When I had the daring idea of making known my "concept of Don Juan," Édouard de Max was still alive. He is dead now, and I no longer consider writing the play in which I wanted him to take the leading part.

"Édouard," I said to him, "how do you feel about it?"

"I'm too old, my dear."

"Exactly. But for my play I need to have you old."

"Then I'm not old enough for the part. You've hurt my feelings."

The expression in the blue-green-gold eyes and the sound of his voice cast a spell.

"But I also need to have you very seductive."

"Well, that I can still be, thank God. Youth is not the time to seduce, it is the time to be seduced. What does your Don Juan do in the play?"

"Nothing yet, the play isn't written. And not much when it is written. I mean to say, he doesn't make love—or at any rate, only a very little."

"Bravo! Is it indispensable to make love? Oh, it's all right to do it, but only with women to whom one feels indifferent."

I am quoting Max faithfully, for the pleasure of putting his words beside those of a great lover, Francis Carco, the novelist. Just listen now to Carco: "Ah," he sighs in moments of simplicity and gloom, "a man should never go to bed with a woman he loves, that spoils everything . . ." And I want further to quote Charles S.: "The difficult thing is not so much to obtain a woman's ultimate favors, but rather, once she has yielded to our desires, to prevent her from setting up housekeeping with us. What else can we do but run? Don Juan has shown us the way."

"Édouard," I went on, "you've got to understand me."

"I'm afraid I will," Max agreed, and his charming smile lost all its gaiety. "Haven't I already understood?"

I explained my famous project and repeated the name Don Juan twenty times. Without our being aware of it, the warmth and magic of that name wove a spell: Édouard's expression changed as, mentally, he assumed the role. I could see his lips compress, his deep-set eyes sparkle blue and gold, the colors of the water salamander; I was aware of his magnificent mane of hair trembling as he moved his shoulders, and could see his hand gradually reach for the hilt of a sword . . .

"You see, after the age of fifty, Don Juan . . ."

The interval of a dress rehearsal at the Théâtre Marigny shed an unflattering light on us and on the gardens, the acid, cold green of springtime. It was there, for the last time, that I promised Max that he should create the part of a misogynous Don Juan. "Make haste," he said to me. Alas, he was more prompt than I and descended forever toward the wavering secondary characters with whom I had not yet had time to pair him off. I had already decided that around him, around Don Juan in his maturity, there should be as many women as possible, and for the most part young, and that he would detest them. For I counted on taking as my model a man known to me, and who no doubt is still more or less alive somewhere or other.

As for that man, it took me quite a while, some years ago, to see that he was Don Juan, because what little he had to say about women was offensive.

A persistent youthfulness clung to his features, without improving his looks, and indeed it was rather a curse. Besides, he had no need of it. I can't figure out whether women were drawn straight to his eyes, bathed in a false and saline mistiness like gray oysters, or to his lips, always shut over his small and regular teeth. All I can say is, they were drawn straight to him. Where he was concerned, they at once acquired the set purpose of somnambulists and bruised themselves against him as if against a piece of furniture, to such an extent did they seem not to see him. They were the ones who designated him to me by his true name, Don Juan. Without them, I would never have thought of applying that name, of humble origin really, born of a very few pages, but eternal, for no other name in any language has ever supplanted it.

One of his most striking characteristics was the fact that he never hurried. Golf, tennis, riding kept his diaphragm flat and his muscles in trim. But I confessed to him my surprise that, except for games, he was always last to arrive at functions where politeness or the obligation to be pleasant should have been his guide.

"It's not out of laziness," he replied very seriously, "but to maintain my dignity."

I laughed and all too readily agreed with his rivals, who sneered at the offhand attitude of this man who was more successful with women than they. "That imbecile, that idiot of a Damien . . ." I am here bestowing upon him a name which recalls his true name, a rather old-fashioned one . . .

Later on, while I was working on *Chéri,* I tried to persuade myself that Damien, young, could have served as model for me, but I soon saw that Damien, a stiff and rather limited sort, was far from having the indulgent whimsicality, the impudence and boyishness indispensable to Chéri. They had nothing in common except a similar melancholy, and a keen intuitiveness, extraordinary in Damien.

One day he showed me, in confidence and out of vainglory, the cabinet where he kept his letters from women. It was a tall piece of furniture, impressive beneath its bronze appliqués, and was provided with a hundred little drawers.

"Only a hundred!" I exclaimed.

"The drawers are subdivided inside," Damien replied, with the solemnity that never left him.

"And do women still write letters?"

"Yes, they write. A great many do, really a great many."

"Quite a few men have assured me that women nowadays merely use the telephone, reinforced by a few *petits bleus!*"

"The men to whom women don't write nowadays are simply men to whom women don't write, period."

I liked being with him, as I like being with swift animals who are motionless when at rest. He talked little, and I believe he was second-rate in everything except the performance of his mission on earth. When I finally overcame his mistrust, I was greatly edified by his sententious and quasi-meteorological manner. It was almost identical to that of country people who forecast the weather, understand the temper of animals and the intentions of the wind—I believe I need look no further for the secret of our apparently unjustifiable friendship.

To amuse and astonish me, he kept me informed as to how he "lured" women to their fall, one misstep after another. Please note that, unlike his ancestor, he did not seduce cloistered little ninnies, whining little Catholic pussycats, warm and weaned. It took little prowess, certainly, to seduce Inés!

I was dumfounded, however, at the monotony and simplicity of the amorous maneuvers. Between Damien and the women there was not the slightest hint of diplomacy. It was rather a question of merely pronouncing the magic word, "Open sesame!"

I believe he concealed a rather modest family background. This would explain his agreeably exaggerated reserve, his discreet vocabulary. His successes were neither retarded nor reduced by this; on the contrary, since a great many women have a secret aversion to men of gentle birth. At the risk of being thought older than he was, he did not use the current slang. When we established our friendship, Damien was becoming almost as hard on himself as on "them," his women. Old age, declining powers, and physical decrepitude were condemned by him according to the code of the primitives who kill off the aged and execute the infirm. Merciless—in a well-mannered way.

I put some questions that must have seemed rather naïve—for instance, the following exchange.

"What memory, Damien, do you believe you left with the women, with most of them?"

His gray eyes, which were usually half closed, now opened wide.

"What memory? Why, without a doubt, a feeling of not having had quite enough."

The tone of his reply shocked me, although it was too curt for me to notice at once its fatuity. I surveyed this cold man, who was not at all affected, whose good looks were not in the least banal or standardized. The only flaws I could find in his physique were his hands and feet, which were too small and dainty, a detail that I find important. As for his gray eyes and dark hair, that is a contrast that vividly strikes us women and we say, complacently, that it is a sign of a strong character.

The man of strong character deigned to add a few words:

"Whether I had them at once or let them languish a little, I had to leave them the minute I was sure they would blame me for ruining them. That about sums it up."

I know that every métier begets its particular lies and litanies, but even so, I listened to Damien incredulously. "I had to . . ." But why did he have to? I put the question.

He replied in his usual firm voice, his usual dry manner, as if he were predicting the bad weather to be expected at the next full moon, or a devastating scourge of caterpillars.

"You surely wouldn't expect me to dedicate myself to their happiness, once I was sure of them? Besides, if I had spent my time making love, I would never have been the Don Juan I was and am."

I recall that this instruction was imparted to me between midnight and two o'clock in the morning, in one of those unpredictable towns where darkness is the glacial opposite of daylight and where only the night makes one aware of the nearness and attraction of the sea. Damien and I were drinking a sweetish orangeade drowned with water, a hotel orangeade, an end-of-the-season orangeade, and were sitting beneath the glass roof of a hotel lobby.

Damien had come to my dressing room to fetch me after my pantomime act. "I'm in this town rusticating," he had briefly explained, using a word that was out of date. He abstained from alcohol. "It brings gray hairs," he said, leaning over his goblet to show his dark hair, which was rather plentifully threaded with gray, glistening like aluminum. He sipped his orangeade thoughtfully through a straw, and as my eyes rested on his fine mouth, I reflected that there was something about it that aroused ideas of sweetness, of sleep, something secret and gentle and sad—and still youthful. And I remembered the adage: "A kissed mouth never grows old."

I have often thought about this man who had neither wit nor gaiety nor the disarming coarseness that women find delightful and reassuring. His only asset was his function. I have tried to persuade myself a hundred times that nothing in him stirred my senses, only to admit a hundred times that this was only a part of the truth, the plain and short, the meaningless part of the truth.

"You had to leave them," I repeated. "But why? Is victory all you want? Or, on the contrary, is this victory of no importance to you?"

He turned my question over in his mind. Then, as if it had reached him from a long way off, he clapped the palms of his hands together and forcefully interlaced his fingers. I expected him to let out a torrent of abuse, to speak out, to say no matter what. I wanted him to give way to anger, to make some kind of row that would prove him to be illogical, weak, and feminine—what every woman wants every man to be at least once in his life. I wanted to see him roll up his eyes pathetically, wanted him to show the ugly empty whites, instead of those eyelids like shutters, slanted down, cautious, sheltering the proud and reproving gaze of his lowered eyes. Nothing that I wanted to happen happened. Instead, Damien began to talk quietly, in short and abrupt phrases that I would be hard put to recall and write down, because the meaning of words cannot be separated from their sound or from the monotonous delivery, with frequent pauses, which helped Damien at times to hide and at others to express the deepest resentment.

Not for a moment did he lose the least dignity, at any rate the physical dignity of a man accustomed to live his life in public. He did not let out any of the crude old words that we all carry in our subconscious since our childhood, since our schooldays. He named no one and committed only one error of taste, the casual reference to his mistresses in mentioning the title or rank or social position of their husbands or protectors. ". . . She was the dear and close friend of a great industrialist . . ." "Her husband was a peer of the realm . . ." "Good God, you can't imagine how boring a Balkan grain dealer can be to a woman!"

He talked for a long time. My hotel darkened; in the late hours we were allowed only a reduced light which fell from the high ceiling. A night watchman in correct livery but wearing preposterous carpet slippers shuffled across the hall.

"Well now, please tell me," said Damien, "what did I get out of all this?"

Listening is an effort that ages the face, makes the neck muscles ache, and stiffens the eyelids looking fixedly at the speaker. It is a kind of studied debauch . . . Not only the listening, but the interpreting . . . the elevating to its secret meaning a litany of dull words, promoting acrimony to grief or wild desire.

"By what right? By what right did they always get more out of it than I did? If only I could doubt that they did! But I had only to look at them. Their satisfaction was all too real. Their tears, as well. But their satisfaction especially . . ."

At this point he did not indulge in any digression on the bold immodesty of females. But imperceptibly he threw out his chest, as if to shake off what in effect he was seeing in his mind, likewise "subdivided inside."

"They allow us to be their master in the sex act, but never their equal. That is what I cannot forgive them."

He took a deep breath, pleased at having so clearly rid himself of the essential motive of his long, low-voiced lament. He turned from one side to the other, as if to call a waiter, but all the night life of the hotel had withdrawn into a single human snore, nearby and regular. Damien therefore satisfied himself with the rest of the tepid soda water, composedly wiped his gentle mouth, and smiled sweetly at me from the depth of his wilderness. The night passed over him softly, and his vitality seemed to be a part of a particular asceticism . . . At the beginning of his confidential talk he had successively singled out, to show them off better, the famous mistress of the great industrialist, the titled lady, the actress, but from then on he used only the plural. Lost among them, feeling his way through a crowd, through a flock, scarcely guided by such landmarks as a breast, a hip, the phosphorescent furrow of a tear . . .

"Sensual pleasure, satisfaction, good, yes, satisfaction, that's understood. If anyone in the world knows what it is, I'm the one. But beyond that to . . . No, really, they go too far."

He shook out what remained of his drink on the rug, like a wagoner in a country inn, and without excusing himself. Were those drops of warm water meant to insult a woman or the entire invisible horde that had no fear of the conjuration?

("They go too far." They go, to begin with, as far as the man leads them, and the man demands a great deal in his conceit, his intoxicating conviction that he is imparting an arcane science. Then, the very next day, he says, "What has become of my innocent girl of yesterday?" He sighs and exclaims, "What have I in common with this she-goat at a witches' revels?")

"Do they really go so far?"

"You can believe me," he said laconically. "And they keep going, they don't know how to stop."

He averted his eyes in a way that was characteristic, ostensibly, like a man who, confronting an open letter, refrains from reading it for fear of betraying on his features what he might thus dishonestly find out.

"Perhaps it was your fault. Did you never give a woman time to get used to you, to become mollified, to relax?"

"What in the world!" he scoffed. "Peace, after all that? Cucumber cold cream for the night and the newspapers in bed in the morning?"

He stretched himself discreetly, his only confession of nervous fatigue. I respected his silence, the elliptical word of a man who had never in his life treated with the enemy or laid aside his armor or admitted the least failure of energy—which is a kind of repose—to enter into his love-making.

"In short, Damien, you have the same concept of love that used to be characteristic of young girls, who could not imagine a warrior except with his weapon drawn or a lover except ready at any moment to prove his love?"

"There's something in that," he conceded, "and on that score the women I've known never have had any reason to complain. I educated them well. But as for what they ever gave me in exchange . . ."

He stood up. I was afraid of recognizing in him another haggling trader, disappointed in a bargain—for I had met and known one elsewhere and at closer range. I was afraid of finding the answer to his riddle and of having Don Juan change before my eyes into merely an unlucky creditor. I therefore hurried to reply.

"What they've given you? Why, I should think, their grief. So you're not all that badly paid after all, are you?"

He showed me then that he was neither governed by his model nor jealous of him.

"Their grief," he repeated, "yes, their grief. That's very indefinable. And I don't appreciate it as much as you think. Their grief . . . I'm not a mean person. I only wish that I could have received —if only for a moment—as much as I gave."

He started to go. Again I held him back.

"Tell me, Damien . . . Aside from the men I've seen you speak to, have you any male friends?"

He smiled.

"Oh, really! *They* wouldn't have tolerated it."

Buried beneath that conglomeration of women, he had had no ventilating shaft to provide him with some fresh air . . . But just as I was about to regard the life of this man with horror, I suddenly thought that any alteration in the design, any "repentence" would have turned a modestly legendary figure into a pitiful caricature. Grotesque, the idea of a jovial Damien being consoled for his wicked women by pals who would slap him on the back and give him their advice: "Forget it. Come along, friendship is . . ." I had just imagined this final downfall when Damien reassured me, with that severity which, for lack of other virtues, constituted his self-respect.

"I have nothing to say to men and never had. Judging from the little time I've spent with them, their usual conversation is sickening. Besides, they bore me. I believe," he hesitated, then concluded, "I believe I don't understand men."

"You exaggerate, Damien. It would have been different had you been obliged to earn a living and been put in daily contact with men, or if women had ruined you materially . . ."

"Ruined? Why, please, ruined? What's money got to do with the topic we're discussing, which, by the way, has kept us up so late here—I really wonder why."

He was losing patience and checked himself.

"You've been told," he went on more gently, "that the idea of money inevitably enters into love affairs. You've been told . . ." He smiled, in good fettle despite the late hour. "Too bad you don't have a son. I would have taught him the few words that a man like me should know . . ."

I protested: ". . . and which would have doubtless been useless, for I simply cannot see myself with a son who would resemble you."

"Have no regrets," he said with disobliging sweetness. "Not everyone can have a son like me. I scarcely know more than two or three such men, and they are quite circumspect. Even so, I will speak the few words to you, which you'll not understand: 'Give nothing—take nothing.' "

I was dumfounded.

"You see," Damien noted gaily, "I'm delighted! I was always a little afraid you weren't any more intelligent than other women. Now, my dear, I must excuse myself for having stayed so long."

"Wait," I exclaimed, catching him by the sleeve. "If you want to keep your prestige with me, explain yourself. I don't always respect what I don't understand. 'Give nothing, take nothing.' What exactly do you mean by 'nothing'? Neither flowers nor jewels nor banknotes nor art objects? Are you thinking of *bibelots,* gold, credit, furnishings, real estate?"

He gravely inclined his well-shaped head.

"Exactly, all that. It is hard, I admit, not to break the rule. But one soon perceives that the bracelet is poisoned, the ring unfaithful, the card case or the necklace disturbers of dreams, the silver eager to land on the gambling table . . ."

It was fun to see him becoming sententious again, glorying in a science he had invented, and as positive as a village soothsayer.

"So one should neither give nor receive?" I laughed. "And if the lover is poor, his mistress indigent, then both she and he must tactfully let themselves and each other die?"

"Let them die," he repeated.

I had accompanied him as far as the revolving glass door of the lobby.

"Let them die," he said again. "It's less dangerous. I can swear on my word of honor that I never gave a present or made a loan or an exchange of anything except . . . this . . ."

He waved both hands in a complicated gesture which fleetingly indicated his chest, his mouth, his genitals, his thighs. Thanks no doubt to my fatigue, I was reminded of an animal standing on its hind legs and unwinding the invisible. Then he resumed his strictly human significance, opened the door, and easily mingled with the night outside, where the sea was already a little paler than the sky.

I treasure the memory of that man. Although I have never lacked close friends, rarer in my life have been the friends who were not close, between whom and me passed a sensual current, a mysterious force that made them, to begin with, rather cantankerous and sparkling, then dull, snuffed out like a candle. I enjoyed seeing Damien fixed in his error—as we call any faith that is not ours. Besides, he satisfied the liking I have always had for the mysterious void, and for certain privileged creatures and their steadiness in a supposedly paradoxical equilibrium, and especially for the diversity and steadfastness of their sensual code of honor. Not only honor, but poetic feeling, as when Damien applied his lyricism to abandoning his mistresses and letting them die. "Let them die," he said, and he said, "I *had* to leave them." He would have been baffled had I told him (as I never did) that in his "I had to leave them" resided his simplicity, and that when he thought he was being coldly calculating, he was being a poet and a fatalist. His thankless and well-loved duties shut him off from everything else, and I could have learned a lot from him and about him had he not, in his hatred of any contest of wits, practiced the empiricism of the wild beast teaching her young: "Look: This is the way I jump, this is the way you ought to jump." "Why?" "Because this is the way to jump."

I linger over this memory. If Damien is still alive, he is now more than seventy years old. Has the time come for his deliverance? And once freed, what does he amount to? If he reads these lines and this book, in which I hope to add my personal contribution to the sum total of our knowledge of the senses, he will smile and shrug, the tranquil little gray-haired gentleman. If in his latter years he has married some stouthearted woman, he will keep it quiet that he was Damien: this will be his last pleasure and his supreme deed of darkness. What could be the avowable end of Damien, other than a premature death? But there is no premature death for a man utterly dedicated to conquest, solitude, and vain flight: he is always at an age to die.

He embodied that type of man whom other men unanimously refer to as "a person devoid of all interest." When, by chance, he had to deal with ordinary men, he was always, I noticed, the one who was embarrassed and momentarily at a disadvantage. And if in his presence they told the usual off-color jokes, he barely gave a sign that he heard. However, surrounding him there was an expanding zone as subtle as a perfume, gradually perceived by the men present, and with aversion. They justified this aversion as best they could. "What does that character over there do for a living?" one of them asked me, adding, "I can't stomach him. I'll bet he's a pederast." I could hardly keep from laughing over the way the suspicious man was betraying his own naïve and equivocal behavior—he was limp with anxiety and as irritable as a prude on the point of letting herself be seduced, as he cast contemptuous glances at the suspected man, the very glances I had seen one of Damien's mistresses dart at him before she succumbed. She, too, had referred to him as "that character," to begin with. And when she stood up after sitting beside him, she brushed her skirt as if to shake off some crumbs. That gesture was, I felt, almost a morbid tic.

"Leave her alone," I told Damien.

"I'm not doing anything to her," he replied.

In fact, he did nothing but hover in her vicinity and make rather trite remarks. And always she stood up nervously and left, in a telltale way, going toward the nearest exit—the terrace of the casino, the french window of the salon, a garden gate. He needed no stronger hint and vacated the place. When she returned, she inexplicably looked for him; to be exact, I divined it from the way the nostrils of her perfect little nose flared, and the impatience with which she pushed aside the empty chairs in her way. Watching her was what made me believe that all of us in that man's presence scented a delightful something, if I may flatter the atmosphere surrounding him by associating it with the most aristocratic of our five senses, the olfactory.

What happened later was the usual thing: the two, of course, became lovers, and the young woman was alternately radiant and pale, unsociable and gay, visibly haggard so long as she resisted, dashingly rejuvenated when she stopped resisting. And when the hour struck that indicated, according to Damien and his particular religion, that "it was really necessary" for the affair to end, she vanished as if Damien had thrown her into a well.

No doubt in describing him I am slurring the character of this dispenser of pleasure, ill recompensed and probably quite incapable, if he had so desired, of giving any woman lasting happiness.

In his own way he also went "too far" when he accorded unlimited credit to the sensual satisfaction that he gave. Can his obsession with potency ever equal, for a lover, his obsession with impotence?

And what would he have said had he ever met the woman who, out of sheer generosity, fools the man by simulating ecstasy? But I need not worry on that score: most surely he encountered Charlotte, and perhaps more than once.

She produced for him her little broken cries, while she turned her head aside, and while her hair veiled her forehead, her cheek, her half-shut eyes, lucid and attentive to her master's pleasure . . . The Charlottes of this world nearly always have long hair.

At a time when I was—or thought I was—insensible to Damien's attraction, I suggested that he and I go for a voyage together, a pair of courteously egotistic companions, accommodating, fond of long silences . . .

"I only like to travel with women," he replied.

His gentle tone was meant to soften the brutal remark. But, afraid he had offended me, he dressed it up with a remark that was even worse.

"You, a woman? Why, try as you will . . ."

HB

❦❦ La Chevalière

A champion, when defeated by another champion, is nonetheless ready to applaud a superior speed, an innate ability to cut the air and cover distance. Damien's remark hurt me for quite a while, and since it happened to be one of the last remarks he ever made to me I never had the opportunity to admit to him that, oddly enough, I was secretly craving just then to be completely a woman. I am not alluding to a former self, a public and legendary figure that I had ostentatiously cultivated and arranged as to costume and external details. I am alluding to a genuine mental hermaphroditism which burdens certain highly complex human beings. And if Damien's pronouncement vexed me, it was because I happened to be making a particular effort at the time to rid myself of this ambiguity, along with all its flaws and privileges, and to offer them up, still warm, at the feet of a

certain man to whom I offered a healthy and quite female body and
its perhaps fallacious vocation of servant. But as for the man, he was
not taken in; he had detected the masculine streak in my character
by some trait of mine I could not identify, and, though tempted, had
fled. Later he returned, full of grudges and mistrust. And I did not as
yet think to put to use the warning Damien had given me.

Of what avail is it to warn the blind? The blind trust only their
own well-known infallibility and are determined to assume the full
responsibility of hurting themselves. Thus I hurt myself in my own
stupid and forthright way.

"There's no reason to be so upset," Marguerite Moreno said to
me one day. "Why don't you just accept the fact that for certain men
some women represent a risk of homosexuality?"

"You and I may comfort ourselves with that thought, Marguerite, at any rate. But if what you say is true, who will realize that we
are women?"

"Other women. Women aren't offended or deluded by our
masculine wit. Think it over . . ."

I interrupted her with a gesture. We had the comfortable habit
of leaving a sentence hanging midway as soon as one of us had
grasped the point. Marguerite Moreno thought I stopped her now
out of decency, and she fell silent. No one can imagine the number
of subjects, the amount of words that are left out of the conversation
of two women who can talk to each other with absolute freedom.
They can allow themselves the luxury of choosing what to say.

"A great many men have a feminine streak in their mental
makeup," Moreno continued. "I emphasize: in their mental
makeup."

"I quite understood," I said gloomily.

". . . Because, when it comes to morals, they are unassailable,
they are quite strict, as a matter of fact!"

Amused, I nodded in agreement.

". . . And they are gallant souls, in the general acceptance of
the term, the military way of using it. But oh, how they shriek if a

caterpillar grazes them or if a bee flies too close; and just notice how they go pale at the very sight of a big black cockroach or the cockroach's cousin, the earwig . . ."

"Them? Are they all that numerous, Marguerite?"

She bowed her head with that grave, donnish air that people who have seen her films find so comic.

"And what about us? What about us women who constitute their homosexual risk? Are we equally numerous?"

"Far from it, I'm sorry to say. With an equal, even an equal in number, one can always get along. I've not finished. I've got only as far as the cockroach. But haven't you noticed, when *they* let themselves go in a violent scene with a woman, haven't you noticed that they never forget to keep their eyes averted from the face of the woman they're blackguarding, and focus on her hands?"

"And if they're quarreling with a man?"

"They never make scenes with another man. They may despise and fear the other man, but rather than be obliged to exchange words with him, they prefer to have it out in a duel."

I burst out laughing—it does one good, when at a safe distance from the claws that have wounded us, to laugh at them, even when the old wounds are still raw and gaping.

"In short," the clairvoyant continued, "if they are often deluded by the expression on our face, they can more safely consult, behind us, the expression on our back . . . Oh, how beautifully they laugh, and how easily they weep!"

She uttered a Spanish oath and made a face at some memory or other. Then she yawned and succumbed to sleep, leaning her head against the high-backed armchair. Her strong, sexless features softened a little as she sank into the sudden sleep of all trained workers, who know how to recoup their strength by taking a ten-minute nap in the bus or the Métro, a quarter of an hour at rehearsals as they sit on the taboret that will serve in one scene as a Regency desk and in the next will represent a flowering hedge, or beneath the tropical lights of the cinema studios. Sitting or leaning, they sleep the sleep of the careworn, the weary, the conscientious worker. Asleep, she rather resembled Dante, or a refined hidalgo, or Leonardo da Vinci's Saint John the Baptist. Now that our woman's wealth of hair is shorn, when our breasts and hands and stomach are hidden, what remains of our feminine exteriors? Sleep brings an incalculable number of women to assume the form they would no doubt have chosen if their waking state did not keep them in ignorance of themselves. The same applies to men . . . Oh, the charm of a sleeping man, how vividly I recall it! From forehead to mouth he was, behind his closed eyelids, all smiles, with the arch nonchalance of a sultana behind a barred window. And I who would willingly have been completely woman, completely and stupidly female, with what male wistfulness did I gaze at that man who had such a delightful laugh and who could respond to a beautiful poem or landscape . . .

That man always comes into our lives more than once. His second apparition is less frightening, for we had thought him unique in the art of pleasing and destroying; by reappearing, he loses stature.

Grudgingly we confer upon him generous and noble attributes and make the inevitable gestures to which he has the right, we employ an anthropometry that renders him commonplace. Fashioned for the use and the hostility of woman, he nonetheless recognizes at a distance, in a man, his own species and the amiable peril his own species represents, and so he steps aside. For he knows that he is stripped of his powers the minute a woman, in talking about him, should say "they" instead of "he" . . .

"Isn't it a fact, Marguerite, that a standardized executioner . . ."

But Marguerite Moreno was sleeping, her Conquistador nose turned toward adventure. Her deep sleep gave to her mouth, small and firm in her waking state, a plaintive look of submission.

Cautiously I reached for a light coverlet and laid it over Ximena and El Cid, closely united in the sleep of a single body. Then I resumed my post at the side of a worktable, where my woman's eyes followed, on the pale blue bonded paper, the hard and stubby hand of a gardener writing.

:

A woman needs a fine and rare sincerity and a good amount of high-minded simplicity to determine what it is in her that tips the scale and adds some standard and approved element to her clandestine sex life. Sincerity is not a spontaneous flower, nor is modesty either.

Damien was the first to designate, in a word, my place in the scheme of things. I believe he assigned to me the place of a spectator; he felt I should have one of those choice seats that allow the spectator, when excited, to rush out on the stage and, duly staggering, join the actors and take part in what is going on.

I was not long deluded by those photographs that show me wearing a stiff mannish collar, necktie, short jacket over a straight skirt, a lighted cigarette between two fingers. Certainly I turned on them a less penetrating look than did that arrant old demon of painting, Boldini. I saw him for the first time in his studio, where the gown of a big unfinished portrait of a woman, a satin gown of blinding white—peppermint-lozenge white—caught and flashed back all the light in the room. Boldini turned his griffin face away from the portrait and gave me a deliberate stare.

"Are you the one," he said, "who puts on a dinner jacket in the evening?"

"I may have done so, for a costume party."

"You're the one who plays the mime?"

"Yes."

"And you're the one who goes on stage without tights? And who dances—*così, così*—quite naked?"

"I beg your pardon! I've never appeared naked on any stage. It may have been said, and said in print, but the truth is . . ."

He was not even listening. He laughed, shrewdly, insinuatingly, and patted my cheek.

"My, what a proper young lady we are," he murmured, "what a proper young lady we are!"

At once he forgot me and returned to his work, expending, for the benefit of the peppermint-lozenge painting, his demonic energy in froglike leaps, gurgles, shrieks, in magical brush strokes, in Italian ballads, and in monologues:

"A grreat meestake! A grreat meestake!" he yelped suddenly.

He leaped backward, eyed the "meestake," recovered his energy and gave it, as if by surprise, a subtle lick of the brush:

". . . meeraculously co-rect-ed!"

He paid no more attention to me. An empty gown, lackluster, not quite white, was posing for him on an armchair. It was from that dull gown that he was creating on the canvas, stroke by stroke, the whites of cream, of snow, of glazed paper, of new metal, the white of the unfathomable, and the white of bonbons, a tour de force of whites . . . I remember that my dog Toby trembled against my legs; he already knew more than I did, certainly, about the misshapen divinity who was leaping about there in front of us . . .

The "proper young lady," offended, took dignified leave, adjusted the knot of a mannish necktie that had been imported from London, and went away, looking as much as possible like a bad boy, to rejoin a strange company of women who led a marginal and timorous life, sustained by an out-of-date form of snobbishness.

How timid I was, at that period when I was trying to look like a boy, and how feminine I was beneath my disguise of cropped hair. "Who would take us to be women? Why, women." They alone were not fooled. With such distinguishing marks as pleated shirt front, hard collar, sometimes a waistcoat, and always a silk pocket handkerchief, I frequented a society perishing on the margin of all societies. Although morals, good and bad, have not changed during the past twenty-five or thirty years, class consciousness, in destroying itself, has gradually undermined and debilitated the clique I am referring to, which tried, trembling with fear, to live without hypocrisy, the breathable air of society. This clique, or sect, claimed the right of "personal freedom" and equality with homosexuality, that imperturbable establishment. And they scoffed, if in whispers, at "Papa" Lépine the Prefect of Police, who never could take lightly the question of women in men's clothes. The adherents of this clique of women exacted secrecy for their parties, where they appeared

dressed in long trousers and dinner jackets and behaved with unsur-
passed propriety. They tried to reserve for themselves certain bars
and restaurants and to enjoy there the guilty pleasures of backgam-
mon and bezique. Then they gave up the struggle, and the sect's
most stubborn proselytes never crossed the street or left their carriage without putting on, heart pounding, a long plain cloak which
gave them an excessively respectable look and effectively concealed
their masculine attire.

At the home of the best-known woman among them—the best
known and the most misunderstood—fine wines, long cigars, photographs of a smartly turned-out horseman, one or two languorous
portraits of very pretty women, bespoke the sensual and rakish life
of a bachelor. But the lady of the house, in dark masculine attire,
belied any idea of gaiety or bravado. Pale, without blemish or blush,
pale like certain antique Roman marbles that seem steeped in light,
the sound of her voice muffled and sweet, she had all the ease and
good manners of a man, the restrained gestures, the virile poise of a
man. Her married name, when I knew her, was still disturbing. Her
friends, as well as her enemies, never referred to her except by her
title and a charming Christian name, title and name alike clashing
with her stocky masculine physique and reserved, almost shy manner. From the highest strata of society, La Chevalière, as we shall
call her, was having her fling, sowing her wild oats like a prince.
And like a prince, she had her counterparts. Napoleon III gave us
Georges Ville, who survived him for a long time. La Chevalière
could not prevent this man-woman, deathly pale, powdered, self-
assertive, from exhibiting herself and signing the same initials as her
model.

Where could I find, nowadays, messmates like those who, gathered around La Chevalière, emptied her wine cellar and her purse?
Baronesses of the Empire, Canonesses, lady cousins of Czars, illegiti-
mate daughters of Grand-Dukes, exquisites of the Parisian bourgeoisie, and also some aged horsewomen of the Austrian aristocracy,
hand and eye of steel . . . Some of these ladies fondly kept in their
protective and jealous shadow women younger than they, clever

young actresses, the next to the last authentic demimondaine of the epoch, a music-hall star . . . You heard them in whispered conversation, but to the great disappointment of the curious ear, the dialogue was banal. "How did your lesson go? Do you have it now, your Chopin waltz?" "Take your furs off here, you will get hot and won't be in voice this evening. Yes, you know better than I do, of course. But I studied with Nilsson, please remember that, my dear . . ." "Tut, tut, my sweet, one doesn't cut a baba with a knife . . . Take a small fork . . ." "You have no idea of time, and if I didn't think for you, my pet . . . What do you mean by putting your husband into a bad humor by going home late every time?"

Among these women, free yet timorous, addicted to late hours, darkened rooms, gambling, and indolence, I almost never detected a trace of cynicism. Sparing of words, all they needed was an allusion. I heard one of them, one only—a German princess with the fresh chubby face of a butcher boy—introduce her *petite amie* one day as "my spouse," whereupon my blunt gentlemen in skirts wrinkled their noses in distaste and pretended not to hear. "It's not that I conceal anything," briefly commented the Vicomtesse de X., "it's simply that I don't like showing off."

It was otherwise with their protégées, who were, more often than not, rather rude young creatures, insinuating and grasping. Not surprising, this, for these ladies in male attire had, by birth and from infancy, a taste for below-stairs accomplices and comrades-in-livery —and, as a consequence, an incurable timidity, which they dissimulated as best they could. Pride in giving pleasure relieved them of the need for any other dignity; they tolerated being addressed familiarly by these young creatures and found again, beneath the insult, the tremulous and secret pleasure of their childhood when dining at the servants' table.

In the servants' quarters, from their first toddling steps, they had found their allies and their tormentors, whom they and their brothers equally feared and loved. It is quite necessary for a child to love. The women of whom I am speaking were considerably older than I, they had grown up in an epoch when the aristocracy, even more than the rich bourgeoisie, handed over their progeny to the domestic staff. It is a question who was worth more to the children, the paid tormentor or the depraved ally. My narrators did not judge them. They did not bother to embroider their tales but calmly described the orgies in the pantry, when strong liquor was poured out for the dazed children, or told how those underlings would one day stuff the babies with food and next day forget to feed them at all . . . They did not speak in the maudlin tone of cheap journalism; none of these women claimed the grade of infant martyr, not even the daughter of the Duke de X., who said that from six to fifteen she had never worn a pair of new shoes, that her shoes had all been hand-me-downs from her elder brother or sister, and with holes in the soles. Blandly, and at times rather mockingly, she described incidents of her childhood.

"In the corridor outside our nursery," she related, "was a small antique lady's desk in rosewood incrusted with a large medallion in Sèvres porcelain, with the monogram of a queen and her crown glittering in diamonds. My mother did not like that small piece of furniture and had sentenced it to exile in the corridor, where it stood between two doors. Well, to please my mother, when we dressed for dinner we always set our muddy shoes on the top of that *bonheur-du-jour,* right on the Sèvres medallion and its diamonds . . ."

Married to a man she hated, my narrator had not dared to confess her despair when she fancied she was pregnant, except to an old footman, an ancient corrupter of princelings, a valet she feared.

"He brought me a concoction to drink," she said, touched at the recollection. "He, and he alone in the world, pitied me . . . What he gave me to drink was pretty horrible . . . I remember that I wept . . ."

"With grief?"

"No. I cried because, while I swallowed that horror, the old fellow tried to hearten me by calling me *niña* and *pobrecita,* just as he had when I was a child."

These women who had been dispossessed of their rightful childhoods and who, as girls, had been more than orphans, were now in their maturity the fond instructors of a younger generation. They never seemed ridiculous to me. Yet some of them wore a monocle, a white carnation in the buttonhole, took the name of God in vain, and discussed horses competently. These mannish women I am calling to mind were, indeed, almost as fond of the horse, that warm, enigmatic, stubborn, and sensitive creature, as they were of their young protégées. With their strong slender hands they were able to break in and subjugate a horse, and when age and hard times deprived them of the whip and the hunting crop, they lost their final scepter. A garage, no matter how elegant, can never equal the smartness of a stable. The motorcar cannot be mounted; a mechanical carriage bestows no psychological glamour on its driver. But the dust of the bridle paths in the Bois still haloes, in countless memories, those equestriennes who did not need to ride astride to assert their ambiguity.

Seated on the handsome back of a lean thoroughbred, mounted on the twin pedestal of a chestnut crupper, where shimmered two ellipses of unctuous light, they were freed of the awkward, toed-out stance of the ballet dancer that marred their walk. The thing women in men's clothes imitate worst is a man's stride. "They raise their knees too high, they don't tuck in their bottoms as they should," was the severe pronouncement of La Chevalière. The exciting scent of horses, that so masculine odor, never quite left these women, but lingered on after the ride. I saw and hailed the decline of these women. They tried to describe and explain their vanished charm. They tried to render intelligible for us their success with women and their defiant taste for women. The astonishing thing is that they managed to do so. I am not referring here to La Chevalière, who by character as well as physique was above them. Restless and uncertain in her pursuit of love, she searched with her anxious eyes, so dark they were almost black beneath a low, white forehead, for what she never found: a settled and sentimental attachment. For more than forty years, this woman with the bearing of a handsome boy endured the pride and punishment of never being able to establish a real and lasting affair with a woman. It was not for lack of trying, because she asked nothing better or worse. But the salacious expectations of women shocked her very natural platonic tendencies, which resembled more the suppressed excitement, the diffuse emotion of an adolescent rather than a woman's explicit need. Twenty years ago she tried, with bitterness, to explain herself to me. "I do not know anything about completeness in love," she said, "except the *idea* I have of it. But they, the women, have never allowed me to stop at that point . . ."

"Without exception?"

"Without exception."

"Why?"

"I'm sure I don't know."

La Chevalière shrugged. The expression that appeared on her face recalled for a minute Damien's expression when he had assured me that "women go too far . . ." Like Damien, she seemed to be recalling something rather sad, rather repellent, and she was about to say more, but like him she contained herself.

"I'm sure I don't know," she repeated.

"But what in heaven's name do they hope for, by going further? Do they give so much credit to the physical act, the idea of the paroxysm of pleasure?"

"No doubt," she said, uncertainly.

"They must at least have an opinion on that special pleasure? Do they fling themselves upon it as upon a panacea, do they see in it a kind of consecration? Do they demand it, or accept it, more simply, as a proof of mutual trust?"

La Chevalière averted her eyes, flicked off the long ash on her cigar, waved her hand as a discreet man might do.

"This is beyond me," she said. "It does not even concern me."

"And yet . . ."

She repeated her gesture and smiled to dissuade me from persisting.

"I'm of the opinion," she said, "that in the ancient Nativities the portrait of the 'donor' occupies far too much space in the picture . . ."

La Chevalière always had, still has wit, a quick sense of repartee. The years have made little change in her and have let her keep her smile that is so difficult to depict, so difficult to forget. That smile of the "donor" who despises his gifts did not however discourage me from questioning her. But she was shy and rejected this subject of conversation, to which, however, I will add a remark she let fall one day when an ugly young woman was being described in detail in her hearing.

"That girl, if she didn't have her two eyes . . ."

"What more does a woman need besides her two eyes?" asked La Chevalière.

In effect, I knew she was mad about blue-green eyes, and when I told her she shared with Jean Lorrain the obsession of "green" eyes, she was annoyed.

"Oh," she said, "but it's not the same thing at all! Jean Lorrain takes off from green eyes to go . . . you know where. He's a man for whom 'the deep calleth to deep' . . ."

The remark is worth more than her epoch and the literature of the turn of the century, swollen with masks and voodoo, black Masses, blissful decapitated women whose heads float among narcissi and blue toads. For a timid soul, exalted in silence and perpetually adolescent, what more seductive depths could one plunge into than the eyes of the loved one, and descend in thought and blissfully lose one's life between the seaweed and the star?

The seduction emanating from a person of uncertain or dissimulated sex is powerful. Those who have never experienced it liken it to the banal attraction of the love that evicts the male element. This is a gross misconception. Anxious and veiled, never exposed to the light of day, the androgynous creature wanders, wonders, and implores in a whisper . . . Its half equal, man, is soon scared and flees. There remains its half equal, a woman. There especially remains for the androgynous creature the right, even the obligation, never to be happy. If jovial, the androgynous creature is a monster. But it trails irrevocably among us its seraphic suffering, its glimmering tears. It goes from a tender inclination to maternal adoption . . .

As I write this, I am thinking of La Chevalière. It was she who most often bruised herself in a collision with a woman—a woman, that whispering guide, presumptuous, strangely explicit, who took her by the hand and said, "Come, I will help you find yourself . . ."

"I am neither that nor anything else, alas," said La Chevalière, dropping the vicious little hand. "What I lack cannot be found by searching for it."

She is the person who has no counterpart anywhere. At one time she believed that she had her counterpart in the features of a young woman, and again in the features of a handsome young man —yes, of a young man, why not?—so handsome that love seemed to despair of him, and who, moreover, clung to no one. He gave to La Chevalière a name that made her blush with joy and gratitude: he called her "my father." But she soon saw that again she had been mistaken, that one can adopt only the child one has begotten . . .

"All the same," the solitary woman sighs at times, "I must not complain, I shall have been a mirage . . ."

Around her, beneath her, a quarrelsome and timid life gravitated. She served as the ideal, as the target, and ignored the fact. She was praised, she was calumniated, her name was repeated in the midst of a subdued and almost subterranean tumult, was heard especially in the friendly little dives, the tiny, neighborhood cinemas frequented by groups of her women friends—basement rooms arranged as restaurants, dim, and blue with tobacco smoke. There was also a cellar in Montmartre that welcomed these uneasy women, haunted by their own solitude, who felt safe within the low-ceilinged room beneath the eye of a frank proprietress who shared their predilections, while an unctuous and authentic cheese fondue sputtered and the loud contralto of an artiste, one of their familiars, sang to them the romantic ballads of Augusta Holmès . . . The same need for a refuge, warmth, and darkness, the same fear of intruders and sightseers assembled here these women whose faces, if not their names, soon became familiar to me. Literature and the makers of literature were absent from these gatherings and I delighted in that absence, along with the empty gaiety of the chatter and the diverting and challenging exchange of glances, the cryptic reference to certain treasons, comprehended at once, and the sudden outbursts of ferocity. I reveled in the admirable quickness of their half-spoken language, the exchange of threats, of promises, as if, once the slow-thinking male had been banished, every message from woman to woman became clear and overwhelming, restricted to a small but infallible number of signs . . .

All amours tend to create a dead-end atmosphere. "There! It's finished, we've arrived, and beyond us two there is nothing now, not even an opening for escape," murmurs one woman to her protégée, using the language of a lover. And as a proof, she indicates the low ceiling, the dim light, the women who are their counterparts, making her listen to the masculine rumble of the outside world and hear how it is reduced to the booming of a distant danger.

HB

✻✻ Amalia X.

"Ghoul," "vampire"—by these names they called a woman now dead who experienced the worst of her ill-fame thirty-five or forty years ago. She was described to me by an actress acquaintance, Amalia X., a former companion of mine on theatrical tours. "Ugly, but chic," was the way Amalia X. described her, adding, "She looked very smart in a tail coat."

"Which only makes one more ill-cut masculine suit," I said.

Her portraits show that she was dark-complexioned, angular, thin-lipped, displaying the insolence of a twenty-five-year-old midinette dressed up in men's clothes on St. Catherine's Day. She was credited with having made a number of young women wretched, of having driven one of them to commit suicide beneath her window, of having broken up several marriages, of having incurred rivalries that at times ended in bloodshed. Her doorstep was heaped with floral offerings, and she had a reputation for behaving with incomparable disdain. Well, now! So many postulants and so few chosen? Surely that is not the balance sheet of an ogress. It looks more like the trifling of someone who enjoyed inflicting mental cruelties. To wreak havoc by practically abstaining from sin is not the behavior of a vulgar woman . . .

A photograph signed with her assumed name, Lucienne de ——, shows her in correct men's evening dress, correct but with traces of bad taste, I mean to say, feminine taste. The pocket handkerchief points two inches too high; the lapels of the coat are too wide, and the style of the shoes is dubious. One feels that a feminine imagination, imprisoned beneath the bared forehead of the spurious man, regrets having been unable to let itself go in jabots, ribbons, silky fabrics. Strange, that a woman like this who rivaled and defrauded men should have as her single ambition to look and act the part of a dashing young-man-about-town. It was hard for her to leave off her look of bravado. She dated, as did her aggressive handwriting, from the epoch of impudent cocottes. Amalia X., that good comic actress of road companies who died at the beginning of the war, had been a rival of La Lucienne in many a conquest and many a risky adventure. Amalia, if one were to believe her, had not hesitated to leave a sleeping and satiated sultan and go on foot, veiled, through the night streets of Constantinople to a hotel room where a sweet, blond, and very young woman was waiting up for her . . .

"And you must realize," the worthy Amalia confided, shuffling the pack of tarot cards on a small galvanized table in a dingy café at Tarbes or Valenciennes—I forget which—"you must realize that Constantinople then, at night, was less safe even than the boulevard de la Chapelle."

Slightly mustached, rheumatic, at the end of her strength, Amalia X. still enjoyed life, was still "touring" at over sixty years of age, and recalled her past with satisfaction. "I had everything," she asserted, "beauty, happiness, misery, men, and women . . . You can call it a life!" Her big handsome Israelite's eyes rolled up at the mere thought.

"But," I said, "if between your little *amie* and you there had not been the dark streets, the risks, and the old man you had just abandoned, in short, had there been no danger, would you have hurried so eagerly?"

The old comedienne looked away for a moment from the Hanged Man, the Cups, the Swords, and the Skeleton who smiled at her.

"Don't bother me with such questions," she said. "I'm an old woman, which is already no joke. Why do you want to deprive me of the illusion that I was once the equal of a young man?"

"So you had the idea, when you left the old Turk, that you stopped being a woman?"

"For heaven's sake, no! How mixed up you are! We never have to stop being a woman. Not on any account, my girl. And even—get this into your head—a couple of women can live together a long time and be happy. But if one of the two women lets herself behave in the slightest like what I call a pseudo-man, then . . ."

"Then the couple become unhappy?"

"Not necessarily unhappy, but sad."

"Oh? Explain, please."

Amalia laid out cabalistically her precious tarot cards, which smelled of greasy cardboard, old leather, and the tallow candles wine-cellar inspectors carry rolled up in a worn-out old bag.

"You see, when a woman remains a woman, she is a complete human being. She lacks nothing, even insofar as her *amie* is concerned. But if she ever gets it into her head to try to be a man, then she's grotesque. What is more ridiculous, what is sadder, than a woman pretending to be a man? On that subject, you'll never get me to change my mind. La Lucienne, from the time she adopted men's clothes, well! . . . Do you imagine her life wasn't poisoned from then on?"

"Poisoned by what?"

"From that time on, my pet, if her lady friends sometimes forgot that she wasn't a man, she, for her part, the little fool, never stopped thinking about it . . . And so, despite all her successes, she never stopped being resentful. That obsession deprived her of sleep and of faith in herself, which is even worse. Oh, she was a good sport, yes. But a discontented one. Mind you, I say discontented, not sad. A little sadness doesn't hurt a ménage of two women. Sadness, you might say, fills the void. Find a woman who hasn't felt wistful over a period in her life when she was sad!' "

"It fills the void"—the remark smacks of unisexuality. It develops from the strict seclusion in which a feminine passion is confined, that period of sensual instruction, that rigorous induction without which, declared the Duc the Morny, a woman remains an unfinished sketch.[1] This enlightened amateur in such matters elaborates his theory to such an extent that, if I remember correctly, we understand he is not merely thinking of a "diploma in sensuality" but seems to consider—since diamond polishes diamond—that a woman refines a woman, leaves her softened, more pliable, one might still better say, bruised. Morny evidently spoke as an experienced man who would seek out a woman for a daring collaboration: "I hand over to you an incomplete marvel . . . See that you perfect her and hand her back to me!"

"It was then," Amalia went on, "that La Lucienne began to make trouble. She began to adopt all the mean ways of love: there were affairs broken off without reason, there were reconciliations, but conditional, and separations, and unnecessary flights, tearful scenes, and I don't know what all . . . An obsession . . . Loulou, a pretty blonde she had with her, well, she threw her out one night half naked into the garden to teach her a lesson and make her decide what she wanted, that is, to choose between her, Lucienne, and Loulou's husband. Before dawn, Lucienne leaned out over the balcony: 'Have you thought it over?' she says. 'Yes,' says the girl, who was sniffling with the cold. 'Well?' says Lucienne. 'Well,' says the girl, 'I'm going back to Hector. I've just realized he can do something you can't.' 'Oh, naturally!' says Lucienne, spitefully. 'No,' says Loulou,

[1] *Journal des Goncourt.*

'it's not what you think, I'm not all that crazy about you know what. But I'm going to tell you something. When you and I go out together, everyone takes you for a man, that's understood. But for my part, I feel humiliated to be with a man who can't do *pipi* against a wall.'"

At the end of this story, Amalia commented: "Did you ever? Lucienne expected almost anything but that. She took it bad. So bad that she never saw Loulou again. Why are you laughing?"

"My goodness, at what Loulou said. It's childish!"

Amalia leveled on me her wrathful big eyes.

"Childish! Why, my pet, Loulou simply found the unkindest thing in the world to say!"

"I don't see why. To me, her retort was childish, rather comic."

"The unkindest thing in the world, I repeat! Such things can't be explained. There are . . . subtleties . . . you have to feel them. If you don't understand, then I can't explain it to you. And I really wonder what interests you in these subjects which you don't at all understand! Let me be, now. You've upset me enough in my 'fate'!"

She lowered her long lashes on her withered cheeks and remained severely silent as she read her fortune, moving a gouty index finger over the cards . . .

How many times did I not "upset her in her 'fate'"? I pretended to be naïve to hear her talk. I loved to search her face, studying the thick eyebrows and the Roman chin for traces of that warrior girl who at night hurried through the alleyways of the Orient, passed through and outdistanced a number of dangers and, on a body exactly like her own, as if fondly patterned on her own, tightened her arms . . . Her arms, the final beauty, polished, greenish-white as are the arms of Tunisian Jewesses, and robust . . . arms that had cradled the confident slumbers of young women and shimmered through the veiling tresses of long hair.

"Listen, Amalia, see here . . . Why do you suppose Loulou chose to go back to her husband? How do you explain it?"

"I have nothing to explain," said Amalia stiffly. "Besides, I never said she did go back."

"What was her husband like?"

"Very good-looking," said Amalia with sudden keen sympathy. "A handsome, fair-haired lad, golden-blond, oh yes, my goodness, one of those big peaceable fellows . . . And no trouble at all to Loulou. In fact, rather too peaceable . . ."

She raised her eyes, focusing them on the golden-haired young man in the far recesses of her memory, then again made her hostile estimate: "Yes, rather shifty. But very, very patient. The patience of an angel!"

Very patient . . . "See that you perfect her and hand her back to me!" As for perfecting her, well and good, but hand her back? When I recall my conversations with Amalia, I feel that masculine imprudence in such a case is great. Supposing the precious hostage, summoned to return to the straight and narrow, told her lover, "No, I'm not coming back to you, I'm better off here than across the street"?

"The important thing, for Loulou, you see, was to revenge herself with a terrible word, to hurt Lucienne."

"Hurt Lucienne! A terrible word? You make me laugh, you sound like a schoolgirl. Such childish goings on! The big peaceable fellow must have laughed harder than I. He was biding his time."

"Childish goings on? How crass you are! How dare you talk like that?"

She surveyed me contemptuously, flaring her nostrils, and her irritation exaggerated the majesty of her features, making them look as if but a mask over that hidden face that spoils the looks of some women, the face of a bad priest, a face which seems to denounce their secret sins. This woman, well past sixty, still stood her ground against her triumphant rival and disputed his advantage with an impatience that imitated the chronically sulky face of Lucienne. Yes, well and good as for perfecting the girl, but as for handing her back . . .

I find it interesting to compare this tartness with the libertine calm of the man who resigns himself, a mocking spectator, to wait for the woman who for a time escapes him, as if to say, "Oh you, I'll nab you once more!" Such arrogance and such confidence deserve to be rewarded, as in fact they nearly always are.

"Amalia, were you faithful?"

"To whom?" said she, sarcastically.

"To your little friend?"

She affected a sudden disdain and raffishness.

"Oh! To women? It depends."

"Depends on what?"

"On the life we led together. If our work did not allow us to live together, my little friend and I, then I wasn't faithful. And neither was she."

"Why?"

I remember that once more Amalia wearily shrugged, raising her vast shoulders weighed down by the disastrous bulk of the breasts which pulled them forward.

"That's the way it is. What do you expect me to say? It's necessary to have gone through it. And me, I did go through it. That's the way it is. A woman isn't faithful to a woman who isn't there."

At this point I did not torment her further, for I felt sure she would never go beyond that boastful, "Me, I went through it."

I liked to touch the absolute limits of her ignorance and her sapience. About two kinds of loves she knew as much as can be learned from experience and a realistic hardihood. The wellspring of her memories having run dry, along with her blustering good humor, I left her to her "Knave of Swords" and, without her, I pursued the subject further.

HB

❧❧ Sodom

Ever since Proust shed light on Sodom, we have had a feeling of respect for what he wrote, and would never dare, after him, to touch the subject of these hounded creatures, who are careful to blur their tracks and to propagate at every step their personal cloud, like the cuttlefish.

But—was he misled, or was he ignorant?—when he assembles a Gomorrah of inscrutable and depraved young girls, when he denounces an entente, a collectivity, a frenzy of bad angels, we are only diverted, indulgent, and a little bored, having lost the support of the dazzling light of truth that guides us through Sodom. This is because, with all due deference to the imagination or the error of Marcel Proust, there is no such thing as Gomorrah. Puberty, boarding school, solitude, prisons, aberrations, snobbishness—they are all seedbeds, but too shallow to engender and sustain a vice that could attract a great number or become an established thing that would gain the indispensable solidarity of its votaries. Intact, enormous, eternal, Sodom looks down from its heights upon its puny counterfeit.

Intact, enormous, eternal. Those are big words which imply consideration, at least the consideration one owes to power. I don't deny it. Women are little acquainted—it goes without saying—with homosexuality, but when they encounter it they adopt the attitude imposed by woman's instinct. Thus, facing the enemy, the rose beetle falls and plays dead; the great crab, immobile, arches its pincers; the gray tarente lizard clings, flattened, to the gray wall. We should not be expected to do more than we can.

A woman whom a man betrays for another man knows that all is lost. Containing her cries, her tears, her threats which comprise the main part of her forces in an ordinary case, she does not struggle, but digs in or says nothing, fulminates scarcely at all, occasionally tries to find the way to an unrealizable alliance with the enemy, with a sin that dates as far back as the human race, a sin she neither invented nor approved. She is far from adopting the mockingly licentious attitude of the man whose wife or mistress forsakes him for another woman: "Oh you, I'll get you back." Disillusioned, she renounces with bitter hatred and carefully conceals her great uncertainty, wondering, "Was he really destined for me?" For she has more humility than is generally believed. But since her subtlety is limited in range and since she judges severely the inclinations of the mind, she can never manage to separate the mental from the physical and stubbornly confuses "homosexual" with "effeminate men."

In a certain period of my youth, I associated for some time with various homosexuals, thanks to one of Monsieur Willy's ghost-secretaries. I am recalling now an epoch when I lived in a singular state of neglect and concealed wretchedness. Still very provincial—isn't it so, dear Jacques-Émile Blanche?—physically unsociable to the point of sometimes avoiding shaking hands or not letting my hand be kissed, I resented being isolated and forgotten in the gloomy flat as much as I resented being forced to appear in society. I therefore took great pleasure in the companionship of the secretary, like me a "ghost." He was young, wellborn, cheerful, impish, and he made no secret of his homosexual inclinations. He and I worked—the expression will still make a few of our colleagues smile, among others Pierre Veber, Vuillermoz, and Curnonsky—in the same "writers' workshop."

He confided in me and brought his friends to see me. With them I felt younger, I recovered my actual age. I laughed, reassured in the presence of so many inoffensive young men. I learned how a well-dressed man dresses—for they were for the most part English and had strict ideas of elegance, and the same young fellow who secretly wore next to his skin a turquoise cross on a neck chain would never have allowed himself unconventional ties or handkerchiefs.

Two rooms had been set aside for me in the conjugal apartment, a bedroom and a studio, which I referred to proudly as my "bachelor digs." In that studio, which was equipped with a trapeze, there was as much laughter as in a boarding school, exaggerated and youthful laughter. But what strange talk went on there between gentlemen!

"What's happened, my dear fellow, to your young boxer?"

"Boxer? I don't have a boxer!"

"I mean, that youngster who made cardboard boxes for milliners and perfumers."

"Oh, that one! I have a poor memory. You should ask me about a certain fireman of the city of Paris!"

"A fireman? How frightful!"

As a visiting card is thrust out under an insult, an unmounted photograph was thrust beneath the nose of the disdainful one.

"How frightful, really? Take a look! This may make you change your mind. And please note the belt with the arms of Paris on it . . ."

Internationally famous, well preserved, my old friend C. de X., who has since died of old age and whose friendship, youthful spirit, and charming manners I still miss, climbed the three flights of stairs not without difficulty. A dyed, square-cut beard concealed, so he said, his "old codger's wattles." The stubborn effort to survive bedewed his temples with sweat, which he lightly dabbed with his handkerchief. I can still see the thinness of his hand, on which great veins stood out, the gray of his jacket, the blue-gray of his silk handkerchief, the blue-gray of his eyes that were already faded, and the fixed smile that widened his mouth . . . That old man, who was ashamed of nothing, managed to shock no one.

"Ouf!" he sighed, as he sat down. "Oh, to be only sixty again!"

Jean Lorrain speaks of him somewhere in *Poussières de Paris*, referring to his exceptional good looks, something about "the best pair of shoulders of the century," if I'm not mistaken.

"Why are you so out of breath? Where have you come from?" asked a young man, insultingly.

"From my mother's," replied C., giving himself the pleasure of not telling a lie, for in fact he was a tender and respectful son and lived with his almost centenarian mother. He looked the young man up and down and made a stinging rejoinder: "She is the only companion I have, sir. Has someone been telling you I have another?"

While the young man was still trying to think of a retort or an excuse, C. burst into a short laugh, then turned toward me and added, "I have no other since the departure of a young friend, who is traveling."

"Ah, yes? Where is he going?"

"Who knows? He had certain troubles that made him decide to leave."

He heaved a deep sigh, took a swallow of weak tea, and once more the blue handkerchief came into play as he dabbed his mouth and temple.

"He's such a nice boy, but absent-minded," C. went on. "Just imagine! A lady invites him to her house for a cup of hot chocolate —he is attractive. He accepts the invitation—and has one of his weak moments. While talking with her, he happens to drop something, I don't know what, into her cup of chocolate. Anyway, the lady wakes up two days later and finds—deplorable coincidence!— that all her furniture has disappeared. She thought she was dreaming, the poor lady. But no sooner did she recover her senses than she lodged a complaint against my absent-minded friend. And so, not wanting to be mixed up in a complicated affair, he went away. May heaven return him to us!"

Giving me a wink of his alert little dark eye, my friend the ghost-secretary questioned C. in a tone of sincerity.

"Tell me, dear sir, isn't that absent-minded young man the same young man who is supposed to have strangled a Turkish-bath attendant?"

Straightening up with a proud jerk that was especially due to stiff muscles, the old man defended himself with a wave of his fine, wrinkled hand.

"Gossip, dear boy, gossip! I'm a wise man, I am never jealous of the past!"

Tartness, theatrical cynicism, affectation, nonsensical jesting comprised the tone prescribed by this type of visitor. Sometimes violence, masculine or morbid, let out its brief cry, injected its brief warmth. For instance, a mere boy, issuing from the distant times when good and evil, mingled like two liqueurs, made one, gave an account of his last night at the Élysée Palace-Hôtel:

"He made me feel afraid, that big man, in his bedroom . . . I opened the little knife, I put one arm over my eyes, and with my other hand holding the knife, I went like this at the fat man, into his stomach . . . And I ran away quick!"

He was radiant with beauty, with roguishness, with a kind of incipient madness. His listeners were tactful and cautious. No one exclaimed. Only my old friend C., after a moment, casually said, "What a child!" and then changed the subject.

Lacking grandeur and malice, C. resembled the Baron de Charlus only generically. But it is this powerful late-comer on the stage, Charlus, who seems to serve as model, for even those who preceded him regard themselves as weak descendants and pay homage. Courage, if we reduce the word to its most ordinary and military meaning, did permit C., as it permitted Charlus, to graze real dangers, sometimes to court them—with this difference, that C., very far from having the masochistic deviation of Charlus, wanted only the best and most available of what he liked best: "At heart, I'm a French milliner," he stated. At any rate, he did not regard at all highly this cosmopolitan youth, gossipy and grasping, who offended the ancestor with their irony and crude familiarity.

Often in their company, rarely questioning them and never indulging in persiflage with them, I reassured these men, of whom I would be the last to say they lacked virility. A human being with a man's face is virile by the very fact that he contracts a dangerous way of life and the certainty of an exceptional death. My strange friends discussed all sorts of things in my presence—violent deaths, inevitable blackmails, fleecings, shameful lawsuits, cravats, cuffed trousers, music, literature, dowries, marriages—avoiding no subject of conversation in front of me, and I still wonder why society regards this category of men as irresponsible.

They know precisely what they like and dislike. They are aware of the perils of their chosen way of life, know the bounds of their particular prejudices, and if they pay lip service to caution, they often forget it.

They allowed me to share with them their sudden outbursts of gaiety, so shrill and revealing. They appreciated my silence, for I was faithful to their concept of me as a nice piece of furniture and I listened to them as if I were an expert. They got used to me, without ever allowing me access to a real affection. No one excluded me—no one loved me. I owe a great deal to their cool friendship, to their fierce critical sense. They taught me not only that a man can be amorously satisfied with a man but that one sex can suppress, by forgetting it, the other sex. This I had not learned from the ladies in men's clothes, who were preoccupied with men, who were always, with suspect bitterness, finding fault with men. My strange homosexual friends did not talk about women, except distantly and condescendingly. "Very pretty, that white on white beading that Bady wears in the third act," they would say. Or: "Oh, really, those enormous hats of Lantelme, I'm fed up with them! Why doesn't she parcel them out?"

Absent yet present, a translucent witness, I enjoyed an indefinable peace, accompanied by a kind of conspiratorial pride.

I heard on their lips the language of passion, of betrayal and jealousy, and sometimes of despair—languages with which I was all too familiar, I had heard them elsewhere and spoke them fluently to myself. But my brazen young men stripped the words and sentiments of their murderous force, played with weapons turned aside from me, for as yet I had neither the strength nor the desire to put myself in a safe place. The "Young Greek God" had nothing to fear from me, not even a kiss; "Namouna" and "Once More" babbled in their maternal tongues; Édouard de Max paid us a visit, escorted by adolescents, like a god escorted by nymphs. He flattered them with his eyes, scolded them with his voice; for them he was nothing but tutelary indifference, hauteur, melancholy, all singularly aloof. A tyro in the career of diplomacy had the unfortunate idea of bringing along with him one day his intimate friend, Bouboule, decked out in a dress of black Chantilly lace over pale blue silk, his face sulky beneath a wide lace hat, as uncouth as a country wench in need of a husband, his cheeks plump and fresh as nectarines—such freshness not surprising in a seventeen-year-old butcher boy. We were frozen with astonishment, and aware that he was meeting with no success, kicking the hem of his skirt with his enormous feet, he left us. He did not go far, apparently, for only a few days later he committed suicide—the unexplained and clumsy act of a big boy, uncertain and chagrined.

He shattered with a revolver bullet his pretty pouting mouth, his low forehead beneath kinky hair, his anxious and timid little bright blue eyes . . . My circle of friends did not even give him the briefest funeral oration. On the other hand, these same young men talked excitedly and endlessly about the murder, in London, of the painter, Z. . . . They classified it as a great curiosity and studied it like men who, both innocent and expert, can easily decipher the cryptograms written with a knife point on a slashed throat or with spurs on bloodstained thighs.

One of these friends received a long letter from London which he brought and read aloud. We all listened, reread, and absorbed it with the delectation of young wild beasts tasting blood. I heard shrill cries, hoarse blasphemies in English, obscure predictions:

"You'll see, it's another stroke of those damned three-shilling prostitutes of the . . ." He named a regiment.

"They? You flatter them!"

"I know what I'm saying. They're capable of anything that will prove they can be real he-men."

It may surprise some people that I could secretly apply the

name "oasis" or "island" to this shore approached only by men tarred by the same brush, who arrived like the survivors of a cataclysm. Variously marked, variously formed, they all came from afar, from the beginning of time. They had traversed unscathed every epoch, every reign, without perishing, like a dynasty sure of its everlastingness. Self-centered, blinded by their own brilliance, they have bequeathed to us only a one-sided and romanticized documentation. But, up to now, were they ever observed by any woman for the length of time they have been observed by me? Ordinarily a woman —and let's say, an ordinary woman—tries to entice a homosexual. Naturally, she fails. She then declares she "despises" him. Or else— and the case is not rare—she wins a physical victory, which gives her a cause for pride; she has achieved a kind of brilliant advantage over him, but futile and misleading, because she gives an exaggerated importance to external signs, if I dare say so. She is bound to be disillusioned afterward and will forever loudly lay claim to what she calls her due. And from this arises deep resentment. She, who easily renounces getting from a normal man the same "due," providing her renouncement remains a secret, will not relinquish her claims on a catch she made by chance and by mistake. Powerless to bring about a repetition of the initial victory through chance and mischance, she hounds him and willfully sinks into an unheard-of amorous despair. I wrote about such a young woman in *L'Entrave,* calling her May and making her unrecognizable.

Jealously and suspiciously she prowled about her lover, subjecting him to such a close watch that I reproached her for it.

"Well, what about me?" May burst out. "Am I not patient, haven't I been patient for almost a year now? Do you think it's natural to be like Jean? A man who doesn't get drunk, doesn't make scenes, doesn't receive in the mail anything but bills and postal cards, doesn't ever have a really good time, and is never in the dumps?"

Wrathfully she clenched her tiny fists and shook them threateningly at her invisible adversary, a cold, solidly built young man, rather common when he talked, irreproachable when he remained silent. Then she shot me a glance that sent me packing and returned to her quest, grumbling and whining. I must say that, with her snub nose, her wide-set, prominent, and glittering eyes, she resembled a blond bulldog. Although he was visibly bored, she kept dragging Jean back to the studio gymnasium.

"What can you see in that couple you first brought here?" I asked my friend, the ghost-secretary, referring to this couple.

"The man is amusing," he said vaguely, after letting his bird-like eyes, alert and black and inexpressive, linger first on them and then on me.

"Amusing!" I exclaimed. "The woman perhaps, that little clown without a nose. But the man?"

"I may be mistaken," said the Ghost, with the punctilious politeness he knew how to make discomfiting.

But from then on I noticed that two people were spying upon May's lover: May and the Ghost.

Insupportable chatterbox, but harmless and friendly, May chatted for the most part with the younger of the two Englishmen, the one who was called "Once More." Those two innocents recovered their childhood on the trapeze, hanging from the rings, improvising circus stunts, and Jean, all smooth surfaces, patient, uncommunicative, laughed at them rather grudgingly.

One evening, May and her gymnastic partner could be seen whispering and plotting together; then they disappeared and May came back, making a grand entrance, simpering, dressed in the navy blue suit of "Once More," a scarf around her neck, the cap slanted over one eye.

"What about it, Jean?"

"Ravishing! Gaby Deslys as an Apache!" exclaimed the Ghost.

"You think!" said May, annoyed. "Why, I'm completely 'Once More'! Deah me, fawncy seeing her heah!" she said, aping the young Englishman. "Can't you see, Jean?"

Wagging her hips, she approached her lover and pressed herself against him like a pet animal. I only saw that he bent his head toward her and that his mouth seemed suddenly to swell. May let out a strange little cry, the scream of a caught rabbit, retreated toward me, and Jean excused himself to me, repeating agitatedly, "I didn't do anything to her, I didn't do anything to her."

But he could still not control his expression, and his mouth was in fact swollen, his eyes pale, glaring with hatred at May, forbidding her to caricature a secret idol secretly revered . . .

Then he controlled himself, and the face he had briefly exposed was soon again masked. May courageously tried to give another interpretation to the weird scream of a wounded rabbit she had uttered by repeating it intentionally, on a variety of notes. And still shrieking "Eee! Eee!" she left the room to put on her dress and her big plumed hat. When she reappeared, Jean stood up, ready to take her home. But she decided otherwise.

"No, no, go home on your own, just let me have the carriage, I want to go to the rue de Rivoli to pick up my fur-lined coat, it should be ready by now."

He went off obediently, as if walking in his sleep, and May, following him, gave me a shrewd and outraged look. But I had not the least desire to bring that poor girl to admit the existence of a category of man who craves men, who is reserved for men and is as noxious as the fruit of the tropical poison tree to any woman he happens to attract.

Despair born of frustration drove women, after the war, to imitate the looks and manners of androgynous young men. They had reckoned on their men being delivered back to them full of frenzied desire. Then, becoming aware that their own apotheosis was not very dazzling, they began wildly to imitate the outward looks of the male tribe that was causing them such heartache. They cropped their hair, squandered a fortune at the shirtmaker's, and drank to excess. And they gained no ground, for they were not disinterested enough.

Without meaning to, this behavior of women contributed to the creation of a type of young man both effeminate and cruel, wearing ocher makeup, thinking only of getting ahead, no matter how. I find this type very different from my friends of 1898 and 1900 as I remember them. They may have been scandalous, but only moderately so, and fatuous, but their extravagance went no further than the moonstone and the chrysoprase. They were ridiculous, certainly, but in those bygone times their behavior did not completely disguise them; I could still recognize in them a primitive bloom, the strength of deceptively frail-looking people; I could still see in them the gravity and the savagery of love.

As I write these words, I am thinking of a couple who never mingled with my usual visitors . . . But I am afraid that if I merely specify that the elder of the two was a scholar, a poet, a writer, beautiful from head to foot, he might be recognized . . . As for his protégé, his skin reminded one of ripe wheat, of apple blossoms, and he had the dignity of a child of old peasant stock, as indeed he was; he spoke little and listened attentively to his tutor and friend. Together they lived a quiet life, outside Paris. I can still see the hostile glances they shot at my flamboyant coterie when they unexpectedly arrived one day.

"Sh . . ." whispered the elder, before he addressed me in a low voice. "Don't disturb these . . . charming individuals. We've just dropped in to say *au revoir*—we're going away, tonight."

"Where are you going?"

"To Touraine, with the youngster, for the harvesting. They need his help."

"And you?"

"I too will help with the harvesting."

He thrust beneath my eyes his weathered hands, the hands of a great traveler, his wrists as hard as saplings.

"We're making the trip on foot," he added. "And not for the first time. It's so much more agreeable."

The "youngster," his impatient eyes a resplendent blue, was already waiting for the signal to depart, eager for the long march beneath the June night sky, the halts along the road and the vagabond meals, the warm bread bought in the villages on the way. Shorter than the elder man, upon whom he modeled himself admiringly, the boy carried himself easily, head high. What would time do to such an attachment?

The elder, killed in action during the war, was not among those who let themselves be forgotten. I will not bequeath his letters to anyone. I wonder about the younger one. When he stirs the windrows with the pitchfork, does he still feel a sinking of his heart that was once full to overflowing? Friendship, male friendship, unfathomable sentiment! Why should the sob of ecstasy be the one release denied you?

I am betraying a tolerance that some will condemn as strange. It is true that the association of the male couple I have just briefly sketched had, for me, the aspect of union and even of dignity. A kind of austerity overlaid it which I can compare to no other, for it held nothing of parade or precaution, nor did it spring from the morbid fear that galvanizes more often than it checks so many among those hounded by society. I find it in me to see in homosexuality a kind of legitimacy and to acknowledge its eternal character. I used to be archly scandalized that the male was attracted less, in the female form, to the charm of a deep snare, a smooth abyss, a living marine corolla, than to the occasional assertion of the woman's most virile characteristics—and I am not forgetting the breast. A man is attracted toward what can reassure him, to what he can recognize in that convex feminine body which is exactly the opposite of his own, disquieting, never familiar, with its ineradicable odor which is not even earthy but is borrowed from sea wrack, from the original slime . . .

Those who helped me at that time when my life was nothing but constraint and a lie imposed upon me made it clear that the antipathy of one sex for the other is not necessarily pathological. As I moved into other milieus, I noted that the viewpoint of "normal" people is not so very different. I have said that what I particularly liked in the world of my "monsters" where I moved in that distant time was the atmosphere that banished women, and I called it "pure." But, for that matter, I would have liked as well the purity of the desert, the purity of the prison. Prison and desert are not, however, within the reach of everyone.

Tenderly, then, I recall the monsters who accompanied me for

a long way during that part of my life which was not easy. Monsters
—that is a word soon said. So much for monsters. Why, as to those
who diverted me from my troubles, I could name them thus and
implore them from the depths of myself, "O monsters, do not leave
me alone . . . I do not confide in you except to tell you about my
fear of being alone, you are the most human people I know, the
most reassuring in the world. If I call you monsters, then what name
can I give to the so-called normal conditions that were foisted upon
me? Look there, on the wall, the shadow of that frightful shoulder,
the expression of that vast back and the neck swollen with blood
. . . O monsters, do not leave me alone . . ."

They and I were confronted with identical dangers: an intract-
able man and a pernicious woman; we knew what it was to tremble
with fright. At times I thought of them as less fortunate than I,
because fright seized them unexpectedly, capriciously, according to
the state of their nerves, whereas I always knew why my heart sank
and why I trembled. But I envied them, since many of them were
apt to confuse panic with the arousing of the senses. I envied them
their chimera, close-shut in a cage and terrified. One of them, of
whom I was very fond, kept his personal folly on a short and timid
leash. He took it for a breath of its vital element in those parts of the
city it and he knew, like the Chinese who go at evening to show their
captive songbird the flowering gardens and the reflection of the setting sun among the reeds.

Pepe was—death now has him in safekeeping—a Spaniard of
the old nobility, a small man, rather stiff and formal, chaste out of
timidity, and agreeably ugly. He was hopelessly in love with blue
and gold, pale gold, the blue and gold of the fair-haired working
men in blue-denim coveralls. Toward six o'clock in the evening,
Pepe would lean against the balustrade of the Métro and watch,
spellbound, all those shades of blue climb up from the dark underground, and the robust necks and the fair heads of hair. He tasted a
pleasure that was purer than that tasted by the men who are attracted to working girls, for he neither made a move nor said a word.
He had given me his friendship and unbosomed himself to me in his

French, which was correct but accented. No one has ever talked to me as he did of the color blue or of golden hair curling like shavings around a reddened ear, or of the pungent populace of blond young working men.

"Pepe," I said, "write down what you have just told me!"

Modest Pepe, shocked to the depths of his lyrical feelings, lowered his eyes.

"That would not be at all amusing, my dear."

On fine warm evenings he took endless walks, searching, finding, and fleeing. The morose Paris of summertime became for Pepe an inferno, voluptuous and almost tropical. He described the wretched streets that I did not recognize, for under the vault of the twilight sky he set, like a tower of silver and gold, blue generator of light, some plumber's apprentice with Venetian blond hair, some metal worker spangled with copper. For a long time he loved those blond, blue-clad young males as one loves the immense sea, its every surge and swell. But one day the tide of six o'clock which empties the metallurgical and electrical workshops out onto the streets of Paris set before Pepe a nameless blue, blue of forget-me-not, of aconite, of gentian, of squill, with a golden pennon streaming across the face of . . .

"Oh!" stammered Pepe. "Vercingétorix!"

He pressed both hands against his heart that was at long last torn, and shut his lips. For a man has the right to murmur audibly "Adèle" or "Rose" and to kiss in public the portrait of a lady, but he must stifle the names of Daphnis or Ernest.

Pale, winged like those who go to their death, Pepe followed Vercingétorix. On the collar of the Gaul, in the folds of the elbow, and even on his boots, a fine fresh powder of metal sparkled, and sometimes his enormous mustache, obeying the evening breeze, almost whipped the back of his neck. He went into a nearby *tabac* so suddenly that he bumped into Pepe, who, stung by a point of the streaming mustache, staggered.

"*Pardon, monsieur,*" said Vercingétorix.

Dazed, Pepe told himself that he must be dreaming. "Or else

I've just died," he thought. "The boy excused himself! He looked at me! He has just looked at me again . . . What's happened to my knees? My knees won't hold me up, but still I keep going, I'm following him, I . . ."

He stopped thinking, for Vercingétorix, turning around like an impudent street urchin, had smiled at him.

"I felt," Pepe related, "that shattering pang which warns us, deep in sleep, that a happy dream is ending. But I could not stop following him, and a half hour later I was climbing behind Vercingétorix a steep staircase and was sitting down in a small bedroom, very clean, very quiet, where there must have been net curtains, for everything seemed white. Vercingétorix had said, 'sit down,' and had gone behind a ground-glass door. I believe I remained alone for quite a while. Such a thing had never happened to me before. I told myself, 'My heavens, he may kill me . . .' And I thought, 'Oh, if only he would kill me.' Because I realized that nothing better could happen. At last the door opened again and Vercingétorix . . ."

He clenched his boyish fists and banged them together.

"No, not Vercingétorix! No more Vercingétorix! Oh, what a horror he was! He had put on a woman's chemise laced with ribbons, cut low. And do you know what he had on his head? A . . . I almost don't dare to say it . . ."

He swallowed hard, made a face as if sickened.

"He had on his head a wreath of pompon roses. Pompon roses. With leaves. And with that soft pretty mustache below it . . . His beauty dishonored! Oh, what a shameful mascarade . . ."

He fell into a bitter silence. I questioned him.

"But then what, Pepe? Afterward?"

"Afterward? Why, nothing," he said, astonished. "You perhaps don't find my story amusing enough. Afterward, I went away. I gave him something, left it on the table."

"Have you seen him again?"

"No, thank you very much," said Pepe, waving his hand. "I can see him well enough in my imagination . . . with the pompon roses. Never again in my life do I want to hear anyone talk about pompon roses . . ."

The fortunetellers that he feverishly consulted—the woman in the rue Coulaincourt who fell into trances, the woman with the candle, the woman with the tarot cards, the woman with pins—kept predicting the same thing, and Pepe went from one to the other, leading a threatened life, for the pythonesses never stopped predicting that a big blond woman was going to bring him to grief. They saw her quite easily through Pepe's small, slender body that was attractive through some hard-to-define invalid's elegance, the hauteur of a hunchback without a hunch, the grace of the lame man without a short leg. When he finally had enough of giving the soothsayers the confused and travestied image of his infatuation, he disappeared, let himself be forgotten, then departed his uncomfortable life by an extremely tactful suicide, carefully prepared, colorless and well-bred, a suicide that disturbed no one.

HB

❧❧ The Pure and the Impure

They have so perfected their art of dissimulation that by comparison everything else seems imperfect. When I had to dissimulate, I had my models right there before my eyes. I had the daily example of a diplomacy laboriously practiced merely in the service of passion and resentment. I recall how a young man and his lover who were obliged to exercise great prudence were unmasked by a chatterbox and rather scandalously separated. The one most hurt of the two spent months on end trying to find a woman who would be attractive to the chatterbox's husband and succeeded all too terribly well.

Submerged in this project, he forgot himself, relegated his grief to a secondary place, studied and compared, arranged meetings, seized opportunities. Out of sheer exhaustion, he confided in me. Arriving with his harmless look of a young intellectual rather worn and haggard from his thankless work of translating, he would sink into a deep English armchair, green and hideous, lean back in it, and say, "I need to rest a while." Which was a lie, for he shut his eyes out of circumspection, as a priest in the confessional shuts his eyes, separating himself from the penitent the better to see the form of the sin.

To dissimulate and keep up the dissimulation over a long period without ever flagging, through silences, through smiles, to appear to be an entirely different person—this relegates the trifling exaggerations of gossips to a quite inferior category. It is a task, as I've had occasion to notice since, which is only possible for the young; it is almost a kind of secretion, as native to young people as an insect's ability to elaborate its horny wing sheath, its casque and corselet of hard chitin . . . It would be a pity to let the memory of all this be lost. I keep it, as I keep, from these experiences, the ability to see beneath the surface and to outwit the admirable artifices of children and adolescents. Through this ability I enjoy better than many adults the forbidden pleasure of penetrating the world of the young, its brash lies, its elaborate and naïve constructions. Far from resenting my clairvoyance, my powerful yet puerile opponent with his multiplicity of faces enjoys the game, gives up when caught, and shows with a delighted blush the exact sensitive point I have struck.

Insight—the titillating knack for hurting! Reward granted for measuring, for intuiting the oscillations, the pendulum swings of "give and take"! A force that decreases does not go without appropriating to itself in passing some juxtaposing and consenting forces. "We come to you for warmth," declare my young friends of both sexes, wearing their youthful wounds like decorations, some of them still glistening with a trace of fresh blood, battered from recent blows. "Warm us, make us well!" they repeat. Many of them come to crouch down close to me and wait, resting a confused head against my knees . . . O innocents! I tremble lest they be mistaken and, starting out as mendicants, may find they are the givers of life. Shall I ever know what I take from those who have trusted me? Did I owe them nothing more than to warm them? To receive from someone happiness—there's no avoiding using that word I do not comprehend—is it not to choose the sauce in which we want to be served up?

Scruples come to me, as usual, by extrahuman routes. The feeling has grown in me that I owe a debt to the animals which have dedicated their brief existence to me. Am I their guardian? My role is more nearly raptorial. Perhaps, after all, the true friend of animals is the one who groans in exasperation, "Oh, how that dog wears me out!" "Take away this cat, I can't think while he's in the room!" While I knowingly exhaust the dog, since he always yields, and usually when I say, "Come, puss," I see the cat hurry forward, even if reluctantly, and the cat is the abundant reservoir from which I draw secret clairvoyance, warmth, fantasy, self-control. Birds are too far removed from us, although the tufted titmouse shows a preference for me. But I remember that "catless" period of my life, which lasted about two years, was a time out of joint, a barren epoch. Whether one has to do with an animal or a child, to convince is to conquer and subdue. Just two hundred steps from this table lives a little four-year-old girl who fears neither spanking nor thunder and lightning nor wasps, and so assured is she of her power of seduction that she is practically uncontrollable. Sometimes, toward the end of the day, when her father is yawning with nervous exhaustion, when the violet shadows that ring the large eyes of her young mother make them seem larger, the child's nurse, white-faced, comes to fetch me: "*She* is terrible. *She* did not want to take her nap this afternoon. We are worn out, but *she* is as fresh as a daisy . . ."

Then I climb the neighboring alleyway, and I confront the All-Powerful. Far from treating me as a scarecrow, the All-Powerful smiles at me, greets me, and starts a conversation on the exaggerated importance given to stewed peaches in her alimentation, for instance, or she criticizes my way of dressing: "You're not at all pretty in pajamas, I like you better in a skirt," or she will show a great

fondness for ancient French folklore and will sing an old ditty for
me:

"Early this morning
Ragotin-dandy
Drank so much brandy
That he's staggering,
Staggering!" [1]

My role is to act indifferent and to read beneath the changing
features of the All-Powerful her real thoughts. Shameful métier, in
which I succeed all too well. Why is it that, without means other
than my eyes and words, I leave the All-Powerful mollified and
overcome with sleep? Seeing her so sensible and smiling with self-
satisfaction, I am reminded of a pair of little horses, glossy with
indolence and oats, which, taken from the stable and harnessed, immediately broke the shafts and the traces. We harnessed them again
and they were soft as soap beneath my hands, trotting sweetly when
I took them again from their master. "You have the hand of an old
coachman, a hand that puts a horse to sleep," he said, by way of
praising me. For some human beings are utterly unacquainted with a
certain kind of piracy.

But my rival, the All-Powerful, will have her turn, when I
become enfeebled. Hovering over me like a dragonfly, she will
murmur, "There, there . . . Rest, go to sleep," and to my astonishment I shall sleep. We've not reached that point, yet—oh, that involuntary start of pride!—I am still strong enough to be lavish with
my gifts as well as to plunder the riches of others. If I had no equals,
I would tire of this twofold occupation, this acting like a robber one
minute and like a spendthrift the next. But, apart from those individuals who hurriedly let themselves be filled by me, leaving me

[1] Ce matin,
Ragotin
A tant bu de brandevin
Qu'il branle!
Qu'il branle!

empty and drawn, and apart from the superabundant ones, still worse, whose indigestible contributions I quickly reject, there spreads a zone where I can disport with my equals. I have more of these than I could have expected. They are usually just emerging from the worst kind of youth, the second childhood. They have lost their solemnity and have acquired a sane notion of what is incurable and what is curable—for instance, love. Ingeniously they fill each day from one dawn to the next, and they have an adventurous spirit. They perceive, as I do, the pernicious element in daily work, and they do not laugh when I repeat the quip of a great journalist who died young and in the harness: "Man is not made to work, and the proof is that work tires him." In short, they are frivolous, as have been hundreds of heroes. They have become frivolous the hard way. And they secrete from one day to the next their own ethics, which makes them even more understandable to me and colors them variously.

The thing we all have in common is a certain diffidence: we never dare to show openly that we need each other. Such reserve acts as a code of behavior and constitutes what I call our "etiquette of survivors." Cast upon a rocky coast by their dismasted vessel, should not the survivors of the shipwreck be the most considerate of messmates? It is wise to apply the oil of refined politeness to the mechanism of friendship. Listen now to my friend, the painter engraver, D., and his Polynesian tactfulness. He had ceremoniously prepared his visit by a telephone call, and now he enters and noiselessly occupies the whole room, like a cloud:

"Madame Colette, I have come to excuse myself, I cannot dine with you tomorrow. I'm sorry, I'm really very upset, but since I've promised . . ."

He lowers his eyes in his reserved way, his wide shoulders fill the window, blocking the light as he stands there, dense and motionless as a wall. He speaks in an almost inaudible voice, without gestures, quite aware that a movement of his body, his suddenly raised voice could bring down the ceiling and shatter to bits my collection of milk glass.

"I would not have allowed myself to promise," D. goes on in a hurried whisper, "but it's a rather exceptional circumstance. I'm expecting a friend. We haven't seen each other in a long time, it will soon be five years, just imagine. I should explain that he has been absent . . . He's a lad who has had troubles, a great many troubles. He's returning from a distance and is going to feel very disoriented. The fact is, he was accused of having killed his grandmother and cut her up into pieces—what won't they think up next! Not only did they accuse him, they condemned him, like that, without proof. And worse still, they unearthed—the word is exact—an old yarn concerning a little girl who had been more or less raped . . . All this was quite badly demonstrated. In short, my friend has been away for five years. Just imagine how changed he will find things! So I promised to meet him at the station and to have dinner with him tomorrow. By jove, all those things that have been said about him . . ."

The rigidly extended arm of D., like a supporting beam, divides the room into two parts, on the one side "the things that have been said" and on the other side the sentimental truth.

". . . I simply disregard. But what I can assure you, Madame Colette, and I know him well, is that the boy is . . ."

A big hand, spread flat, marks and covers the location of an even greater heart, while his voice, muffled with tenderness, murmurs like the rustling of leaves:

". . . is infinitely gentle and refined. I might have asked your permission to bring him with me to dinner, but I felt I must refrain from making such a request . . ."

While speaking, the big man is tenderly handling a tiny frigate in spun glass; now he looks up at me, flashing me a facetious glance, his eyes as innocent as those of a young girl:

". . . because my friend is so shy . . ."

I allow this last word to keep all its naïve value. Not that, when listening to him, I am duped by so much artlessness—no more than D. himself is—or if so, just barely. That an assassin may be prudish or nervy, one can allow; it is by no means surprising. What I find significant when listening to D. is his respect for my personal conception of his character. An ideogram is comprised of heavy and light strokes, one must often press down hard when tracing a pattern, must use in a decorative way the dark stain in the background. Instinct and unbridled Herculean strength do not alone impel my friend D. to settle a public row by knocking two crazed heads together. Not in one day or spontaneously is a thoughtful "Polynesian" like D. fashioned, or a "child of nature" such as I. He and I and others like us come from the distant past and are inclined to cherish the arbitrary, to prefer passion to goodness, to prefer combat to discussion. Taken together and in good company, are these mental liberties enchanting? Certainly. Yes, yes. And without danger—without any other danger than not to have any more danger to run.

But scarcely have I praised these parallels and affinities than I cease to enjoy myself and begin to feel a malaise such as one experiences in the great museums among the crowded masterpieces, the painted faces, the portraits in which life continues to surge with baleful abundance.

Remove from me everything that is too sweet! Arrange for me, in the last third of my life, a clear space where I can put my favorite crudity, love. Merely to have it before me and to breathe it in, merely to touch it with hand or tooth, it keeps me young.

What then has changed between us, between love and me? Nothing, unless myself, or love. Everything that proceeds from love still wears its color and spreads it over me. But this jealousy, for example, which blooms in its side like a dark carnation? Have I not too soon plucked it? Jealousy, debasing suspicions, inquisitions, reserved for the hours of night and nudity, the ritual ferocities, have I not too soon said goodbye to all those daily tonics? Jealousy leaves no time to be bored; does it even leave time to grow old? My grandmother, the mean one—that was the way I distinguished her from the other grandmother, who was apparently kind—at sixty years of age and more, followed my grandfather to the door of a certain *petit endroit*. When my mother was scandalized, the jealous old Provençal lady haughtily instructed her: "Eh, my girl, a man who wants to deceive us manages to escape through even smaller holes."

Her gray-green eyes were shaded by low reddish eyebrows, she moved with a dense corporeal majesty, in wide black taffeta skirts, and when so close to the end, she did not hesitate to treat love familiarly, with suspicion. I believe she was right to do so. It is right not to deny one's self too soon all familiarity with the big impressive gestures which only jealousy can teach us, the big facile and murderous gestures, meticulously premeditated, so masterfully accomplished in imagination that it is foolish and pointless to carry them out.

The feminine faculty of anticipating or inventing what can and will happen is acute, and almost unknown to men. A woman knows all about a crime she may possibly commit. Maintained, if I may so express it, in a platonic state, amorous jealousy stimulates our gift of divination, strains all the senses, reinforces self-command. But what woman has not been disappointed in her crime, once she has committed it and the murdered lover lies there at her feet? "It was finer, the way I planned it. Is blood on the rug always dull and black like this? And that strange look of discontent, that disapproving sleep on a face, is it death, really death?"

She preferred her dreadful crime when she was carrying it within her, heavy and vibrant, finished in every detail and ready to break out into the world, like a child in the last hours of gestation. "But it didn't need to have all this reality . . . Reality makes it seem so old, so commonplace and boring. But now here it is, the hour of my greatest torment, the hour when I organize each day a new setting for my great torment, for the ups and downs that I had not yet imagined, a catastrophe, a miracle. I did not want to exchange my great torment except for peace—if I have been mistaken, what will become of me?" She perceives that murder is always a fool's bargain. But she accepts it with difficulty, stubbornly she regards as an end what is only a beginning. Hence she must go on humiliating herself until she realizes there are only two kinds of human beings: those who have killed and those who have not killed.

I have had occasion to descend to the very depths of jealousy, have settled into it and thought about it at great length. It is not an unendurable sojourn, although in my writings in bygone days I believe I compared it, as everyone does, to a sojourn in hell, and I trust that the word will be put down to my poetic exaggeration. Rather, I would say, it is a kind of gymnast's purgatory, where the senses are trained, one by one, and it has the gloom of all training centers. Of course, I am talking about motivated, avowable jealousy, and not about an obsession. The sense of hearing becomes refined, one acquires visual virtuosity, a rapid and hushed step, a sense of smell that can capture the particles deposited in the atmosphere by a head of hair, a scented powder, the passage of a brazenly happy person—all this strongly recalls the field exercises of the soldier or the hypersensitive skill of poachers. A body absolutely on the alert becomes weightless, moves with somnambulistic ease, rarely collapses and falls. I would go so far as to affirm that it is so protected by its state of trance that it escapes the ordinary epidemics, provided, naturally, that one respects the rigid and special hygiene of the jealous person, eating enough and disdaining drugs. All the rest is, according to one's character, as boring as any solitary sport, as immoral as a game of chance. All the rest is a series of wagers lost or won, especially won. "What did I tell you? I told you He was meeting her every day at the same teashop. I was sure of it!" All the rest is competition: in beauty, in health, in obstinacy, in salacity, even. All the rest is hope . . .

Jealousy even thrives on homicidal desires. Inevitably. Checked, then released briefly like an elastic band, it almost has the virtues of an exercising apparatus. Leaving aside the hours darkened by sensual desires, when one is always ready to shout "Stop thief!" and to pose as being mistreated and starved for love, I deny that the pangs of jealousy keep us from living, working, even behaving like respectable people.

However, I see I have just employed, carelessly, the expression "to descend into the depths of jealousy." Jealousy is not at all low, but it catches us humbled and bowed down, at first sight. For it is the only suffering that we endure without ever becoming used to it. I am calling upon my memories for this, my most faithful memories, that is to say, those that do not demand the help of superfluous accessories such as a night of wind, a mossy stone bench, the barking of a dog in the distance, arabesques of light and shadow on a wall or on a dress. Jealousy, by its tinctorial power, instills a strong and definitive color to everything it encounters. If I wish, for example, to resuscitate a carnal moment—"thus I was caressed, thus I caressed, yes, thus, thus . . ."—an ironical mist hides and deforms what happened, what is no longer timely.

But let a certain phase of the moon take, at my order, its customary place in the sky, and simultaneously let a certain decaying elbow-rest at a window splinter beneath my fingernail, as it did thirty years ago, and the two compose an escutcheon of jealousy, and I see, on a field vert, the green of fine, stiff woodland grass piercing the dead leaves with its lances and brandishing them in the air. O flat Moon, round, then waning and less round, worm-eaten old wood, various other allegories, are you all that remains to me of a possession hotly and vainly disputed? No, I now have the ability to think about jealousy without experiencing burning transports, and can hear the echo of a name as if it were merely the distant and musical drone of an enormous swarm of bees. That is what constitutes one of the by no means negative recompenses, considerable, though vague, like one of those diplomas in which the whole place of honor on a parchment is filled with the word DIPLOMA. Who would think of trying to decipher the fine and complicated calligraphy below that word, faded and dim in the gloom of a parlor?

Like everyone, I have wanted death and a little more to claim a woman, two women, three women . . . I am talking now about those acts of sympathetic magic which do not seriously harm anyone, not even the one who casts the spells, provided the people concerned are strong and hearty. They will get off with a confused and transient uneasiness, a feeling of languor, a few slight shocks such as might be caused by a finger laid on one's shoulder. But these are the messages that are sent by love as well as by hate, so I cannot guarantee their complete harmlessness.

During a rather burning season of jealousy, I myself ran some risks. A rival of mine, very insecure in her happiness, thought of me strongly, and strongly I thought of her. But I made the mistake of letting myself go back to my writing, which demanded my attention, and to abandon my other task of antagonism, of daily and secret defiance. In short, I postponed my curses during three or four months, while Madame X. continued hers, devoting her long hours of leisure to this. And I soon became aware of the results of such inequality. I began by falling into a ditch in the Place du Trocadéro, then I caught bronchitis. Then, in the Métro, on my way to the publisher, I lost the last part of a manuscript of which I had not kept a duplicate. A taxi driver shortchanged me, leaving me on a rainy night without a sou. Then a mysterious epidemic bore off three of my Angora kittens . . .

To put an end to the series of misfortunes, I had only to arouse myself from an inexcusable negligence and to return once more to an even exchange of mental trajectories with Madame X. And we lived on mutually bad terms until the bond between us was worn out and space ceased to be a pathway of wicked beams of thought, a harp of resonant waves, a starry ether hung with signs and portents. I was not the only one to regret it, for we had quarreled without feeling any fundamental antipathy. Time recompenses honorable adversaries. Mine, as soon as she stopped being an adversary, had some delightful anecdotes to tell which could amuse only ourselves.

"One day when I was going to Rambouillet to murder you . . ."

The rest of this story was a gay vaudeville, an involved tale of a missed train, a stalled car, a gold-mesh handbag that burst open at the bottom, spilling out an indiscreet revolver upon the Rambouillet pavement, of inopportune encounters, of a friend who read in the periwinkle blue eyes of Madame X. a homicidal intent and by some fond diplomacy diverted her from it . . .

"My dear," she exclaimed, "just count all these little happenings which raised chance obstructions between you and me in the town of Rambouillet! Can you deny that they were providential?"

"God forbid! There is one, especially, that I would hate to forget."

"Which one?"

"You see, I wasn't in Rambouillet at the time. I didn't set foot there that year."

"You weren't in Rambouillet?"

"I was not in Rambouillet."

"Well! That is the absolute limit!"

This limit revived, for some unknown reason, a little of the former resentment in the periwinkle eyes that questioned mine. But it was only a fleeting gleam. In vain we tried—in vain we still try—to upset each other by violent arguments, a tone of defiance quite out of keeping with our calm remarks: we soon recover our cordial relations. The powerful bond that was our youthful and mutual hatred can no longer unite us.

With that beautiful blue-eyed woman, whose light chestnut hair was exactly the shade of mine—and with such and such another and still another woman—I have ceased to exchange, shall never more exchange because of a man and through a man that menacing thought, those reflections from mirror to mirror, that tireless emanation which wronged the lover himself . . . "What are you thinking about?" he asked them. They were thinking about me. "But where are you, please?" he asked me when he saw I was not listening to him. "In the moon?" I was in spirit close to some woman, my invisible presence was upsetting her. We lacked nothing, those women and I: we had every kind of trouble.

Halfway between them and me, in an immunized zone, "He" lorded it, not as umpire but rather as the prize over which we fought. "They"—the men—are not fond of such subtle games and dread the fury of two females locked in combat. But a contest, even a terrible one, demands something more than passion. It demands sportsmanlike qualities and an equable temper even in the very midst of ferocious feelings. I do not have one jot of the sporting spirit, and therefore I indulged in fantasy, dealt blows below the belt that must be counted as foul or as failing to obey the rules of a game. I committed only one real fault, but I repeated it and was duly punished. Which was only just. An old saying warns us never to give either a boat or a bird. I would add: or a man. To begin with, because a man never—even when he swears it on our head or on the Holy Book—a man never belongs to us. And if by chance he lets himself be treated as our property, even gladly, he is so constituted that he would never forgive us for it. And since he rarely forgives the happy beneficiary, once again renouncement will have spoiled everything.

If you succeed, as I did, in sublimating the sexual drive and putting it in the service of heaven knows what mortifying joy or egalitarian madness, you will see the furious flower of jealousy stripped of its thorns, along with the condign egotism of the human couple.

What would a father confessor think of these agreed-to abdications, the handing-over of the rights of the bed? I am sure of his response, I who have never had an authorized confidant. He would think, as I do, that there is something about certain conjugal permissiveness that reminds one of the stuffiness of a closed room, and that the calm surface of these spurious families of doubtful respectability is worse than equivocal. Can one exist on lukewarmness? No better than one can live on vice—which, incidentally, stands to lose nothing in such conjugal arrangements.

What a lot of time wasted in absolutions! The most imbecile of all is that which literature has sanctified as "the eternal triangle." Its shocking variations, its acrobatic aspects of human pyramid very quickly discouraged the hesitating polygamous societies. What woman, no matter how foolish and unsettled, could be made to believe that one plus one equals three? Speaking as an onlooker, a cool-headed woman I know, unconventional but not without lucidity, assured me that in an eternal triangle there is always one person who is betrayed, and often two. I like to think that the one most constantly betrayed is the patriarch *in camera*, the clandestine Mormon. He well deserves it, in his traditional role of *agent provacateur*, and as a small-scale pasha.

His snare, a crude one, since it is nothing but sexual satisfaction, is set against him, if one of the two women he brings together improperly has some strength of character and withholds herself for the benefit of the weaker woman, withdrawing from the arrangement that has set them face to face, or to put it more coarsely, mouth to mouth. The weak one normally yields, sheds her veil, demands a tender relationship with the other woman and gives her unquestioning devotion. "Trust me utterly, since I now have nothing to hide from you, I feel pure, I am your ally and no longer your victim."

Women pair off like this oftener than one might think. But having entered this state by a narrow tunnel, they prefer and are entitled to keep their union secret. Not long ago, one woman of such a pair died, and her friend quite literally sank into a decline. She did not make haste, she did not woo death, nor did she seek what she could never again possess, what she had never hoped for, what she explained so confusedly: "No, she was not like a daughter to me, for I doubt that genuine maternal feeling ever rids itself, even momentarily, of all hostile feeling. No, she was not like a lover to me, for I forgot that she was beautiful, that we had come together in despite of a man, in the deep and growing indifference we felt toward that man. We were joined in an infinity so pure that I never thought of death . . ."

As that word "pure" fell from her lips, I heard the trembling of the plaintive "u," the icy limpidity of the "r," and the sound aroused nothing in me but the need to hear again its unique resonance, its echo of a drop that trickles out, breaks off, and falls somewhere with a plash. The word "pure" has never revealed an intelligible meaning to me. I can only use the word to quench an optical thirst for purity in the transparencies that evoke it—in bubbles, in a volume of water, and in the imaginary latitudes entrenched, beyond reach, at the very center of a dense crystal.

HB

PART Six ❦❦ [1939-1954]

Another War—Old Age—The Blue Lantern

. . . *la règle guérit de tout*

. . . discipline is the cure for everything

❧❧ World War II

Letters to Renée Hamon

Hotel Métropole, Dieppe

[August 27, 1939]

We return to Paris tomorrow morning. For how long? No one knows that, [but] if war breaks out, Maurice won't allow me to live in Paris, as you can well imagine. We both send you big hugs. What lovely weather! Almost as lovely as in 1914.

9, rue de Beaujolais, Paris

[September 2, 1939]

My little Renée, I'm afraid there is no question of my moving from here. My eyes are not good and I can't see very well from a distance, consequently I shall stay here in Paris.

DC

"Colette speaking"

This report on Paris in the first months of the war was written to be read over the Paris Mondial radio for listeners in America, with Maurice Goudeket standing by to translate Colette's text into English.

When I became a spokesman for this hemisphere, I was obliged to remind myself of the difference in time between our continents. At this moment, America is glittering in that multicolored evening glare I once glimpsed on a short trip to New York, the letters of fire, the arrows, the quivering garlands of the advertisements, the cinemas, the big stores. But here, it is two o'clock in the morning, nighttime, wartime . . .

As in 1914, I still find intact in my heart—a heart no different from the hearts of thousands of other Parisians—that egotistical love which, heedless of all caution, has summoned us back from the peaceful countryside at the height of a magnificent summer, and since the last days of August has held us captive here. Nothing could prevail against it, neither the threat hanging over us in the sky, nor the prospect of being evacuated by force, nor that of acute discomfort. I would like you to know that Paris has never been more beautiful. Emptied, in part, of its civilian population, it now seems to us to be larger. Now the familiar congestion has been removed, it has found its former harmonious proportions once again. The dimensions of its squares are more easily perceived; some of the very old roads leading to its heart, normally filled with commercial traffic, have become narrow streets intended for pedestrians once again. One glimpses old buildings suddenly surrounded by the empty spaces that the architect envisaged for them, long ago.

In the silence of the nights, Paris is once more hearing sounds which it had long forgotten: the chimes of the Angelus and the bells ringing for early Mass glide down, with the pigeons whirling like dying leaves, from the tops of the spires, and the catarrhal bellow of a barge on the Seine comes before daybreak to where I lie in sleep,

crossing the spread-eagled surfaces of silence, of gardens and colonnades which are the gardens of the Tuileries, the Louvre, the Car-
rousel and the garden of the Palais-Royal. These historic gardens,
these palaces built by kings, have lost, during this past month of
war, as during the four years of the former war, not a single flower
from their flowerbeds, not a single sculpted floweret from their im-
mortal walls. Their gardeners still tend to their attires, their keepers
are still maintaining the masterpieces to which the entire world, as
soon as they are threatened, turns its anxious thoughts. I have just
walked past these palaces, these bridges, this river, these gardens
which the fall of the year has not yet deflowered, all this magnificence standing in the heart of Paris, in the dead of night.

It is two o'clock in the morning, and it is wartime. There were
a few blue landmarks, a few feeble, flickering lights to guide my
steps. At such an hour, and at such a time, one feels what such a
walk is truly worth. Dawn is still a long way off. As it breaks, a
population will awake composed of units, each of which will go
about its separate task. Paris wakes up, like certain tropical flowers,
all at once. I should feel proud if I could show you the bustle that
follows its sleep. The men—old or very young—are sprightly. The
old men have grown young again, the adolescents try to be older so
as to look like men. The women, on their way to work, living proofs
of the city's moral and physical health, have abandoned none of
their essential coquetry, thanks be to God. Since our heads of industry made the carrying of gas masks obligatory, the women, in the
space of a single week, have made their cylindrical cases into accessories that can express their personal tastes. They can be tartan-
covered like little kilts, sheathed in leather like a dressing case, clad
in brightly colored silk like a little parasol, or else matched, as to
fabric and color, with a daytime suit. Masks hung from the belt,
masks slung over shoulders, masks strung over backs, masks in baskets, masks in *pochettes* looking like handbags—there is every sort
of mask to brighten our streets. I would not swear that all these cases
are used to house their regulation contents, not, that is, if I am to
judge by my own, which I find so handy for bringing back one of the

last of the season's tiny melons from les Halles, or a pound of golden grapes, or some fresh walnuts . . . But I will delve no deeper. The Parisian, derisive by nature, will always put his comfort before his security. I need only offer as a very topical proof of this the contempt with which the people of Paris spurned the shelters made necessary by our policy of passive defense, during the two or three alerts that we had in September. When the one daylight alert sounded, I was able to watch from my window as the police in charge of the defense of the city were forced to round up the men and women in the streets like so many recalcitrant goats.

I am afraid that this prosaic little account of mine may be giving you an inadequate idea of the humdrum life we are leading here, we civilians who don't wish to be separated from our beloved city. I am afraid it may give you a very poor picture of what it means to be a civilian in Paris. If I am wrong, so much the better. For I have the impression that we have been conducting ourselves, since the beginning of September, very well indeed. Most of us have a very good idea of what we mustn't do, and even of what we must do. We go on living without fuss, we don't get in the way, almost all the women have given up wearing the sort of hat which is an offense against common sense and aesthetics, and, except for those who are displaying an excess of zeal and wasting their time in wanting to put it to good use, I have never found them so charming. They are already talking in less high-flown terms, and perhaps this war is even beginning to reeducate us . . . But it is right that I should tell you, above all, that their double solitude—after the departure of their husbands and the evacuation of their children—has found these women armed with a dazzling courage. They are firm, in some cases perhaps a little hard, and one never sees them displaying reddened eyes or any other outward symptoms of their grief.

DC

June 1940

All that is silence in the garden now recalls that summer morning in 1940, which brought its benison to the elm-tree bowers, the flowering rose trees, the lawns with their blue mist of dew from the watering spray, the whole quadrangle of the Palais-Royal so soon emptied of its quiet inhabitants by the heat, and above all by the imminence of something other than the dog days. . . . In the morning shade, a man was cleaning out his bird cages, changing the inmates' water and seed, giving them fresh lettuce leaves, and squeezing fresh slices of fruit between the bars. When certain moments of a fine day become too beautiful, the human animal interrupts his labor or his play, gives his veneration to all that is silent or singing around him, and unconsciously purifies himself by seeking contact with all that the sky, the earth, and the city have granted him—unless he has been given knowledge of the future and is mourning for them in advance. And that perhaps is what he was doing, that man busy with his cages, at one moment drinking in the solitude and peace of the deserted garden, at another standing motionless, a bunch of millet held idly in his hands.

Just then, a civilian made his way into the garden. He seemed surprised when he found it empty, save for some chattering sparrows, some pigeons taking delight in their own amorous garglings, a single dog whose name was—and still is—Kiki, and the man with the cages, whom he hailed with an ease and courtesy of manner that forcibly recalled the theater.

"You appear to be most pleasurably occupied, monsieur."

"It's the best hour of the day, monsieur," replied the man with the cages. "The garden attendants are having their breakfast. If they were to catch me cleaning my cages outside the arches, they wouldn't half give me a going over! But at this hour of the morning, everything's peaceful and quiet."

These last words appeared to make some impression on the sociable civilian.

"Peaceful and quiet . . ." he echoed. "Monsieur, did you not know that the German Army has entered Paris?"

The man with the cages threw him a brief backward glance over one shoulder: "I know you've told me so, monsieur. But I'm not forced to believe it. I'll wait till they get as far as here and tell me so themselves."

"Monsieur, I have just come from the Place de l'Opéra, where there are German troops, even as I speak to you . . ."

"Yes, monsieur, you are speaking to me indeed; but if I may be allowed to say so, I didn't ask you anything."

The civilian walked away two steps, then, attempting to be humorous in his turn: "Doubtless you find the events I speak of without interest, monsieur."

"Monsieur, the important thing for me, today as on all other days, is taking care of my canaries. Remember that my canaries are Saxons, monsieur, Saxons!"

The civilian stood dumfounded, gazing at the beautiful walls of stone and foliage around him, listening to the silence, which was less disturbed by the distant noises from outside than by the song of the Saxon canaries.

"Are all the inhabitants of the Palais-Royal displaying the same serenity of mind at the moment as you yourself, monsieur?" he said at last.

"All of them, monsieur," said the man with the cages. "You would think they were all my brothers if you could see them."

"If I may judge by the present aspect of the Palais-Royal, your brothers are . . . absent, are they not?"

"By no means, monsieur. It's just that they're all sleeping late this morning."

The civilian frowned, searched for a biting retort, failed to find one, and finally decided to walk away. Left alone, the natural of the Palais-Royal glanced around at the carved windows, tight shut for the most part on apartments emptied by the exodus, and returned to his tasks. But noticing that the civilian was moving off rather slowly and with circumspection, he began to whistle a little tune—a gay little tune, of course.

DC

Late June 1940

Beyond the oxcarts, the haycarts, the big automobiles swathed in dust, the wheelbarrows and the charabancs, beyond the lines of rounded hills, the darkened regions with their blue foliage, the meadows full of hay ready to be mowed, where each little valley enfolded the sleep of a wandering tribe, of a carriage caparisoned with mattresses, the slumber of a child wrapped in a toweling bathrobe, of a pair of doves in a cage, of a fox terrier tied to a tree, of a young girl hugging a man's topcoat about her; beyond the 350 miles of highway covered by the chaos of a France slithering onward over itself, a credulous and oblivion-filled fatigue was filling me with beneficent illusions. Extreme fatigue and its accompanying fever are pitiful in their treatment of us, since they admit, since they invent the approach of a single place, a single moment in happiness and unhappiness alike. There was no need of a long rest to help us regain our balance amid the common lot. Wherever the writer stops, aging though he may be, exhausted though he may think himself, his favorite enigmas, his passions still glitter there: the human face and the secrets that overwhelm it, the vertically slit pupil and phosphorescence of a night-piercing eye, the language of a bird, the tricks of a child . . .

A profession, though of long standing and ingrown in us, departs when an honor, a disaster, or an exodus happens suddenly to all the inhabitants of a nation, and carries us out into its ocean swell . . . But it comes back. At the end of a long road, I had not foreseen that I would go so far, only to stumble into a table—winning post, obstacle, or reef; a trustle, a tray with folding legs for serving meals in bed, a rickety occasional table in a hotel—across a writing table. Everything perceived produces but one identical duty, which is perhaps only a temptation: to write, to describe. I have seen none of this war's violence, no scenes lit by the glare of incendiaries. Each writer has incumbent upon him the task decided by his abilities, by chance, by the decline or the vigor of his years. I found my stopping place among the people who live by the land, those who, according to the caprices of successive wars, have watched the invaders, always disguised in armor, pass across their plow lands. The peasant did not always even know the name of this faceless flood, which in one age was called the Saracens, in another the Spaniards, and then the Revolution . . . But he did not move, and they did no more than trample the green shoots of a future harvest and move on. When they were gone, he prepared the land for seeding once again. He is always there. I spent my childhood as a peasant, I like to put my faith in him and to contemplate him as he stands, unmoving, between his greathearted wife, his children, and his flocks, against a background of modest village spires, fresh streams, and a hesitating dawn.

It may perhaps seem strange that since I was cut off, on June 15, from the homes I think of as mine—four rooms in Paris, in the 1ᵉ arrondissement, and the same number outside Montfort-l'Amaury —I should sometimes worry less about them than about the changes which the war and the Occupation have inflicted, as I fear, upon the village where I was born. The only homage I have ever paid it was a single, and brief, visit, sixteen years ago. My reason for the journey was a desire to observe the exact relation of memory to the sites which shaped it. One of the gardens of its deserted château still has its old rosebushes trained into swags, the warmth of warm bread on the façade where they bloom: I knew all I needed to know, everything was in order. The house where I was born also—aging, in all conscience, less quickly than I myself. As for the little town as a whole, I passed a verdict of guilty on several new roofs and some swan-necked street lamps, but the remainder still fitted faithfully beneath the tracing which I always carry with me.

But the war? . . . A beloved ghost, Sido, now draws the whole town back with her into a far-distant past, a past I never knew, since the war in question is that of 1870, and I was not born until three years later. "Your father," Sido told me when I was little, "swung himself out of the village on his crutches, despite the snow, accompanied by a few of the other men. He was the only one who could speak a little German, and he managed to make himself understood. Thanks to him, there was no looting, and very little panic. *They* were rather impressed by him."

"And you, where were you?"

"I was taking care of the house and the children. Your sister was twelve, your elder brother was seven, and Léo was three."

"What did they say?"

"Say? Nothing. I don't know what they said! What can it possibly matter, what they said then?"

At the first shock of resistance, her intolerance reappeared and rose up to confront the interrogator, the contradictor. She had never learned even the first word of the language people use to dull the minds of children. So that even her invective left us feeling honored and more grown-up.

"Ask them yourself what they were thinking at the time. They're still alive, aren't they? And I didn't give birth to a lot of idiots without memories."

She became gentle again as quickly as she had flared up.

"Though I expect they have forgotten, in fact. Your sister was at Mlle Ravaire's boarding school. Léo . . . well, he was only three. How can you expect him to have understood or remembered anything at all about the war?"

"But I don't expect it, that is precisely why I'm asking you . . ."

"Achille . . . Yes, you can ask Achille, obviously."

She smiled, swelling up with infinite pride.

"He was seven. He trotted about the streets, already quite tall for his age, in among the Prussian soldiers. And as he passed, they would stop and look around at him for a moment. You see, they had never seen such wavy, chestnut hair before, such dark blue eyes, and especially such a mouth . . ."

"But you, Maman, did you see them?"

"Yes," Sido answered with indifference. "But I've rather forgotten them too, I only remember the very first one I saw."

"Was it terrifying?"

"Why should it have been terrifying? Heavens, what a commonplace child it is! It was up in Fox Lane . . . At dusk there is almost always a mist up there, along Fox Lane, because the spring is smoky then. So there I was, and I saw a soldier with a spike on his helmet standing in the middle of the lane. He was holding his rifle as though it was a shotgun. I could just make out that he had a thick, short beard. I think he was a Bavarian. Because of the dusk and the mist, there was no way of telling the color of his uniform or of his beard. And for a moment I had the impression that the whole German Army must be composed entirely of gray men just like him, gray clothes, gray faces, gray hair, like people in engravings . . ."

"What did you do?"

"I went straight home and buried all the best wines," Sido replied, not without pride. "The wine dating back to my first marriage, Château-Laroise, Château-Lafite, Chambertin, Château-Yquem . . . Wines already ten, twelve, fifteen years old. That beautiful dry sand in the cellar made them ever better still."

She blinked her gray eyes and lifted her chin with the air of a great wine-drinker and connoisseur. Though in fact, though she had very good taste in these matters, she scarcely ever drank anything but water, being mistrustful of wine, since even a half glass of it made her laugh and sent the blood rushing to her cheeks.

Nothing could be less like what is happening today than this image with which my mother won my admiration by making it so very striking with so very few words. So striking that now, seventy years after the Franco-Prussian War, when it is a question of envisaging the outward aspect of another German occupation, I can accept no other: a gray soldier against a gray background of mist, and then, walking toward him, a nimble and rather plump little lady who suddenly catches sight of him, turns on her heel, and hurries back home to provide a place of safety, behind the ramparts of her ample crinoline skirt, behind the aura of courage that surrounds her like the radiant plumage of some exotic bird, for her entire household: her children, her timorous servants, and her bottles of old wine.

DC

Letter to Renée Hamon

[*July 22, 1940*]

. . . I am now beginning to receive letters again. We have been here, in this lush green tomb which is Curemonte, *a whole month* without mail, without telegrams, without the telephone, without gasoline, and without newspapers. We could have won the war and still not have heard about it. This silence is much more difficult to bear than danger. I had no idea that such isolation was possible. We have been here since June 15. We had to leave on the fourteenth or the thirteenth, because the Germans had reached Méré. And I wanted to stay. And despite everything, I regret not having stayed. Curemonte, in ruins, has been loaned to my daughter by one of her brothers. We are waiting, and with such a hunger, to go back to Paris as soon as there is a route open. Not enough gasoline.

DC

Ruins

When it rains, the damp soaks into and revives the colors of the little dome, twelve or fifteen feet above our heads, which forms the roof of a little circular room in the ruin. In dry weather, the same paintings, apparently dating from the Renaissance, turn pale and powdery. We gaze up at them from below, there is not a single wall solid enough to lean a ladder against. These inexpungeable frescoes, consisting entirely of geometric decorations converging on the keystone of the dome, are painted very closely over a background of dark stone. They once enlivened with their yellows, their blues, and their olive greens, the solitary state of a Lady who kept herself warm without the aid of a fire, her feet tucked up in her great skirt edged with vair.

It is her bedroom that we are burning, its wooden panels carved into flowers and picked out in colors; under the paint, it is crumbling away and as soft as sponge. From her little square window, the Lady used to see the invader, the ally, and the merchant mount the hill; she used to watch for the approach of what we lack: her freshly churned butter, her honeycombs, her rents paid in kind with chickens strung up by their legs, and fine-ground flour . . . Whether she came from Plas or from Saint-Hilaire, the Lady of this place was at least accustomed to her fixed life in this place. The curfew was not, as it is for us, the moment to be dreaded above all other, the moment when we all know that we can no longer count on anyone but ourselves until the coming of the clear dawn, cold as in all mountain districts, and heralded by a hundred goldfinches perched on the tips of the pea sticks.

The great windows flapping out from their frames, long innocent of all their small, square panes, bear witness that under Louis XV the masters of this double château decided to catch up with fashion. Outside one of them, a balcony spreads its lip into a gentle concavity inspired by a shell. Since the first few days of July, the last rays of the setting sun, no longer impeded by the west front, now collapsed, reach around to this window and then, as though they are arriving from some late night festivity, tinge the lip of the balcony with red. "Ah," says my daughter, who is a poet, "the Phantom Ball . . ."

A cold July, storms coming one after the other, always at the same time in the afternoon, eight days in a row, and pouring their waters out of the heavy sky. Then, unfailing in its punctuality, a double rainbow arches itself across the screen of the receding rain . . . So many omens, whose meaning will later become clear, say the villagers. But why try to read our fate in the clouds? Welling slowly up in all of us, there is the serenity that comes to those who have lost everything. And for us there can be no omens, either good or bad. The rainbow is but an incomparable feat of architecture, one foot resting in a meadow, the other, with its seven ethereal metals, firmly planted in the middle of the little stream. The rest of the arch is missing: an azure breach that allows free passage to the birds and clouds. Then the seven-tinted miracle completes itself again, confronts the setting sun, and straddles the peaks and valleys with its curve. The rain, having brought it into being, then erases it.

For the past few days we have been seeing soldiers. Encumbered by their disencumbered arms and their packless backs, they all cut walking sticks from the hedges and peeled them white. At first they went into the various bars and dark, low-ceilinged inns, talking rather loudly, tossing their soldiers' jokes into the void and employing the limited repertoire of new words they had picked up in the barracks; but that didn't last long. They were for the most part country boys, and the peasants' silence regained its hold on them. They have given up their white sticks, their military vocabulary, their shy loquacity. When they have no tool to carry on their shoulders, they walk along in silence, their arms dangling at their sides. Once more, they are looking and listening instead of talking. They can tell from a long way off the name of the man sharpening his scythe in the distance, or of another calling orders to his team of oxen, or the name of the bird whose short song makes a sound like glass alleys shaken in a closed fist. And when they pass a woman they do not know, instead of looking her up and down they give her a pensive good day.

"When I've got nothing to read, I scratch myself."

"And I have to stop myself from biting my nails when I have nothing to read."

"It's only because there's nothing to read that I've started sewing."

"If there were a library here, I'd smoke less . . . They say that just over a mile from here there's an ex-schoolteacher who has a collection of two or three hundred books . . . If the rain stops, I shall take a walk over there, just to take a look . . ."

". . . And all you'll find will be a lot of old books given out as school prizes," put in the least talkative one among us, in a grating voice. *The Lady's Country Housekeeping Book* or *The Complete Handyman's Manual* if the teacher is less than seventy, and a few volumes of Alexandre Dumas if he's over seventy."

We arrived here, all of us, borne by the dreadful tide; the strange thing is that our various routes should have all reached their crossroads here. Not one of the voyagers on this ruined ark possesses anything more, or better, than a single suitcase and its contents. We thought we would be stopping here for just a few days . . . The woman who runs the grocery-drapery-tavern in the village sold us her last few pairs of blue overalls, which spare our precious suits and blouses, and even shirts. But we would all willingly exchange the shirts off our backs for ten pounds of printed goods. The real shortage is that of books. We have a score or so of them that move around from bedroom to bedroom, come back to the beginning, and then start the rounds all over again. There are five or six volumes of Proust and three Balzacs which are very much in demand. We are learning how to read again; we find a use even for the scratches and imperfections in the paper. For the first time in many years, reading is losing its egotistical aspect. "Did you see this? There, at the bottom of the page, read it, it's delicious." We are also learning how to share.

But pleasure gives birth to pain. What is the small hardship of having to soak our dry bread in coffee not sweetened with milk, beside the certainty that we shall not receive—neither this evening nor tomorrow nor after our meal nor during the night—a fresh, unopened paper, or a novel with the pages still uncut? Ah, the books stacked up behind their glass! That prodigal display in Stock's store window. Those victuals spread before one like a multicolored harvest home! As for the *éditions de luxe,* with their sumptuous pages,

translucent "Japan," blue-tinted "Chinese," or creamy sheets from
Holland, I think back, but coldly, to those overdressed creatures. Like
all who reread a great deal, I like my copies to be well broken in,
their binding thread hanging off their backs, and so well worn that at
whatever page you open them, they fall flat on their backs, out for
the count.

The twenty or so books we have here, the companions of our
insomnias and mangled sleep, are crying out for mercy, including
the green, clothbound copy of Montaigne. "It is two o'clock . . . it
is three o'clock in the morning . . ." chimes out the tiny church.
The smell of the garden comes in through the half-open window:
that means day is about to break. A fine rain is dusting down onto the
leaves outside; I shall switch on my lamp again. The book at my
elbow can by now predict the shortness of my sleeps, my frequent
awakenings. I have almost reached the point where I can recite it
like a familiar score, like the music one still follows with one's eyes,
even though one can sing it all by heart.

As in all regions where they have not been decimated, the birds
here are very bold. At the top of every one of the stakes supporting
the bean plants, there blooms a goldfinch in full flower. Yesterday,
two chaffinches, having started a quarrel on a branch, flew down to
the ground to continue their fight with greater ease. A wheel of
russet wings and furious beaks began flailing up the dust. Neither of
the combatants took any more notice of my presence than if I had
been a wall or a cloud. On nights brimming with moonlight, the
barn owls and the tawny owls freely hurl their invectives at the
bright and unseemly light; the white splashes of their droppings
signal the presence of screech owls on the topmost steps of a staircase that ceases in mid-air, the perfect height for a night bird or an
angel to take wing.

There is a charm residing in the presence, in the constancy of a
welling spring that derives from our astonishment. The more subterranean, the more secret the water is, the greater the reverence we
feel for it. Our ruins conceal no water; it is only with the greatest
indifference that the forked wand will curve, very slightly, at this or

that point, in my hand. The water for the garden and for washing is drawn up from a square well. Though it is better not to look too closely at the skin that forms, like a coat of collodion in the process of solidifying, over the contents of the pails and pots. But twenty feet farther down, out of the rock itself, there springs the water which serves to slake both our thirst and that of the villagers. It is a seignioral spring, which means that everyone has the right, a right they have possessed for centuries, to all its benefits. It is held by all the villagers in common, as the bread oven used to be. Its flow has never been seen to change or diminish, even by the oldest inhabitants, or by their grandfathers before them. At six in the evening, we go down the hill with our buckets. One of our neighbors, a woman who lives opposite the spring, keeps the rope, also common property, always wet, and glistening like a snake, with a loop at one end that can be passed over the hand and wrist, and terminated at the other by a big, iron snaphook.

The water, set in a shaft at the foot of one of the ruin's great walls, wells up out of the rock about ten feet below ground level and breathes its pure fragrance up into your face. It has grown itself a decorative fringe of toadflax and maidenhair fern which places a crown on the reflection of your head as you lean over. As the bucket is drawn up again, it is resplendent with the faintly blue-tinged limpidity and shimmer of the cold sweet dancing water. The fairy presiding over this spring is wholly good. But the wicked fairy is not far away. She dozes idly, turning yellow when it rains, in the deep recesses of her lair. "But what would happen if the bad water seeped through into the water we drink?" I asked the woman-with-the-rope. It would not have far to go. The woman-with-the-rope looked at me with a shocked expression. "Them's things as can't happen." And she knotted the snake of dripping hemp back around the railing of her porch.

The human hand: powerful, delicate, clumsy, perfectible . . . It is attempting here to relearn what it has forgotten. The women's hands are more successful in this than the men's. The women are discovering that beneath the great display of physical strength usually associated with manual labor, what really counts is skill. Two women, wielding a great double-handed saw, are finding that they can produce their day's output of logs quite quickly. When a man expresses astonishment, they tell him: "There's nothing to it; you always insist on pushing the saw as well as pulling it, so of course you get tired. All it really needs is for both of us to pull in turn." In the heat of the day, a man will chase the flies away by waving his handkerchief, and simply makes himself irritable. One of the young women tore the remains of a wire-netting cover from an old window, cut out a rectangle from it, fixed it to a handle made of thick wire, and in two minutes flat had produced an efficient "anti-fly" weapon, derived from the American fly swatter. Even the felling axe and the hatchet are obeying these same delicate hands. But it is their epiderm that turns traitor on them. It tears like silk, bleeds, swells into blisters; and you may see one of our pioneering women, encircled an instant before by an oblique, blue, whirling blade, suddenly drop her axe, suck at her palm, moan over a splinter, and blench at a tiny cut.

The men, once transplanted into the country, admit their clumsiness and apply themselves with diligence. Humble in the face of necessity, they display patience and astonishment. "What," they cry, "am I capable of nothing more than knotting a necktie, filling a fountain pen, and then emptying it, nibful by nibful, on sheets of paper? To what depths have we sunk?" And in consequence, they regard the expert handyman with unlimited admiration. They become his pupils. They learn how to make a fishing line and how to lay the firewood in a star under the copper; they shell the peas and whistle like little boys let out of school. But why should this gentle way of life, this mutual aid among fellow castaways, become poisoned at certain times? There is nothing to prepare us for the sudden pain of feeling ourselves to be each other's enemies. But this is the inevitable price we pay for living in human society. An unpleasant glance, a false laugh, the terrible desire to wound, to crush another with a few well-chosen words, the horror of being part of a group, the cruelty that prisoners inflict on one another, all these hover over us. They're all going to stop work suddenly; there's going to be a trial, and one of us will be convicted . . . No, there will be no outbreak. But there is something more, something better to be suffered. A girl sits sewing. Without stopping work, she sends a tear that was clinging to her lashes flying over one shoulder with a vehement shake of the head. Young and untamed, on the very point of cursing us she restrains herself, and comes over to rest her head on my shoulder . . . She is inoffensive once more as we gaze at her. Alas, how beautiful she is! Alas, how vain are all her weapons in this place, this crumbling and verdant tomb! . . . Alas, how much rather she would be thrown into the heart of the fire, torn to pieces by love, pierced with his arrows! . . . Once again I am free to love that tanned brow, that hair she hacks off without pity, that mouth she will not allow to complain. And free also to voice in silence the promise for which she yearns: "There, there, you shall feel the flames . . . I promise you."

DC

❧❧ The Occupation

❧ PARIS FROM MY WINDOW: 1940–41

A pink roof, guttered tiles . . .

A pink roof, guttered tiles, what are called roman tiles. A cypress like a rocket, black in the lovely light, and a few willows with big knobbly heads and tender new leaves that the wind combs, blows into streaming locks, parts, then brings together again. Behind the cypress, a little patch of rye sparkles with a green, vernal brightness; and a wide, pale April sky overhead is the crown of this peaceful corner of the universe.

"How do we know that we're in France?" my companion asks. He explains what he means:

"I don't mean in terms of geographical knowledge. I mean, why is there this emotional and disturbing certainty inside us that says: 'This is the beauty that belongs to France, so balanced, so composed that it seems some art has had a part in it . . .'? The solitary cypress tree, the old willows with their fresh leaves, the pink roof, you could find them all tucked away in any little corner of Italy as easily as in the South of France. The dry stones scattered down the hillside might belong to Spain, and as for that wide, vaporous sky, we have seen its bleached suavity before, over Morocco. But bring me here even in my sleep, lay me down, and when I wake up, I shall cry: 'I am in France!' Why?"

I made no reply to my companion, for he is a poet. To a poet, silence is an acceptable response, even a flattering one. The lyric gift itself contains part of the truth. A poet perceives and gives whole-hearted expression to that which our sensibilities, not less lively but less musicianly, keep stored inside. So that when he cries out: "How beautiful it is!" we remain silent, stirred by his words . . . But when the subject in question is France, and the beauties of France, then we all become poets in our different ways; we all sing of her bruises and her diminution, we all lament for her as she lies in her bonds, with her great wound cutting her in two, and her borders gnawed at by the firing guns. Could this feeling of tenderness not have come to us sooner, some might ask. But it is a love that is harbored in the hearts of the French people always, as incurably and as discreetly as the feelings of a woman, too faithful for her own good, exploited by a lover who is sure in advance of every pardon. We were children denied nothing by a country worth all the other countries in the world, and now the portraits painted of it in years gone by can tear our hearts to pieces.

I was brought up in an age when the French, still more or less ignorant of their own country, had not yet begun to travel. When restlessness became the fashion, they left France behind them. Then they returned; and when they wished to describe an Italian lake, a

North African forest, or icebergs swimming like swans upon the sea, they would sit down at the edge of one of those French landscapes whose composition was the work of careful chance and the prevailing climate, rich of earth and subsoil, and whose delicate nuances, harmonious lines, and engaging nobility seduced so many foreigners and made so many passing travelers into inhabitants.

Before the war, the young people of France were accustomed to travel; or let us say rather that they were accustomed to covering great distances, that they knew by heart the stopping places along innumerable itineraries, and that they could reel off the correct numbers for all the national highways. Among these young people so preoccupied with speed there were some, naturally enough, who became attached to the beauties of their own country. It was easy enough to recognize them by the way they slackened their speed, abandoned their preconceived itinerary, sometimes garaged their car in a town, and then set out into the countryside with rucksacks on their backs. Or else they would forget themselves between a hill, a blue-black river, a stretch of flame-colored heath, and you would find them still there a month later . . . The genuine travel lover loves to stop.

I frequently find myself back among the pages of a certain book by Taine: *Voyage aux Pyrénées*. I wonder if the author, in his three hundred pages, covers the daily three hundred and fifty miles regularly devoured by any motorist before the war? I doubt it. But he did discover the universe that lies between Arcachon and Bagnères-de-Bigorre. Better still, he described it in such a way that we, his readers, are able to discover those French peaks with him, their legends, their flora, and their dangers. The true traveler is he who goes on foot, and even then, he sits down a lot of the time.

I have the pleasure of being one of those stay-at-homes who cannot set foot outside their own home without exclamations of wonder. Lazy but farsighted, enamored of church spires ringed with pigeons, of washing sheds on river banks, and shady village squares, I have not, when all is said and done, visited very many places. A stretch of Burgundy, a few cantons in Switzerland, in Savoy, in the

Franche-Comté, Provence, some places and stretches of seashore in Picardy and Brittany, some fiords, Morocco superficially, Algeria in a rush . . . I haven't forgotten much, and I don't greatly desire to see more, for I can still wander to a very limited extent here in France. I know that in France there is no need to arrange in advance how to make my approach to a certain site or a particular prospect. The one always came to me when I was thinking of other things; the other simply fell into my arms. For me the flowers and the springs poured forth, and the old, worn steps of a ruin were covered with birds and children. It has also happened that landscapes I desired to see have been refused me; the Tours de Merles, for example, the chasms of Padirac, Albi, all these have interposed some mischievous accident, a screen, a slight mischance, between themselves and me. What does it matter? Chance took them from me, chance will bring them back. Or provide me with compensations in their stead.

It is providing me with them already: I live in the Palais-Royal. Like many French people who are a little too soft, a little peevish, but capable of spending long hours admiring what they like, the worship I offer to my country is a slow-burning fire deep inside me. We were spoiled when young by the succulence and the grace of the French earth, warm in its every fold from having provided shelter to the human race. At a bend in the road, at the corner of a street, on beaches, or standing on a hill, we were loaded with inestimable gifts in a currency of phosphorescent waves, of apple trees in bloom, of meadowlands, of historic palaces, of fruits from the valley of the Rhône. We did not know that the blows destined to fall one day upon a country so filled with beauty would reverberate through each and every one of us. We know it now. It is with this kind of love as it is with the other: we find out very little about it from the joyful times. We are certain of its presence and its power only when it brings us pain.

DC

Like flies after honey . . .

Like flies after honey they pour in, mass together, and feed
. . . The simile is by no means new, but it is inevitable. Everything about the scene forces it into my mind: the noontide hour and
the splendor of these autumn days, as well as the haste and assiduity
of the open-air readers themselves.

Their place of meeting is old, beautiful, and venerated. There
are too few passers-by to clutter or disguise the lines of this ancient
square which lies adjacent to a famous theater, a garden, and a palace, all of them at one time royal.

The Louvre and its flowerbeds, the rue de Rivoli and its arcades, the Stock Exchange and the Bank all pour out at noon their
diligent and hemmed-in floods of people, all of whom, in less than
two hours, must take their lunch and recreation. Though it certainly
seems to me that they are concerned much more nowadays with the
one at the expense of the other. In the avenue de l'Opéra, another
bookstore receives the same kind of homage, and I am assured that
the treacherous drafts below the Odéon still fail to discourage any
true lover of reading. But here, in my neighborhood, which is also
that of the Comédie-Française, the honey that attracts them, the
books, seem to flow as from a generously yawning sluice, offering
themselves joyfully to avid hands and eyes. The old atlas, engraved
on copper plates, in which wind gods blow their cheeks out by the
islands and dolphins gambol between two continents, lies there op-
pressing Giraudoux and Victor Cherbuliez with its evenly divided
weight. The second-hand books, old before their time, dog-eared and
warm, the thread of their bindings hanging off their backs, are there
for you, for me, for everyone. But leave them, as I do, to those who
will not buy them, those who will read fifty pages today, as many
again tomorrow, and the rest the day after . . .

They are easily recognizable. Most of them are young; they
read standing up and rest as they do so, shifting their weight from

one foot to the other. Bareheaded, boys and girls, they are not yet wearing topcoats or winter jackets; perhaps they won't do so all through the winter . . . For the moment this is no deprivation, because the autumn sun, as it moves gradually around to the south, is warming their shoulders, and because, in addition, they are all holding opened books. Using the convenient height of the outside display shelves as a desk, they turn the pages with one hand and keep the other free, because as they read they are also eating their lunches. I would much rather—such is the extent of our cowardice, our desire to escape what pains us—I would much rather not know that this is how they must eat their hurried, and so frugal, lunch. They too, being proud, would prefer us not to know, for example, that the objects looking like great flutes, which they raise up to their mouths, are in fact small loaves of bread, some filled with meat, some not, and rolled in pieces of paper for disguise. There is also, alas, the meal hidden in the pocket, or in the handbag, from which, as though they were doing it absent-mindedly, they tear off little mouthfuls with two fingers . . .

Standing thus, chained to their dreams, there is a section of French youth that reads passionately. They have always existed, they have always read at bookstore shelves, or along the river embankments, caught beneath the lids of the metal boxes like sparrows in a trap. But I think that in former days they did so with less passion and less determination. To convince myself of the truth of this belief, I have only to read my "letters from strangers" file attentively:

> Mme Colette, I would like to get hold of some books, how can one exchange books? We have a somewhat ill-assorted collection here—travel books, novels, natural-science books—which we have all read and reread, and it's almost impossible to buy new books at the moment . . . Mme, why are there no small circulating libraries these days?

People will perhaps point out to me that these young people of both sexes, so avid for reading matter—that is, borne up by a painful aspiration, a need to escape in spirit toward lighter regions of the mind, to relax from their daily hours of toil—are now at the stage of reading "anything they can lay their hands on." I agree. My own experience assures me that this is true. Where is the harm in that? They are reading and pondering over works of entomology, odd issues of art magazines, a fine old novel by Alphonse Daudet, an incomplete set of medical yearbooks, manuals of practical science, a thick tome on law, or perhaps an eighteenth-century travel book, a miracle of leisureliness, of simplicity, of tender curiosity; they turn the pages of a marvelous *Paris in History*, raise their eyes, and are amazed to recognize what they have just seen on every side of them . . . They are making contact with a past which, in their ignorance, they had been rejecting, with a capital city where they were born and at which they had not even been looking; they are being moved by the thought that it could have perished without their having truly loved it . . .

So let them continue to read whatever they can lay their hands on. That is what I did when I was young. I was let loose upon a library, and everything in it became grist to my mill, though you would have found nothing there that could be called suitable for a girl of six, or ten, or even fourteen . . . Forbidden books, books that were too serious, and books that were too frivolous as well, rather boring books, dazzling books, suddenly lighting up at random and closing their temple doors behind a spellbound child . . . A disorder in reading is noble in itself. Each book, incompletely annexed at first, eventually becomes a conquest. Its jungle of ideas and words must open, in the end, upon an ordered and friendly landscape.

DC

Every morning . . .

Every morning, I see them hurrying their various ways, the men to work, the women toward their problematic shopping. It is still so dark, it is still so scarcely morning when the six official chimes ring out from the Bibliothèque Nationale at four o'clock, that there is a constant display of flashlight beams that leap out through the dark like signals from tiny lighthouses. "But since you get back in the afternoon what you lose in the morning . . ." We know that, but it is colder at four in the morning than it is at six. The first few hours of the working day are dark. And all living creatures, since they all have the instinct for hibernation still within them, have difficulty in shaking the numbness from their limbs before day breaks.

Man experiences the night in the same way as a plant. All birds do not rise early. We know there are some flowers that bloom only at night. Between midnight and three in the morning the white sand lily effects a complete physical transformation, stretching its petals wide, stiffening its stamens into claws, and casting its nets of scent into the surrounding dark. The human species, too, abounds in nightwalkers whose pleasures lead them to delay the hour at which they will retire, but even they feel no instinct inciting them to leave their beds in the middle of the night. The daily effort demanded from workers of both sexes by this extra daylight-saving hour is quite considerable. Let us hope it will not last all winter.

Even children refuse to make up in the evening the two hours they are being cheated of in the morning. As with the birds, as with livestock on a farm, that tutelary syncope we call sleep refuses to bow to our human decisions and descends on our children again when they are already up, dressed and washed. Heads drooping, they return to their unfinished dreams and curl up again in the way of children, a way which is also, toward the end of the night, the way of the cat coiled into a turban, of the pigeon sunk into its own breast, of the curling bracken frond, of the delicate anemone petal closed against the chill of dawn.

Since I myself have passed the age of long sleeps and regular working hours, I sometimes find myself watching as the little flashlights flicker in the distance between six and seven in the morning. They move swiftly, without stopping, growing larger; some of them, as they arrive level with the Stock Exchange, decide to turn down the rue du Quatre-Septembre; others fork off along the rue des Petits-

Champs. The rest plunge beneath the arches of the Palais-Royal. Their rounds of brightness, directed down onto the sidewalk, ring the feet of the torch bearer with a halo of light. So many transparent stockings, so many open-toed, high-heeled shoes! . . . The silk stockings and the slim-soled shoes betray the women's stubborn determination not to abandon their costly, unreasonable, unseasonable fashions.

I date from an era far enough in the past to have known, in my childhood, several old, well-off, middle-class women, or provincial ladies of the manor whom their advancing years had fixed once and for all by their firesides, like a great armchair, or like a pair of andirons. When my mother called, they used to display the relics of their youth to her: a sprigged frock, a veil of malines lace, a counterpane pierced with innumerable hemstitched holes and incrusted with lace; a nightgown worn on a wedding night, stockings donned for long-past cotillions. "Feel the weight of them!" they would say with pride. And so saying, they laid in Sido's hands two silk stockings as heavy and as cold as a pair of little snakes.

Whether natural silk or not, a pair of stockings today is composed of no more than eight to ten grams of thread. A frail protection against frost, against rain and tempest, against Métro stairs and thin-soled shoes, a mere ten grams of thread! But the disconcerting thing is that these women go on putting up with such things and won't give in, except for the wealthy, or the reasonable ones, who wear woolen stockings. But even they pay dearly for this privilege, since it does not automatically bring with it the further privilege of owning the proper shoes to complement their thick hose.

"Ever since I began wearing these lovely, thick, warm stockings," one of my illogical acquaintances confided in me, "I've been getting chilblains! Can you understand it?"

And she showed me the chilblains caused by the pressure of her shoes, the chilblain running in a little roll around the tendon above her heel—the worst—and the string of chilblains all across her poor, hunched-up toes.

Several women, unmarried working girls and widows without children, have asked me to suggest a way of employing their days off.

"Deliver us," one wrote to me, "from the house 'scrubbed from top to bottom' and from the movies! Do people think that our tiny apartments need such a great deal of attention, or that we do nothing to them in the week? And going out just constitutes an extra fatigue . . ."

I am very much afraid that my young, tired working girls are going to make nasty faces at the piece of advice I am going to give them. But the winter cold, the animal law that slows down our lives in the cold months, thrift, and the interests of their health are all at the moment on my side when I say to them: sleep. The country is a long way away, the daylight hours are short. Are you one of those lucky ones—or bitter ones—who live on your own? Then sleep. Once the Saturday meal—or the Sunday meal—and your household chores are over and done with, sleep. With a hot-water bottle at your feet and the window half opened on the dry cold or the steely downpour outside, let yourself go . . .

The worst that can happen is that you won't wake up again until the following morning (all the better for your ration coupons) at your usual hour, feeling relaxed, a little lost, light of body, and then you can stretch until your joints crack, and cry out, as I once heard a little girl of my acquaintance do: "I grew an incalculable amount last night!"

I am writing in the heart of a darkened dawn. It is seven o'clock in the morning if I am to believe my clock—but I don't believe it. The little flashlight beams are crisscrossing outside in the street. A parasol of light is moving toward me, its double handle suddenly revealing itself as two slender legs terminating in two open, pointed shoes. At what time did they get up, those graceful legs? On which day will they rest? They climb the steps up into the Passage du Perron with such nimble lightness! Be of good heart! The time of day is so ambiguous that I hesitate, up above in my window, whether I should bid them good morning or good night . . .

DC

"I'd like to see you in my place!"

"I'd like to see you in my place!" writes one of my readers. She is a woman encumbered with two young children, a boy seven and another nine, who are confined to the house by the bad weather and deprived of their open-air games.

Madame, and dear reader, I would very much like to see myself in your place too, first of all because I would then be only a very little more than thirty, but also for another reason . . . There is a certain melancholy in having to tell oneself that one has said goodbye—unless of course one is a grandmother—to the age and the circumstances that enable one to observe young children closely and passionately. It is a kind of study that I have enjoyed very much in my time.

There you are then, and you are by no means alone in this predicament, saddled with two little boys who are buzzing at the windows like captive bees and demanding to be set at liberty. Paris is not a city for children, and even less so this winter than during other winters. I suspect you of being a mother at once young, tender, and gay, a rather weak mother who allows herself to be ruled quite often by her nerves. If I risk explaining to you my personal ideas on how to bring up children, it is possible that you will think me a child torturer. But I have not relinquished those ideas. I persist in believing that the happiness of one does not necessarily mean the unhappiness of another, and that although the child has its rights, the parent has his or her rights too: the right to rest, the right to silence at certain hours of the day, the right to work undisturbed.

I also cling stubbornly to my belief that a child can grow and prosper without yelling all the time, and that tears—provided the child is not sick—are simply a bad habit and proof of a bad upbringing. I maintain that there is nothing inhuman in depriving city children of toys such as the drum, the rattle, the trumpet, and the whistle; that savage whoops and yells of all kinds do not constitute a necessary exercise for the respiratory tracts, and that the vetoing of wheeled toys unless they have rubber tires does not necessarily produce rickets or chronic depression in a child. Already, madame, you can see what a pitiless kind of mother you have to deal with.

My principal victim, a little girl, was always bursting with health, and even beauty, despite my ill treatment. Having been made aware at a very early age of my insensitivity on certain points, she very quickly accepted the agreement, which, I would like to point out, we also make with animals living in an apartment: be as wild as you like outside the house, as long as you behave sensibly inside it. Though it may not be very difficult for a mother to establish her authority, it is less easy to consolidate it, for a child, with its fresh and subtle instincts and its various cunning, is constantly on the watch for opportunities to undermine it. It is up to us—I have already suggested that we treat them as so many enemies—to outwit them. Though shaking the floorboards like thunder may be an entertaining diversion, walking on tiptoe can be another, suggested by us, and quite as amusing.

Have you acquired the habit, madame, of saying no to your sons with a smile, and then making sure that that no is as unshakable as it is pleasant? Yes? So much the better. You have gained a great deal of time and spared yourself a great many painful words. An old English nanny, from whom I learned a lot, used to say in her pidgin French: "If I take a dog, or a very young child for their education, it's the same thing with both. The first two days and the first two nights are bound to be a hell, but you must not give in. After that, everything goes all right, because both the baby and the little dog have made up their minds about you by then."

You tell me that your boys are "intelligent and difficult to manage." These two adjectives seem to me almost irreconcilable; the intelligent child is the one most easily won over of all. Are you sure you appeal to them often enough? That you appeal above all to their capacity for comprehension? Are you one of these reprehensible parents who prefer vetoes to explanations, scoldings to warnings? I very much hope not. Are you of the "Don't-touch-it" school? Do you include the effects of innocent clumsiness on your list of childish crimes? If not, then I am very relieved, for I was subjected, very early, to the contrary course of instruction, the guiding principle of which is: "Touch this." It is a system of education that can never be forgotten, and one that I tried to pass on to my beloved "victim," though doubtless in less masterly a fashion than it had been taught to me . . .

"Touch what you please . . . which is to say: enter into contact with everything around you. Touch, beneath the cat's fur, the violent movements of its little ones trying to be born. Hold the little yellow chick in your hand, and don't hurt it. You want to drink out of the beautiful Chinese cup? Drink then. But if you break it, you will be deprived, forever, of the pleasure of drinking from it. Take care: the wasp has a sting. But when all is said and done, whether you get yourself stung or not is your own affair. Knives cut, pliers pinch. Yet another reason for learning how to put both to their proper use . . . Do you see? You are bleeding. Next time you'll handle it better; my advice is to try again, to touch it again . . ."

Nor have I ever been afraid, madame, and dear reader, that a child was too young to understand me. For from its earliest years any child is capable of thinking us childish. On a beach once, in Provence, I knew a young mother completely unable to cope with, and completely controlled by, two little boys—one seven, one eight—who were so good-looking, so strong, and so full at that early age of virile majesty that I nicknamed them "the supermen." Like many children, they had hacked out in the bosom of their family a retired, tranquil, impregnable existence, like two explorers on an island. There were frequent allusions, in their conversations with each other, to a certain person whom they always referred to as "the little girl."

"We'll go to Pampelonne on Sunday," the elder would say.

"With the little girl?" his brother would ask.

"I'd rather go without the little girl. She'll want to take so many things along with her, the way she always does . . ."

"And anyway, she'll be late . . ."

"We'll go without the little girl. We won't tell her we're going."

And their mother searched among the many children on the beach to try to discover which little girl it was for whom her pair of supermen had conceived this deep but somewhat severe affection. She searched, and was not a little crestfallen, as they say, when she discovered that "the little girl" was none other than herself . . .

DC

A dry spring . . .

A dry spring is bringing desolation to still another year. The short wheat stalks will provide us with neither straw nor proper grain. In vain, their feathers dulled, the pigeons stretch out one wing, and then the other, imploring the benison of rain. We shall have no fruit in June, or in July. We shall not have . . . The list of those things that will be refused us would be a long one.

Beneath my window, each at his own hour, my familiar neighbors move past in procession. In four years, some of them have been transformed from passers-by into my friends: in other words, the war and my own immobility have not deprived me of everything. But there are others who no longer pass by, who will never pass by again. Among those who are determined to go on living, many spend their time in remaining recognizable. It is an admissible activity to one who is growing old at the heart of so long an agony. What else am I doing myself? There is the will to hold ourselves straight, not to permit the formation, just below the neck, of the "camel's hump," that bolster of flesh that pushes forward the head and neck and drags down the shoulders . . .

"Hold yourself straight, my girl," said the slender-waisted mothers to their daughters in other days.

Their granddaughters, these days, curve their backs and hollow their stomachs. Mauriac assures us that in old age the women who once wore those cruel armatures of whalebone and stays can always be recognized by the inalienable liveliness of their carriage . . .

"Ah!" cried one of these pleasant women, sometimes so old, sometimes rather young, "I've had enough! If only the war would end, I could get on with it to my heart's content!"

"On with what, my dear?"

"Growing old, of course! But while the war's still on, I daren't. I'd be too ashamed."

And she described to me with anticipation and delight the white hair she would have, the fine, wrinkled, unpowdered skin she would have, the comfortable dresses she would wear, and all her carefree life to come . . .

"A year in wartime," she said, "seems as though it will never end. Two years of war, that's a very long time. Three years, four years . . . one lives through them. But only at the price of acquiring a sort of art of passivity. And during all that time there is still, on top of everything, the business of not deteriorating physically . . . I'm very tired."

As I listened to her, I searched her outward appearance for the person she used to be, the champion of feminine activity that she was between 1914 and 1918. What magnificent stand-ins she provided for us during the Great War! In factories and offices, in hospitals and business houses, those women and their initiative sometimes went far beyond what we could have expected of them. The war lent them virility, clothed them in the girt-up tunic of Éliacin, cropped their heads into banister knobs, slicked them down into Argentinian dancers.

One of the singular things about the present war is the exclusively, the dangerously feminine appearance it is imposing on women. Is it because of the total occupation of our territory, because of the omnipresence of a foreign and virile horde, that our women are assuming the outward aspect of urchins and the behavior of schoolgirls? I bring no accusations against any of their hidden thoughts, knowing as I do full well that they never display the best part of themselves. But the scattered profusion of their hair, the indiscretion of their curls, the insufficient length of their skirts, together with a width that allows free play to wind and gaze, are errors when seen on these women whose natural grace, as they are Frenchwomen, has transformed into so many provocations. One longs to say to these young girls, whatever their ages, disheveled and excessively revealed: "Please! . . . There are other people here . . ."

But then, they are often beautiful, and they take such care of what poor clothes they have. And doubtless they could very well reply to me that spring, no matter how barren it may seem, still brings back the urgent need to flower. They might say that there is some merit in setting off their beauty, in improving on it in a hundred little ways, and that to adorn it, barbaric though the setting may seem to be, is to await, and even to honor in advance, the coming peace . . .

DC

❦❦❦

Three letters

[December 21, 1941]

It is already ten days since they took Maurice away at six-thirty, when it was still pitch dark. At least I have been able to find out that he is in Compiègne . . . All communication is *impossible*. I am waiting. I've had a few good words. That's all.

[December 23, 1941]

No more news of Maurice except what I was given over the telephone by someone who'd been moved out. Morale is excellent. 36 in a room. Food less disgusting than we feared. The prisoners all do their best to help one another. Straw on the floor to sleep on. I just wait. It's the most difficult part.

[*February 13, 1942*]

If I haven't written to you before, it was because for the last eight weeks I have been carrying something far too heavy inside me, my Marguerite. Maurice, who's been "away" since December 12, has just been given back to me. I didn't want to tell you about it, what was the good of loading you with an extra worry? There was always a great, hopeful obstinacy in my heart of hearts. At the moment I am allowing myself the luxury of being very tired. But there are two of us once more to send you our kisses. Always your *Colette*

DC

Fifteen hundred days: liberation, August 1944

Fifteen hundred days. A thousand days, and then more than five hundred on top of that. As many days and nights as it takes a baby to be born, to grow, to start talking, and to become an intelligent and delightful human being; enough days for other human beings, completed and flourishing, to go down in terrifying numbers to their deaths. After fifteen hundred days of war and oppression, of organized destruction, does a people not abandon everything, even its hope? The French people astonished its torturers, and survived the demoniacal caprices with which they thought to display their sense of humor.

I have my humble place among those who did nothing except wait. When it must prolong itself for four whole years, such waiting encounters opportunities of raising itself just a little above the level of a mere exercise in passivity. If nothing was able to make me leave this place, to make me sleep one night elsewhere, to banish me for even twenty-four hours, it is because my sufferings and felicities were better borne here than in any other place in the world. Sustained by a hunted companion, then deprived of that same companion when he was imprisoned, I squeezed myself up against the host of other women who were waiting. To wait in Paris meant to drink from the spring itself, however bitter. Perhaps a woman who was born in the provinces draws a particular kind of faith from Paris, in the light of which it is easier for her to bear the threat of foreigners, to receive and to transmit the imponderables of a beleaguered capital, to adapt herself to the nighttime raids, to assimilate an atmosphere loaded down with war, blackened and made fetid by the war, to admire the children, to admire the men and women of Paris, gazing with mockery at the crude propaganda slogans on the posters . . .

Their virtues and their defiant bravery kept these incorruptible city dwellers on their feet; meanwhile, winter followed winter, and the dismal summers charred our arbors as early as July. After which there came a time when a light began to break in people's hearts, and in the air there trembled some great news. When we strained our ears, was that not the even-tenored, stifled thunder that the earth gives out when it is shaken by a great advance? No. We had not yet progressed beyond those troubled days of contradictory reports, of radio broadcasts listened to in secret, of whispered denials. But Paris was already packed with hidden men, with invisible allies, with enemies wilted by long, wakeful nights who no longer had the time to sleep, while across the camouflage of their great trucks our shattered forests were casting their deep shade . . .

Then the voices, our own, grew louder, shouting out the names that the days before were only whispers: Leclerc and Koenig . . . And in the final hours, the great leaders lost their names entirely and were called, simply and gloriously, "they."

"*They* have reached Anthony! . . . *They* have taken the hills at Châtillon . . . No, *they* are still fighting . . . *They* are repairing the road to get the tanks through . . . *They* are coming . . . *They* are here . . ."

At all the windows, threadbare and badly dyed, cut out and sewn together in advance, in darkness and in danger, the flags wave like foliage along the rue Vivienne . . . That is as far as I shall see, because of my leg. But when the night rose like a dawn, a glow in the East shone over the Hôtel de Ville, over its lights, the crowd, the armies, the new color of the soldiers' clothes . . .

How strange a thing it is, how poignant, a street that is laughing and dancing, and crying at the same time! Paris has not laughed or wept publicly, freely, for so long . . .

The gun saluted, the sound of the bells flew up over the darkened garden, whose windows, once blinded every evening, opened both their lids and poured light into the space between. All the windows were singing the *Marseillaise,* all the windows, opened wide, were stretching black arms out against a backdrop of gold . . . A celebration, but a discreet one, for all the voices were husky with love . . .

Happy those who did not restrain their frenzy on that night! Happy those who wept, who laughed, who cheered, who waved their arms, who embraced strangers in the street, who took each other's arms, walking at random forward into the night, dancing, carrying lights, waving flags with horizontal bands of red and white and blue, with stars, with upright and diagonal crosses . . . Happy all those who cast off their chains, children, white-haired elders, and girls with blond curls, all those whom an order had at last hurled forth into this great celebration, drunk without wine, hurling themselves upon their saviors as they wound along the streets! Happy all those who were beside themselves!

What calm . . . Were it not for the printer who likes to work at night, printing away on the first floor, the nights would be even more calm than the days. During the time when all the shooting was at night, this was until quite recently—the snipers up on the roofs would never give up, running all around the courtyard and interspersing their shots with warning cries: "Don't shoot, it's me!" "Shoot now, I can see him, against that pillar!" "Look out, be careful, he's behind the chimney!" These "helmet hunters" were not always, alas, the heroes they should have been. One of them, who used to plug away calmly along the rue Vivienne, had 1,100,000 francs on him when he was caught . . .

The shots, echoing and reechoing from wall to wall across the garden, provided a rather theatrical display. The most difficult part was always keeping a little way away from our windows. The average inhabitant of the Palais-Royal tends to spend some of his time leaning out of his open window, or at the door of his shop. My exhausted traveler, who used to sleep sometimes here, sometimes there, like a chimney swallow, insisted I swear a solemn oath never to lean out to watch the shooting at night. "These fellows are dangerous," he told me, "they're such bad shots."

In the evening he would move on from attic to attic, either in our neighborhood or around the Place de l'Étoile.

For eighteen months altogether, he experienced in such places the discomfort of extreme heat and numbing cold, setting both, with secret delight, against his memories of the internment camp, and always resisting the friendly temptations offered him by the Palais-Royal.

"Do you know how to climb down a knotted rope?" Mme X., the owner of the bookstore, asked him once point-blank. "If you're caught here, it's quite simple, you tie a knotted rope to your window frame, you climb down, and there you are in front of my shop door, which I shall leave ajar. I've put a cushion and a little lamp behind the big Gustave Dorés for you . . . But don't let the cat get out."

Another neighbor, the one who with her needle picks out on pieces of canvas the blue ribbons and the bunches of roses that pay no heed to any war, came up with her mouselike tread to hand my nightly fugitive, with fewer words, a key.

"It's the one to the back door of my shop," she said. "It's best that you should have it with you all the time, monsieur."

It was at that time, more or less, that we used to be visited by a series of almost elegiac Germans, lovers of art and beauty, who came in and wandered around our garden. One of them, a plump and tightly belted fellow, Commandant Lust or Lutz by name, was always trying to strike up an acquaintance with the tradespeople in their glass-fronted cages where trade is always half asleep, always dozing off, scarcely awake even at those hours when the Banque de France is buzzing with people . . .

"I love," Commandant Lust or Lutz stated in good French, "only three things in the world: birds of paradise, novels about love, and works of art."

As to the novels about love, his purchases in that field were volumes with titles such as *Spurs and Riding Crops, Flagellation, The Empress in Shiny Leather,* and other high-class works of that kind.

He would always insist, with a stubbornness that she found it hard to bear, on coming into the shop of my rose-and-ribbon lady, who also sells antiques. It was all she could manage to hide her claws, perpetually ready to strike, beneath a cloak of extremely impertinent politeness. As soon as she heard the step of this art-and-bird lover ringing out beneath the empty arcades, she would flush with irritation. One day I was in there gossiping with her when she heard her enemy approaching. She leaped to her feet and began doing something to the spring lock on her door, one of those cumbrous objects bequeathed to us by successive revolutions, which are partly boomerang, partly truncheon, and partly adze. I saw that my lady of the embroidery was unscrewing it, then replacing it, unscrewed, on its shaft.

The voluminous Lust or Lutz darkened the tiny shop with his square body, made a stiff gesture of greeting, and proceeded to inquire about every object in the place. My neighbor, suddenly very voluble, was as quick to stifle the words on his lips as she was to snatch her wares from his fingers.

"The candlestick? I've just sold it, monsieur, just a moment ago, there! I'll just take the ticket off . . . The little chair? Oh, monsieur, it's not genuine, you know: just a poor imitation, no connoisseur would ever be taken in by it. I'm sorry, monsieur, the opaline lamp isn't for sale; it was just brought in by a customer to be repaired . . ."

She fluttered around him like a tomtit driving off a pillaging jay. He gave up, turned heavily and politely toward the door, and was obliged to open it himself. To this end he seized hold of the spring lock—one half of which remained in his fist, while the other half went bouncing away under the arches.

The object, gripped in his German soldier's hand, looked suitably like a weapon, and standing there stiffly in front of my tiny neighbor he looked as though he had come there to smash in her skull.

"Oh, it's broken . . ." he murmured in confusion. "I'm sorry . . ."

My neighbor was suddenly all smiles.

"Yes, monsieur, you've broken it. Don't apologize, monsieur, it's really not worth it. No, no, monsieur, we can get it repaired ourselves . . . We'll just have it repaired . . . at the same time as all the other things. Goodbye, monsieur."

Right up till the end of the war, my angry little tomtit's attitude remained the same. And so did that of the other sparrows who led their sedentary existence in the Palais-Royal. They are miraculous in their lack of caution, cheeky, scornful, always ready to defend their miserable "rights"; yet they never forgot during the war the wisdom of gulling their victors, or lost their instinct for it.

This royal palace during the Occupation was the domain of thin-lipped, adventuresome old men, of mocking children, of shopkeepers without stock, of sneering adolescent girls, of all the pure Parisian types which the occupying forces never understood the first thing about.

DC

Who would not have offered his cellar, his house, his bed? One Jew who is dear to me—the services he rendered in the 1914–18 war did not prevent them from sending him to the camp at Compiègne—had the following offer made to him by a woman who lives up in one of the attic apartments: "If they come to take you back again, run into my room, because it isn't bolted, and then quick, no hesitation, no silliness about it, hop under the bedclothes with me!

You can rest assured they won't think of looking for you there!"

This warm and tacit agreement lasted as long as it was needed. Very few of the occupiers came in to trample our royal garden. Sometimes there was an occasional squad with nothing better to do, walking around with a civilian guide muttering an educational commentary: "This was the cradle of the French Revolution . . ." Sometimes there were pairs—one green soldier, one gray mouse— who sat on the benches conversing in gestures. The few that came in on their own, through the arch from the Place du Théâtre-Français, would idle along, dragging their great boots behind them, in front of the little meditating shops, and lose no time in leaving again through the Passage du Perron. "Melancholisch . . ." The unanimous refusal emanating from every stone, from every passer-by, from every woman sitting by her baby carriage forced them out again. An intense, compact refusal, a blind and deaf refusal, and dumb as well. A refusal to notice the presence of the invader, to read Paul Chack's poster or any of the other degrading placards they put up, a mental regurgitation rejecting the propaganda hammered out by the newspapers and the radio . . . A refusal to smile, to be seduced, to be terrorized. Not to be wooed, not to be broken into by foreigners, not to be intimidated by violence, Paris refused everything they tried. Let us now caress with happy hands its still gaping gashes, its shattered columns, and its crushed flagstones: these wounds apart, it has emerged from the ordeal intact.

DC

But I feel no love for anything that those years of war bequeathed to me. Not even that painfully preserved passivity, less of which was consumed in deceiving the occupier than in inspiring optimism in the occupied, for optimism is a matter of contagion. Dark, dark, a deep well of dissimulation, raging inside, hidden behind a smiling mask, dry-eyed, I yearned, as we all did, for the return of a time before the war which we had thought of as scarcely passable before experiencing the years that followed it. Among other earthly advantages, I longed for the license it would bring me to explore my sadness. "Oh, when everything is all right again, I'll have my fill, I'll drown myself in tears . . ." One says that at the time.

DC

🌿 The Evening Star

"I'm going out"

"I'm going out."
"In this weather! I pity you."
"Are you all right? Are you expecting anyone?"
"No, no one."

The truth of my answer is relative. But after all, I could scarcely admit to my best friend that I'm waiting for the spring. What is there for me to wait for, if not the spring? I am one of its creditors this year. It still owes me that second helping in the autumn that we didn't have, the sudden attack of fever that relights the candelabra on the chestnut trees, forces the lilacs out in mid-October, and draws unexpected leaves from the denuded branches, that crisis in fact to which we give the name St. Martin's summer. For no one thinks of calling what is springlike "spring" twice in one year.

This feeling of expectation applies only to the spring. Before it, and after it, we anticipate the harvest, we take the ripening of the grapes for granted, and we hope that winter will one day thaw. Summer forces itself upon us, we do not wait for it; and the winter we dread. For spring alone we become like the bird behind its screen of tile, like the stag when on a certain night it breathes, deep in the winter forest, the unexpected mist warmed by the approach of a new year. A deep and yearly credulity takes hold on all the world, freeing the voice of the bird and the flight of the bee too soon. For a few hours—and then we fall back into the common wretchedness of enduring winter, and waiting for the spring . . .

"It's freezing in here, Pauline!"

"Of course it is, madame. It's to be expected, we can't be in the middle of spring just like that."

. . . Which never comes when we expect it to. It comes—as we said when we were children—in a big carriage, that is, it rolls in, breaks its way in, on a thundering chariot lashed at by the huge zigzags of the lightning. Another year, before the dawn, it lays big panes of glass on everything; on the chickens' water trough, on buckets of water, even on the footprints of the cattle at the edges of the pond. As soon as the sun touches them they shiver into slender, tinkling slivers of ice, and the frost, just as we had decided to entrust our names to it, scrawled with a fingertip, the frost vanished away like misty breath from a mirror.

Or else, as on my last wedding day, the spring will erase in a single morning all the good work done by an April already far advanced, filling the sky with gray flock that untangles into snow like a burst eiderdown. And it wasn't even cold that morning either; oh, how soft and white that snow was! It clung to the yellow catkins on the hazel bushes and fell so thickly that I begged my old friend, the new bridegroom, to stop the car so that I could listen to the whispering of the snow on its bed of dead leaves. It makes such a gentle murmur, it almost seems to be speaking. I have tried to describe it more than once. If I compare it to the whispered orisons of a praying crowd I shall fail yet again, especially if I forget to mention that it is accompanied by another sound that underlines it, a rustling as of silky pages leafed through with diligence. Beautiful April snow . . . The wild honeysuckles in the Vaux-des-Cernay held it balanced in tiny piles on their tiny, new ears, and the impetuous torrents streaming from the springs were all a serpentine and glistening blue.

Nor did the menu of our wedding breakfast give the lie to that wintry interlude of spring. It included some small and melting hams cooked in a casserole, garnished with pink bacon and their own rind, bathed in their own stock, which was scented slightly with celery, slightly with nutmeg, slightly with horse-radish and slightly too with every healthy vegetable fit to be the aromatic servitor of such a mistress as that meat. We had crêpes too . . . Can one be married without champagne? Yes, if champagne is erased from the mind by one of those chance meetings that brighten our French inns with their golden light, in this case with a wine from an anonymous vineyard, dark and gilded like some Spanish reliquary, which matched the ham and the cheeses blow for blow . . .

"Here I am back again. What weather! Are you all right?"

"Perfectly, thank you."

"You're not working, I hope?"

"May God forbid! Quite the contrary: I'm playing."

. . . Another time the spring will make one think of a submerged rose. It glows beneath the water, all made of gaily sparkling showers and mosses grown in the space of a few hours. Like a green fingernail at the end of a twig, endlessly there drips a drop of rain, another drop, always another drop, falling to swell the song of the tiny, subterranean waterfalls. The embryos of the seeds are full of juice, the grass is lush, the bark is splitting, and syrupy clay betrays the unwary foot. But a hidden glow clings to each fold of the brimming waters, the water flag is about to unsheathe itself, and the rain is warm. In the dusk, the stream smokes like a bonfire of dead leaves . . .

A first coat of green foam spreads over the surface of the tree trunks that face northeast, and in our grates the fire sweats, dribbles, and splutters in protest. Insidiously, a smell creeps up from the cellar and reaches the first floor . . . "What is it that's smelling like that?" The thing that's smelling like that is a full barrel changing its nature under the influence of this damp, moldy spring and turning from wine into vinegar. The barrel is delivered, too late, of an enormous "mother," a sort of horrible squidlike mass, purplish and gelatinous . . .

A terrible clamor from the housewives: "The cider is all dead!" They emerge from the stillroom, all in mourning for their cider, each brandishing a pitcherful of a liquid as dark and muddy as old beer, from which all the virtue has departed.

Everything smells sharp and sour, like gherkins that have stood too long, like crushed apple pulp, like sugarbeets in a silo . . . It is your smell, rotting spring! And yet if only the sun and the wind would change their minds, you are still the muddy and fertile path, the acid gully that can lead us to the best part of the year: there is just time to freeze up all these dripping molds, to serve one last little dessert of April rain on the traylike flower of the laurustine, and the torrid spring will hurl itself with violence onto a budding world.

This is the most difficult part to evoke. I take hold of it by a bud, by a spiraling shoot, a vigurnum sprout, and I pull it toward me, very gently . . . The silence and the heat hold sway over the naked fields. A world of weak and various creatures is dragging itself across them, fluttering, falling back to earth. Feeble legs and claws are groping and limping, bellies squirm; everywhere there are insects succumbing on the brink of life, a milky grub pours out its white blood, a chrysalis explodes like a pod. A massacre is about to take place in the dark dungeons of the subsoil. In front of the perfected creature a door was about to open and has not opened. Will the fury of its death surpass the fury of its birth?

Now it is a burned-up spring, shortening the blades of the grass, the spears of the wheat. East wind, no dew, the rosebush is losing its unopened buds, the cherry tree its wrinkled fruit, the young garlic and the sensitive shallot are swooning away—have mercy on the winged pea flower as it prays for the rain to turn it into a pod . . .

Over the vehemence of this spring season I superimpose also the idea of love, if only to remind myself of that hard core of self-interest behind the lover's view of things, the little pink snout of love, its secret barracks-room language—for what modest young girl, possessed by love, does not blast her rival secretly by calling her a foul-faced bitch and a stupid cow? . . . It is strange that this sort of spring should still have its place among my mysterious old woman's recreations.

"What are you looking at?"

"The American airplanes going by. A flight of fishes in the falling dusk . . . They swim into the rain clouds like a stickle back into his downy nest . . ."

For it is always wise to dissemble. To confess that one is entirely occupied with one's memories might well be wounding to some innocent soul. And how could I make this innocent questioning me now believe that though I am more than seventy years old I am even now looking back with regret, and with such stubborn strength and refusal to submit, to a season of the year, to a bush, to a sky, to a landscape, to all my boundless and inalienable possessions? We must retire then, my dead springtimes and I, behind the blown-up foregrounds of my pretended turbulence, and then creep into the shelter of my real patience.

"But the pain in your leg is no worse?"

"Not in the slightest. I'm thinking!"

I'm thinking. Already something of an admission, but it is said with enough comic emphasis to reassure the person who is worried about me. Should I really give the name of thought to a walk, to a sort of contemplation without goal or specific reasons, to a sort of virtuoso playing upon memory that I am alone in not condemning as vain? I set off, I plunge off down a once familiar path at the pace I walked along it then; I aim for a big, crooked oak, for the poor farm where the cider and the bread spread with butter were doled out to me with such a generous hand. Here is the fork in the yellow path, the creamy umbrellas of the elder bushes so thickly surrounded by bees that their noise, like a threshing machine, can be heard twenty paces away . . . I can hear the sobbing of the guinea hens, the snorting of the sow . . . That's what it amounts to, my method of working. Then, quite suddenly, a hole in the mind, the void, everything ceasing to exist—a perfect resemblance, it flashes through my mind, to what the beginning of death must be like. One's way lost, barred, erased . . . It does not matter: I shall have had a good time on the journey . . .

I don't always have a good time. I can spend a whole night

pursuing a scrap of memory, a name, a word, things not even useful to me in my work. A sport, a challenge. Do other unfortunates, other writers, set out on similar hunts? The object of my pursuit leads me through the roughest country, it is as cunning as a quarry that has been stalked ten times already. Sometimes, so that it will allow me to catch up with it, I find myself trying to sing it, as well as its mistily perceived homonyms, trying to catch its half-heard rhythm. If it falls asleep, I sleep too. My slumber renders it incautious, and in the morning I am able to capture it as it lies in an unsuspecting doze. I wake up before it and leap upon it . . . I would like very much, for example, to recall the name of the traveler who assured me that in Martinique—perhaps it wasn't Martinique, though—at about the time of the feast of St. John—but it may well have been some other saint—the ground is completely covered in the space of a single day—or rather, in a night of frenzy—with pink flowers. You can see that not only do I hesitate as to the place, the date, and the time of day, I don't even know the name of the flowers. What do I mean, of the flowers? Of *the* flower. A single flower, a coating, an unbroken layer of flowers, each inch of the ground an open flower's mouth . . .

"I've ordered that book you wanted, but it won't be here till tomorrow. Did you count on having it today?"

Not at all, my dearest friend. And yet I shall allow you to think I did. At this time of day I make only unavoidable appointments. According to whether my bed, which follows me as faithfully as its shell does the snail, occupies one or another of the window bays, commands a view of the south or of the east, I perceive or do not perceive certain stars that a nephew of mine, familiar with the sky of the astronomers, knows all about. When the stars he has taught me by name are inaccessible to my view, I invent them and nail them up where they are not. To one who scarcely ever moves at all, it is simple, with head comfortably leaning back, to rearrange the firmament and its strict rule.

"We can't see the Great Bear from here," one of my neighbors once remarked.

In exactly the same pinched tones, she also says: "We are at a great disadvantage in this district insofar as the sale of fish is concerned."

The tiny, pointed lights of the distant stars, panic-struck and lost when a cloud draws its smoke in front of them; the spacious palpitations of the planets; the whole turning sky . . . I can't see the great planet Venus with her humid brilliance. This nephew of mine has explained to me why she is so often inaccessible to view. But I only like to remember the sort of things about her that please the ignorant. For example, that she had already begun deceiving the men who raised their eyes to her in ancient times, because they did not know that their Venus of the evening was also Lucifer, the sparkling morning star . . . Or that we say: "Venus is rising," just when she is about to set . . . With this planet's third name, Vesper, I associate, to it I harness my own decline. In earlier days it poured its splendor on my childhood, seeming to rise out of the wood at Moûtiers, from the heart of a fading and contented sunset. My father would raise his finger, speak its name: "Vesper!," and recite some poetry. Then he would plant his feeble little telescope on its tripod and aim it at the stars . . .

We shall soon reach the season for sleeping out of doors, that is, for fitting my bed into the frame of the open window. If it were not closed at night, you would be able to look up from the garden below and see my hair through the balusters, like a badly built nest. That in it I am able to sleep outdoors is one of the charms of this apartment. Big raindrops come rushing up from the south, the wind changes direction and scatters papers about, a night bird cries. Everything penetrates into the open room and wanders there, everything that the nights lavish upon the light-filled sky, the elastic moon, the dawn, the lightning flash, and the stars—all save the great planet which crosses the skies of Paris invisible, dimmed by the sun and submerging itself almost at the same time as he. To Vesper with the triple name, the handmaiden of the sun, I dedicate my own vespers and I read her celestial adventures across the night.

"After every eight-year period, Venus shows herself with such great brilliance that one can see her shining in bright daylight, and at night she throws shadows, like the moon. People still remember that in the year 1849 . . ." *Dictionnaire Universel,* you make no small claims, and I should like to be able to juggle with time as you do. In 1849 you were a young encyclopedia, twenty-seven years old, gazing up at a Venus in her glory, visible from December until May, during which time she changed from a disk into a crescent. Tell me then, hoary-headed old Dictionary, tell me how, on April 4, 1847, Venus in the evening, or Lucifer in the morning, "attained its maximum size and brilliance, then shot rapidly [*sic*] up to the highest point of its orbit, then fell back into the rays of the great star and vanished with it."

So difficult is it to avoid lyricism when we talk about Venus . . . Casting all restraints aside, the Great Dictionary then pursues this vein, inviting its readers to make sure they do not miss this planet's passages and apogees, occurring at intervals of a hundred and thirteen years and a half . . . I am perfectly prepared to make the attempt, but I'm afraid I shall not succeed.

DC

❧ FLOWERS

They say now . . .

They say now that flowers are altogether capable of sensation, that they have a nervous system and rudimentary eyes; there is even a part of the scientific world still groping toward the final discovery, their heart, the source and regulator of the translucent blood that irrigates the whole . . . And from the greatest advances in our knowledge must come, yet again, an even greater distress of mind. Uneasiness, scruples, the perpetual certainty henceforth that we shall be inflicting real death at every step, remorse as we see swooning and succumbing at our hands all that we press against our bosoms, against our mouths, all that we most cherish—is that what we must look forward to? By speeding them up, the movie screen can now reveal to us the drama hidden in the growth and flowering of plants. We know that their petals only attain full freedom at the price of what are apparently conscious efforts; just so does the still sticky larva struggle inside its final shell the instant before it blooms into a moth or glittering dragonfly.

Before our eyes, the sensitive mimosa, in order to deceive its aggressors, bends all the elbows of its little twigs, allows its leaves to droop down from their shoulders, and proffers no more than a wilting husk of itself. One by one, the secrets of the plants, their magical defenses, are falling to us. The mechanisms of their traps are now laid bare, revealing their predatory instincts and their taste for murder. The shiny sides of one hairy calyx, rounded to form a lip, constitute a fatal trap. Another flower imprisons its insect victim behind two interlocking harrows of inflexible hairs . . . What! are the flowers cruel too? Are they too the slaves of a demanding sexuality? Do they too have savage and cruel caprices?

It is not impossible that witchcraft, that peasant magic we once thought so naïve, that fund of information on how to cull simples, how to distill juices, how to gain knowledge from the flowers, may now recover its prestige. The motion picture, the enlargement possible on the movie screen will help in its recovery by showing us the gloxinia and the birthwort, like abysses full of ghosts, the cotyledons of the haricot bean, like a hinged trap, and the budding lily, a long crocodile's mouth as it yawns open for the first time . . . Can that be you, gentle iris, that monster with the hair-covered tongue? And what maleficent grimace is this, twisting the mouth of the opening rose? Twenty devil's horns ring the tops of the cornflower and the carnation. The climbing pea strikes like a python's head, and the germination of a fistful of lentils gives motion to a writhing mass of hydras . . .

Such spectacles, which hold me spellbound in front of the screen, will one day compete, if my wishes are fulfilled, with the toy

train smashing through its bridge and tumbling into the water below, or with the arctic cataclysm made to carry off, riding on the
safest of its little icebergs, an overweening starlet. Human imagination does not reach far; only the vagaries of reality are uncheckable
and limitless. Consider, as they are projected before your eyes, many
times enlarged, the refracting planes of these delicate crystals, archi-
tectures of pure light, dizzying perspectives, geometric fanta-
sies . . .

I am easily astonished when I see such secrets being torn from
flowers blown up till they are monstrous and unrecognizable. But I
also forget them easily when faced with the flower itself. Our clumsy
human eyes, once freed from their too powerful aids, recover their
traditional poetry. There is a sort of calendar religion that makes us
feel attachment to a flower, even a sickly one, when it is the symbol
of a season, or to its color when it commemorates a saint, or to its
scent if it brings back the pain of some dead happiness.

Almost an entire nation demands lilies of the valley in spring,
much as it demands its daily bread. Were it not for its excessive
fragrance, flouting all logic—and even, I am inclined to add, all
decency—the lily of the valley is merely a tiny slip of a flower with
little greeny white, round bells. It thrusts up through the dry leaves
at that time of the year when the first warm rains are falling, heavy
drops that unwind and pull down with them the simple arabesques
escaping from the thrush's beak, and the first notes bursting with
luminous sphericity from the early nightingales . . . I am feeling
my way cautiously, I am discovering an inexpressible communion
between the milky droplets of the lily of the valley, the tears of the
warm rain, and the crystalline bubble floating upward from the
toad . . .

The first stir of spring is such a solemn thing that the accession
of the rose, coming after it, is celebrated with less fervor. Yet everything is permitted to the rose: splendor, conspiring scents, petals
with flesh that tempts the nostrils, the lips, the teeth. But all has
been said, everything has been born already in any year when once
the rose has entered it; the first rose but heralds all the other roses

that must follow. How assured, and how easy to love it is! Riper than fruit, more sensuous than cheek or breast. Every painter's brush has painted it and will go on painting it. I have twenty portraits of it, like everyone else. Plump roses, cabbage roses, flat roses like the roses of Persia . . .

Here an anonymous water colorist has given it pleated petals like a dahlia; there, a once young girl has hollowed it into a little carmined navel. These little flower paintings go with me everywhere, all modest but each one highlighted by some arbitrary, mysterious detail that attracts me in the same way as a word whose meaning is only half apparent. The rose abounds in them. It is not that I love it more than I did before, but simply that I seek it out more. I am fascinated by its prodigious and inexhaustible gift for metamorphosis, always following the horticultural fashion of the day. In the gardens of my childhood it was most prized when it was huge, and unashamedly rose-pink. Carrying its head upright and stiff, it listened without tiring to the long canticles of the month of Mary, and disdained to swoon away between its two burning bushes of candles. "Have you seen Madame Léger's rose, up on the altar? As big as a lettuce, my dear, as big as a lettuce—Monsieur Léger measured it before it was brought to the church. Eight inches in diameter!" Rose-pink roses, blue larkspur reddened by some mysterious process of oxidization, and you, black roses, concocted of pure fragrance, I loved you enough to watch you changing as I changed myself. Who still takes the trouble to extol the cabbage rose and its Second Empire crinoline? As for the larkspur, it reigns now, twenty times bigger than before, under the title of delphinium. The black rose you may still see in the province where it was born. Cheek to cheek, one pale, one purple and black like sin, a solitary woman and an inexhaustible flower intoxicated by each other's nearness . . .

Twenty-five years ago, in the garden of a tree specialist in Besançon, chance brought me face to face with a rosebush that produced edible fruit. I was less struck by its rough, harsh leaves whispering in the wind and its red, dog-nose flower than by its smooth hips with their tiny pomegranate-like crests, tart to the tongue, and with a subtle, sweetish aftertaste. The old tree man died, and his rosebush with him. I talked about them both a hundred times, a hundred times I asked in vain: "Who can tell me where there is a single rosebush with edible hips still living?" It grew larger in my memory, I depicted it with ardor and without hope, as one does a lover whom death has cut off in his prime. And then, the other day, in Versailles, walking through a laboriously disheveled American garden, I realized that I was walking between two hedges of the rosebushes I had so long been seeking. But they bore no fruit. They had been packed tight together, trimmed, treated like box or yews . . . "They're very good for hedging," was the brief comment of my host, a connoisseur of humble country gardens, and very, very rich. Then he led me toward his rose garden, and I was introduced to all the very latest novelties in this field: roses the color of nasturtiums, with a scent of peaches; starved-looking roses tinged with dirty mauve that smelled of crushed ants; orange roses that smelled of nothing at all; and finally a little horror of a rosebush with tiny yellowish flowers covered in hairs, badly set on their stalks, bushing out all over the place, and giving off an odor like a musk-filled menagerie, like a gymnasium frequented exclusively by young redheaded women, like artificial vanilla extract—which plant my flower lover proceeded to give the name of "rose," and I did not have the courage to appeal, other than with my eyes, to those sovereign blooms, as white as snow, as dark as blood, apricot-colored, pale on the outside, troubled in the depths of their heart, which universal homage has given the right to bear that name . . .

Rose, increasing your dimensions, shrinking once more, perverted, disguised, and docile in the capricious hands of man, you still have the power, despite all this, to draw out from us, to calm in us all that remains of love's old madness. Rose, it is right that you should be the final ember around which the circle of former lovers gathers in contemplation. If they are seized by the great shiver that comes with spring, and if they sigh, "I am trembling with the cold," you may be sure that more than one is listening within himself to the long confession of yesteryear: "I am trembling with morning, with March, with flight, with hope that has no face, with sprouting seeds, and with forgetfulness . . . I am trembling with hyacinths, with hawthorn flowers, with tears . . ."

DC

I used to love to visit the flower shows . . .

I used to love to visit the flower shows that marked out the stages of the year so faithfully, along the Cours-la-Reine. The azaleas came first, then the irises and the hydrangeas, the orchids, and last of all the chrysanthemums. I can recall an extraordinary prodigality of irises, in May . . . Thousand upon thousand of irises, a mass of azure blue next to a mass of yellow, a velvety violet clump confronting another of pale, pale mauve, black irises the color of spiders' webs, white irises that were about to turn into a rainbow, irises as blue as a storm by night, and Japanese irises with great wide tongues. There were also the American irises with their gaudy finery, like magnificent strolling players. Thousand upon thousand of irises, busy being born and dying at exactly the correct time, never resting, ceaselessly mingling their odors with the fetid smell of a mysterious fertilizer . . .

However noisy our Paris of those days was, it did still have its unexpected moments of tranquillity. Along the Cours-la-Reine between one o'clock and half past one, when the last trucks had been parked outside their drivers' eating places, those of us who loved flowers and silence could enjoy a strange truce, a solitude in which the flowers seemed to be recovering from the effects of human curiosity. That heat filtering through the canvas roof, that total absence of movement in the air, the sleepy weight of an atmosphere loaded down with scents and dampness, these are all gifts of which Paris is usually very sparing. The irises, massed in the thousands, seemed to be feverishly hatching the summer. The peace of the place was complete, but not the silence; it was disturbed by an insistent feather-light noise, more delicate than the nibbling in a silkworm farm, a noise as of silk being gently scratched . . . The noise of the chrysalis crackling open. The noise of an insect's delicate legs, the noise of a dead leaf dancing. It was the irises loosening the dry membrane rolled down over the base of their calixes in the propitious and dappled light; the irises, in the thousands, opening.

The scraping sound of an existence and a need that are very real; the violent thrust of a bud; the jerks of a drained and wilting stalk as it fights its way upright after being returned to the liquid that gives it sustenance; the avidity of juicy stems such as those of the hyacinth, the tulip, or the narcissus; the fantastic growth of the mushroom thrusting its way upward and brandishing on its rounded head the leaf that watched it sprout—such are the spectacles and the harmonies for which I have acquired a respect that has grown with my curiosity. Does this mean that I have sentimental scruples, that I cannot bring myself to inflict the slightest suffering on the sensibilities of the vegetable world, that I recoil at slicing through a fiber, at snipping off a head, at cutting off a supply of sap? No. Greater love need not bring a greater pity.

There is not one of us who does not start when a rose, unfolding in a heated room, abandons one of its conch-curled petals and leaves it to float, reflected, on a polished marble top. The sound of its fall, very low, distinct, is like a syllable of silence, enough to stir a poet to creation. The peony drops its petals all at once, its whole corolla loosed in a crimson wheel about the bottom of the vase. But I have no taste for such spectacles of graceful death, or for its symbols. I would much rather hear about the triumphant sighs of irises in labor, about the arum unfolding its trumpet with a harsh grating sound, or the big scarlet poppy that forces open its green and slightly hairy sepals with a little "plock," then makes haste to unfurl its red silk flower, impelled by the seed-bearing capsule below, with its silky head of blue stamens. The fuchsia is not silent either. Its reddish bud does not divide its four pointed shutters, does not curl them up into a pagoda roof without a slight smacking of their lips, after which it shakes out, whether white or pink or violet, its charming wrinkled skirts . . . Confronted with this, or with the moonflower, how can one prevent the image from rising of other births, the huge and imperceptible crash of the breaking chrysalis, the damp wing stretching, the first leg feeling its way out into an unknown world, the fairy-tale, faceted eye receiving ᵗhe shock of its first image on this earth . . . The death agony of a orolla has the power to move me. But a flower making its debut in ɩhis world exalts me, as does the beginning of a butterfly's brief longevity. What is the majesty of any ending beside these tottering beginnings, these disordered dawns?

Defense, attack, the struggle to endure and overcome: we in our climate do not see the worst combats, the attacks that the great cannibalistic flowers of the tropics make on one another, but here the gentle little butterwort folds its hairy leaf over the insect and devours it, the sump of the birthwort is filled with minute victims. If the appetites of a plant make it resemble an animal, then I do not like it any more than I like humanized animals. "You wouldn't like me to give you a little monkey?" someone once suggested to me. "No, thank you," I replied, "I would prefer an animal." I forbid my house to all fly-trapping flowers, with their hinged mandibles and their fatal secretions. How many crimes perpetrated by one kingdom upon another! And this spring, my beautiful pink-flowered chestnut tree, I expect I shall be obliged once more to free the bee stuck on the shiny surface of your gum-covered buds. At least you are beautiful. But what am I to think, to the great shame of the arum family, of a certain devil-in-the-pulpit I know? . . . Its phallic pistil spreads all around it a smell of rotting flesh, misleading and making drunk the clouds of insects it attracts. They hurl themselves into their intoxication, then decline into torpor, and one sees them in writhing masses, heaped at the bottom of its trumpet, fighting among themselves for all the flower can dispense, including death, and then, in immobility, forget all their antagonism. With horror, I should like to know . . .

No, I would rather not know. Let the little black secret remain lying there in the depths of that flower-of-ill-repute. What advantage would there be in being able to define, name, or predict what my ignorance now permits me to think of as a miracle! Flowers are not explainable, nor is their influence over us. The leaves of a plant may be miracles of form and color, but it is to its modest flower that we direct our curiosity all the same. I know a young boy in his teens who suddenly lost a great deal of his admiration for the bougainvillea, that cape of orange, violet, and rose-pink flame that covers so many Algerian walls. "It's ever since I found out that the flowers are just bracts . . . ," he said, without further explanation.

But yes, exactly. Only bracts. We wish to expend our veneration on nothing but the crater, which is the flower.

DC

. . . If I had a garden. . . .

. . . If I had a garden. But it just so happens that I don't have a garden any more. There is nothing so terrible about not having a garden any more. The worrying thing would be if the future garden, whose reality is of no importance, were beyond my grasp. But it is not. A certain crackling noise the dry seeds make in their paper packet is enough to sow the very air around me with their flowers. The fennel's seeds are black, shiny like a mass of fleas, and even if you keep them a long time they still give off a smell of apricots when they're warmed, though they don't pass the scent on to their flowers. I shall sow the fennel seeds after the dream, after all my plans and memories, in the shape of what I have possessed and what I now anticipate, have taken root, have taken their places in my tomorrow garden. The hepaticas, I know, will certainly be blue, since I am always irritated these days by the ones that are that winy pink. They will be blue, and there will be enough of them to make an edging all around the basket ("all the baskets must be raised in the middle . . .") that will display the dielytras hanging down in pennants, the weigelas, and the double deutzias. I shall have no pansies but those—with wide faces, beards, and mustaches—that look like Henry VIII; no saxifrages, unless, on some fine summer eve-

ning, when I politely offer them a lighted match, they will reply to
my gesture with their little, harmless explosion of gas . . .

An arbor? Naturally I shall have an arbor. I'm not down to my
last arbor yet. I must have a trellis for my purple dragon-tongued
cobaeas to perch on, and for my cane melons . . . Cane melons?
Why not a wickerwork marrow? Because the melon plant I am talking about hauls itself up the canes that are stuck up to support it,
then runs between them like a green pea plant, marking every stage
of its progress with little green and white melons that are very sweet
and full of flavor. (See Mme Millet-Robinet on the subject.)

Then, if all those lovers of horticultural novelties have banished all the old prince's feathers from their gardens, I shall certainly take a few of them in myself, even if it's only so that I can call
them by their old name: nun's scourge. They will go well with another feathery plant, silver colored this time, the pampas grass, a
good solid flower, though slightly stupid, which spends the winter to
the left and right of the fireplace in trumpet-shaped vases.

In summer, we shall turn up our noses at the pampas grass and
stuff the vases with those suffocating white lilies, those lilies, more
imperious than the orange blossom, more passionate than the tuber-
ose, which climb up the staircase at midnight and come to find us in
the very depths of our slumbers.

If it's a Breton garden—how I love this ideal flower bed of
mine with its sumptuous border of "ifs"—then there will be the
daphne, that flower, so tiny and so timid, yet so immense too because
of its fresh and noble fragrance, piercing and filling the Breton winter with its scent even in January. A bush of daphne in one of the
showers that ride in with the tide from the west seems to have been
watered with perfumes. If it is beside a lake, this garden of mine, I
shall have, besides the load of shrubs that the late Old Gentleman
always dragged about with him, some winter Japan allspice instead
of the daphnes. The Japan allspice, which flowers in December, is
about as bright and colorful as a small chip of cork. Its merit is
unique and always reveals its whereabouts. Once, in the countryside
outside Limoges where I did not know it was growing, I looked for

it, stalked it, and found it, by following the traces of its fragrance through the icy air. Dull and grayish on its twig, but endowed with an immense power of attraction—when I think of the Japan allspice I think also of the nightingale. So I shall have some Japan allspice . . . Don't I have it already?

I shall have many other plants too, rose windows of verbena, pipes of birthwort, powder puffs of thrift, crosses of St. Helena's cross, spikes of lupine, night-blooming bindweed, the marvel of Peru, nebulas of bent grass, and clouds of feathered pinks. Beggar's staff to aid the last steps of my journey; asters to fill my nights with stars. Harebells, a thousand harebells to ring at dawn just as the cock starts crowing; a dahlia pleated like a Clouet ruff, a foxglove in case a needy fox should visit me, and a rocket. Not, as you might think, a rocket to send into the sky, but a rocket to edge my flower bed with. Yes, to edge my flower bed with! And for that I need lobelias too, for the blue of the lobelia has no rival either in the sky or in the sea. As for honeysuckle, I shall choose the most delicate, the one that is wan with the burden of its own scent. Finally, I must have a magnolia, a good layer, one that will be covered all over with white eggs when Easter comes; and wistaria that will let its long flowers drip off it one by one till it turns the terrace into a lake of mauve. And some lady's slipper, enough to make shoes for everyone in the house. But no oleanders, if you please. They call the oleander the laurel rose, and I want only laurels and roses.

There is no guarantee that the flowers I have chosen would flatter the eye when assembled. Besides, there are others I can't call to mind at the moment. But there's no hurry. I shall dig them all into their storage trenches, some in my memory, the others in my imagination. There, thanks be to God, they can still find the humus, the slightly bitter water, the warmth and the gratitude which will perhaps keep them from dying.

DC

❧❧❧

Autumn

This shows imagination; but one senses a deliberate attempt to appear original.

It has always remained in my memory, this note written with red ink in the margin of a French composition. I was eleven or twelve years old. In thirty lines I had stated that I could not agree with those who called the autumn a decline, and that I, for my part, referred to it as a beginning. Doubtless my opinion on the matter, which has not changed, had been badly expressed, and what I wanted to say was that this vast autumn, so imperceptibly hatched, issuing from the long days of June, was something I perceived by subtle signs, and especially with the aid of the most animal of my senses, which is my sense of smell. But a young girl of twelve rarely has at her disposal a vocabulary worthy of expressing what she thinks and feels. As the price of not having chosen the dappled spring and its nests, I was given a rather low mark.

The rage to grow, the passion to flower begin to fade in nature at the end of June. The universal green has by then grown darker, the brows of the woods take on the color of fields of eel grass in shallow seas. In the garden, the rose alone, governed more by man than by the seasons, together with certain great poppies and some aconites, continues the spring and lends its character to the summer. The elder flowers are turning into berries, and the mown fields are waiting for the second crop of hay.

All the scattered yellows that in April echoed the colors of the new-hatched chick have passed. Wild chicory, cornflower, and self-heal: those are the last blues of the season, drowned in the waves of fading wheat. But already the wild harebell, the knapwort, and the scabious are reminding us that the meadow saffron will soon be here, its pale night light sparked into a glow by the first cold nights.

Depths of dark greenery, illusion of stability, incautious promise of duration! We gaze at these things and say: "Now this is really summer." But at that moment, as in a windless dawn there sometimes floats an imperceptible humidity, a circle of vapor betraying by its presence in a field the subterranean stream beneath, just so, predicted by a bird, by a wormy apple with a hectically illuminated skin, by a smell of burning twigs, of mushrooms and of half-dried mud, the autumn at that moment steals unseen through the impassive summer. Only for a moment. Then July becomes a torrid miser once again. The apple and the pear are as sour in the mouth as the green hazelnut. The hardened remains of once juicy fruit dangle from a few cherry trees; the strawberries, the red currants, and the black currants have all melted into jam . . . When, oh when will the autumn come with its abundance? . . .

It is already here, as you would know if you could but translate those glittering drops transpiring from the underside of that leaf, fallen with no cause, or construe that diamond-studded zigzag the spider has hung along the box-hedge top. At both extremities of a day that still seems endless, both the dawn and the dusk are suffering from the same dry heat, the drought is upon us, and there are only the storms to hurl down their crushing dews. Meanwhile, the sorb apple grows red, all the birds have lost their fledgling twitter, and a few oval coins are dropping from the acacia trees, then hovering uncertainly before falling lifeless to the ground. Two months ago, fluttering with wings tinted the same pale yellow as these falling leaves, we saw the brimstone butterfly . . . But the fate of the brimstone is already settled. Now, in its place, there is the wonderful peacock, its wings eyed with glinting blue planets, the suspicious tortoise-shell who can never be too warm, and the beautiful painted lady, for they all last until the first frosts come.

There still remains a long corridor of darkening greenery for us to travel through. High summer, wishfully we call it. High and grave, fleecy, gentle when it is a near neighbor of the sea or lakes, yet even in France it has its awful regions, and there the wild animals grow thin beneath its weight. The hares, lying flat against the earth, pant in terror. And where is it to find moist clay to dress its wound, the woodcock with its broken leg?

As the water in them sank, August, fall's precursor, used to spread a thin film of tin over the ponds in my native regions. When a water snake, long and vigorous, its little nostrils level with the surface, crossed a pond and drew his triangular wake behind him, I hesitated, as a child, to swim there. So much hidden life was rising in circles, in glistening films and bubbles from the haunted mud below; so many springs were bubbling; so many tubular stems were vaguely waving . . . And yet the marsh frog, green on his green raft, as well as the brutal and doubtless nearsighted dragonfly still tempted me. Even a child cannot respond to everything. But its antennae quiver at the slightest signal, and best of all it always likes those things that are closed, misty, unnamed, mysteriously impressive. It is to my childhood ponds, thickened by the summer, stirred up by the fall, that I owe the love I was able to feel for a little Mediterranean marsh whose russet water was always rendered salty by the equinoctial gales. Meadows, moors, and undergrowth are all less life-filled than a marsh. From the swallow that scythes through the morning air to snap up the early mosquitoes, right on to the last slither of the marsh warbler down the stems of the rushes, what a world of joy! . . . Birds, yellowish rats and field mice, heavy-winged butterflies pressing down on the layer of overheated air that shimmers like a feverish mirage; the leaps of the big female toads who venture into the water only very briefly, because they don't like the salt; the slow convolutions of a strange, black and white water snake; the first and none too assured flight of the first bat at last; and the miaowing of the sparrow owl that makes the cats so angry—what joy there is in the little marsh at Cannebiers! . . . There are no wasted hours there, as time flows indolently along the edges of the water, neither sweet nor yet entirely bitter, almost hidden from the eye, masquerading as a meadow of reeds with edible seeds, of sedge and yellow St.-John's-wort . . . From August onward, my marsh was covered with the mauve flowers of the wild thrift that does not wither. You must not be afraid, if you decide to go and pick wild thrift, either of the invisible water that gulps down your foot and holds it fast, or of the plants' inhabitants when they leap, fly, coil, and swim away in flight. The stems of the mock bamboos, recently cut back, gouge into the flesh with their obliquely sliced-off ends.

August, in the village where I lived in the North, was a long month suffered in silence. The children, torn away like myself from school, found the days slow. They spent their interminable leisure hours huddled up together in the shade of the houses, for they were tired of the shaved stubble fields and the silent woods. As the sun moved higher in the sky, so they pulled back their dusty legs farther and farther away from its heat. They played, we played, at scissors-and-stones, at guess-the-pebble, at knucklebones. They bit into the first peaches, still half green—I didn't write "we bit" because I always contented myself with the taste of the fruit when it was ripe and juicy. We watched the great candlesticks of the teasels slowly rising out on the sterile, untilled waste patches, their flowers, ringed with spiky weapons on every side, catching fire and bursting into purple flame just before the summer began to sink. The mulleins came out at that time too, entirely covered—hairy leaves and road-colored flowers—with the gray dust of the dog days. Bloated with idleness, pining because we missed school and could not admit it, we counted the days as they passed, and lied to one another, saying: "Oh goodness, how the days fly by!"

Nothing flies by in summer, unless it be the summer itself. An August storm would begin on the dry, flinty ground, raise itself on columns of white dust up into the sky, then fall again in a deluge whose first gusts grated between the teeth and sucked up whole flights of little frogs from the dried-up ponds, knocking them quite silly as they came down again with little plopping sounds. The storm would move away, and the great wake of vertical rain it left behind would last all night. In the morning, we could see that everything had changed and, what is more, that all the female cats were pregnant . . . September! September! It wasn't there yet, but it was breathing its strong scent of delicate corruption everywhere, a second spring with a scent of plums, of smoke, of hazel husks. September soon! The children came to life once more in the rain, and the light pouring out from the ballooning West was blue, less generous, more swiftly gone. "But it's evening!" my mother would cry. "Time for the lamp already." To myself, I said: "Time for the lamp at last . . ." Another week and the ripe peaches were falling, the red sage plants were stretching up their spikes of seed, and the acid opacity of the grapes was turning to translucent agate . . . Another two weeks and the two cats were giving birth, both on the same day, to their punctual broods of kittens, proof positive that this time September really had arrived.

The fire, the wine, the red and windy skies, the flesh of the various fruits, the heady dishes of game, the barrels, and so many pulpy globes all roll before it. Chestnuts in their spiky cases, squashy medlars, pink sorbs and tart-tasting sorb apples—the autumn drives before it a profusion of modest fruits which one does not pick but which fall into one's hands, which wait patiently at the foot of the tree until man deigns to collect them. For his eyes and mind are all on his second crops, and on his grape harvest.

Above the Loire, however, it must be admitted that the grape harvest is a somewhat grim matter for the peasant, poor creature of the soil, whose work becomes a constant punishment of hail, rain, numbing cold, and invisible attacks. Even the daylight in which it is carried out is cut short by the advancing season, and it is a task, constantly harried by October's bitter moods, for which the farmer's wife ties on her kerchief tightly and the farmer buttons up his woolen jacket. It is the South alone that experiences with its grape harvest the expression of a joy that springs partly from the climate, partly from the unbroken weather, and partly from the punctual and perfect ripeness of the grapes, sometimes so warmly caressed by the sun that they call their chattering militia in among the vines as early as late August. The entire department of Var—and its neighbors too, I believe—was forced to begin stripping its laden vines as early as the twenty-sixth of August a few years ago. Otherwise the long, purple bunches of fruit, already trailing heavily upon the ground, would have been scorched and spoiled. What sweetness and what warmth, what a bloom of blueness on that bulging fruit, what depths of violet in the skin of the oval grape they call the olivette! . . . The clairette is pinkish and round, the luxurious picardan weighs down its vine, the golden muscat and the little, very black pineau burst their skins if they are made to wait, and all their richness drains away. One year of wild abundance produced bunches of legendary dimensions. The little vine which is now no longer mine proudly displayed one bunch that year that was brandished aloft with cries of: "A champion, this one! Eight pounds if it's an ounce!"

Down there, in the South, the women with their black hair go grape-gathering dressed in white. They cover their heads with great wide hats, pull their sleeves down over their wrists, and put on coquettish shows of fear: "Ahh, a tarantula! Holy mother, there's a snake!" There is coquetry too in the way the men "drop" their coats and throw aside their shirts. When the men are beautiful and naked above the waist, then the women brim with laughter, and sing between the rows of vines. Delicate, high voices carried by the western wind from gulf to gulf . . . Drunk and defenseless, the wasps glue themselves to the sticky juices; the sun in September is as warm as the sun in August . . . Only privileged climates can paint such pictures and retain such pagan pleasures on their easeful shores. The old, hand-driven wine press still visits Saint-Tropez, still stops at every door, surrounded by swarms of children and golden flies. From its purple girths, from its wooden body dyed an indelible violet, there flows, thick with clots, the new wine to which anyone may hold up his glass . . . From that day on, in all the low, dark kitchens, the *vin marquis* is being made. Would you like it plain—new wine boiled down to one third its volume—or refined, spiced with aromatic herbs, filtered, then put in bottles? The second for Sundays, the first for weekdays—you can do no better than that . . .

After the grapes, down there in the South, there comes the "second fig," which is all honey. Its pink-tinted heart resembles that of the strawberry we call June beauty. After the figs come the last hard peaches from the lower slopes. The hazelnuts and walnuts are already piled up on echoing wooden floors. And then there begins a sort of rustic idleness, a time of leisure throughout those parts, while the fig is shriveling on its wicker bed, sweating a dry coat of sugar on its skin . . . If I could choose, I should take my vacations at the same time as Provence.

Then I should go home, climbing up France "from the bottom to the top," as children say. Such a journey can never be accomplished without melancholy. But I have never been in the habit of loving things because they are the gayest, of preferring only what is proof against all bitterness. To leave the South of France in September is to tear oneself away from a festivity that still goes gently on when we have left, inviting the naked striplings, the women in holiday attire to go on dancing to the same old tunes behind us. Beyond Avignon, the summer grows yellow, the vine leaves are curling, and at the same time that the sky begins to descend, a strange dawn rises from the earth; France is gathering the pride of its four seasons, the sparing, limited, but great and glorious vintages, and its migrating birds.

Long, subtly shaded progress of the fall, stubborn determination to bear fruit . . . The perfected, strong, and fragrant time that has for so long been gathering the starlings, whistling like silk being scratched, or like a sibilant wind, above my head, that has for so long been stretching the great V of flying ducks across the sky, and the flights of cranes and wild geese, massing together, then whirled away from the congregating councils of the swallows . . . When these celestial movements are accompanied below by the opening of all the most ardent flowers there are, the flaming sage, the chrysanthemum with its romantic locks, the dahlias darker than even the black rose, and the scarlet cannas, how could I associate the ideas of sleep and abdication with them? Add to this the prodigality that grants us the possession of such freely offered gifts as the russet medlar, the mulberry, the mushroom, the three-sided beechnut, the four-horned water chestnut . . .

I am aware that there are many regions, including Paris, which have never heard of this latter, the *cornuelle*. Also, it is quite rare and won't grow in just any pond. To gather it, you needed a flat-bottomed boat, a stern oar, an old pair of pants, and a willingness to splash about in cold water. Failing these, it was always possible to buy some, as I used to do—a hundred and four *cornuelles* for four sous—after watching out for the arrival of Frisepoulet, a majestic old man of the woods whose white flax hair and beard provided an admirable foil to the black brilliance of his sorcerer's eyes . . .

> Prickly chestnuts!
> Tickly chestnuts!
> They tickle your thighs,
> And prick your pocket!

He cried his wares in the street, he sold them, but he never addressed a word to the ordinary village folk or to the children by way of conversation. With Frisepoulet came the first chestnuts. After him there was nothing more to come but the blue sloes on the hedges, and as soon as the frost arrived to lay its thin sheets of glass over the water in the buckets by the pump, I would go out to gather these sloes, shriveling on their bushes, so that my mother could use them to flavor her bottles of spirits with. Can so many little miracles still take place today, without the aid of Frisepoulet? I doubt whether the cheeses in the village where I was born can reach the same pitch of perfection in the irremediable absence of a little man whom I never heard referred to by any other name than "God above," and who also repaired our umbrellas, sitting under a staircase . . .

"Do go and fetch my unbrella. It must be all repaired by now. And tell that God above to reach you down a cheese . . ."

Stripped of these picturesque originals, what would our childhood memories become? If the man-with-the-rose, passing by in a fragrance of young shallots, of scallions and bay, if he was forever mute, it was because the rose he gripped eternally between his aging teeth had closed his lips. For the man-with-the-rose alone, the Bengal rosebush would neither flag nor cease . . .

The style of things, the kind of things that we shall love in

later life are fixed in that moment when the child's strong gaze se-
lects and molds the figures of fantasy that for it are going to last. I
set my own up against backgrounds that will never fade, such as fir
trees overwhelmed with snow, narcissi growing in a circle around a
hidden spring, flaming geraniums, family meal tables and little family feasts arranged like a set piece of flowers, and an English teapot
whose little hat was a bindweed flower. All around the table were
the Chinese cups, the stemmed glasses for the Frontignan wine, and
in the middle, the cake flavored with rum. Autumn, autumn yet
again, that burning cake, seasoned with honest rum. For the teas we
ate in the warm summer garden, the meringues filled with fresh
cream, and the raspberries, they were all lost in the excess of heat
and light. But in autumn, Sido's wide sleeves, fluttering above the
table, shed on the tea things a faint, night-light glow. Her bare fore-
arms were even more graceful than the neck of the slender pitcher
in which the slices of fresh fruit floated in cooled white wine, enclosed in thick crystal entwined with filigree . . . Household objects
at that time were still not entirely free of all the Gothick claptrap
that cluttered up the mid-nineteenth century. But the impression they left on the memory was all the more striking for this,
imbued as they were with a sort of frantic elegance, which resulted
in excessively frail handles stuck on excessively bulging flanks, and
emaciated backs on ponderous chairs . . . Where would it not lead
me, the memory of Sido's arm extended by a chocolate pot, and the
chocolate pot itself, with its pretentions, or the chair that had been
imitated from a Louis XV style under Napoleon III? Nothing could
have been purer than the style of Sido's arm. But even if I wanted
to, which I do not, I would be unable to separate it from those agreeable errors of taste we see scattered around people we know, which
play a part in their conservation, in their ideal commemoration.

Her forty years scarcely weighed at all upon the principal character in my life, upon Sido, when she brought me into the world. But
after my birth she put on weight, became plump without losing her
looks, and was forced to give up wearing the dresses which had
highlighted her young and girlish figure. I did keep a blue dress of

hers in fact, one she told me she had missed not being able to wear. It had a skirt of fine linen with a white embroidered garland around it, very full at the hemline, but with a waist band that measured scarcely more than twenty inches around.

It was because of me, therefore, that she advanced into her autumn as a woman and that she settled into it with such serenity. She even tried to wear the insignia displayed once upon a time by aging ladies; that is, she wore a frilled cap for a time, and on Sundays a bonnet that tied under the chin. But then her children, independent but united, knowing no other ties than an obscure and hidden family tenderness, rose up against her. They saw her and were outraged, they laid their curse upon the frilly cap, they heaped invective upon the bonnet, its strings, and its funereal violets. They thrust forward into the future— "the future," said one of us, "is what doesn't happen"—this inadmissible and outward shape their mother had assumed, and set up inflexible limits beyond which Sido was not permitted to decline. Autumn, but no further! For them, she made it a point of honor that her October should often appear like August. Where the cursory glance of the stranger would have seen no more than a tiny aging woman dressed like a peasant, her delicate feet shod in garden clogs, we her children reaped the spontaneous riches of her language, its sprinkling of fresh images, a voice whose wide-ranging tones ravished the ear, the gaiety of those who have nothing more to lose and so excel at giving, and the names allotted to us by a love that made us perhaps too harsh in judging other loves: "Minet-Chéri . . . My beaming sun . . . Beauty! . . ." This last was not her name for me but for my eldest brother, for no autumn is ever quite pure of passion. To the heart of a woman chastely caressing her favorite creation, to her eyes as they proudly examined that perfect specimen, her son, I should not have blushed to confess what living aid it was that masked, gave brilliance to, and later prolonged, my own decline. But Sido left us too soon.

Even as I write, it is approaching once again, the season that a schoolgirl celebrated long ago because, precociously, she loved it. It comes back decked in gold, so as to inspire wisdom, or its opposite, so that the chestnut tree may flower a second time, so that the cat, which weaned its last litter in June, may feel the need for further adventures, so that the swallow may be misled and start another nest, so that a ripened woman may glow with sunlight and sigh: "I'm sure there'll never be another winter . . ."

DC

❧❧ Under the Blue Lantern

We should not be unreasonably perturbed . . .

We should not be unreasonably perturbed when our precious senses become dulled with age. I say "we," but I am the text of my own sermon. My chief concern is lest I should mistake the true nature of a condition that has come upon me gradually. It can be given a name: it keeps me in a state of vigilance, of uncertainty, ready to accept whatever may fall to my lot. The prospect gives rise to little that is reassuring, but I have no choice.

More than once of late, turning my eyes from my book or my blue-tinted writing paper toward the superb quadrangle that I am privileged to view from my window, I have thought "The children in the garden are not nearly so noisy this year," and a moment later found myself finding fault with the doorbell, the telephone, and the whole orchestral gamut of the radio for becoming progressively fainter. As for the china lamp—not the blue lantern that burns by day and night, of course, but the pretty one with flowers and arabesques painted on it—I was forever scolding it unjustly: "What can this wretched thing have been eating to make it so heavy?" Discoveries, ever more discoveries! Things always explain themselves in the long run. Instead, then, of landing on new islands of discovery, is my course set for the open sea where there is no sound other than that of the lonely heartbeat comparable to the pounding of the surf? Rest assured, nothing is decaying, it is I who am drifting. . . . The open sea, but not the wilderness. The discovery that there is no wilderness! That in itself is enough to sustain me in triumphing over my afflictions.

RS

My juniors in the prime of life . . .

My juniors in the prime of life sometimes look sternly at me; they feel anxious. They gather the recalcitrant fold of a shawl across my shoulder with a "You're not feeling a draft?" No, I am not feeling chilly, I am not feeling *that particular* draught you have in mind. My thoughts are too out of joint for me to feel it. I have so many reasons for avoiding what you tactfully call "the dangerous draft." Chief among them is pain, pain ever young and active, instigator of astonishment, of anger, imposing its rhythm on me, provoking me to defy it; the pain that enjoys an occasional respite but does not want my life to end: happily I have pain. Oh, I know perfectly well that by using the adverb "happily" I sound affected, like someone putting on the brave smile of an invalid! Very few invalids do remain entirely natural, but I would not like it thought that I am making my infirmity an occasion for sinful pride, that I require respect and special consideration, or that it fosters an inferiority complex, that root cause of acerbity. I am not referring to those who pretend to be sufferers, who are of no interest and are in any case a small minority, nor am I alluding to a category of sufferers who are far from reluctant when surprised or discovered in the very act of suffering. My doctor brother summed up in a few words the pleasure enjoyed by such as these. "It is," he said, "a kind of ecstasy. It's akin to scratching the hollow of your ear with a matchstick. Aphrodisiacal, almost."

So, as luck will have it, I am fated to suffer pain, which I reconcile with a gambler's spirit, my ultra-feminine gambler's spirit, my instinct for the game of life, if you prefer it; the Last Cat, toward the end of her life, gave every indication by the movement of a paw, by the smile on her face, that a trailing piece of string was still for her a plaything, food for feline thought and illusion. Those who surround me will never let me want for pieces of string.

RS

In anticipation of the time . . .

In anticipation of the time when I shall no longer be able to move, I make no effort to move.

I ride at anchor beneath the blue lantern, which is quite simply a powerful commercial lamp at the end of a lengthy extensible arm, fitted with a blue bulb and a blue paper shade. Though a permanent fixture, it has nonetheless suggested to my neighbors the name they have chosen to baptize it with—*fanal*—the light that rakes the seas. "Madame Colette, you can't imagine how pretty your lantern looked yesterday, shining through the fog. . . . Oh, but you can't tell me that you make sparing use of your blue lantern! It's on at all hours, in the early morning, at eight, sometimes at seven-thirty even!" There is nothing I can hide from them, not even the moment—at cockcrow, perhaps—when the beam from my lantern casts a blueness over the brown coffeepot and the white milk jug. I tend to make less and less distinction between the hours of night and the hours of day, the hour for reading, for writing, for looking about me, all are equally good.

RS

Beyond the need to see . . .

Beyond the need to see only very few faces, to hear only a very small number of voices, there takes shape another, contradictory need: that of continuing to try to decipher that fine but bungled masterpiece comprising no more than a pair of eyes, one nose, and one mouth. It is in the name of this thirst, this minimal desire for human society that I allow people to enter. And then the old politeness, learned and never forgotten, which requires that to a greeting there be joined a second greeting, that to a request there should succeed assent . . . The glass door in the archway opens, the stranger enters . . . He has his plan of campaign. His weapons are the inquiry, the request for an article, pure curiosity, and the money-making proposition. Of such as he, or her, I know little since the war, whereas they already have an old, stereotyped picture of me. He tells me, she assures me, that a very important newspaper, about to "appear" shortly, would like to know . . . They evidently suppose that it is impossible for me to withhold from the world some startling opinion on the subject of women's votes, removing collaborators from office, the role of young women in modern society, the reform of the theater, the closing of restaurants, the paper question and the housing question. He asks me for, she requests a list of my literary projects . . .

There they are, by the side of the divan I use to work or suffer on, the divan raft on which I have been floating now for years. They are sitting on the little chairs I had such pleasure covering with an old tapestry-work design, which bear witness to my well-ordered solitude. And I, for a time that happily is under my control, lie here their prisoner. I assume an air of finding their presence natural, but I am the one who has been summoned to appear. What could be more normal than to tremble before youth? It is possible that they too, at bottom, are uncertain of themselves. They think I possess a store of general ideas. It is not for me to enlighten them, to explain that I am living off that fund of frivolity which is provided for the aid of those who live a very long time. Or that there comes an age when one must choose between bitterness—pessimism, as we used to call it once—and its contrary, and that it is a great while now since my choice was made, or rather, more truthfully, since it was made public.

I have no other defense against them but to look at them. It is difficult for them, this job they're doing, this job they're making up as they go along. The war has not taught them any lessons. Their greenness shows clearly through their unconcern, and it is quite possible that their easy manner is as much a cheat as my own. Nevertheless, it is they who have the considerable advantage of being able to brandish the interrogation mark, the weapon of the aggressor. I can interrogate only their faces. What was the cause of that premature wrinkle? Of that raised scar? Of that sad gaze in one so young? That profound weariness betrayed by such long and frequent intakes of breath?

"It would not be indiscreet of me, madame, to . . . ?"

Yes it would. Even before the question is finished, I know quite well that it's going to be indiscreet.

"And among your literary plans, madame, do you . . . ?"

The speaker must be about twenty-two or twenty-three; he has all the volubility of an old hand, and a lock of blond hair falling over one eye. If I could not see his fountain pen shaking, I should take him for the patron saint of gall in person. Plans, my boy? Oh, of course. At seventy-three, minus three months, one still has plans. I have no lack of these. I am planning to live a little longer, to go on suffering in an honorable fashion, which is to say without noisy protest and without rancor, to rest my gaze upon brows like yours—you look something like my daughter, but an inferior copy—to laugh all to myself about things in secret, and also to laugh openly when I have reason to, to love whoever loves me, to put in order all that I shall leave behind, my bank account as well as the drawer of aging photographs, my few clothes, the few letters . . . But all those plans are not for you. So to you, young man assigned to make this inquiry, and so responsible, so young, I gravely reply:

"My plans . . . er . . . I'd rather not tell you at the moment. Perhaps in a few months . . . No, no . . . In that time there may be a volume of memoirs . . . As for the novel . . . Oh, no! There is nothing I could tell you about my method of working . . ."

I keep my face quite straight. He makes a note. I add a few

ambiguous words, a gesture, behind which he can perhaps conjure up a whole avenue of great thoughts . . . And now it's over. He is leaving with the square of American chocolate I gave him bulging in his cheek. As he goes out, he opens the wrong door—Pauline is not here—walks into a little shower cabinet and offers it his apologies, walks through into the icy little room with the glass skylight that lets in the rain, blunders into the toilet leading off the hall, tries to close the front door after him, though it's impossible unless you know the password—in short, he has gone, and I am left alone to muse over what this young drone referred to as my method of working. "Perhaps, madame, among your notes there is . . ."

He appeared to find it quite natural that I should have a method of working, and even that I should want to keep it secret. So he must certainly have one himself . . . I should have interviewed him . . .

Among my notes . . . What notes? When I am gone they won't find a single one. Oh, I tried! But everything I made a note of became as sad as a dead frog's skin, as sad as a plan for a novel. Trusting to the advice of writers who did make notes, I made some notes on a sheet of paper, then lost the paper. So I bought a notebook, one of the new spiral ones, and I lost the notebook, after which I felt that I was free, forgetful, and prepared to accept the consequences of that forgetfulness.

DC

The only living animal left to me . . .

The only living animal left to me that I can call my own is the fire. It is my guest, and the work of my hands. I know all about covering a fire, succoring a fire. I know the art of surrounding a fire in the open air with a circular trench, so that it may burn up well without "marking" the stubble and setting the ricks ablaze. I am well aware of its dislike of even numbers, that three logs burn better than two and seven than four, and that like every other animal it likes having its belly scratched from underneath.

Between it and me lies an old question which it takes me most of my time to resolve since it burns on my hearth for three quarters of the year, there in my bedroom, which has adopted its colors, red and white, and its presence. I burn it ceaselessly. Ceaselessly, but with a certain thriftiness. I pile it up, but with the air of doling out beggarly alms. I show it that I am a native of a distant province, where everyone learns not to waste wood and bread. I give it its quota of splinters, twigs, and dried leaves, and I intend always to have the last word with it—that stand-by of trainers acquired through long dealings with animals. It repays me, by hurling itself upon the least of my offerings; it makes much of me, encourages me in my by now automatic incantations to it: the business of incantation loses nothing by it.

The hearth at which I solemnize my fire worship is of ancient construction and required, I don't mind betting, no more than the hand of a simple mason to build it. Within the precincts of the Palais-Royal we do have here and there some doorknobs and wainscot paneling of artistic merit, along with a few fine fireplaces. The marble has been stripped away from my own and replaced by a sort of pink and beige galantine. No matter, it has kept its intrinsic nature and its appetite for heat, together with that allegiance of permanent fixtures devised to share intimately in the life of man and his rudimentary needs.

Anyone who is given to meditating in front of a fire, during the hours when the shades of night beyond the windowpanes guarantee him safe protection, need no longer fear being joined at the fireside by the dog and the wolf of twilight—the shudder and the sudden start. Only novices in the art are liable at that time to be assailed so powerfully by age, fright, evil, or a guilty conscience. Let me run through my little incantation.

A fire affords such genial company
To the chill prisoner, the drear night long!
Close by my side there sits a good fairy
Who drinks, or smokes, or sings an ancient song . . .

Whose lines are those? I might almost go so far as to say they are my own, since once upon a time a competition for reading aloud was held in my canton for those of us who, when twelve or thirteen, were made to read with meaning and expression from both verse and prose. A certain well-intentioned man, having heard in our chief town that no child in the district had any conception how to read other than in a monotonous drone, was roused to indignation and, after pointing out the dire peril into which the ignorance prevailing in the department of Yonne could not fail to plunge the whole of France, founded an elocution prize. A red and gold volume, and a diploma, confirmed that at the age of twelve and a half Gabrielle-Sidonie Colette knew how to read, and consoled me for having slurred my words while reading, so that I said "who drink sore smokes," and inadvertently altered the prose of Mme de Sévigné.

> A fire affords such genial company
> To the chill prisoner . . .

Perhaps these second-rate verses really are mine. Mine as is the fire, as is everything that surrounds me at night.

Poetry does not necessarily have to be beautiful to stick in the depths of our memory, there to occupy most mischievously the place doomed to invasion by certain melodies which, however blameworthy, can never be expunged.

> "A fire affords . . ."

Reading at night is a fickle ally. More reliable than a book is the setting I have arranged in honor of the minutes and the hours. I am not always equal to my bouts of insomnia, but I usually succeed in getting even with them by the application of a sort of mental restorative, which drives away fear of the unwonted from my mind and my surroundings. It is not later than three in the morning, nothing at roof level is yet beginning to pale. Because there is a lamp on every pillar, I could count the number of arches along the Palais-

Royal from my bed. The inhabitants of this house are so quiet that I never hear a soul at night; but the clatter of my tongs into the grate would ruin the fitful rest of even someone sleeping two doors away. Now, if I am lying here motionless tonight, there is good reason for it, for I can feel stirring within me—apart from the twisting pain, as if under the heavy screw of a winepress—a far less constant turn-screw than pain, an insurrection of the spirit which in the course of my long life I have often rejected, later outwitted, only to accept it in the end, for writing leads only to writing. I am still going to write; I say this in all humility. For me there is no other destiny. . . .

RS

I grow less and less afraid . . .

I grow less and less afraid of the presence of skeptics and of their opinions. Little by little, I am escaping from their grasp, on the understanding that they provide me with food for my ohs! and ahs!, which don't make a great noise but come from a long way down, and on condition also that they furnish me with my daily subject of amazement. A lack of money, if it be relative, and a lack of comfort can be endured if one is sustained by pride. But not the need to be astounded. Astound me, try your hardest. These last flashes of astonishment are what I cannot do without.

DC

We have close friends . . .

We have close friends who sometimes ask in amazement as they are shown in: "What were you two laughing at in here? What's the joke?" There are times when we could well reply: "No joke at all. But I was here with him, and he was here with me."

DC

It has taken me a great deal of time . . .

It has taken me a great deal of time to scratch out forty or so books. So many hours that could have been used for travel, for idle strolls, for reading, even for indulging a feminine and healthy coquetry. How the devil did George Sand manage? Robust laborer of letters that she was, she was able to finish off one novel and begin another within the hour. She never lost either a lover or a puff of her hookah by it, produced a twenty volume *Histoire de ma vie* into the bargain, and I am completely staggered when I think of it. Pellmell, and with ferocious energy she piled up her work, her passing griefs, her limited felicities. I could never have done so much, and at the moment when she was thinking forward to her full barns I was still lingering to gaze at the green, flowering wheat. Mauriac has consoled me for this with a stinging piece of praise: "Where has she not burrowed her way in, this great honeybee?"

At the moment she is making herself a very tiny amount of honey from the two flowers—there are two now—on the pink chestnut tree. The day is sinking into evening. But is everything not evening now for me, O Evening Star? The days are not miserly, but they are swift. The sixth little boy who was just born this week below my windows, is he not beginning to walk already? The eldest of the six, the shepherd to the masculine gang, leads them into the garden, where they disport themselves, and then, when the time comes to leave, he gathers them together and carries off one of his lambs under each arm. They grow as quickly as little chicks; the one who was crawling a moment ago has started to run, the one who had long curly locks so recently now has the shorn head of a man, and all this confuses me. If I turn away my eyes for a single moment, everything has changed. The life of a creature that was more or less immobile has become a whirlwind of haste and variety.

I must have an appearance of activity to take the place of what for so long was a source of pride for me: my proficiency as a handyman, my friendship with the hammer and the nail, the trowel and the dibble.

After all, at the age I have now reached, was Sido not engaging in arm-to-arm combat with the great "Prussian cupboard," pierced by a bullet in 1870? But for me, the time when I took pride in my plumbing and my cabinetmaking is over. I now claim no other usefulness than my simple presence, and even then I have limited that usefulness to those who love me. And having for a half a century written in black and white, I have now been writing with colored threads on canvas for what must be almost ten years.

With the blunt needle held in my fingers, I guide the wool held captive in its oblong eye. My women friends say that it is my way of amusing myself; my best friend knows that it is my way of resting. It is simply that I have found my purpose in it and have decided that the greenery shall be blue, the marguerite multicolored, the cherry huge and marked across its equator with four white stitches . . .

My vocation for tapestry work is not, as can be seen, a recent acquisition. I did not dare to make the cross-stitch, simple as the childhood of art itself, my own childhood's art. The "boy who sews" delivers himself in this way of a secret, takes up a pleasant occupation, and assumes a virtue nourished by tradition. The same tradition that served your dark diplomacies, shadowy young ladies of the nineteenth century, stifled in the maternal shade and plying your bright needles . . . Balzac had his eye upon you. "What are you thinking of, Philomène? You've gone over the line . . ." Three stitches too many in the pattern of a slipper intended for her father, and Philomène de Watteville is about to divulge the criminal preoccupation lurking in her soul . . . But she unpicks the three stitches that have gone over the line and sets herself, ringed invisibly with perils, to weave the downfall of Albert Savarus. My intentions are more innocent.

It is the task of the parallelogram made by a cross-stitch to give us the illusion of curves. Four stitches must represent the round pupil of an eye and sixteen its iris, two hundred are a plump and well-fed dove. Cross-stitch samplers are all held in the spell of a passionate ingenuousness. What form of art has ever required so many hearts and turtledoves, so many forget-me-nots, sheep, button roses, cushions exclaiming *Papa!*, and medallions swearing *Friendship?* On a tombstone—am I not right, dear Dignimont?—there prays a dog made up of little squares, while all around the tomb there flutter cabalistic words like ABC, DEF, GHIJK, ORSTU . . . But once we have made our way through these stammering beginnings and emetic emblems, we discover in the best periods of the cross-stitch those impetuous flowerings, those electric eels of color that galvanize its most remarkable achievements. I may be mistaken, but it certainly seems to me—judging by the set of the canvas, by these woolen riggings, by those convolvulus flowers hatching purple starfish in their azure throats—it seems to me that I have reached a haven.

Christian Bérard was tempted by tapestry work a few years ago. He could only succeed where others would have failed, and indeed inspired a group of aristocratic sewing maids to follow his lead. We know that such ladies are not the soul of constancy. Of the fine flame they kindled there now remains, I think, here a sky-blue armchair scattered with ermine tails, there some little Negro serving-maid with hair dressed à la Sévigné, against a red-currant background. Then came the mannerism, the excess of enthusiasm that caused the cross-stitch to sink back into an oblivion it shares with macramé work and embroidered net. I can think of no one other than Mme Lanvin who still does tapestry work for the sake of doing tapestry work, by which I mean in order to project onto canvas the otherwise unemployable excess of her raging creative faculties.

It is not for me to say whether my cross-stitch work involves the expenditure of some similar superfluity in me. I pierce my canvas, then pierce it again. My sand eel—my needle—glitters up between two threads, towing its tail of wool behind it. My memoirs are inscribed in greenery that is blue, lilacs that are pink, and multicolored marguerites. I shall begin a portrait of my star Vesper, embroidered from nature. The movement of my arm, a thousand times repeated, knows all the tunes there are. "We scribblers, you know," Carco used to say, "we poor writers are the only ones who can't sing at our work." My new work does sing. It sings the *Bolero* like everyone else. It sings: "I thought I glimpsed a woodcock at the bottom of the field . . ." It sings: "When I was in my father's house—little freckled girl . . ."

Learning how not to write—it shouldn't take too long. I am going to try in any case. I shall be able to say, "I'm not at home to anyone, except for this quadrangular forget-me-not, for this rose in the shape of a wishing well, for the silence in which the sound made by the mind when searching for a word has just died away."

My goal has not been reached; but I am practicing. I don't yet know when I shall succeed in learning not to write; the obsession, the obligation are half a century old. My right little finger is slightly bent; that is because the weight of my hand always rested on it as I wrote, like a kangaroo leaning back on its tail. There is a tired spirit deep inside of me that still continues its gourmet's quest for a better word, and then for a better one still. Happily, my ideas are less insistent, they are quite accommodating as long as I dress them properly. They have grown used to waiting, half asleep, for their feed of fresh words.

All my life I have gone to a great deal of trouble for strangers. This was because as they read my work they suddenly found they loved me, and sometimes told me so. Obviously I am not counting on my tapestry work to win their hearts from now on . . . How difficult it is to set a limit to oneself . . . But if all I need to do is try, then all is well; I'm trying.

Along an echoing road, beating in time at first, then out of time, then coming together again, can be heard the trotting hoofs of two horses in double harness. Controlled by the same hand, the pen and the needle, the habit of work and the wise desire to put an end to it make friends with one another, part, and then are reconciled . . . Oh, my slow coursers, try to pull together: I can see the end of the road from here.

DC